PLAYING THE CELLO,

To Lydia

Playing the Cello, 1780–1930

GEORGE KENNAWAY
University of Leeds, UK

Routledge
Taylor & Francis Group

LONDON AND NEW YORK

First Published 2014 by Ashgate Publisher

2 Park Square, Milton Park, Abingdon, Oxon OX14 4RN
711 Third Avenue, New York, NY 10017, USA

Routledge is an imprint of the Taylor & Francis Group, an informa business

First issued in paperback 2016

British Library Cataloguing in Publication Data
A catalogue record for this book is available from the British Library

The Library of Congress has cataloged the printed edition as follows:
Kennaway, George.
  Playing the cello, 1780–1930 / by George Kennaway.
    pages ; cm
  Includes bibliographical references and index.
  ISBN 978-1-4094-3833-5 (hardcover : alk. paper)
  1. Cello--Performance. 2. Performance practice (Music)–
History. I. Title.
  ML915.K44 2014
  787.4'14309034--dc23

                                                          2013031546

ISBN 978-1-4094-3833-5 (hbk)
ISBN 978-1-138-27029-9 (pbk)

Bach musicological font developed by © Yo Tomita

Contents

List of Figures

List of Tables

List of Music Examples

Preface

This treatment of historical performance practices is not intended to be a simple guide to how to play the major works of the cello repertoire in a convincingly nineteenth-century style. It does examine some quite basic topics, such as posture and bow hold, but this is done in part to show that changing approaches to the fundamentals of cello performance, and by implication historical performance practices in general, have an intellectual interest in themselves in terms of ideas that, while connected, can be shown to change at widely varying speeds. This in turn suggests a direction from which the concept of historically informed performance can be re-assessed, and current generalizations questioned. The chapters on the gendered associations of the cello and potential implications for performance are offered as only one possible area for further study of the role that the audience's expectations might play in altering the performer's perspective on historical style. With this comes a suggestion that the current historical performance discourse creates difficulties because of an underlying assumed aesthetic model of the musical work.

The existing historical literature that focuses specifically on the cello is patchy, and often draws heavily on earlier sources. The works of Wasielewski and Edmund van der Straeten, from the later nineteenth and early twentieth centuries respectively, are still used as sources for much biographical detail. They underpin much in the current edition of Grove, especially those articles concerning minor, or under-researched major, figures.[1] At the time of writing, for example, there exists no detailed study in English of either Adrien Servais or Friedrich Grützmacher. Servais is therefore still erroneously supposed to have adopted the tail-pin because he was overweight. His compositions have not been studied at all by scholars, and the only significant biographical work on him is in Flemish.[2] There has been no modern research on Alfredo Piatti, apart from Barzanò and Bellisario's idiosyncratic overview of biographical material. This contains much

---

[1]   William Jos..D. Wasielewski, trans. Isobella S. E. Stigand, *The Violoncello and its History* (London: Novello, Ewer & Co., 1894; 1st. pub. 1888); Edmund van der Straeten, *A History of the Violoncello, the Viol da Gamba, their Precursors and Collateral Instruments* (London: William Reeves, 1914). See, for example, Lynda MacGregor, 'Alfredo Piatti', 'Friedrich Grützmacher', 'Pierre Chevillard', *Grove Music Online. Oxford Music Online* [last accessed 16 March 2009].

[2]   Peter François, *'Ah! Le metier de donneur de concerts! Adrien François Servais (1807–1866) als rondreizend cellovirtuos* (Halle, Belgium: vzw Servais, 2007), and exhibition catalogue for Zuidwestbrabants Museum, *Adrien François Servais 1807–2007 Halse cellist met wereldfaam* (Halle, Belgium: vzw Servais, 2007).

reference material, such as a catalogue of his compositions, and selections from his correspondence, along with anecdotal material, but is inconsistently referenced, and confusingly structured.[3] Grützmacher is still chiefly identified with his notorious edition of Boccherini's B♭ major 'concerto', leading to a lack of interest in his performing editions in general.[4]

Existing studies of individual cellists are uneven. An experimental approach is adopted in Elizabeth le Guin's study of Boccherini.[5] She attempts to incorporate the physicality of performance (and of composition-as-performance) into the musical meaning of the work itself, showing how physical tension and harmonic or melodic tension can combine or be at odds. This idiosyncratic work has yet to be fully assessed with regard to other repertoires. It is open to a charge of excessive subjectivity, in that as a cellist herself her own perceptions of the physicality of performance may be quite different from another player's, but it suggests stimulating future lines of research. The only biography of David Popper, written by one of his last pupils, is an invaluable source of material from Hungarian journals in particular, and contains many revealing personal anecdotes. De'ak's citations are, however, often inadequate.[6] The literature on Casals, though extensive, generally examines his later teaching and politics rather giving detailed attention to his playing itself, even though his recorded legacy is considerable.[7] The most recent study of a cellist, Anita Mercier's monograph on Suggia, is almost entirely biographical in orientation, with much useful information about concert programmes and repertoire, but with very little broader historical context (especially concerning Suggia's critical reception), and no detailed examination of her relatively small recorded output.[8] More recent broadly-based histories of the cello intended for a non-specialist readership recycle much older work or contribute peripheral anecdotal material.[9]

The position with regard to larger-scale studies is broadly similar. Lev Ginsburg's substantial work on nineteenth-century Russian cellists has never been translated into English, with the result that no comprehensive study of the work of Carl Davidoff

---

[3] Annalisa Lodetti Barzanò and Christian Bellisario, trans. Clarice Zdanski, *Signor Piatti – Cellist, Komponist Avantgardist* (Kronberg : Kronberg Academy Verlag, 2001).

[4] Luigi Boccherini, arr. Friedrich Grützmacher, *Konzert in B* (Leipzig: Breitkopf & Härtel, [1895]).

[5] Elisabeth le Guin, *Boccherini's Body: An Essay in Carnal Musicology* (Berkeley: University of California Press, 2006).

[6] Steven De'ak, *David Popper* (Neptune City, NJ: Paganiniana Publications, 1980).

[7] Lillian Littlehales, *Pablo Casals* (London: J. M. Dent & Sons, 1929); J. Ma. Corredor, trans. André Mangeot, *Conversations with Casals* (London: Hutchinson, 1956). See, for example, David Blum, *Casals and the Art of Interpretation* (London: Heinemann Educational, 1977); Robert Baldock, *Pablo Casals* (London: Gollancz, 1992).

[8] Anita Mercier, *Guilherminia Suggia* (Aldershot: Ashgate, 2008).

[9] Elizabeth Cowling, *The Cello* (London: Batsford, 1975); Margaret Campbell, *The Great Cellists* (London: Gollancz, 1988).

as a cellist, let alone as a composer, has appeared outside Russia.[10] In modern times, only two significant treatments of the cello have appeared – the Cambridge Companion to the Cello and Valerie Walden's monograph concentrating on the period 1740–1840.[11] The former covers a very wide area with variable depth and detail. Some chapters, especially those on the leading players in the classical, romantic and twentieth-century periods, are particularly poorly referenced (with much use of van der Straeten and Wasielewski), while others simply attempt too much in the limited space available.[12] Walden deals with the period between Corrette and Romberg and is largely concerned with material drawn from the more prominent cello methods of the period by well-known players. She uses very few other primary sources, especially the smaller, cheaper cello tutors published anonymously. She tends to presuppose the validity of the concept of 'schools' of playing, and also uses sources from much later than her defined period in order to give additional importance to topics which that are of marginal significance. However, her discussion of 'good style', though inconclusive and unfocussed, constitutes an admirable attempt to broaden the traditional parameters of the discourse of performance practice historiography.[13] Christiane Wiesenfeldt's recent treatment of the German nineteenth-century cello sonata contains virtually no material on performance, focussing instead on formal analysis.[14] The same is true, though to a lesser degree, of Sylvette Maillot's examination of cello music in eighteenth-century France.[15]

Traditional studies have generally adopted an evolutionary, teleological model. Cellists are normally assessed in terms of their contribution to the 'development'

[10] Lev Ginsburg, *Istoriya violonchel'novo: iskusstva russkaya klassicheskaya violonchel'naya shkola (1860–1917)* [History of the cello: the art of the Russian classical cello school] (Moscow: Musiyka, 1965). The second part of his survey, published as *Istoriya violonchelnovo iskusstva* (Moscow: Muziyka, 1978) is available in English: Lev Ginsburg, trans. Tanya Tchistyakova, *Western Violoncello Art of the 19th and 20th Centuries* (Neptune City, NJ: Paganiniana Publications, 1983).

[11] Robin Stowell (ed.), *The Cambridge Companion to the Cello* (Cambridge: Cambridge University Press, 1999); Valerie Walden, *One Hundred Years of Violoncello: A History of Technique and Performance Practice, 1740–1840* (Cambridge: Cambridge University Press, 1998).

[12] See, for example, Margaret Campbell, 'Masters of the Baroque and Classical Eras', 'Nineteenth-Century Virtuosi', and 'Masters of the Twentieth Century', in Stowell, ibid., pp. 52–91, or Peter Allsop, 'Ensemble Music: in the Chamber and the Orchestra', ibid., pp. 160–177.

[13] Walden, 'Elements of aesthetics and style', *One Hundred Years of Violoncello*, pp. 270–300.

[14] Christiane Wiesenfeldt, *Zwischen Beethoven Und Brahms: Die Violoncello-Sonate im 19. Jahrhundert. Kieler Schriften zur Musikwissenschaft, band 51* (Kassel: Bärenreiter, 2006).

[15] Sylvette Maillot, *Le violoncelle en France au XVIIIième siècle* (Paris: Champion, 1985). 15

of technique, and the overall emphasis is on the leading virtuosi or on the most influential teachers. This has led some cello treatises to be down-valued, and to a privileging of technical innovation. This evolutionary view can be found, perhaps unsurprisingly, in the late nineteenth-century work of Wasielewski, but a concept of history as progress is of course considerably older. There is clearly a change in many aspects of cello performance practices during this period – or, to put it more accurately, cellists play differently at different times and places. But a Darwinist view of an instrument's historical development can both distort and obscure matters. Admittedly, it is hard to avoid a developmental view of a topic presented, in its different manifestations, chronologically.

At the turn of the last century, there were two distinctive, and problematic, views about the 'development' of the cello. One was based on its repertoire, the other on its pedagogical history. The first was expressed by Wasielewski, who maintained that in the nineteenth century the cello set aside inappropriate violinistic mannerisms and gradually assumed its 'true' character.[16] The twentieth-century literature for the cello would certainly not reinforce this essentialist view, not least because the very concept of an inherent 'character' becomes increasingly unsustainable, as the most cursory glance at contemporary writing for cello will confirm. The second view, expressed by Emil Krall, at even greater length by Diran Alexanian, and implicit in almost every pedagogical work on the cello, was that its pedagogical history was that of a search for fundamental principles.[17] Krall describes 'the continual endeavour of players to find and establish laws'.[18] Casals's preface to Alexanian describes the Traité as 'a well elaborated plan for the analysis of the theory of violoncello playing [...] a serious effort towards the casting off of the shackles of superannuated prejudices'.[19] Here, 'progress' is from the straightforward pragmatism of much nineteenth-century cello teaching (where one is basically taught what one will need in order to play cello pieces) to a more thoroughly scientific approach based on systematic thinking and a knowledge of anatomy. This brings with it the pursuit of technical development for its own sake, far beyond the immediate requirements of the most difficult music written for the instrument.[20] Yet even this apparent transformation is not straightforwardly linear. The late-eighteenth-century scale fingerings of John Gunn mark a decisive shift towards more ergonomic fingerings which that are independent of apparent musical structures, based on principles which that can be applied to any scale.

---

[16]   Wasielewski, *The Violoncello and its History*, pp. 212–13.

[17]   Emil Krall, *The Art of Tone-Production on the Violoncello* (London: The Strad Office, John Leng & Co., 1913); Diran Alexanian, *Traité théorique et pratique du violoncelle* (Paris: A. Z. Mathot, 1922).

[18]   Krall, ibid., unpaginated preface.

[19]   Alexanian, ibid., p. 4.

[20]   See, for example, the transcendental studies of Bazelaire, based on much earlier studies by Kummer. Paul Bazelaire, *10 Etudes transcendantes d'après des études mélodiques de F. A. Kummer* (Paris: Alphonse Leduc, 1936).

The very short, repetitive, left hand exercises of Bideau (1802) anticipate the standard work of this kind by Feuillard.[21] Gunn, and to a degree Bideau, are being analytic, over a century before the much more obviously, and explicitly, scientific approaches taken by Alexanian or Becker.

Therefore, while a diachronic study of the evidence predisposes towards a developmental narrative model, this study will frequently stress the synchronic diversity of practices, with the intention of discouraging over-simplified generic approaches to historically informed performance. This diversity will also be examined in the light of the frequent apparent contradiction between 'theory' (verbal instructions of whatever form, such as pedagogical material or concert reviews) and 'practice' (performing editions, the evidence of early recordings, or individual performance reception). Concert reviews can fall into both categories, in that the critic may express a general stylistic preference as well as record what actually took place. The theories and practices recorded here are presented with a view to retaining their variety, rather than seeking an over-arching normalizing narrative. This is because such narratives, whether couched in evolutionary terms, or in terms of 'schools', are hard to justify empirically, and tend to pre-determine routes of inquiry. The source materials used here are mostly conventional, and relate directly to matters of musical performance. But there are some materials that are less frequently encountered in studies of this type, in particular as they concern ideas of the character of the cello and its gendered identity. This entails the use of sources familiar to researchers in other fields, including literary representations of the cello in novels, poetry, drama and miscellaneous newspaper and journal articles, mostly written by non-expert musicians. It is hoped that the material and ideas presented here which may be unfamiliar to readers – whether cellists, performing musicians, or researchers of historical performance practices – may suggest ways in which they can find common ground.

George Kennaway
February 2014

---

[21] Dominique Bideau, *Grand nouvelle méthode raisonnée* (Paris: Naderman, [1802]); Louis R. Feuillard, *Tägliche Übungen* (Mainz: B. Schott's Söhne, 1919).

Acknowledgements

I should first acknowledge that my interest in some of this repertoire began when as a young cellist I explored the remarkably good collection of the music department of the Edinburgh Central Public Library, a collection that is still intact today. The librarians of the Mitchell Library (Glasgow), the Royal Academy of Music, the Juilliard Conservatoire, Edinburgh University, the Conservatorio Civico di Bergamo, the Wighton Collection at Dundee Public Library, the Baldwin-Wallace Library (Ohio), the Manx Museum, the New Orleans Public Library, the Hill Memorial Library (Louisiana State University), the Gemeentemuseum (The Hague), and the Brussels Royal Conservatoire all gave additional, and very time-consuming, help and information. Peter François, director of the Servais Museum in Hal, Belgium, gave invaluable assistance. Andrew Streit and Martin Pickard gave essential help with much of the German translation, as did Petra Bijsterfeld with material in Dutch and Flemish. Dr Rita Steblin supplied and translated a passage from Anton Gräffer's MS memoirs.

My own cello teachers unwittingly sowed the seeds of some of the ideas in this thesis: Marie Dare, Valentine Orde, Michael Edmonds, Christopher Bunting and Ioan Davies. Many other cellists have lent and even donated rare music from their own collections, including Ioan Davies, Jo Coles, Jenny Langridge, Robert Truman and Moira Philips, and particular thanks is due in this respect to Anna Shuttleworth. I have benefited from discussions with other cellists actively researching in this field, particularly Elizabeth le Guin, Christine Cyprianides, Bonnie Smart, and Kate Haynes. Jerome Carrington kindly gave me a copy of his unpublished work on Servais and Haydn, and Jeffrey Solow assisted with several enquiries about American cellists. My colleagues in the Orchestra of Opera North were unfailingly encouraging, even if privately baffled, and the amateurs of Yorkshire Late Starters Strings have been willing guinea-pigs for my experiments in posture. Professor Clive Brown was the benign supervisor of the PhD thesis that has given rise to this book. The examiners of my doctoral dissertation, Dr Michael Allis and Prof. Simon McVeigh, both made invaluable and thought-provoking suggestions. I am also grateful to Professors Derek Scott and Rachel Cowgill and many other generous colleagues and friends for their responses to my work. Rehearsals and further discussions with Dr David Milsom, Dr Peter Collyer and Duncan Druce have been constantly stimulating. I also wish to thank the anonymous reviewers of this book at various stages of its preparation for their constructive and stimulating help. Errors are, of course, entirely my own.

However, the greatest debt I owe is to Lydia Kennaway, for her constant encouragement, patience and tolerance in times of stress, and it is to her that this book is dedicated.

Notes and Abbreviations

Notes

Unless otherwise stated, all translations are the author's, with the original given in a footnote. When quoting from a text originally published in a multilingual edition, only the English version is given unless there are significant differences.

Quotations retain original spelling and punctuation. Unless otherwise stated, italicization or other emphases are as in the original. In particular, ellipses not within brackets are as in the original text; this especially concerns French texts quoted in Chapter 7.

Typeset music examples use modern clefs. Markings in square brackets in music examples are editorial additions for clarification.

The most frequently used Italian terms such as arco, pizzicato, staccato, vibrato and portamento are not italicized.

Note-names are in Helmholtz notation, with octaves beginning on C: middle C = c′. However, cello string names are standardized as C, G, D, A.

Dates of publication within brackets are not supported within the text of the publication. However, dates in brackets without any further qualification have been verified from the *Hofmeister Monatsbericht*.[1]

Abbreviations

Journals and Periodicals

AmZ	*Allgemeine musikalische Zeitung*
AmZmbR	*Allgemeine musikalische Zeitung mit besonderer Rücksicht auf den österreichischen Kaiserstaat*
AwMZ	*Allgemeine wiener Musik-Zeitung*
BamZ	*Berliner allgemeine musikalische Zeitung*
MT	*Musical Times*
MW	*Musical World*

---

[1] F. Hofmeister, et al., *Musikalisch-literarischer Monatsbericht: über neue Musikalien, musikalische Schriften und Abbildungen* (Leipzig: F. Hofmeister, 1829–1907); online at http://www.hofmeister.rhul.ac.uk.

References

Brown, *CRPP*
>   Clive Brown, *Classical and Romantic Performing Practice 1750–1900*
>   (Oxford: Oxford University Press, 1999).

Grove Music Online
>   *The New Grove Dictionary of Music and Musicians*, ed. Laura Macy,
>   URL: http://0-www.oxfordmusiconline.com.

The Recorded Cello
>   *The Recorded Cello – The History of the Cello on Record, 6 discs* (Pearl Gemm
>   CDS 9981–86, 1992).

Performer Abbreviations

cond	conductor
movt	movement
pf	piano
pt	part
vc	cello
vn	violin

Chapter 1
Basic Posture and Bow Hold

Broderip and Wilkinson's *Complete Treatise* is an anonymous work costing three shillings, quite modest in its scope, typical of several from the 1790s onwards. The frontispiece shows a man, perhaps the intended reader, or the sort of person the reader aspired to be, playing the cello in a small music room (Figure 1.1).[1] Another instrument, possibly a bass viol, lies neglected in the shadows, while a chamber organ dominates the opposite wall. Elaborate wall hangings and side panels hung with musical instruments frame the player like a proscenium arch – the cellist is playing to an unseen audience, the reader. His melody is 'unheard', not in any Keatsian sense, but because of his general posture. He holds the bow a

Figure 1.1   Frontispiece illustration, Broderip and Wilkinson's *Complete Treatise for the Violoncello*

---

[1]   Broderip and Wilkinson's *Complete Treatise for the Violoncello* (London: the Editors, [c.1800]).

considerable distance from the heel, almost at the balance point, and it is at least 3 inches from the bridge. His left hand looks like a violinist's, and his left elbow sags behind the instrument in a way that most modern cellists would find lazy. The cello itself may be resting on the ground or held precariously between the legs (as in many such illustrations, the artist's perspective drawing is poor). He turns his head sharply to his right to read the music, which would otherwise obscure him from the reader. Almost every aspect of his general deportment minimizes the amount of sound he can produce.

This chapter considers the most basic topics in cello playing: posture and bow hold. They are often ignored in studies of historical performance practices, or treated superficially. Nonetheless, without a clear understanding of this groundwork there is no foundation for studying many other aspects of performance.

Throughout the nineteenth century, cellists sat in fundamentally the same way, with the left foot slightly forward of the right, the back edge of the cello against the left calf, and the front edge against the right. This simple formula occurs in virtually every cello tutor, but with variations, additions and shifts of emphasis.

Before the later nineteenth century there are very few references to a tail-pin in the pedagogical literature. Corrette mentions it once, briefly and disapprovingly:

> note that the instrument does not touch the ground at all, since that makes it muted: sometimes one puts a stick at the end to support the cello, when one plays standing up: not only is this posture not the most attractive, but it is moreover the most contrary for difficult passages [...].[2]

Robert Crome gives a brief but interesting recommendation:

> ...the lower part is to rest on the Calves of the Leggs supported with the Knees, but for the greater ease of a Learner we wou'd advise him to have an hole made in the Tail-pin and a Wooden Peg to screw into it to rest on the Floor which may be taken out as he pleases.[3]

Some tutors, such as Bréval's, rely on an illustration to convey correct posture, rather than words. But his illustration (Figure 1.2) has some curious features.[4] The player's heels are off the ground, he leans markedly to his left, and his left calf is

---

[2]   'observer que l'Instrument ne touche point a terre, attendu que cela le rend sourd: quelque fois on met un bâton au bout pour soutenir la basse, quand on joue debout: non seulement cette posture n'est pas la plus belle, mais elle est encore la plus contraire aux passages difficiles [...].' Michel Corrette, *Méthode théorique et pratique* (Paris: Mlle. Castagnery, [1741]), p. 7.

[3]   Robert Crome, *The Compleat Tutor for the Violoncello* (London: C. & S. Thompson [1765?]), p. 1.

[4]   J.B. Bréval, trans. J. Peile, *Bréval's New Instructions for the Violoncello* (London: C. Wheatstone & Co., [1810]), p. 6.

Figure 1.2   Bréval, *Méthode*, posture illustration

against the lower ribs of the cello rather than the back edge. This posture would quickly create physical tension and affect tone quality. The illustration shows the feet turned out (as does Romberg's drawing, Figure 1.3), visibly contradicting the Paris Conservatoire cello method, which expressly forbids this.

Peile's 1810 (extremely free) translation of Bréval is a little more detailed:

> The holding the Instrument is particularly to be observed and the following directions will serve to give a proper idea of it. The learner being seated as forward as convenient on a Chair or Stool rather low, is to extend his legs with the feet turned outwards, and receive the Instrument between so that the upper edge of the Violoncello may press against the Calf of the right leg, and the opposite lower edge against the Calf of the left leg together with the lower part of the left thigh, this position inclining the fingerboard inwards which must always be observed.[5]

---

[5]   Ibid.

John Gunn and Bernhard Romberg also recommend a low stool. In the first detailed explanation of cello posture in any language, John Gunn explains posture at exhaustive length (this topic receives less attention in the first edition):

> The mode of holding the instrument is far from being indifferent, and we see several ways adopted, which are exceptionable, from the obstructions they oppose to good tone and a facility of expression. The position which in these respects possesses the greatest advantages, is the following. The player sitting as forward as he can on a chair or stool, rather low, is to extend his left leg nearly as far as he can, so as not to rest solely on the heel, but with the foot flat on the ground; this is done in order to depress the left knee, which would otherwise oppose the proper action of the bow. The right knee must be extended a little outwards, so as exactly to receive the Violoncello between both legs, the toes of the right foot being turned quite outwards, so that the Calf of that leg which will be perpendicular to the ground, may be pressed against the upper rim or edge of the instrument, while the opposite lower edge is pressed against the lower part of the left thigh a very little above the knee, the upper rim will thus project beyond the knee, and the bridge will be on a line with the right knee, as it necessary the bow should pass on the fourth string in the direction of the bow, a___b at fig: 11 of the annexed plate, about three inches above the bridge: for if the instrument be held lower, the bow must be drawn on that string in the direction of the dotted line d...b. The finger board should incline to the body and towards the left shoulder, as at fig: 17.[6]

Duport deals with the subject in rather fewer words:

> The hold of the cello between the legs varies a lot, according to people's different habits and sizes. One can very well play, holding the instrument a little higher or lower. This is the manner most used, which must be the best. One must first sit towards the front of the chair, bringing the left foot well forward, and the right closer: then place the instrument between the legs, so that the lower left hand corner bout is by the left knee joint, and the weight of the instrument is borne by the left calf: and above the left foot. If the knee is opposite this bout, it will prevent the bow passing easily, when one wishes to use the A string. The right leg is placed against the curve below the instrument, to hold it securely.[7]

---

      6   John Gunn, *The Theory and Practice of Fingering the Violoncello* (London: the Author, 2nd edn. [c.1793]), pp. 5–6.
      7   'La tenue du violoncelle entre les jambes varie beaucoup, suivant les habitudes et la différente taille des personnes. On peut très-bien jouer en tenant son Instrument, un peu plus haut ou un peu plus bas. Voiçi la manière la plus usitée et qui doit être la meilleure. Il faut premièrement s'asseoir sur le devant de sa chaise, porter ensuite le pied gauche loin de soi en avant, et rapprocher le droit: alors placer l'Instrument entre les jambes, de façon que le coin de l'échancrure inférieure d'en bas a gauche, se trouve dans la jointure du genou

Dominique Bideau is even more concise:

> 1mo. To sit on the edge of the chair, 2do. To place it between the legs, 3o., to put both feet forward, to advance the left foot especially, so that all the weight of the instrument can rest on the calf of the left leg, and by this means can hold it with confidence, 4o. to bring the right foot closer, so that the bout is found at the left knee joint.[8]

Robert Lindley emphasizes the readjustment of posture according the string in use:

> The Instrument should be supported by the calf of the left leg, whilst the right leg affords the pressure requisite to keep it in its place. The Instrument must be under the control of the right leg, so that it may be made to slant one way or the other, as the first and second, or third and fourth strings may be most required.[9]

Romberg places his feet differently from the conventional posture (Figure 1.3):

> The heels may be six inches apart, and one foot not more advanced than the other.[10]

Georg Kastner agrees with Romberg (the feet must be 'sur une même ligne' [on the same line]), but it is still a minority view.[11] Note that Romberg's right leg does not just press against the front edge of the cello, but almost envelopes it. In Figure 1.3 Romberg is leaning slightly to his left, but his shoulders appear to be more or less level. The net effect is to distribute the weight of the cello more

---

gauche, afin que le poids de l'Instrument, soit porté sur le mollet de la jambe gauches: et le pied gauche en dehors. Si le genou se trouvoit au contraire dans cette échancrure, il empecheroit l'archet de passer aisément, lorsqu'on voudroit se servir de la Chanterelle ou première Corde. La jambe droite se pose contre l'éclisse d'en bas de l'Instrument, pour le maintenir en sûreté.' Jean Louis Duport, *Essai sur le doigté du violoncelle* (Paris: Imbault, [1806]), p. 5.

[8] '1mo. De s'asseoir sur le bord de la chaise, 2do. De le placer entre ses jambes, 3o. de mettre les deux pieds en dehors, d'avancer surtout le pied gauche, afin que tout le poid de l'instrument puisse poser sur le mollet de la jambe gauche, et par ce moyen le tienne avec assurance, 4o. de rapprocher de soi le pied droit, et de faire en sorte que l'éclisse se trouve entre la jointure du genou gauche.' Dominique Bideau, *Grande nouvelle méthode raisonnée pour le violoncelle* (Paris: Naderman, [1802]). p. 3.

[9] Robert Lindley, *Hand-book for the Violoncello* (London: Musical Bouquet Office, [1851–55]), p. 5.

[10] Bernhard Romberg, trans. anon., *A Complete Theoretical and Practical School for the Violoncello* (London: T. Boosey & Co., [1840]), p. 7. Orig., *Violoncellschule* (Berlin: Trautwein, [1840]), p. 6. Illustration, ibid., unpaginated, p. 6 verso.

[11] Georges Kastner, *Méthode Élémentaire pour le Violoncelle* (Paris: E. Froupenas & Cie., 1835), p. 2.

Figure 1.3   Romberg, *Violoncellschule*, posture illustration

symmetrically than Duport, Bideau or Lindley suggest, and experiment shows that this posture places the instrument more vertically.

The question as to whether the calves held the cello by the ribs, or by the edges, is important. Gripping the ribs dampens the resonance of the instrument. Kummer was among the first to acknowledge this problem, stressing holding the cello by the edges:

> The Violoncello should be held between the legs, so that the lower part of the front edge of the Instrument comes exactly on the right calf, and the back edge exactly on the left calf of the player. But it must be especially remembered that the sides of the edges be not too much covered by the calf of the leg; as thus the vibration of the Instrument will be impeded.[12]

Concern for tone quality, rather than the comfort of the player, was to lead eventually to the general use of a tail-pin, but it is clear that, throughout at least the first half of the nineteenth century, if used at all, it was rare. Adrien-François Servais (1807–66) appears to be the first cellist to have used it regularly (Figure 1.4).[13]

---

[12]   F.A. Kummer, trans. anon., Violoncello School op. 60 (London: Ewer and Co. [1850]), p. 4. Orig., *Violoncelloschule* op. 60 (Leipzig: Hofmeister, [1839]).

[13]   Photograph, Servais Collection, Halle (Belgium).

Figure 1.4   Photograph of Servais, c.1862

Although it seems he taught all his students to play in this way, it would be at least another half-century before it became virtually universal.

Several cello tutors from even the late nineteenth and early twentieth centuries do not mention the tail-pin at all. Junod's 1878 method simply gives the standard warning that: '[The player] must avoid covering the sides (or ribs) of the instrument so as not to check the vibration of the sound.'[14] The same is true of Edward Howell's much-simplified version of Romberg's tutor.[15] August Schultz's cello method (c.1882) has a very clear illustration of the instrument with no mention of a tail-pin, and he stresses the importance of holding the cello by the edges so as not to dampen the vibration.[16] Olive Vaslin makes a similar point:

[14]   Laurent Junod, trans. F. Clayton, *New and Concise Method for the Violoncello* op. 20 (London: Lafleur, 1878), p. 3.

[15]   Edward Howell, *Edward Howell's First Book for the Violoncello adapted from Romberg's School* (London: Boosey & Co., [1879]), p. 1.

[16]   'Die Waden dürfen dabei niemals die Flächen der Zargen ganz deden, um nicht die Vibration der Töne zu hemmen.' August Schulz, *Elementar-Violoncelloschule* (Hanover: Louis Oertel, [1882]), p. 5.

> The pressure necessary to retain the instrument can be exerted without an audible alteration of the vibration, for the simple reason that in this posture the legs only reach the parts [of the cello] already essential to the solidity of the framework.[17]

Gaetano Braga's 1873 revision of Dotzauer's method expands Dotzauer's illustrations considerably but makes no mention of a tail-pin.[18] Piatti's 1877 revision of Kummer's cello method includes Kummer's illustration of the cello without a tail-pin.[19] As late as 1902, Hans Dressel, a pupil of Friedrich Grützmacher and Ernest de Munck (himself a Servais pupil), could describe the cellist's posture without any reference to a tail-pin at all:

> The student should sit erectly on the chair, placing the right foot firmly down, and stretching out the left. The 'Cello should be placed in a slanting position, and tilted slightly to the right, leaning on the middle of the player's chest, and held by the legs.[20]

When the tail-pin does begin to be recommended in cello tutors or methods it is still very much in the context of the more traditional posture. Both Henri Rabaud (1878) and Jules de Swert (1882) advocate the tail-pin, but the basic posture is not very different. In fact, Rabaud tells the student to master the 'classical' posture first:

> Several artists make use of a spike, rod or extension to hold up the cello, which fits the button: I advise pupils not to use it before being well familiarized with the classical posture.[21]

De Swert recommends using a tail-pin for better tone quality, and thus answers Kummer's reservations:

---

[17] 'La pression nécessaire au maintien de l'instrument peut s'opérer sans altération sensible des vibrations, par la raison toute simple que dans cette attitude les jambes n'atteignent que des parties déjà maintenues par la charpente indispensable à la solidité.' Olive Vaslin, *L'art du violoncelle* (Paris: Richault, 1884), pp. 2–3.

[18] Gaetano Braga (ed.), *Metodo per Violoncello di J. J. F. Dotzauer* (Milan: Regio Stabilimento Ricordi, 1873).

[19] F.A. Kummer, rev. A. Piatti, *Violoncello School for Preliminary Instruction* (Leipzig: Friedrich Hofmeister, 1877), unpaginated plate.

[20] Hans Dressel, *Moderne Violoncell Schule Modern Violoncello School*, 2 vols. (Leipzig, London, Paris and Vienna: Bosworth & Co. 1902), Vol. 1, p. 2.

[21] 'Plusieur [sic] artistes se servent pour soutenir le Violoncelle d'une pique, tige ou rallonge qui s'adapte au bouton de l'instrument: j'engage les élèves à ne pas en faire usage avant d'être bien familiarisés avec la tenue classique.' Henri Rabaud, *Méthode Complète de Violoncelle* op. 12 (Paris: Alphonse Leduc [1878]), p. 1.

Nearly all the modern players use a stem made of wood or metal (wood is preferable) about seven or eight inches long, which is fixed to the lower part of the Violoncello, and on which the instrument rests. In my opinion this is perfectly right, because, by this system, not only is the position of the body freer, but also the tone is favourably influenced by the instrument resting on this stem instead of being held by the pressure of the legs, the latter plan necessarily interfering with the development of the tone.[22]

(Although metal replaced wood, Max Merseburger still suggested that wood was an option as late as 1920.)[23] De Swert's accompanying illustration shows that the near-vertical cello and the placing of the feet are still virtually as they would have been without a tail-pin. The near-vertical upper right arm, dropped left elbow and pronated right wrist, would be familiar to a cellist from the beginning of the nineteenth century as well. However, this illustration is as misleading as Bréval's, with a rather glum cellist leaning perceptibly to his right, away from the instrument, which would be difficult to sustain for any length of time (Figure 1.5).[24]

Even in 1909, Otto Langey describes posture in terms familiar from a century earlier, and simply adds the tail-pin:

The performer should sit well forward on his seat, with the left foot in advance of the right, the feet turned outwards. The instrument should be placed between the legs with the lower edge of the back on the calf of the left leg and the edge of the belly on the calf of the right leg. [...] The instrument must rest entirely in this position without the assistance of the left hand, and high enough, so as to prevent the bow touching the knees. An End-pin should be used for this purpose.[25]

The upright posture is also described by Carl Davidoff:

The player sits forward on the seat, grasps the cello with the left hand on the neck, and secures it with the spike, so that it stands perpendicular to the feet...[26]

---

[22]   Jules de Swert, *The Violoncello* (London and New York: Novello, Ewer and Co. [1882]), p. 4.

[23]   'The spike, whose use has now become general, which has made the holding of the cello easier, will, if made of wood, be about 15 mm thick...' ('Der Stachel, dessen Verwendung jetzt allgemein geworden ist, da er die Haltung des Cellos sehr erleichtert, soll, wenn aus Holz bestehend, etwa 15 mm durchmesser haben...'). M. Vadding and Max Merseburger, *Das Violoncello und seine Literatur* (Leipzig: Carl Merseburger, 1920), p. 30.

[24]   Ibid., p. 4.

[25]   Otto Langey, *Practical Tutor for the Violoncello. New Edition, Revised & Enlarged* (London: Hawkes & Son, 1909), p. 7.

[26]   'Der Spieler setzt sich vorn auf den Stuhl, faßt das Violoncell mit der linken Hand am Halse und fixiert es mit dem Stachel, sodaß es vertikal den Füßen steht...' Carl Yu. Davidoff, *Violoncell-Schule* (Leipzig: Peters, [1888]), p. 2.

Figure 1.5   Swert, *The Violoncello*, posture illustration

Josef Werner (1883) gives the standard advice about the length of the tail-pin relative to the player, but still implies that it is optional:

> When using a peg at the bottom of the instrument, it is necessary to have it so long, that the lowest screw [the C string peg] reaches the left ear at about two or three inches distance, so as not to run the risk of knocking the left knee with the bow in striking the A string.[27]

Swert's illustration shows roughly this length of tail-pin, seven or eight inches, similar to that used by Servais.

Edmund van der Straeten (1898) recommended the tail-pin even more firmly:

> The use of the peg is now generally adopted, and offers the double advantage of steadying the instrument and strengthening its tone by an additional amount

---

[27]   Josef Werner, trans. anon., *Praktische Violoncell-Schule* op. 12 (Köln: P.J. Tonger, [1882]), p. 3.

of resonance, resulting from the communication established by it between the body of the violoncello and the floor. If the peg be of steel, as is now generally the case, it will prove even a stronger medium than a peg made of wood... [Playing without a tail-pin] which is still practised in isolated cases, has the disadvantage of giving the instrument a rather upright position, rendering it somewhat stiff, and necessitating the covering, by the legs, of a greater part of the ribs, which prevents the free emission of sound.[28]

Note that van der Straeten (Figure 1.6) is shown with his feet opposite each other, like Romberg; the drawing is a portrait, copied from a photograph of van der Straeten.

Other sources confirm that the tail-pin was in widespread, but not universal, use around the end of the nineteenth century. The revised versions of Romberg's and Kummer's cello methods, by Jules de Swert (1888) and Hugo Becker (1909)

Figure 1.6   Van der Straeten, *Technics*, posture illustration[29]

---

[28]   Edmund van der Straeten, *History of the Violoncello, the Viol da Gamba, Their Precursors and Collateral Instruments* (London: William Reeves, 1898), pp. 17–18.

[29]   Ibid., p. 30.

respectively, add clearly defined editorial comment to bring them up to date half a century later.[30] De Swert comments on Romberg's description of posture without a tail-pin:

> This stance has almost completely disappeared. The majority of modern cello virtuosi use a spike 7–8 inches long attached below the instrument. The earlier stance is in my opinion uncomfortable and ungraceful; besides it is clear to all, that through the pressure of the leg and the contact with the clothing that the tone must suffer considerably.[31]

Similarly, Becker adds to Kummer's description of posture:

> In more recent times a spike is generally used. This innovation brings many advantages: greater stability and better resonance of the instrument, by being less tiring to the player.[32]

In Becker's edition of Sebastian Lee's method he mentions another benefit, while making it clear that the basic posture was unchanged:

> Latterly, the use of the tail-pin has been pretty generally adopted, as it permits of greater freedom in the handling of the instrument. The above mentioned fundamental principles on position, however, are thereby not altered in their salient features.[33]

---

[30]   This contrasts with the approach taken by August Lindner in his trilingual edition of Duport's *Essai*, who claims to retains elements that are no longer current, leaving it to the teacher to explain them, but who also makes several silent alterations. Jean Louis, trans. August Lindner, *Anleitung zum Fingersatz auf dem Violoncell und zur Bogenführung. Instruction on the fingering and bowing of the violoncello. Essai sur le doigté de violoncelle et sur la conduite de l'archet* (Offenbach: Jean André, Philadelphia: G. André & Co., Frankfurt: G.A. André, London: Augener & Co., [1864]), p. 1.

[31]   'Diese Haltung ist fast ganz abgekommen. Die Mehrzahl der modernen Violoncello-Virtuosen gebrauchen einen Stachel van 7–8 Zoll lang der unten im Instrument eingeschraubt wird. Die fruehere Haltung ist meiner Ansicht nach unbequem und ungrazlös; ausserdem wird es jedem klar sein, dass durch das Druecken der Beine und den Contact des Beinkleider der Ton bedeutend leiden muss.' Bernhard Romberg, ed. and rev. Jules de Swert and Heinrich Grünfeld, *Violoncelloschule* (Berlin: E. Bote & G. Bock [1888]), p. 4.

[32]   'In neuerer Zeit bedient man sich allgemein des Stachels (Stütze). Diese Neuerung brachte manche Vorteile: großerer Stabilität und bessere Resonanz des Instrumentes, bei geringerer Ermüdung des spielers.' F.A. Kummer, rev. Hugo Becker, *Violoncelloschule* op. 60 (Leipzig: Peters, 1909), p. viii.

[33]   Sebastian Lee, rev. Hugo Becker, *Violoncello Tecnics* op. 30 (Mainz: B Schott's Söhne [1900–03]), p. 2 (English and French). First edition, Lee, *Méthode pratique pour le Violoncelle (Praktische Violoncell-Schule.)* op. 30 (Mainz: B. Schott et fils, [1846]).

Carl Schroeder also describes the older posture as out of date:

> In former times the violoncello was held in such wise as to grip it between the calves of the legs, whereby the position was rather upright, and the entire manner of holding somewhat stiff. Now a peg is used, secured underneath through the button (tail-pin). The holding is by this means rendered more free and comfortable, and the free emission of the tone is no longer hindered by the pressure of the legs against the sides. When a peg is used, the instrument is so placed between the legs as to give it a slanting direction.[34]

Nonetheless, the illustration shows a disposition of the feet and an adjustment of the height of the right leg which would have been easily recognized by any of his predecessors (Figure 1.7).[35]

Although the recommended length of tail-pin appears to have been 7–8 inches (both in words and illustrations), a somewhat longer one is shown in Thomas Eakins's 1896 portrait of the cellist Rudolph Hennig (1845–1904), although this

Figure 1.7   Schroeder, *Catechism*, posture illustration

---

[34]   Carl Schroeder, trans. J. Matthews. *Catechism of Cello Playing* (London: Augener & Co., 1893), pp. 19–20.

[35]   Ibid.

may be a matter of remaining in proportion with the length of the player's leg.[36] An American composite cello method from 1895 shows a diagram of the instrument including a tail-pin without any comment.[37]

If the majority around 1900 preferred to use a tail-pin, it was clearly optional for some time later. The 1910 revised edition of Piatti's cello method by Piatti's pupil William Whitehouse gives both stances:

> There are two ways of holding the cello – without the peg (Piatti's method), and with the peg, the latter being that generally adopted at the present time.[38]

Whitehouse's description of posture is essentially the same with or without the tail-pin, rather like Langey's quoted above. Even in 1919 this approach was still recommended by Alfred Earnshaw:

> It is probably only in comparatively recent times that ladies have taken up the cello, and the fact that few, if any, 'cellos were fitted with the sliding peg by which the 'cello could be held up, proves that it was considered only possible for a man to play it. Therefore, the best way to find the correct position in which to hold the instrument is to revert to the old method and hold the 'cello by the knees and calves, when the correct adjustment is assured, then we can use the peg, which to my mind, is certainly easier and more comfortable.[39]

Earnshaw's photograph shows clearly that his posture is 'the old method', with the instrument turned so that the front right edge of the cello rests against the player's right leg, and the the C string peg just clearing the player's shoulder.[40]

The tail-pin was sometimes thought to bring problems of its own. The Yorkshireman Arthur Broadley thought it actually encouraged self-indulgent playing:

> Piatti, who does not use a 'cello peg, holds his instrument in a correct manner, not shuffling about or varying his position. Now if the reader ever has a chance of hearing Van Biene, let him observe the manner in which that artist holds his cello. We have here the two extremes; as Piatti is of the strictly correct order,

[36]   Thomas Eakins, *The Cello Player* (1896), oil on canvas, 163 cm × 122 cm, formerly Joseph E. Temple Fund, Pennsylvania Academy of Fine Arts (sold privately 2007, current whereabouts unknown). Available online, URL: http://arthistory.about.com/od/from_exhibitions/ig/Americans-in-Paris/amerinpar_18.htm [accessed July 2012].

[37]   Carl Weber (ed.), *The Premier Method for Violoncello from the works of [...] Dotzauer, Bach, Laurent, Romberg [...] and others* (Philadelphia, PA: J.W. Pepper, 1895), p. 7.

[38]   Alfredo Piatti, rev. W.E. Whitehouse and R.V. Tabb, *Violoncello Method* (London: Augener, 1911), Vol. 1, p. [ii].

[39]   Alfred H. Earnshaw, *The Elements of 'Cello Technique* (London: Joseph Williams Limited, 1919), p. 1.

[40]   Ibid., p. 3.

Van Biene is of the exaggerated artistic order, all the time he is playing constantly striking some fresh attitude. If Van Biene had again to take to concert work, I have no doubt that he would calm down a little in this respect … his exaggerated style while being every effective on the stage, would not be tolerated on the concert platform.[41]

Auguste van Biene was probably the most widely heard cellist in Britain at the turn of the century, performing as a cellist in a play written for him, *The Broken Melody*, which received nearly 6000 performances in the period 1892–1913 in Britain and abroad. His own recordings demonstrate some of the most extreme portamenti of any musician from the period, and his acting style was equally exaggerated.[42] In spite of his reservations, Broadley's own charming illustration (Figure 1.8) shows him using a tail-pin.[43]

Figure 1.8   Broadley, *Chats*, posture illustration

[41]   Arthur Broadley, *Chats to Cello Students* (London: 'The Strad' Office, E. Donajowski and D.R. Duncan, 1899), p. 7.

[42]   George Kennaway, 'The Phenomenon of the Cellist Auguste van Biene: From the Charing Cross Road to Brighton via Broadway', in M. Hewitt and R. Cowgill (eds), *Victorian Soundscapes*. Leeds Working Papers in Victorian Studies 9 (Leeds: LCVS and LUCEM, 2007), pp. 67–82.

[43]   Ibid., p. 8. Broadley uses a similar photographic illustration in his *Adjusting and Repairing Violins, Cellos, &c.* (London: L. Upcott Gill, 1908).

A little later, Hugo Becker sounded another warning note:

> Unfortunately, simultaneously with the use of the spike a negligent, unattractive posture has crept in, which is detrimental to the handling of the instrument.[44]

Carl Fuchs was criticized for showing posture illustrations that had *omitted* the tail-pin in the first edition of his cello method, but he defended himself in the 1907 second edition:

> Fault has been found with pictures 3 & 4, because the player uses no end-pin. Although it is not advisable to allow beginners to play without a spike, I think it very useful to practise without. The body must then of necessity be kept still, and anyone who has fallen into the habit of holding the legs in an ugly position, can remedy this evil by practising without a tail-pin. Often too a player not accustomed to playing without a spike might be debarred from playing altogether by finding only a 'cello without an end-pin or with too short a one.[45]

The majority of cellists, certainly at the professional end of the spectrum, appear not have used a tail-pin until around the last quarter of the nineteenth century.[46] The principal reason for the increased use of the tail-pin was improved tone quality rather than physical comfort. In fact, if followed correctly, the traditional advice to hold the cello at its edges and not the ribs minimizes the problem, but this can be uncomfortable. A natural tendency to apply pressure to the ribs of the instrument may well have created the perceived disadvantage. For all the care that earlier cellists took in describing this method of holding the cello, there were many who, like John Peile in the early nineteenth century, over-simplified to the almost certain detriment of the instrument's resonance:

---

[44]   'Leider schlich sich aber mit dem Gebrauch des Stachels gleichzeitig eine nächlässige, unschöne Haltung ein, die nachteilig auf die Behandlung des Intruments einwirt.' Kummer, rev. Becker, *Violoncellschule*.

[45]   Carl Fuchs, *Violoncello-Schule Violoncello Method*, 3 vols (London: Schott & Co. Ltd., 2/1907), Vol. 1, unpaginated preface.

[46]   Tilden Russell has argued that there was a widespread use of some sort of support for the cello amongst amateurs from long before the nineteenth century, and that method books rigidly codified what had been more flexible in the eighteenth. His iconographical evidence is inconsistent, however, depicting scenes from a very wide range of social situations and historical periods. If anything, he overstates the prevalence of the tail-pin by the end of the nineteenth century by not considering enough early twentieth-century evidence, and does not sufficiently stress the retention of the older posture when using a tail-pin. Tilden A. Russell, 'The Development of the Cello End-Pin', *Imago Musicae* 4 (1987), pp. 335–56.

The Learner should be seated forward in a chair or stool and the Violoncello held between the two calves of the legs and inclined to the right in order to have a better command of the first String – the Thumb is then to be placed without pressure on the back of the neck of the Violoncello [...].[47]

If there was general agreement in the nineteenth century about the cellist's basic posture, there is rather less agreement on how to hold the bow and how to explain this to the student. There are two main topics to consider: how to hold the bow (including the shape of the right arm), and the distance between bow and bridge.

The most widespread view throughout the nineteenth century is that the bow should be approximately 2 inches from the bridge, with some variation for dynamic effect or different tone colours. However, the recommended distance ranges from a minimum of 1–3 inches. Crome, Raoul, Lindley, de Swert and Alexanian place it approximately 1½ inches from the bridge (the latter two are slightly closer at 3 centimetres). Azaïs, several anonymous late eighteenth-century tutors, Bréval, Eley, Schroeder, and Langey, opt for 2 inches, and a small group of eighteenth-century cellists suggests that the bow is normally 3 inches from the bridge (Corrette, Hardy, Gunn). Among the less specific teaching on this point, the Paris method only says that the point of contact should be adjusted for volume; Bréval's illustration looks as if the bow is 2–3 inches from the bridge, but there is no supporting text; Crouch says that it should be 'rather nearer the bridge than the fingerboard'; Romberg's illustration suggests roughly 2 inches.[48]

The position of the point of contact between bow and string is extremely important with regard to tone quality and tonal projection. This is recognized by some, but by no means all, writers, who are in general more concerned with the loss of quality further away from the bridge than with enhanced projection close to it. In 1741, Corrette found 'sons sourds et faux', but a century later Robert Lindley was less critical, simply noting that 1 inch from the bridge produces a 'metallic or reedy' sound, becoming 'soft and fluty' 3 inches away.[49] The difference between these distances and modern practice can be shown in Christopher Bunting's specific insistence that the point of contact should divide the vibrating length of the string in the proportion of 1:13, which means that as the notes are played in higher positions the bow moves closer to the bridge and *vice versa* (irrespective

---

[47]   John Peile, *A New and Complete Tutor for the Violoncello* (London: Goulding, D'Almaine, Potter and Co. [1819?]), p. 11. This is a quite separate work from his 'translation' of Bréval quoted above.

[48]   Corrette specifies 3–4 'doigts' from the bridge ; i.e. either finger-widths (= 2–3 inches) or ½-inches (= 1½–2 inches). Raoul uses the 'ligne', a twelfth of a French 'pouce' (a unit slightly longer than the English inch). He recommends 18 *lignes* from the bridge, but says that since others prefer 24, one can compromise at 20 to 21, moving closer to the fingerboard for nuances.

[49]   Corrette, *Méthode*, p. 9; Lindley, *Hand-book*, p. 5.

of dynamic).[50] The concept of the 'sounding point' – the point of contact that produces the most resonance and projection, and a central part of modern cello pedagogy – is almost entirely absent from nineteenth-century cello methods, with the interesting exception of Raoul. He describes how, if the bow is correctly placed:

> The vibration of the string is then accompanied by a certain 'biting' which adds to the beauty of the performance. Moreover, because this 'biting' is most difficult to acquire, and that only when one is the master of tone quality, one can bring the bow nearer to the bridge to soften or moderate the voice of the instrument.[51]

Playing 3 inches from the bridge on gut strings produces a soft-grained, unprojected sound (even more so in higher positions), suitable for small-scale domestic music-making but inadequate for public performance in larger venues. Lindley may have described this favourably as 'fluty', but he was exceptional. There is a slight trend through the nineteenth century towards a point of contact closer to the bridge, but, apart from John Gunn, those who recommend placing the bow more than 2 inches from the bridge are generally writing for amateurs. Such tutors were published anonymously, covered a smaller range of topics, and offered the pupil a range of simple tunes to play in easier keys with limited *tessitura*. Apart from these, 2 inches is almost standard.

There is less agreement on the manner of holding of the bow and the general disposition of the right arm, than on the distance from the bridge. Most cellists agreed on these points:

* fingers spread naturally, and curved;
* stick inclined towards the fingerboard (except when on the C string);
* wrist curved outwards on upper strings, less so on lower;
* second finger touches the hair;
* first finger used to increase pressure for more sound;
* upper arm barely used;
* most movement comes from forearm; and
* string crossing is done mainly with the wrist (this is discussed at more length in Chapter 3).

Some of these points coincide with a natural physical tendency, such as the different relation of bow to string on the C' and A strings, with the stick leaning

---

[50]   Christopher Bunting, *Essay on the Craft of 'Cello Playing*, 2 vols. (Cambridge: Cambridge University Press, 1982), Vol. 1, pp. 23–4.

[51]   'La vibration de la corde est alors accompagnée d'un certain mordant qui ajoute à la beauté de l'exécution. D'ailleurs comme le mordant est ce qu'il y a de plus difficile à acquérir et que quand on est maître de la qualité de son, on peut rapprocher l'archet de la touche pour adoucir ou pour nuancer la voix de l'instrument.' Jean Marie Raoul, *Méthode de violoncelle* op. 4 (Paris: Pleyel, [c.1797]), p. 6.

more towards the fingerboard on the upper strings and less so on the lower, or the differing curvature of the wrist on low and high strings.

But in the agreement over the last four points above, which concern the positioning of the upper arm and elbow and the use of right index finger, we encounter some of the most striking differences between nineteenth-century practice and our own time. Illustrations often clearly reinforce the advice not to use the upper arm and to keep the right elbow low (even when playing at the tip). Since using the weight of the arm itself as a source of pressure on the string is not possible in this position (to say nothing of the basically vertical position of the instrument), the first finger has to vary the bow pressure on its own, and for louder playing it has to stretch forward on the stick with a larger gap between the first and second fingers. The examples in Figures 1.9–1.12 cover a wide historical period.

The illustrations of Romberg and Kummer share the highly angled instrument embraced by the right knee, and the low right elbow when playing at the tip. However, in other respects they differ significantly. Romberg's right wrist is naturally curved at the heel, and is held very low at the tip, while Kummer's right hand (shown in the 'ghost' arm in the illustration) is more naturally curved at the heel and leans forward at the tip. Because it leans forward in this way, Kummer's fourth finger rests on top of the stick when playing at the tip, but

Figure 1.9   Romberg, *Violoncellschule*, bowing at the tip[52]

---

[52]   Kummer, *Violoncelloschule*, p. vii.

Figure 1.10   Kummer, *Violoncelloschule*, posture illustration (note 'ghost' right
              arm)[53]

Romberg's remains somewhat over the stick. Becker recreated Kummer's image
photographically in his revision of Lee's method, but with a more recognizably
modern right arm shape, especially when playing at the tip of the bow. Romberg
appears to maintain the same position of the right hand at each end of the bow; the
right wrist and elbow are low, and the right hand curiously lifted towards the first
finger. Keeping the right elbow as low as this is, for modern players, extremely
unnatural, but there can be no doubt that this was an essential part of nineteenth-
century cello technique. Romberg says that both elbows should be low, implying
that his left hand shape was not the only element of violin technique incorporated
into his own playing:

> Stiffness in the arm generally proceeds from bending the body too much
> forward, and raising the elbows too high. The great French Violinists have long
> perceived this defect, and they therefore hold the elbows as low as possible in
> playing and never raised; because an elevation of the elbow forces the shoulder
> out of its natural position.[54]

---

[53]   Kummer, *Violoncelloschule*, p. vii.
[54]   Romberg, *Violoncellschule*, p. 8.

Figure 1.11   Schroeder, *Catechism*, posture at tip[55]

There is altogether less consensus on these other details of bow hold:

- distance of first finger (or thumb) from nut;
- bow hold 'shallow' (held towards fingertips) or 'deep' (stick running closer to second knuckle, mid-finger);
- position of thumb relative to first and second fingers;
- shape of thumb (straight or bent);
- thumb flat to the stick;
- shape and position of first finger;
- third finger touching hair;
- fourth finger passive on stick or active (pressing); and
- balancing function of first and fourth fingers.

The standard modern bow hold, with the thumb more or less opposite the second finger, did not evolve quickly. Many cellists earlier in the nineteenth century placed the thumb between first and second fingers, freeing the first to vary the stick pressure. However, some thought the thumb should be opposite the second finger, including Reinagle, Schetky, Bréval/Peile and Gunn. Romberg and Duport are unusual in placing the thumb between the second and third fingers. Lindley is clearly anachronistic in keeping the thumb opposite the first finger in the 1850s.

---

[55]   Schroeder, *Catechism*, pp. 20–21.

Figure 1.12   Lee, rev. Becker, *Méthode*, posture illustration[56]

Dotzauer acknowledges a wide range of practice in the distance of the hand from the heel of the bow:

> among the strongest players one finds those who hold it as close as possible to the heel; others who hold it much shorter [away from the heel]; excess in both is dangerous. Holding the bow too long so that the little finger is on the button, it is impossible to press with enough force to play *forte*, one risks seeing the bow escape from the fingers. It is even worse to hold it so short that the little finger is several inches from the heel; this puts all the weight of the bow behind the hand where it serves no purpose, in this way one cannot draw the tone, and one acquires a bad habit.[57]

---

[56]   Lee, rev. Becker, *Méthode*, Figure 1, unpaginated.

[57]   'parmis les plus fort joueurs, on en trouve qui le tiennent le plus près possible de la hausse; d'autres qui le prennent beaucoup plus court; des deux façons l'excès est nuisible. En prenant l'archet trop long de manière à ce que le petit doigt se trouve sur le bouton il est impossible de l'appuyer avec assez de force pour jouer un forte, on risquerait de le voir échapper les doigts. Il est encore plus vicieux de le tenir si court que le petit doigt se trouve à quelque pouces en avant de la hausse; ce qui met tout le poids de l'archet en arrière de

His objection to holding the bow too close to the nut – that the first finger is powerless to increase the pressure of the bow on the string – arises because this puts the thumb *opposite* the first finger, and it cannot exert leverage. Dotzauer is the only cellist to make this point.

He is also the earliest to state that the thumb must be next to the frog. There is some variation in the recommended distance between the right hand and the frog, compounded by its being measured in different ways – the distance from the thumb to the frog, or the distance of the hand, measured from the fourth finger (that is, the size of the gap between *hand* and frog). Some tutors are quite vague in any case. 'Near the nut' is the advice of Crome, Hardy and several anonymous tutors.[58] Many specify 1½ inches between the thumb and the nut.[59] A few give the size of the gap between the hand and the nut; Azaïs specifies 1 inch, and Crouch half an inch.[60] Dotzauer was the first to specify the bow hold that was to become standard, with the thumb touching the nut with one side of the thumbnail, but in 1825 he was asserting this at a time of wide variation in practice. There is clearly a move from a bow hold some distance from the nut to the modern bow hold, reaching the latter position during the second quarter of the nineteenth century.

Some aspects of posture come into a different focus when we look at them in their social context. The advice given to cellists often resonates with wider concerns, such as the importance of elegance and grace. Many cellists observe the importance of the visual aspect of the player's posture. This can be as important as the actual playing, so that an unattractive posture can in itself detract from the enjoyment of the performance. John Gunn touches on this in the first edition of his *Treatise*, when he recommends raising the right arm when playing on the A string. As well as enabling more 'natural power' and making string crossing with the wrist easier,

> this position of the arm looks much better than a lower one; and I think it will always hold true, from some general principle in nature, connecting pleasure

la main, ou il ne sert à rien, de cette manière on ne pourrait filer le son, et on contracte une mauvaise habitude.' J.J.F. Dotzauer, *Méthode de Violoncelle. Violonzell-Schule* (Mainz: B. Schott fils, [1825]), p. 7.

[58] Including *New and Complete Instructions for the Violoncello* (London: Goulding, [c.1787]), and *New and Complete Instructions for the Violoncello* (London: Clementi, Banger, Hyde, Collard & Davis, [c.1805]).

[59] *A New and Complete Tutor* (London: Preston and Son, [1785?]); *New Instructions for the Violoncello* (London: Thomas Cahusac & Sons, [c.1795]); Broderip and Wilkinson's *Complete Treatise for the Violoncello*. London: the Editors, [c.1800]; Eley, *Improved Method* [1827].

[60] Pierre-Hyacinthe Azaïs, *Méthode de basse* (Paris: Bignon, [c.1775]), p. 1; Frederick Crouch, *Compleat Ttreatise on the Violoncello* (London: Chappell & Co., [1826]), p. 7, and unpaginated prefaratory illustration. Crouch's work was criticized for plagiarizing the Paris Conservatoire method on its appearance, but this is not quite accurate. Anon., *Harmonicon*, 4 (1826), pp. 28–9.

with utility, that whatever movement is best adapted to attain its end, will also be the most graceful. In this view, practising before a glass will be an excellent lesson to acquire good habits, and prevent bad ones.[61]

Cello tutors certainly discouraged excessive physical effort in performance, albeit to varying degrees. Dominique Bideau refers to this aspect of the cellist's craft almost laconically:

Grace and ease [*aisance*] in the manner of holding an instrument contribute much to success in playing it well.[62]

Duport agrees with Gunn that the most effective movement will also be the most graceful, when he discusses the importance of a flexible wrist in ensuring a straight bow:

There are some people who do this to excess, and all useless movement is ridiculous; others think by this to acquire grace [of movement], but I think that there is nothing more graceful than facility, and all useless movement destroys this.[63]

Dotzauer warns of the awkward use of the feet:

One must carefully avoid stretching out the feet too far or folding them under the seat, these positions are ungraceful.[64]

The Paris Conservatoire method is particularly emphatic about graceful deportment:

the head and body must be held erect, avoiding every thing that might have the air of negligence or affectation. We cannot too strongly recommend pupils to endeavour to acquire a noble and easy attitude. A secret relation exists between the sense of sight and hearing. If the former be offended, if anything constrained or negligent be observed in the position of the player, seeming to contradict

---

[61]   John Gunn, *The Theory and Practice of Fingering the Violoncello* (London: the Author, [1st ed., 1789]), p. 63.

[62]   'Les grâces et l'aisance dans la manière de tenir un instrument contribuent beaucoup au succès de le bien jouer.' Dominique Bideau, *Grande et nouvelle méthode raisonnée*, p. 3.

[63]   'Il y a quelques personnes qui le font à outrance, or tout mouvement inutile est ridicule; d'autres croyent par-là se donner de la grace, mais je pense qu'il n'y a rien de plus gracieux que la facilité, et tout mouvement inutile la detruit.' Jean Louis Duport, *Essai sur le doigté*, p. 159. This passage is omitted in Lindner's trilingual edition.

[64]   'Il faut éviter avec soin de trop allonger les pieds ou de les plier sous la chaise, ces positions ont mauvaise grâce.' J.J.F. Dotzauer, *Méthode de Violoncelle. Violonzell-Schule* (Mainz: B. Schott fils, [1825]), p. 5.

whatever he may do with expression and grace, he will give pain to his hearers in proportion as the contrast is more striking between his playing and his attitude. We will go farther, and say, it is extremely rare and almost impossible, to see a virtuoso at the same time delight the ear and offend the sight. Real talent unfolds every expedient of art, and this development cannot have place without a natural easiness of position which is always attended with grace, and which augments the pleasure of the auditors by leading them to forget the vanquished difficulty, and allowing them to be more affected by the music performed.[65]

This method also mentions an alternative posture, apparently used by orchestral players, where the cello actually rests on the player's left foot, but criticizes it because it is 'ungraceful, and fatiguing'.[66] Crouch, like Dotzauer, is equally concerned with elegance. He follows the Paris method very here closely, but omits the 'orchestral' posture.[67]

The recommended posture had much in common with prevailing notions of correct deportment in general. Turning the feet out was recommended not only by cellists, but by eighteenth-century dancing masters, who taught rules of general deportment:

All masters impressed upon their pupils that in order that 'in order to attain a graceful Manner of Moving, it is first necessary to know how to stand still'. Hence they turn their attention to the placing of the feet. The feet and legs should always be turned out to a moderate degree. 'Always turn out your feet, because that makes you stand firm, easy and graceful', is the instruction given in a little book of polite behaviour for 'Masters and Misses'.[68]

Even in walking, the feet could be somewhat turned out:

neither must he swing his Arms backward and forward, nor must he carry his Knees too close, nor must he go wagging his Breech, nor with his feet in a straight line, but with the in-side of his Feet a little out [...].[69]

Adam Petrie's book was reprinted frequently throughout the eighteenth and nineteenth centuries, and in the nineteenth century it was still thought elegant to

---

[65] P. Baillot, J.H. Levasseur, C.-S. Catel and C.-N. Baudiot, *Méthode de violoncelle* (Paris: Janet et Cotelle, [1804]), p. 8; trans. A. Merrick, *Method for the Violoncello* (London: Cocks & Co. [1830]), p. 17.

[66] Ibid., p. 6 (Merrick, p.14).

[67] Frederick Crouch, *Compleat Treatise on the Violoncello*, p. 9.

[68] Joan Wildblood, *The Polite World: A Guide to the Deportment of the English in Former Times* (London: David-Poynter, 2nd. edn 1973), p. 128.

[69] Adam Petrie, *Rules of Good Deportment, or of Good Breeding. For the Use of Youth* (Edinburgh: [no publisher], 1720), p. 7.

turn the legs and feet out a little.[70] However, overdoing this was discouraged as it might make the person look like a professional dancer.[71] Around 1875, Eliza Cheadle remarked that:

> Horace Walpole is described as always entering a room with knees bent and feet on tiptoe, as if afraid of a wet floor; but we are told that this affected style was quite *a la mode* in his day.[72]

Although Macaulay called Walpole 'the most eccentric, the most artificial, the most fastidious, the most capricious, of men',[73] this 'affected' demeanour is repeated in Zoffany's depiction of Charles Gore playing the cello at a family gathering to celebrate his daughter's marriage, which shows this posture very clearly – the feet turned out, the heels off the floor (Figures 1.13a and 1.13b).

Placing the left foot forward, specifically, would have been familiar advice for a man who had had dancing lessons:

> In order to follow his master's detailed instructions, the pupil should place his weight upon the right foot, the left foot slightly advanced, with the knee relaxed and the foot turned a little outwards.[74]

Similarly, a popular guide to a young man's education from the mid-nineteenth century offered advice on physical deportment that had much in common with the cellist's posture. As well as general advice ('The carriage of a gentleman should be genteel, and his motions graceful', 'Awkwardness of carriage is very alienating'),[75] Edward Turner notes that:

> In dancing, the motion of the arms should be particularly attended to, as these decide a man's being genteel or otherwise [...] A twist or stiffness in the wrist will make any man look awkward. [...] Those who present themselves well, have a certain dignity in their air, which, without the least mixture of pride, at once engages, and is respected.[76]

---

[70]   Wildblood, *The Polite World*, p. 155.

[71]   Ibid., p. 160.

[72]   Eliza Cheadle, *Manners of Modern Society* (London: Cassell Petter & Galpin, [c.1875]), p. 44. Horace Walpole, 4th Earl of Orford (1717–97), author of *The Castle of Otranto* (1764), architect of Strawberry Hill (1749–76).

[73]   T.B Macaulay, *Edinburgh Review* 58 (1833), pp. 227–58, quoted in Peter Sabor (ed.), *Horace Walpole: The Critical Heritage* (New York: Routledge & Kegan Paul, 1987), pp. 18–19.

[74]   Wildblood, *The Polite World*, p. 128.

[75]   Edward Turner, *The Young Man's Companion* (Halifax: Milner and Sowerby, 1861), pp. 274, 278.

[76]   Ibid., pp. 278–9.

Even the advice to cellists to sit forward on the edge of the chair had connections with polite behaviour:

'It is painful to see the want of ease with which some men sit on the edge of a chair.' These are the words of Lord Chesterfield quoted in the nineteenth century. In his day, deportment commended in the sixteenth century would be considered absurdly stiff. In the nineteenth century, however, the complaint was not against too much rigidity, but against too much lounging. 'The manner in which others throw themselves back and stretch forward their legs savours too much of familiarity.'[77]

An 1825 review of Josef Merk (1795–1852) stressed the importance of the appearance of ease in performance (*aisance*, used earlier by Bideau), and compared him with Romberg:

Prof. Merk performs the most difficult passages with the greatest clarity and certainty, without it appearing difficult for him. This *aisance* (had we a word for it, but we only have the thing) in performance is the most attractive quality of great virtuosi, and nobody had this to a higher degree, and with good reason, than our Bernhard Romberg, whom we admittedly only *in imperfectio* can call our own. Yet Herr Merk approaches him in that respect, as in his entire playing style, and I could not give a greater compliment in praise of this splendid virtuoso.[78]

The unpublished memoirs of Anton Gräffer (1786–1852), written c.1850, describe the effect of Romberg's deportment:

I heard Bernhard Romberg perform. [...] Rather than looking at his cello, he used to direct his eyes either upwards or out at the audience, using a friendly, smiling expression, and not like certain cellists who perform so deeply bent over their instruments that one is afraid they will fall off their chairs in order to embrace their instruments on the floor.[79]

---

[77] Wildblood, *The Polite World*, p. 156, quoting Anon., *Habits of Good Society* (London: J. Hogg & Sons, [1859]).

[78] 'Herr Prof. Merk [...] mit grössester Reinheit und Sicherheit die schwierigsten Passagen ausführt, ohne dass es ihm schwer zu werden scheint. Diese aisance (hätten wir nur ein Wort dafür, aber wir haben nur das Ding) der Ausführung ist die bestechendste Eigenschaft grosser Virtuosen, und niemand hatte sie, und mit begrundetem Recht, in einem höhern Maasse, als unser Bernhard Romberg, den wir freilich nur im Imperfekto den unsern nennen können. Doch Herr Merk nähert sich ihm darin, wie überhaupt in seiner ganzen Spielart sehr, und kaum wuste ich etwas ehrenvolleres zum Lobe des trefflichen virtuosen zu sagen'. *BAmZ*, 2 (1825), p. 170.

[79] This material kindly supplied and translated by Dr Rita Steblin.

Figure 1.13a   Johann Zoffany, *The Gore Family with George, 3rd Earl Cowper*, c.1775 (Yale Center for British Art, Paul Mellon Collection)

Romberg's portrait on the frontispiece of his tutor (Figure 1.14), with his benign expression directed out of the frame, bears out this description. He himself was concerned equally with a healthy posture and a graceful attitude:

> The best [posture] to be adopted for sitting is that which is most conducive to bodily health. [...] that posture [must] be adopted, in which the Instrument can be played freely and with ease. During play, no change of posture should take place; least of all, any thing like an affected attitude, which may betray the trouble employed in playing.[80]

Georg Kastner makes a similar point:

> it is necessary, as far as possible, to keep the body in an upright and relaxed position, because a cramped posture is both ungraceful and tiring.[81]

---

[80]   Bernhard Romberg, trans. anon., *Complete Theoretical and Practical School for the Violoncello*, p. 7.

[81]   'il faut, autant que possible, maintenir le corps dans une position droit et aisée, car une position courbée est aussi disgracieuse et fatigante.' Georges Kastner, *Méthode Élémentaire pour le Violoncelle*, p. 2.

Figure 1.13b   Zoffany, *Gore Family*, detail of Charles Gore

Figure 1.14   Romberg, frontispiece illustration (*Violoncellschule*, 1840)

However, at least in the first half of the nineteenth century, most cellists stress the aesthetics of appearance rather than physical health. Kummer is particularly emphatic on how deportment can conceal difficulty from the audience:

> Expression can only originate in the correct use of subtle nuances of tone, not through affected bodily movement, because the composer will work on the listeners' feeling through the ears and not the eyes. Also with passage-work and difficult positions, the greatest possible composure of the body is an advantage, which the learner should emulate, and although the multitude may imagine that the player only executes something extraordinary when he makes visibly violent efforts, nonetheless the artist and connoisseur know very well, that an essential requirement of virtuosity is: difficulties must not appear as such to the listener.[82]

Such remarks provide a context for occasional criticisms of Robert Lindley's concert demeanour. Twice within a fortnight in 1828 the *Harmonicon* drew attention to his implied lack of *aisance* (perhaps combined with additional histrionics):

> The trio [Corelli, played by cellists Lindley (father and son) and contrabass Dragonetti] was as well executed as *such* an adaptation of it would admit; but could old Corelli have heard it, how he would have stared! Poor Lindley's uniform features of placidity were *bewrinkled* into all manner of comical distortions during his exertions, and well they might be.[83]
> The difficult arpeggio accompaniment in the trio [of Beethoven's 8th symphony], for the violoncello, made even Lindley something more than warm upon its repetition. He should be allowed two or three cambric handkerchiefs at the expense of the Society, on such occasions.[84]

Lindley's histrionic playing to the audience even took place apparently at Dragonetti's expense:

> Lindley and Dragonetti played their old sonata in A in a manner that would have astonished Corelli; the former indulging in all those licenses of roulade and

---

[82]   'Der Ausdruck kann nur durch richtige Nüancierung der Töne, nie durch affektierte Körperbewegungen hervorgebracht werden, da der Tonkünstler auf das Gefühl des Zuhörers vermittelst des Ohres und nicht des Auges wirken soll. Auch bei Passagen und schwierigen Stellen ist möglichste ruhe des Körpers ein Vorzug, dem er nachstreben soll, und wenn auch die Menge zuweilen glaubt, er sich dabei sichtbar abmüht, so weiß doch der Künstler und Kenner recht gut, daß eine wesentliche Bedingung der Virtuosität die ist: dem Zuhörer Schwierigkeiten nicht als solche erscheinen zu lassen'. F.A. Kummer, rev. Hugo Becker, *Violoncelloschule*, p. 46.

[83]   Anon. review, 'Ancient Concert', 28 May 1828, *Harmonicon*, 6 (1828), p. 165.

[84]   Anon. review, Philharmonic Society, 9 June 1828, *Harmonicon*, 6 (1828), p. 167.

ornament, against which both good taste and all the genius of the old Italian school have long pleaded in vain; the latter articulating the divisions of the running bass with an *aplomb* and distinctness that are the admiration of all hearers in every succeeding repetition. The encore produced as usual the pleasing pantomime of these genial old comrades. Dragonetti having his arduous work to do over again, was rather coy in his compliance. Lindley having nothing to do was of course quite the reverse, and when the whole was over, the violoncellist handed the contrabassist out of the orchestra, with all the attention and deference that one would bestow on some very remarkable old lady, laughing immoderately, but with great good humour, as though the *encore* of a difficulty were one of the best jokes in the world against Dragonetti.[85]

In fact, Lindley's deportment is frequently praised more when he is *not* actually playing, but simply appearing as a benign presence on the concert platform:

> Instead of a concertante by Messrs. Lindley, Miss Cann, a highly-talented girl,
> [...] played Drouet's variations to 'God save the king,' on the flute; and her
> performance excited astonishment and admiration, both in the room and in the
> orchestra. We were pleased to see the leader, Cramer, nodding mute approbation;
> and Lindley, leaning upon his silent violoncello, smiling as the rapidly-executed
> notes struck on his ear.[86]
> [T]he sight of the comely old man winding his way into the orchestra was, in nine
> cases out of ten, signal for a hearty round of English applause and welcome.[87]
> Endowed with an even temperament and simple manners, Lindley always
> dressed very modestly. The benevolence of his nature will for a long time make
> his memory mourned by artists and lovers of art.[88]

Just over a decade after Lindley's death, Henry Chorley suggested that Servais's performing style lacked grace and *aisance* rather more fundamentally than suggested by the *Harmonicon*'s reviews of Lindley.

> [...] this brilliant mastery [...] was impaired by a certain violence and eccentricity
> of manner which disturbed the pleasure of the hearer. The deepest expression,
> the most vehement passion, is still consistent with grace and composure.[89]

---

[85] *MW*, 9 (new ser. 4) (1839), p. 166.

[86] *Harmonicon*, 3 (1823), p. 204: review, Hereford Music Meeting, 18 September 1823.

[87] Anon. [Henry Chorley], Lindley's obituary: *Athenaeum*, no. 1443, 23 June 1855, p. 739.

[88] 'Doué d'un caractère égal et de manières simples, Lindley portait toujours un costume fort modeste. La bienveillance de sa nature rendra sa mémoire longtemps regrettable aux artistes et aux amis de l'art'. Anon., Lindley's obituary: *Revue et gazette musicale*, 22 (1855), p. 207.

[89] [Henry Chorley], Servais's obituary, *Athenaeum*, no. 2041, 8 December 1866, p. 759.

Chorley's point of view becomes clearer in his review of the French cellist Lamoury:

> M. Lamoury, a new violoncellist from Paris, made a favourable impression. His command of the instrument was shown in a troublesome, patchy, and ineffective *solo*, composed by M. Servais; but there seems to us in his playing that elegance which, in *solo* playing, may attract more than marvellous execution.[90]

Elegance can actually trump technical virtuosity, not merely enhance it. Not only that – Chorley praised Piatti's performance of Beethoven's cello sonata op. 102 no. 2 as a demonstration of how gracefulness could conceal not just the technical difficulty of the piece, but also its compositional complexity:

> In few other hands than those of M. Halle and Signor Piatti would such a feat have been prudent: because, in the last movement, *fugato*, after the enormous manual difficulties have been conquered, an amount of shrewd yet liberal perception is required for the disentanglement on the licentious intricacies of the composition, and by such partial disentanglement, in some degree to conceal them.[91]

Later in the nineteenth century, teachers become less concerned with the aesthetics of appearance as opposed to the simple details of posture, like Laurent Junod:

> [The player's] body should be maintained in a good, easy, natural, and above all, erect position.[92]

When van der Straeten, explaining the holding of the bow, describes the smooth curve of the forearm through the wrist to the fingers, he repeats the idea that functionality and aesthetics are linked:

> This being the most perfect and pleasing line from an artistic point of view, is also the most natural and unconstrained. In fact all thoroughly natural attitudes are always the most pleasing to the eye, and those best adapted to ensure elasticity and agility in movements of all kinds.[93]

He also hints at the associations of certain posture faults with notions of lower-class physical labour:

---

90   [Henry Chorley], *Athenaeum*, no. 1785, 11 January 1863, p. 56.

91   [Henry Chorley], *Athenaeum*, no. 1844, 28 February 1863, p. 302.

92   Laurent Junod, trans. anon., *New and Concise Method*, p. 3.

93   E. van der Straeten, *Technics of Violoncello Playing* (London: 'The Strad' Office, 1898), pp. 28–9.

It is necessary to guard against anything which will bring out the elbow too much, and thereby raise the shoulder. It should never remind one of the position of a tailor sewing up a coat.[94]

In Emil Krall's *Art of Tone-Production* (1913) there is scarcely any such word as 'grace' or 'elegance', so frequent in earlier discussions. Alexanian's even more quasi-scientific treatise actually rejects elegance:

> we learn to place the fingers of our right hand on the stick of the bow in the way that is deemed by our teacher, by experience, to be 'natural' and 'simple'. [...] We have a general idea of the exterior aspect that convention has imposed on our right hand while we are playing. As for the [pressure of the fingers on the bow, and the exact place of each finger [...] the teacher usually decides according to the conformation of the hand. This appears to me to be a faulty procedure. [...] nothing concerning the 'grip' can be absolute, and that if all the artists formed by the same teacher have a slightly personal 'manner' this has originated in the dissemblance of their physical aptitudes. These small differences in the synthesis of appearance can, by a strict observance of its 'analysis' be reduced to an inoffensive relative elegance in the 'aestheticism' of the holding of the bow. As far as technique is concerned it is, if not negligible, at least of secondary importance.[95]

Hugo Becker also does not discuss the aesthetics of posture, focussing instead on the importance of posture being individually adjusted to the requirements of each player – 'each individual cellist possesses his own unique bowing height', which dictates all such matters as the length of the tail-pin or the height of the chair.[96] Those who cannot find an effective posture that will let them play difficult passages such as those in Romberg's concertos are advised to give up the instrument as unsuitable.[97] Practicality is Becker's only concern.

A posture based, by modern standards, on excessively low elbows, putting more strain on the fingers of both hands, deliberately privileges an aesthetically more 'pleasing' posture at the expense of 'good' (more resonant, projected) tone production. This in turn makes playing the cello look less like hard work, which might be associated with a more physically efficient use of the weight of the

---

[94]   Ibid., p. 36.

[95]   Alexanian, Diran, trans. Frederick Fairbanks *Traité théoretique et pratique du violoncelle* (Paris: A.Z. Mathot, 1922), p. 10.

[96]   'jedes cellospielende Individuum seine ihm eigentümliche Strichhöhe besitzt'. Hugo Becker and Dago Rynar, *Mechanik und Aesthetik des Violoncellospiels* (Vienna: Universal Edition, 1929), p. 28.

[97]   'Individuen, welche bei dieser Haltungsart infolge ihres anormalen Körperbaues eine schwierigere technische Aufgabe (z. B. ein Romberg-Konzert) nicht lösen können, eignen sich eben weniger zum Berufs-Violoncellisten.' Ibid., p. 29.

arms. Graceful deportment is partly, perhaps largely, used to conceal the difficulty of playing the piece. This attitude seems more prevalent in the first half of the nineteenth century, though Piatti is a prominent later example. Conversely, an artificial deportment is associated with the appearance of 'hard work', and also with exaggerated histrionics rather than a natural communication with the audience.

This material shows that certain patterns of ideas about cello posture sometimes come together in a general consensus, but sometimes not. The majority view can change, but there are also substantial minority views, never dominant, but which nonetheless persist. There are also occasional individual dissenting voices, some of whom in retrospect seem to be ahead of their time, and some who were clearly old-fashioned even at the time of writing. This is particularly relevant to the use of a tail-pin. It was clearly not universal even as late as the first decade of the twentieth century – and even when it was used, the older posture was still held up as a model. This material has interesting implications for performance practice, or rather, practices. If one wishes to play any nineteenth-century cello music in a historically-informed way, rather than addressing the simple externals of performance such as vibrato, portamento and different types of bowing (considered in later chapters), one should first acquire a physical posture based on a more or less upright instrument, much lower elbows and a virtually inactive upper right arm. This in turn has a considerable effect on tone production – on the actual quality of the basic sound of the instrument.

Robert Lindley's marvellous tone, attested by many accounts, both during his lifetime and posthumously, was largely obtained by his use of particularly thick strings and an unusually heavy bow, unlike many players on the continent:

> The performers on the continent use thinner strings than our own players; and the bridge is generally of *lower* construction; consequently the strings approach nearer the fingerboard, thereby rendering the execution more facile with regard to rapidity. This may in part account for the English player producing a more powerful tone than the foreigners.[98]
>
> If the tone of Lindley's violoncello playing is to be taken as the proper standard, then Batta [...] must be accused of wanting that richness and fullness of tone which is the characteristic of the violoncello [...] Breadth of tone is produced by mounting the instrument with thick strings, playing with a heavy bow, and with the pressure of Lindley's fingers, which seem made for such resources. Unless born a Hercules, it would be in vain to attempt the pleasing effects of modern violoncello playing with such obstacles [...] If M. Batta be content with the flattery of a limited circle, then he will spurn our advice to use stronger strings [...].[99]

---

[98]   Anon. review, *MW*, 2 (1837), p. 130.
[99]   Anon. review, *MW*, 4 (1839), p. 29.

Lindley was an exception, and it may well be that, with his right thumb opposite his first finger, his heavy bow and thick strings compensated for the enforced weakness of the first finger because of its lack of leverage when positioned directly above the fulcrum of the thumb. If the weight of the arm is not used because of the dropped right elbow and passive upper arm, the position of the first finger relative to the thumb becomes essential for varying volume. Putting it directly opposite the thumb effectively removes this option. The net effect is to minimize the amount of sound that can be produced and also the amount by which it can be varied. This effect is magnified if combined with a low elbow, a virtually immobile upper arm, string crossings done mainly with the wrist, a bow-stroke made mostly with the forearm, and the cello held almost vertically. All these factors combine to limit the use of arm weight to deliver pressure to the string. If they were also combined with a point of contact 2 inches or perhaps more from the bridge, tone projection and volume would, in terms of modern performance expectations, be severely compromised. Amateur cellists working from tutors that recommended all of these elements would probably have played with little dynamic contrast. Modern players seeking to explore these historical styles must therefore decide just how far they wish to go.

Chapter 2

The Left Arm and Hand,
and Scale Fingerings

This chapter considers the most basic aspects of the use of the left hand as described by nineteenth-century cellists. In this period, there was some basic common ground concerning the shape of the left hand, with a clear consensus on such simple things as that the fingers curve outwards, the fingertip presses firmly on the string, the thumb pad touches the back of the neck, and the left elbow is low. The last, extremely important, point is the only one that differs substantially from modern practice, and it will be discussed later in this chapter. However, even with the other topics on which there was general agreement, which to a modern cellist might seem quite obvious, there are several distinctions to be noted.

Although the need for firm finger pressure on the string was widely acknowledged, there are some differences of emphasis. Baillot and Dotzauer said that the left hand finger pressure should be greater than that of the bow on the string (advice that is still given today, even when using metal strings), but several cellists in the late eighteenth/early nineteenth centuries warned about excessive finger pressure and the noise of the finger landing too heavily on the string. Laborde said that the fingers should be rounded, but that this was 'in order to attack the string, all the time without force or roughness, which is called "touch" [*le tact*]. One cannot say too often that this is an essential element for playing the instrument well.'[1] For similar reasons, Dotzauer thought it 'vicieux' to have the fingers too high above the string, and Romberg even made the rather exaggerated claim that excessive pressure strains the sinews, so 'that they require whole years of rest before they can again be used for playing'.[2] Some later teachers seem to have agreed that the noise of fingers hitting the string was considered unacceptable. Herbert Walenn appears to have taught a 'soft' left hand technique at the turn of the nineteenth century, as four of his pupils continued to teach it well into the twentieth. These include Valentine Orde, Michael Edmonds, William Pleeth (with all three of whom the writer studied in the 1970s and 1980s), and Zara Nelsova. Nelsova eventually rejected the 'Russian' approach (high left-hand fingers and some percussive noise): 'I learned later that this isn't the way to create perfect

---

[1]   'afin d'attaquer la corde, toutefois sans force ni roideur, ce qui s'appelle *le tact*. On ne saurait trop observer que c'est une partie essentielle pour bien jouer l'instrument'. Jean Benjamin Laborde, *Essai sur la musique* (Paris: Enfroy, 1780), p. 310.

[2]   Bernhard Romberg, trans. anon., *A Complete Theoretical and Practical School for the Violoncello* (London: T. Boosey & Co., [1840]), p. 97.

articulation.'[3] On the whole, the 'hammered' approach to the action of the fingers was discouraged.

The placing of the left thumb is variable. Most tutors recommend that it lies somewhere between the first and second fingers, but a substantial minority (Bideau, Baillot, Schetky, Crouch, and Romberg from the first half of the nineteenth century, and de Swert later) put it opposite the second or even between second and third fingers. Jules de Swert, uniquely, tells the cellist to place the thumb round the neck in fourth position so that it touches the ribs of the instrument.[4] In an illustration, Crouch shows the thumb much further round the neck than most, in the manner depicted in the previous century, and between second and third fingers.[5]

Most tutors recommend keeping the fingers down on the string as much as possible – Eley even gives a substantial exercise for this.[6] Dotzauer is a little more flexible on this point, saying that in some circumstances one need not keep all the fingers down in a short rapid group of stepwise notes, saying: 'It is not vitally necessary for the fingers to remain fixed to the string in passages such as these.'[7] However, the most important aspect of the left hand is its basic shape, and on this point there are several different views. A small minority of nineteenth-century cellists seem to have adopted a 'violinistic' left hand, with the fingers slanted backwards at an extremely oblique angle to the fingerboard and the thumb towards the opposite side of the neck rather than directly beneath it. Romberg is very clear about this in his illustration (Figure 2.1).[8]

His left hand leans well back rather than being perpendicular to the fingerboard, and the left elbow is dropped. This is not merely careless drawing, for Romberg also gives a uniquely detailed verbal description of this left hand shape:

> The hand should so hold the neck, that the 1st finger should clasp it round, the 2nd should be bent so as to form three sides of a square, the 3rd should be bent half round, and the 4th held straight. The thumb should lie exactly opposite to the 2nd finger [...] The palm of the hand should [...] be kept hollow, nor must the hollow of the thumb be pressed close to the 1st finger. The neck also must remain quite free in the hand [...].[9]

---

[3]   Zara Nelsova, interview with Tim Janof, http://www.cello.org/Newsletter/Articles/nelsova.htm [accessed September 2012].

[4]   Jules de Swert, *The Violoncello* (London: Novello, Ewer & Co., 1882), p. 38.

[5]   Crouch, *Compleat Treatise on the Violoncello* (London: Chappell & Co., [1826]) ibid., unpaginated plate.

[6]   C.F. Eley, *Improved Method for the Violoncello* (London: Clementi & Co., [1827?]), p. 79.

[7]   J.J.F. Dotzauer, *Méthode de Violoncelle. Violonzell-Schule* (Mainz: B. Schott fils, [1825]), p. 5.

[8]   Romberg, *Violoncellschule* (Berlin: Trautwein, [1840]), plate facing p. 6.

[9]   Ibid., p. 7.

The thumb must [...] fall exactly opposite the 2nd finger. The third joint of the first finger ([...] the joint next the hand), should be laid upon the neck of the Violoncello. The fingers should be held at the distance of at least a thumb's breadth above the strings, and all of them curved, except the fourth, which should be held straight, but not further removed from the strings [...] To [play] B on the A string, the 1st finger (still curved) should be pressed down, without disturbing the position of the other fingers [...].[10]

Romberg's description of the first finger, both in words and pictures, is quite exceptional. Keeping the lower joint of the first finger in contact with the neck drastically limits its movement, and makes even occasional ornamental vibrato very difficult (which may explain why Romberg barely discusses it, limiting it in practice to the second finger – see Chapter 5).

Figure 2.1   Romberg, *Violoncellschule*, left hand

Valerie Walden has maintained that 'a select group of virtuosos continued to teach and play with [the slanted] hand position', specifying Tricklir (1750–1813), Janson (1742–1803), Romberg (1767–1841) and Vaslin (1794–1889).[11] She could also have mentioned Georg Banger's *Méthode* of 1877, where a highly slanted left hand is also shown, with a very similar illustration to Romberg's but no explanatory

---

[10]   Ibid., p. 10.
[11]   Valerie Walden, *One Hundred Years of Violoncello A History of Technique and Performance Practice 1740–1840* (Cambridge: Cambridge University Press, 1998), p. 100.

text.[12] However, these players only exist as a group in the sense that they used this hand-shape. Given the relatively early deaths of the first two, the frequently old-fashioned nature of Romberg's treatise, Banger's marginal status and Vaslin's generally highly idiosyncratic approach, the importance of this 'group' should not be overstated. Vaslin's case is interesting. Like Romberg and Lindley, Vaslin did not set down his teaching ideas on paper until near the end of his life, at the age of 90. He enthusiastically promotes the violinistic left hand, which he first adopted during his early years in Paris in 1809 aged 15. But it transpires that he adopted it as a means of compensating for a double-jointed third finger:

> [In the Orchestre des Variétés] I met M. Ropiquet *père*, a modest violinist [...] He was struck by the weakness of my left hand, and he had little trouble in making me understand that the size of this large instrument need not preclude the logical, rational principles of the small one, of the same family [*congénère*]. So I abandoned the position of the thumb relative to the second finger in order to obtain this end, that of fingers which held on to the string. I had at the same time to work on the difficult correction of a third finger whose nature was to flex [...].[13]

Figure 2.2 shows him using this left hand shape, in an illustration dating from shortly after Romberg's death when Vaslin would have been just over 30 years old.[14] In this illustration he is not in the act of playing, but in his treatise he describes how this left hand shape is that by which one takes hold of the instrument:

> It is easy to understand and obtain if one can carefully keep the hand in the position which it takes to grasp the neck at the moment of placing the cello between the legs [...] the thumb goes around the neck and the fingers are found to be arranged curved outwards, offering only the tips to the strings.[15]

---

[12]   Georg Banger, *Méthode pratique de violoncelle Praktische Violoncell-schule* (Offenbach am Main: André, [1877]). Banger composed several works for the cello (published 1856–81), but is not mentioned in either van der Straeten or Wasielewski, and is not reviewed in any of the more important musical periodicals of the period.

[13]   '[...] j'entrai à 15 ans à l'Orchestre des Variétés. [...] Là je rencontrai Monsieur Ropiquet père, modeste violoniste [...] La défectuosité de ma main gauche le frappe il n'eut pas de peine à me faire comprendre que la dimension du gros instrument n'était pas une raison d'exclure les principes logiques et rationnels du petit, son congénère. Donc j'abandonnai la pose du pouce vis-à-vis du second doigt, afin d'obtenir que ce fut le bout, mais bien le bout des doigts qui portât sur la corde. J'eus en même temps à opérer la rectification pénible d'un troisième doigt dont la nature était de fléchir [...]'. Olive Vaslin, *L'art du violoncelle* (Paris: Richault, 1884), p. 1.

[14]   Emil Lassalle, lithograph portrait of Olive Vaslin, 1842; Bibliothèque national de France, Richelieu Musique fonds estampes Vaslin.

[15]   ' Ceci est facile à comprendre et à obtenir si l'on veut bien conserver à la main la position qu'elle prend pour saisir le manche au moment de placer le violoncelle entre les

Figure 2.2   Emil Lassalle, portrait of Vaslin, 1842, Bibliothèque nationale de France

As Walden notes, John Gunn had already dismissed the slanted left hand in the first edition of his tutor, saying that the modern hand has a 'great advantage [...] over that formerly in use'.[16] In fact he puts the point even more firmly in the second edition:

> The position [...] formerly much in use, and originating probably from the position of the hand on the Violin, in which it is the best practicable, *is given as a beacon to avoid*; the fingers tending to an oblique direction, as expressed by the dotted lines, cannot be corrected without very long practice ... [17]

jambes [...] le pouce embrasse le manche et les doigts se trouvent tout disposés à se placer en arc-boutants et par conséquent à ne présenter aux cordes que leur extrémité'.Vaslin, Vaslin, *L'art du violoncelle*, ibid., p. 3.

[16]   John Gunn, *The Theory and Practice of Fingering the Violoncello* (London: the Author, 1st edn. [1789]), p. 61.

[17]   Gunn, *Theory and Practice*, 2nd ed. [c.1793], p. 6. Emphasis added.

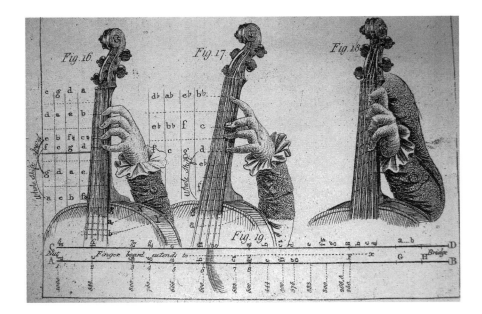

Figure 2.3   Gunn, *Treatise*, left hand shapes – left to right: closed, extended, and the violin hold

Gunn's illustration of the violin hold is very similar to Romberg's, especially in the extreme curling of the first finger (Figure 2.3). Something very like this hand shape is seen in Gainsborough's portrait of the Rev. Chafy from 1750–52 (Figures 2.4a and 2.4b), where the player's left thumb is just visible.

Duport had likewise rejected the violin hold:

> By holding the hand faultily we mean the manner and habit of holding the neck of the instrument as is done with the violin, in the palm of the hand; by this the fingers are shortened, and the stretch from the first to the fourth finger [...] will be found almost impossible [...] Those therefore who have adopted this vicious manner, are obliged continually to change the holding of the hand, even while playing one and the same position.[18]

---

[18]   'Ce que nous appelons mauvaise position de la main, est d'empoigner le manche comme on fait sur le Violon, cela raccourcit les doigts et rend presque impossible, l'écart du premier au quatrième [...] ce qui fait que les personnes qui jouent avec cette position du main, sont obliges de sauter la main a tout moment, même en jouant la même position'. Jean Louis Duport, *Essai sur le doigté* (Paris: Imbault, [1806]), p. 8. The English translation above, from the later trilingual edition, is much more strongly worded than the original. Duport, trans. August Lindner, *Anleitung zum Fingersatz auf dem Violoncell und zur Bogenführung. Instruction on the fingering and bowing of the violoncello. Essai sur le*

Duport and Kummer each give an example of a short passage that cannot be played without moving the hand if it is slanted.[19] Duport points out that backward extensions become difficult, giving the notes E♭, F, and G in first position on the D string; Kummer finds that it inhibits the independence of the fingers, especially the second and third when alternating between F and F♯ in the same position. They fundamentally agree: the violinistic left hand hampers the freedom of the fingers to move, and forces a constant readjustment of the whole hand.

The 'square' shape of the left hand normal today is asserted particularly firmly by some, and quite early in this period – Gunn has already been mentioned. According to Bideau it is vital for good tone:

> Execution and accuracy depend on the position of the [left] hand. This point is so essential, that it is necessary to work for a long time before becoming able to place the hand on the instrument. [...] One must put the four fingers on the fingerboard, two inches from the nut, rounding them as much as possible. It is essential in order to produce a good sound to press them firmly on the string, and at the tip. One must then place the thumb behind the neck without holding it, and in the middle, so that it is between the middle and ring fingers.[20]

In his version of Bréval, Peile manages to criticize the violin hold by implication:

> The Learner is then to bring the left hand to the neck of the Instrument, by placing the Thumb without pressure on the back of the Neck, and bend the fingers in an arch like form over the Strings, stretch'd from each other about an Inch, the first joints of which from their points being nearly perpendicular to the strings, *which position must be particularly observed, as any other would be bad*, that is to say, the hand must be square with the fingerboard.[21]

Crouch gives a particularly good illustration (Figure 2.5) of the square left hand.[22]

---

doigté de violoncelle et sur la conduite de l'archet (Offenbach: Jean André, Philadelphia: G. André & Co., Frankfurt: G.A. André, London: Augener & Co., [1864]), p. 7.

[19]   Duport, *Essai*, p. 8 ; Kummer, *Violoncellschule* op. 60 (Leipzig: Hofmeister, [1839]).

[20]   'De la position de la main dépend l'exécution et la justesse. Cet article est si essentiel, qu'il faut travailler longtems avant que de pouvoir parvenir à fixer la main sur cet instrument. [...] Il faut poser les quatre doigts sur la touche, a la distance de deux pouces du sillet, les arrondir autant qu'il est possible. Il est essentiel pour tirer un beau son de les appuyer fortement sur la corde, et de l'extrémité, il faut placer ensuite le pouce derrière le manche sans le tenir, et au milieu, de sorte qu'il se trouve entre le doigt du milieu et l'annulaire.' Dominique Bideau, *Grande nouvelle méthode raisonnée pour le violoncelle* (Paris: Naderman, [c.1802]), p. 3.

[21]   J.B. Bréval, trans. J. Peile, *Bréval's New Instructions for the Violoncello* (London: C. Wheatstone & Co., [1810]), p. 6. Emphasis added.

[22]   Crouch, *Compleat Treatise*, unpaginated plate.

Figure 2.4a   Thomas Gainsborough, *The Rev. John Chafy Playing the Violincello in a Landscape* (c.1750–52), Tate Gallery

Significantly, whereas de Swert quoted Romberg's description of posture without a tail-pin and commented that it was quite out of date, he omitted Romberg's violinistic left hand shape entirely, without comment, simply teaching the square left hand.[23]

However, although the violin hold did not last, not everyone advocated a strictly square left hand either. Later in the nineteenth century a third shape appears, somewhere between the two. Carl Schroeder illustrates it well (Figure 2.6).[24] His left hand is somewhat slanted, but not as much as Romberg's.

Indeed, Schroeder's fingers look almost as if pointing vertically to the floor, as opposed to perpendicular to the fingerboard. This may well be what Junod intends when he says that the first finger should land 'perpendicularly on the string', rather

---

[23]   Bernhard Romberg, rev. Jules de Swert and Heinrich Grünfeld, *Violoncelloschule* (Berlin: E. Bote & G. Bock [1888]), p. 4.

[24]   Carl Schroeder, trans. J. Matthews, *Catechism of Violoncello Playing* (London: Augener & Co., 1889, trans. 1893), p. 21.

Figure 2.4b   *The Rev. Chafy*, detail showing the left thumb

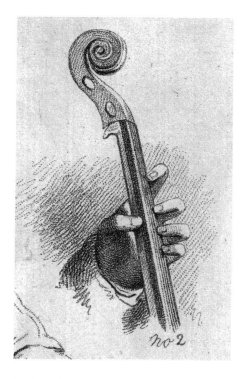

Figure 2.5   Crouch, *Compleat Treatise*, left hand

Figure 2.6   Schroeder, *Catechism*, left hand

than *to* the string – in other words, vertically.[25] However, Schroeder's left hand attracts a dissenting footnote from the translator Matthews, who himself quotes the cellist Edward Howell at some length:

> Considerably greater variety exists in the manner of holding and the playing the Violoncello than the violin, and the following observations upon this point by the well known English violoncellist, Mr. Edward Howell, will be read with interest: – 'The English (really Duport's) style consists of holding the fingers stretched out over the finger-board in the first position, with every finger over its proper note in the scale of C [*sic* – Howell means semitones]. Under the French system, the fingers are not stretched out at all, but are held sloping back as in playing the violin. The advantage of [the English hold] is obvious. The English method [...] keeps the fingers and hand always in readiness; the fingers have only to be dropped on the note required and with a large amount of certainty. Moreover, a firmer pressure is obtained upon the strings as the flat of the finger is used. Added to this is the certainty and ease with which the hand can be shifted, and an enormous amount of pressure to be gained when using the thumb.

[25]   Laurent Junod, trans. F. Clayton, *New and Concise Method for the Violoncello* op. 20 (London: J.A. Lafleur & Son, 1878), p. 3.

The French style of fingering is illustrated by playing with the tip of the finger, each finger being shifted with each note of the scale. The result of this arrangement, which necessitates the bringing forward of the finger for each note, is a loss of power of grip, and a perpetual *glissando* effect. The labour of the performer is increased to a large degree, with results scarcely satisfactory, or even pleasing.' If the English method is adopted, the left arm must be held out straighter than as shown in the engraving. *Tr.*[26]

This interesting, if confusing, comment shows that a sloping left hand was perhaps more widespread than other evidence would suggest, in spite of the obvious objections. Given that a moderately sloped hand need not, in fact, necessitate a continual readjustment of the fingers (see Becker below), it may be that Howell's criticisms are directed at a more extremely sloped hand than that, say, of Schroeder himself. Howell, a pupil of Piatti, must have known of Romberg's violinistic hand, since his own cello method is a simplified and drastically abridged version of Romberg. However, Howell's method omits all reference to the violinistic hand, replacing Romberg's detailed explanation of it with two simple sentences:

The hand should hold the neck so that the thumb may be exactly opposite to the second finger. The palm of the hand should not be pressed close to the neck, but should be kept hollow.[27]

It is not clear why Howell should call the violin hold 'French', as there is no evidence for this in French cello methods, apart from the special case of Olive Vaslin (whose book appeared in the following decade). Indeed, Duport, whom Howell sees as the founder of the 'English' hold, advocated playing as close to the fingernail as possible, and not, as Howell would have it, with 'the flat of the finger'. The translator's own addition concerning the different angle of the left arm if using the square hand exemplifies a trend towards holding the arm further away from the body, discussed below.

Diran Alexanian (1881–1954) who also supplies exercises to train the spacing of the fingers, gives a much more detailed version of the slightly sloped left hand.[28] The additional photographs supplied by Becker for his revision of Kummer's method also show this sloped hand clearly, although as with Alexanian it would seem that Becker had large hands and a particularly long fourth finger (Figure 2.7).[29]

---

[26]   Schroeder, *Catechism*, pp. 22–3.

[27]   Edward Howell, *Edward Howell's First Book for the Violoncello Adapted from Romberg's School* (London: Boosey & Co, [1879]), p. 1.

[28]   Dinan Alexanian, *Traité théoretique et pratique du violoncelle* (Paris: A.Z. Mathot, 1922), p. 25.

[29]   Friedrich August Kummer, rev. H. Becker, *Violoncelloschule* op. 60 (Leipzig: Peters, 1909), plate 2.

Figure 2.7   Kummer rev. Becker, *Violoncelloschule*, photographs of Becker's
left hand, extended (L) and closed (R)

Becker wrote about this hand shape as well:

> It should be noted that the thumb should exert an opposing pressure (Kummer
> speaks of a 'fulcrum') in a diagonal direction; more specifically: with the
> fingering on the A and D strings the thumb lies more on the inner part of
> the neck (thus, under the covered strings); with the fingering on the G and
> C strings, however, more to the outside. The hand is correctly positioned if
> the channel created by the finger placement runs across (not parallel, but in a
> sharp angle to the nails) the fingertips. The first joint of the first, second, and
> third fingers remains almost vertical on the string. The fourth finger, however,
> is more extended, due to its shortness. With the fingerings in extended positions
> (two consecutive whole tones) only the second finger is curved; the two others
> are extended. As a general rule, one can say that the finger position, wherever
> practicable, should be curved; but where a longer reach is required, extended. [30]

---

[30]   'Hierzu ist zu bemerken, daß der Daumen den Gegendruck (Kummer spricht von
Stützpunkt) in diagonaler Richtung ausüben soll; besser: Bei den Griffen auf A- un D-saite
lege man den Daumen mehr an der inneren Teil des Halses (also unter die besponnenen
Seiten), bei Behandlung von G- und C-Seite hingegen mehr an den äußeren. Steht die Hand

Becker shows here that the partly sloped hand need not involve continual readjustment for passages requiring extensions in the way that the 'violinistic' hand did. Given the length of his fourth finger, his comment about straightening it because of its shortness is somewhat disingenuous (something similar is true of the illustrations in Maurice Eisenberg's *Cello Playing of Today*).[31] Nonetheless, the importance of this passage lies in the fact that Becker does not advocate a square hand, even for cellists with smaller hands. All those cellists who recommend a moderately sloped left hand place the thumb centrally behind the neck. Several short Pathé newsreel films from the late 1920s/early 1930s also show cellists using a sloped hand.[32] This hand shape was also advocated in modern times by among others William Pleeth, who explicitly related it to that of the violin – this, for Pleeth, being a good thing.[33]

Whereas the left hand was employed in a shape, or shapes, still recognizable today, the left arm as a whole, rather like the bowing arm, was generally lower. This is the most obvious difference between nineteenth-century and modern practices. Many tutors ignore the left arm altogether, concentrating entirely on the placing of the fingers. This is true of basic, cheaper, methods such as Crome's (though his frontispiece shows a cellist playing with a dropped left elbow) and most of the anonymous ones, but it applies to Gunn, Duport and Lindley as well. Some illustrations are quite clear, such as Bréval's, with a dropped left shoulder and elbow and a smooth wrist, and Romberg's similar picture. Reinagle puts the ball of the left hand close to the neck, which in effect lowers the arm.[34] Crouch says the upper arm should be close to the body (note that in this he differs from

---

rightig, so läuft die durch das Aufdrücken der Finger entstehende Rinne quer (nicht parallel, sondern in einem spitzen Winkel zu den Nägeln) über die Fingerspitzen. Das erste Glied des ersten, zweiten und dritten Fingers steht dabei fast senkrecht auf der Saite. Der vierte Finger hingegen wird, seiner Kürze halber, mehr gestreckt. [...] Bei Griffen in weiten Stellungen (zwei aufeinanderfolgende ganze Töne) [...] wird nur der zweite Finger rund aufgesetzt; die beiden anderen sind auszustrecken. Dies bezieht sich jedoch nur auf die unteren Positionen. Als allgemeine Regel mag dienen, die Finger, wo immer angägig, rund aufsetzen, wo größere Spannungen zu bewältigen sind, aber auszustrecken.' Ibid., p. x.

[31]   Maurice Eisenberg, *Cello Playing of Today* (London: Novello, 1959), pp. 14–15.

[32]   *British Pathé* newsreels at http://www.britishpathe.com> [last accessed September 2012]: No. 3254:12 (1929–30): a short musical item, un-named soprano performing 'Marie' with an un-named pianist and a cellist named Samehtini (probably the Dutch cellist Joachim Samehtini, 1889–1942) who is shown in close-up. No. 1612:23 (10 August 1933): the tenor Frank Titterton singing 'Once in a blue moon' with the Esmond Trio (three women, un-named). No. 1163:05 (20 August 1934): the 'Celebrity Trio' (piano – Reginald King, violin – Alfredo Campoli, cello – Otto Fagotti[?]) in 'A Song of Paradise'.

[33]   William Pleeth, *Cello* (London: Macdonald & Co, 1982), p. 160.

[34]   Joseph Reinagle, *A Concise Introduction to the art of Playing the Violoncello* (London: Goulding, Phipps, and d'Almaine, [1800]), p. 4.

the Paris method), and Kummer is quite firm: 'The left elbow must not be raised.'[35] Cellists in the second half of the nineteenth century move slightly away from this position. Junod puts the arm 'in an easy position and at some distance from the body', with the left elbow neither raised nor resting against the instrument.[36] Carl Schroeder keeps the upper arm and elbow a little away from the body.[37] Van der Straeten describes the arrangement of the left arm, not in the context of a more or less static position, but one that allows the greatest freedom of movement:

> The upper arm should therefore be kept as steady as possible, so as to allow perfect freedom to the left hand and its movements. To find out the proper position of the left hand and arm, stretch out the latter straight from the shoulder. Then stretch out the fingers […] and bend the first and second joints, as if for the purpose of scratching. Now, turn the forearm towards you from the elbow joint, and, without altering the relative distance of the fingers, place *their* tips on the A string […] the left hand standing almost at right angles to the fingerboard. […] The position of the left arm must of course be modified for comfort's sake; but on no account should the elbow hang quite down, as that would cause the left hand to turn too much sideways [backwards], and when shifting beyond the fourth position, the arm would have to be brought forward […] If the left hand and arm are placed in the proper manner […] the latter can shift right up the fingerboard without the least change in position of the upper arm.[38]

Later cellists raise the left arm still more. Schroeder places the upper arm away from the body and not touching it, with a wrist slightly curved outwards, especially on the C string. Rabaud says it should be neither raised nor rested against the cello, and kept some distance from the body, and Becker indirectly contradicts Kummer:

> To achieve a proper placing of the left arm the elbow should be held far enough from the body so that the upper arm creates an angle of 45 degrees with the torso, and the forearm is a direct continuation of the back of the hand. The wrist, consequently, should be neither raised nor lowered.[39]

---

[35]   Crouch, Compleat Treatise, p. 7. 'Der linke Ellbogen darf nicht gehoben werden.' Kummer, *Violoncelloschule*, p. x.

[36]   Junod, *New and Concise Method*, p. 3.

[37]   Schroeder, *Catechism of Cello Playing*, p. 22.

[38]   Edmund van der Straeten, *Technics of Violoncello Playing* (London: 'The Strad' Office, 1898), pp. 69–71.

[39]   'Um eine gunstige Stellung des linken Armes zu erreichen, halte man den Ellbogen so weit vom Korper entfernt, dass der Overarm zum Oberkorper einen Winkel von etwa 45° und der Vorderarm die Fortsetzung des Handruckens in gerarder Richtung bildet. Das Handgelenk darf also weder gehobennoch gesnkt werden.' F.A. Kummer, rev. Hugo Becker, *Violoncelloschule*, p. x.

Becker's version was to become the twentieth-century standard. Schroeder's outwardly curved wrist looks like an element of an older playing style when compared with Becker's forearm continuing in the same line as the back of the hand. In this context, Casals's account of his early tuition with José Garcia (in 1888, at the age of 12) at the Municipal School of Music in Barcelona may reflect an unusually rigid approach: 'We were taught to play with a stiff arm and obliged to keep a book under the armpit!'.[40] No cellist in the nineteenth century advocated a stiff arm, even if there was a general view that the left elbow should be kept low, so Casals's teacher may have adopted an extreme version of this posture.

Having established the principal characteristics of the shape of the left hand, the next pedagogical priority in nineteenth-century cello methods was the fingering of scales. While different cello methods go about the teaching of scales in different ways, the fundamental issue of fingering is one that all must address. From the mid-nineteenth century until the present day, standardized fingerings have been in use for diatonic and chromatic scales. In some specific contexts, other fingerings can be required depending on the particular problems involved, but the standard fingering is the default option. The slow emergence of what are now considered 'normal', or even self-evident, fingerings shows how persistent certain habits of thought could be. Indeed, the very concept of a 'default' fingering has little validity prior to c.1850 even though the 'normal' fingerings were first put forward half a century earlier.

From the later nineteenth century onwards, there is a consensus on scale fingering, which arose from a perceived need for some sort of systematic approach, and today's standard fingerings originated at that time. Earlier cello methods are quite inconsistent, so that the fingerings recommended to cellists from Crome (1765) until approximately 1840, the date of Romberg's *Violoncellschule*, are surprisingly varied.[41] Some finger each scale in a more or less *ad hoc* manner, whereas others look for a recurring pattern. This is particularly important on the cello because of the frequent shifting that even a simple scale requires – the only two-octave scales playable on the cello entirely in first position are C major and D major.

Fingerings proposed much earlier in the eighteenth century had surprising longevity. In particular, Michel Corrette's fingerings, repeated by Crome and subsequently copied in later cello tutors, persisted into the early years of the nineteenth century (Examples 2.1 and 2.2).[42] Crome repeats Corrette's scale fingerings exactly. Both use semitones played with the second and fourth fingers (marked '+' in Crome's 'Gamut'), that is, with the third finger in between them but not lying on a note, and not used in low positions.

---

[40]   J.M. Corredor, trans. André Mangeot, *Conversations with Casals* (London: Hutchinson, 1956), p. 25.

[41]   Robert Crome, *The Compleat Tutor for the Violoncello* (London: C. & S. Thompson [1765?]).

[42]   Michel Corrette, *Méthode théoretique et pratique* (Paris: Mlle. Castagnery, [1741]), pp. 21 and 18; Crome, *The Compleat Tutor*, ibid., p. 6.

Example 2.1   C major scale fingering given by Corrette and Crome

Example 2.2   Chromatic scale fingering given by Corrette and Crome

Example 2.3   Crome, *Compleat Tutor*, scales on one string

Corrette does not explain why the third finger is not used in low positions, but Crome does: 'the distance is great and the Finger shorter'.[43] Crome is writing with reference to the standard violin fingering 0123 – he uses 4 as an alternative to 3. It is in this context that the third finger is, he argues, unsuitable for the cello. He does use the third finger in the course of an octave of a scale on one string, in fourth position, although this is actually more problematic than using the third finger in first position (Example 2.3).[44] Corrette also does this when he explains fingering in higher positions, but he advises against using the fourth finger there. However he does use the second and third fingers a whole tone apart even in third position, which is less feasible than Crome's fourth position example.[45]

Corrette does offer an alternative chromatic fingering with all four fingers taking adjacent semitones.[46] However, he points out that violinists who play the cello will find this fingering difficult, and that they should use the other fingering. He also identifies the chromatic left hand with the bass viol, and is at pains to state the superiority of the cello, adding that the chromatic fingering is useful for string crossing in augmented fourths with the second and third fingers. However, he calls

[43]   Crome, *Compleat Tutor*, p. 2.

[44]   Ibid., p. 18.

[45]   Ibid., p. 2.

[46]   Corrette, *Méthode*, p. 42.

it 'this false position [...] a gothic relic of the bass violins [...] which are excluded from the Opéra and from all foreign countries'.[47]

There is a further possible explanation for the Corrette fingering in terms of tuning systems. In mean-tone temperament, with 'sharp' minor thirds, 'flat' major thirds, and 'narrow' fifths, the second and third fingers become noticeably closer together, and the fourth finger sharper than in equal temperament. This bunching of the second and third fingers is also a natural physiological tendency, which beginners work hard to counteract. While this correction is essential when playing in equal temperament (and there have been many exercises designed to this end), in mean-tone tuning the positioning of the notes matches this natural tendency much more closely. However, this does not explain the continued currency of the Corrette fingering when mean-tone tuning had become obsolete.

Crome's teaching, generally very close to Corrette, was borrowed extensively in turn by several later English tutors. Parts of his *Compleat Tutor* reappear in Goulding's *New and Complete Instructions* (c.1787). Crome was published originally by C. and S. Thompson, so it is unsurprising that *Thompson's New Instructions for the Violoncello* (c.1800) is a revised version of Crome, retaining many of his characteristic turns of phrase, cutting some passages and adding new ones. Crome is also clearly a source for Clementi's *New and Complete Instructions for the Violoncello* (c.1805), though the latter also addresses topics not found in Crome. Crome's chromatic scale reappears exactly in both Goulding and Clementi.

Crome limits scales to C major and a chromatic scale, but later cello tutors quickly added more. Table 2.1 shows that it was only after the 1820s that cellists were shown fingerings for all the diatonic scales. There is a general tendency to limit scales to keys with no more than three or four sharps or flats in the key signature, especially in the smaller anonymous cello methods such as those published by Preston, Goulding or Cahusac. Hardy's range of scales is particularly limited at this time. Surprisingly, for what is quite a basic tutor, Goulding gives major scales in four octaves. Several of these tutors begin and end their scales on notes other than the tonic – this becomes very much less common in later methods. Reinagle gives all major and minor scales but only in two octaves. When a more limited range is offered, it is sometimes out of sympathy for the pupil's difficulties. After showing the fingering for E major, Romberg observes that:

> It would be wrong to torment the beginner with scales that have more than four sharps. He will have enough difficulty with those preceding.[48]

---

[47] 'cette fausse position [...] un reste gotique des grosses Basses de violon [...] qui sont exclués de l'Opéra et de tous pays Etrangers'. Ibid., p. 43.

[48] 'Es wäre unrecht wenn man der Schüler im Anfänge mit den Tonleitern, die mehr als vier Kreuze haben, belästigen wollte; ist dieses hier gegebene doch beinahe schon zu viel.' Romberg, *Violoncellschule*, p. 26.

Table 2.1   Scales in cello methods c.1765–c.1851 (all are given in two octaves unless indicated otherwise)

Method	Scales
1765 Crome	Major: C Minor: none
1785 Anon., pub. Preston	Major: to E and E♭ Minor: none
1787 Anon., pub. Goulding	Major: to E and E♭ (3 octs.) Minor: A
1789 Gunn (1st edn)	ALL (some 3 octs.)
1795 Anon., pub. Cahusac	Major: to E and E♭ Minor: to F♯ and C
1800 Reinagle	ALL
1804 Baillot et al.	Major: to B and D♭ Minor: all relatives
1806 Duport	ALL (some 3 octs.)
1806 Hardy	Major: to B and A♭ Minor: A
1810 Bréval/Peile	Major: to E and D♭ Minor: all relatives
1815 Gunn (2nd edn)	ALL (some 3 octs.)
1819 Peile	Major: to A and E♭ (3 octs.) Minor: all relatives
1820 Muntzberger	Major: to A and E♭ Minor: to B and F
1824 Dotzauer	ALL (3 octs.)
1826 Baudiot	Major: to B and D♭ Minor: all relatives
1827 Crouch[a]	ALL (inc. enharmonic G♯, D♯, A♯ minor)
1827 Eley	ALL
1839 Kummer	ALL
1840 Romberg	Major: to E and A♭ Minor: all relatives (no. of octs. varies – some 1½, some 2)
1850 Lee	Major: to E and A♭ Minor: all relatives
1851–55 Lindley	Major: to E and A♭ Minor: to G and F♯

[a] Eley and Kummer omit C♭ and C♯ major and their relative minors, but there is no technical difference from their enharmonic equivalents. The acoustic distinction between enharmonic pitches ceases to be a topic in these tutors after the turn of the century, so Crouch is unusual here.

Sebastian Lee agrees: 'these studies do not go beyond four sharps or flats, in order not to tire the pupil'.[49] Similarly, Robert Lindley gives only a limited range of scales, fingered 'from the admirable "Méthode" of Duport', adding reassuringly that:

> There are many more Gamuts, or Scales, both major and minor, than are given in this little work, but the pupil will not miss anything that is essential to his practice during a long and industrious period.[50]

When Hugo Becker revised Lee's method, he added that while he understood Lee's point of view, nonetheless:

> in the editor's opinion, the pupil should, however, know the diatonic scales in all keys [...] for that reason he appends the missing scales.[51]

Not only does Becker add the missing scales, but he also gives some enharmonic equivalents such as D♯ minor and G♭ major.

The emergence of standardized scale fingerings in the early nineteenth century was slow. As Example 2.4 shows, there was no consistent approach to those scales that did not use open strings.

Example 2.4   Non-standard scale fingerings[52]

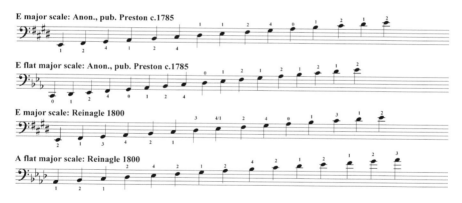

---

[49]   'Les études ne vont pas au de là de quatre dièzes et quart bémols, pour ne fatiguer l'élève.' Sebastian Lee, *Méthode pratique pour le Violoncelle (Praktische Violoncell-Schule.)* op. 30 (Mainz: B. Schott et fils, [1846]) p. 33.

[50]   Robert Lindley, *Hand-book for the Violoncello* (London: Musical Bouquet Office, [1851–55]), p. 9.

[51]   Sebastian Lee, rev. H. Becker, *Violoncello Tecnics* op. 30 (Mainz: B Schott's Söhne [1900–03]), p. 29.

[52]   The E♭ scale is given as such in the Preston method, although it starts on C.

The Scottish cellist John Gunn was the first cellist to give worked-out fingerings for all scales, based on a simple underlying universal principle: all scales can be played in groups of three fingered notes. It follows from this that the difficulty of a scale is not related to the number of sharps or flats in the key-signature: 'two octaves in the key of C♯ show that notwithstanding its seven sharps, it may be taken with as great facility by means of this analysis as any other key'.[53] From Gunn's point of view, 'the four open strings are an exception, and the only one, to general rules of fingering'.[54] These fingerings are given in the 1789 edition of Gunn's *Treatise*, with some additional explanation in the second edition of 1793. Gunn therefore anticipated Duport's *Essai* in this respect by some 17 years. He was the first cellist to seek to clarify a fingering system through analysis based on natural laws, beginning with minutely detailed acoustic explanation of the distribution of notes on the fingerboard:

> to show that the principles upon which the following system of fingering proceeds, are founded in immutable laws of nature; and, with these for our guide, we do not despair of conducting the learner, with ease and satisfaction, through the whole of this hitherto unexplored labyrinth; and of evincing to him, that what has been deemed complex and intricate, is in reality simple and plain.[55]

The analytic breakthrough that produced ergonomically-based finger-patterns, independent of apparent 'musical' structures, was crucial to the development of cello technique, but this intellectual advance was not recognized at the time; Gunn's position in the context of the Scottish Enlightenment is a subject still awaiting research. A 1793 review of a reissue of his treatise was sceptical of his approach and ignored his scales; the differences between Gunn and Lanzetti or Tillière are far greater than the reviewer suggests:

> we are ready to allow that the scientific part of this work is well executed, and that there are few elementary tracts so replete with science, expressed in such clear and accurate language. We are only doubtful whether the mixture of mathematical theorems with practical precepts will smooth or shorten an incipient musician's road to excellence in the first stages of his progress. We have compared these directions with [Lanzetti and Tillière] and we find no other difference than that Mr. G.'s work is more copious [...].[56]

Though the Gunn/Duport fingering eventually became the standard, other cellists were also working towards systematic fingerings. Some of these persisted well into the nineteenth century, even though many were impractical, especially at speed.

---

[53]   Gunn, *Theory and Practice*, 2nd edn, [1793], p. 32.

[54]   Ibid., p. 36.

[55]   Gunn, *Theory and Practice*, 1st edn, [1789], p. 43.

[56]   Anon., *The Monthly Review, or Literary Journal, Enlarged*, 12 (1793), p. 326.

Thus, nearly 30 years after Duport, and 50 after Gunn, Crouch was still proposing scale fingerings based on the pattern 1134 (Example 2.5).[57] This meant that the left hand stayed in lower positions, with shorter, but more frequent, shifts between neighbouring positions. Note that this fingering matches the two tetrachords that make up the scale.

Example 2.5   Crouch, *Compleat Treatise*, C♯ major scale fingering

Several tutors offered three or four alternatives. Bréval was particularly good at this (Example 2.6).[58]

Example 2.6   Breval, *Traité*, variant fingerings, E minor (slurs indicate notes to be played on the same string)

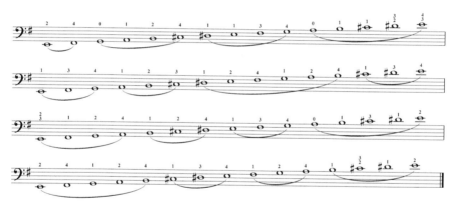

These fingerings have some notable features: the second octave of his first fingering is tetrachordal, using 1134; the second fingering is the standard three-note one; all four fingerings explore the possibility of playing up to six notes on the same string; and the third and fourth fingerings work in terms of extending the scale to three octaves.

The harmonic minor scale is almost always omitted from cello methods at this time, only making an appearance towards the end of the nineteenth century. Duport and Romberg give fingerings for some harmonic minor scales, but they are inconsistent, limited in range and sometimes even impractical.[59] Olivier-Aubert

[57]   Crouch, *Compleat Treatise*, p. 20.

[58]   Jean-Baptiste Bréval, *Traité du violoncelle* op. 42 (Paris: Imbault, [c.1804]), p. 22.

[59]   Duport, *Essai*, p. 11; Romberg, *Violoncellschule*, p. 22.

gives C and F minor scales ascending in the harmonic form, but descending in the melodic (Example 2.7).[60]

Example 2.7   Olivier-Aubert, *Kurze Anweisung*, C minor

From a purely technical point of view, the melodic minor scale, being composed entirely of tones and semitones, poses no fingering problem that does not occur in major scales. However, the augmented second in the harmonic minor scale can be awkward if played with the second and fourth fingers, especially at speed. Nonetheless, the harmonic minor is ignored; even the thorough John Gunn does not address this issue. Admittedly, at this period the player was far more likely to encounter melodic minor scales in the actual music played.

From a modern viewpoint, chromatic scale fingering is even more disorganized in the late eighteenth/early nineteenth centuries. Henry Waylet's fingering (c.1750?), like most eighteenth-century fingerings that became redundant, depended on consecutive same-finger shifts. His enharmonic equivalents are omitted here (Example 2.8).[61]

Example 2.8   Waylet, *Gamut*, chromatic scale

This represents a small advance on Corrette's chromatic fingering, which compresses the second and fourth fingers into a semitone, but it is clearly still crude as the final octave on the A string shows. Example 2.9 shows some more or less unsystematic alternative fingerings from the later eighteenth century.

Laborde's fingering was still being proposed by Muntzberger c.1820.[62] Gunn offers chromatic scales on one string, with the fingering 0112341234 on the lower strings (also used by Eley, discussed below), and 0121234 on the upper.[63] The British Library copy of the Cahusac tutor contains pencilled additions including

---

[60]   P.F. Olivier-Aubert, *Kurze Anweising zum Violoncellspiel* (Vienna: Artaria und Comp., [1819]), p. 16. According to Schroeder, Olivier-Aubert (1763–1805) was a self-taught player. Schroeder, *Catechism*, p. 80.

[61]   Anon, *The Gamut for the Violoncello* (London: Henry Waylet, [c.1750?]).

[62]   J. Muntzberger, *Nouvelle Méthode* (Paris: Sieber, [c.1820]), p. 46.

[63]   Gunn, *Treatise* 2nd ed., [c.1793], p. 37.

Example 2.9   Late eighteenth-century chromatic scale fingerings

the old-fashioned Corrette fingering, which suggests that this fingering was still in use among amateurs at least in the early decades of the nineteenth century.[64]

There are several attempts at a systematic chromatic scale fingering, particularly in Laborde, Raoul, and the Paris Conservatoire method.[65] Raoul continues up the scale from the example quoted above thus, hinting at the repeated 123 fingering familiar today. Raoul continues up the scale from the example quoted above thus, hinting at the repeated 123 fingering familiar today (Example 2.10).[66]

Example 2.10   Raoul, *Méthode*, chromatic scale, upper octave

The Paris Conservatoire method offers two variations, which are repeated in Crouch (Example 2.11).[67] Both these fingerings are systematic, but only up to a point. The upper fingering uses 0121234 on each of the lower three strings and 123 repeated on the A string, while the lower uses the 123 fingering on the lower three strings and a complex, highly unsystematic, A string fingering using the thumb. Only Duport gives the systematic fingering 0123123, now standard, always shifting on the first finger (ascending) and applicable in all keys.[68] Duport uses open strings for better intonation and avoids the fourth finger because it is

64   Anon., *New Instructions for the Violoncello* (London: Thomas Cahusac & Sons., [1795?]), pp. 10–11.

65   JLaborde, *Essai sur la musique*, p. 313.

66   Jean Marie Raoul, *Méthode de violoncelle* (Paris: Pleyel, [c.1797]), pp. 14–15.

67   P. Baillot, J.H. Levasseur, C.-S. Catel and C.-N. Baudiot, *Méthode de violoncelle* (Paris: Janet et Cotelle, 1805), p. 69. Crouch, *Compleat Treatise*, p. 61.

68   Duport, *Essai*, p. 41.

Example 2.11   Baillot et al., Paris Conservatoire method, chromatic scale fingerings

'contrary to the regularity of the fingering'.[69] Hus-deforges, Baudiot and Lindley follow Duport, with Hus-desforges quoting him *verbatim*.[70] Baudiot singles out this fingering for special praise:

> We here pay a tribute of acknowledgment to our master, M. Duport; it is he who found and established this fingering, and, surely, it is not the only service which he has rendered for the cello.[71]

However, the chromatic exercise given in the Paris method (Example 2.12)[72] and reprinted in Crouch, uses older fingerings such as 112233 and a 3232 descending fingering which is also suggested by Dotzauer (Example 2.13).[73] Dotzauer gives three possible chromatic fingerings in first position (all using open strings) and two for higher positions, although he expresses a clear preference for the Duport fingering, 'la meilleure'.

Charles Eley gives this chromatic 1234 fingering (Example 2.14) that avoids open strings (the example from John Gunn mentioned earlier uses the 1234 fingering but only in low positions, not as a general solution).[74]

Eley then notes that 'Some Professors [...] prefer playing this Scale with only 3 fingers & the open strings', and gives the Duport fingering. This would suggest that, at the very least, Duport's fingering was by no means universal even 20 years

---

[69]   'il s'oppose à la régularité de la doigté'. Ibid.

[70]   Pierre Louis Hus-deforges, trans. anon., *Method for the Violoncello* (London: R. Cocks & Co., [1840]), p. 12. French original; *Méthode* (Paris: the author, [1829]). Lindley, *Hand-book*, p. 9.

[71]   'Payons ici un tribut de reconnaissance à notre maître Mr. Duport, c'est lui qui a trouvé et arrêté ce doigté, et, certes, ce n'est pas le seul service qu'il a rendu au Violoncelle.' Charles Baudiot, *Méthode pour le violoncelle* (Paris: Pleyel et fils ainé, 1826), part 1, p. 18.

[72]   Baillot et al., *Méthode*, pp. 78–80.

[73]   Dotzauer, *Violonzell-Schule*, p. 27. The section in treble clef is fingered in the same way when descending.

[74]   Eley, *Improved Method*, p. 75. This fingering also occurs briefly in Louis Feuillard's *Tägliche Übungen . Exercices journaliers. Daily Exercises* (Mainz: B. Schott's Söhne, 1919), but it is of limited practical application.

Example 2.12   Baillot et al., Paris method, chromatic exercise (extract)

Example 2.13   Dotzauer, *Violonzellschule*, chromatic scale

Example 2.14   Eley, *Improved Method*, chromatic scale

Example 2.15   Chevillard, *Méthode Complète*, chromatic scale

after its first appearance. Indeed, even c.1850, Chevillard was proposing this bizarre chromatic scale fingering in low thumb positions (Example 2.15).[75]

Baudiot is more consistent. In his prefatory remarks about chromatic scales, preceding some ten pages of chromatic exercises, he praises the Duport fingering as 'very ingenious and very regular'.[76] His exercises in the neck positions (as far as c″) only use the Duport fingering, but in higher thumb positions he uses

---

[75]   A. Chevillard, *Méthode Complète* (Paris: J. Meissonier, [c.1850]), p. 74. Chevillard gives this fingering for thumb position chromatic scales beginning on tonics as high as G♭.

[76]   'fort ingenieux et très regulier'. Baudiot, *Méthode*, pt. 3, p. 180.

the 112233 fingering used by Chevillard in low positions. The apparent difficulty of establishing a standardized fingering for chromatic scales – a process that took longer than for diatonic scales – may have been due to the relative rarity of such scales in cello music of the period, coupled with a persistent view of such scales in terms of using all four fingers. The chief distinctions between these fingering approaches is whether or not they use open strings, and whether or not they are in any sense systematic.

The gradual emergence of modern fingerings, over a period of some eight decades from the eighteenth into the earlier nineteenth centuries, means that for most of this period several different approaches were current. It is striking that, whereas harpsichordists explore the articulation and phrasing possibilities described in sources like Couperin's *L'art de toucher le clavecin* (to name only the most obvious), string players working in nineteenth-century repertoire do not generally address such apparently fundamental questions when deciding how to finger scales. A historically-informed performance of a moderately difficult work intended for amateur performance could legitimately adopt one of the more old-fashioned fingerings given in tutors written for this market. That of a sonata written for more advanced performers could plausibly use Gunn's or Duport's fingerings, but alternative fingerings could be equally historically appropriate. In the end, obviously, players will use the fingering that seems to them to be the most secure rather than the most 'historically informed'. A fingering that creates an awkward string crossing or an unclear shift (as opposed to portamento, discussed in Chapter 4) will be rejected. But the contrast here is not between a pragmatic and a historically appropriate fingering. Even historically-informed performers of works that include scales cannot be sure that their fingering would have been used by more than a minority of players. The foregoing discussion of minutiae has shown that the wide range of fingerings, even if influenced by what now appear to be obsolete or irrelevant ideas, means that in practice a 'pragmatic' and a 'HIP' fingering may be identical – differing only in the motivation of the performer.

Chapter 3
The Bow in Motion

In Chapter 1, we looked at aspects of bow hold and the placing of the bow on the string. This chapter will deal with the bow in terms of changing perceptions of the physical movements of the wrist and arm, and some specific bow-strokes.

In order to execute any straight cello bow-stroke longer than an inch or so (which can be done by the fingers alone) the right wrist must be able to bend. It is possible to obtain a very short bow movement just with the wrist, using the limited amount of available lateral movement, and this forms a part of some later nineteenth-century approaches to bow technique. However, virtually all cello methods of any substance describe how, in the course of a down-bow, the wrist will begin raised (pronated) and gradually sink so that when playing at the tip of the bow it is much lower (supinated).

Most eighteenth-century tutors, and some early nineteenth-century ones (including those aimed at advanced students), such as those by Corrette, Crome, Tillière, Lepin, Azaïs and Bréval, largely ignore the movement of the wrist. Others, like Schetky, give it only cursory attention:

> The arm from the Shoulder to the Elbow should move as little as possible, the wrist should act freely and be rather supple.[1]

This may indicate that they thought it too obvious to mention, or that they expected a teacher to deal with this in the lesson, or that it was simply not important. John Gunn is one of the first to look at the wrist in a little more detail, stressing its role in string crossing. He claims that a sufficiently high arm on the A string gives more power, and

> it will prevent any unnecessary motion of the arm in passing from a lower string to an upper one, or the contrary, which can be sufficiently accomplished by a small turn of the wrist alone [...].[2]

His second edition goes into more practical detail, introducing an exercise still practised today. Keeping the arm still, he asks the pupil to move the wrist both horizontally and vertically to show how much can be done without the arm (this

---

[1] J.G.C. Schetky, *Practical and Progressive Lessons for the Violoncello* (London: R. Birchall, 1813), p. 2.

[2] John Gunn, *The Theory and Practice of Fingering the Violoncello* (London: the Author, 1st edn [1789]), p. 63.

exercise was still being used in the 1970s by Valentine Orde, 1889–1983, who had studied with Herbert Walenn and Feuermann):

> This serves to move the bow in either direction; and the movement of the arm [...] to extend it to the necessary length.[3]

This flexibility means that:

> the least elevation possible of the wrist will raise the bow from any string to the next higher string, and an equally small depression will, of course, bring it down to a lower string; consequently, no elevation or depression of the arm can even [sic] be necessary to bow alternately on two contiguous strings.[4]

This basic point – that string crossing should be executed with as little arm movement as possible – is usually omitted entirely in the smaller cello tutors, but otherwise it is found throughout the pedagogical literature of the cello in varying degrees of detail. Raoul's formulation, when recommending the study of arpeggios to encourage the flexibility and agility of the wrist ('nothing contributes so efficaciously to the development of the bow'),[5] posits a relationship between the forearm and wrist that, unremarkable as it seems at first sight, was eventually to be revised:

> The bow must be held firmly; but without stiffness; the wrist free; that is its action; it is from its suppleness that the bow derives all its advantages. The forearm leads the wrist: but it must only guide it and follow it in all its movements.[6]

Leading, but also guiding and following – this paradox was not to be resolved until Emil Krall devoted much more space to the topic over a century later. Bowing plays a subsidiary role in Duport's *Essai*, but nonetheless he notes that 'The wrist plays a great part in the bowing' and that in string crossing 'the arm has hardly anything to do'.[7] He also describes the wrist as acting as a hinge (*charnière*) when changing bow:

---

[3] Gunn, *Theory and Practice* (London: the Author, 2nd edn, [c.1793]), p. 38.

[4] Ibid.

[5] 'Rien ne contribue aussi efficacement au développement de l'archet que cet exercice et pour entretenir la souplesse et l'agilité du poignet [...]'. J.M. Raoul, *Méthode de Violoncelle* (Paris: Pleyel, [c.1797]), pp. 30–31.

[6] 'L'archet doit être tenu avec fermeté; mais sans raideur; le poignet libre: c'est de son action; c'est de sa souplesse que l'archet tire tous ses avantages. l'Avant-bras conduit le poignet: mais il ne doit que le conduire et le suivre dans tous ses mouvemens.' Ibid., p. 5.

[7] Jean Louis Duport, *Essai sur le doigté du violoncelle* (Paris: Imbault, [1806]), pp. 159–60. Translation from trilingual edition trans. August Lindner, *Anleitung zum Fingersatz auf dem Violoncell und zur Bogenführung. Instruction on the fingering and*

the wrist must obey, as [if] it were the hinge of a machine [...].[8]

Bréval himself does not deal with the wrist at all, but Peile adds the topic in his translation:

> It is also to be observ'd that on crossing from one string to another, the least depression of the Arm must take place, which may all be effected by the wrist[;] at all times the motion of the Bow must proceed from the first joint of the Arm and Wrist.[9]

In his own tutor Peile merely advises the pupil to 'let the motion proceed from the wrist as well as the arm'.[10] Dotzauer stresses that the wrist 'must move with the greatest lightness [...] transitions from one string to another are only made by the wrist'.[11] Crouch and Eley make very similar points, with the latter emphasizing the wrist's role in producing good tone by avoiding a stiff arm.[12]

Later German cellists go rather further into the role of the wrist and exercises for its development. Romberg insists upon it, repeating the importance of maintaining a flexible wrist in various contexts:

> a flexible wrist is indispensable to a fine execution, and who ever does not acquire this suppleness at first, will not attain it afterwards without infinite labour and pains.[13]

---

bowing of the violoncello. Essai sur le doigté de violoncelle et sur la conduite de l'archet (Offenbach: Jean André, Philadelphia: G. André & Co., Frankfurt: G.A. André, London: Augener & Co., [1864]), p. 140.

[8] Duport, *Essai*, p. 159. This point will recur in the discussion of Davidoff's 'hand-bowing' below.

[9] J.B. Bréval, trans. J. Peile, *Bréval's New Instructions for the Violoncello* (London: C. Wheatstone & Co., [1810]), p. 6.

[10] John Peile, *A New and Complete Tutor for the Violoncello* (London: Goulding, D'Almaine, Potter and Co. [1819?]), p. 16.

[11] 'qui doit se mouvoir avec la plus grand légèreté. L'archet conserve sa place dans la main et les transitions, d'une corde à l'autre ne s'operent que par le poignet.' J.J.F. Dotzauer, *Méthode de Violoncelle. Violonzell-Schule* (Mainz: B. Schott fils, [1825]), pp. 7–8.

[12] See Frederick Crouch, *A Compleat Treatise on the Violoncello* (London: Chappell & Co., [1826]), p. 8; C.F. Eley, *Improved Method of Instruction for the Violoncello* (London: Clementi & Co., [1827?]), p. 2.

[13] Bernhard Romberg, trans. anon., *A Complete Theoretical and Practical School for the Violoncello* (London: T. Boosey & Co., [1840]), p. 8. This comment is retained in Edward Howell's abridgement of Romberg (*Edward Howell's First Book for the Violoncello adapted from Romberg's School* (London: Boosey & Co., [1879])).

The chief object of this study is to exercise the wrist in drawing both the up- and down-bows. All these exercises must be practised with the wrist only, and without moving the arm in the slightest degree from its natural position.[14]

The shifting of the bow from one string to the other must be done by means of the wrist only.[15]

[In arpeggio bowing] everything must be managed with the wrist.[16]

At the end of the century Arthur Broadley ruefully observed that he himself had suffered from a faulty wrist and 'had this knowledge [been] imparted to me a couple of years earlier [...] much unlearning and relearning at more than double the expense would have been saved'.[17] Kummer suggests a way of practising similar to Gunn's:

String crossing (string change) must always be the focus of the cellist's greatest attention, since all changes of the bow should be conducted only by means of the wrist, without moving the upper arm. To achieve this skill the student should diligently undertake the following exercises while limiting in their execution a concomitant movement of the right upper arm by leaning it on a table or cupboard.[18]

Lindley, however, is more relaxed:

the other fingers must assist in governing the Bow without impeding the freedom of the wrist.[19]

The bow must be drawn across the strings almost at right angles with them, subject merely to the natural play of the wrist. The motion of the bow should proceed from the wrist and elbow exclusively. It needs not that the upper joint

---

[14]   Romberg, *Complete Theoretical [...] School*, p. 14.

[15]   Ibid., p. 16.

[16]   Ibid., p. 61.

[17]   Arthur Broadley, *Chats to Cello Students* (London: 'The Strad' Office, E. Donajowski and D.R. Duncan, 1899), p. 11.

[18]   'Der Saitenübergang (Saitenwechsel) muß dem Violoncellisten stets gegenstand der höchtens Aufmerksamkeit sein, da alle Wendungen des Bogens nur vermittelst des Handgelenks, ohne den Oberarm zu bewegen, ausgeführt werden sollen. Um diese Fertigkeit zu erlangen, nehme der Schüler die nächstfolgenden Beispiele mit allem Fleiß vor und verhindere bei deren Studium eine Mitbewegung des rechten Oberarmes dadurch, daß er ihn an einen tisch oder Schrank lehnt.' F.A. Kummer, rev. Hugo Becker, *Violoncelloschule* op. 60 (Leipzig: Peters, 1909), p. 21.

[19]   Robert Lindley, *Hand-book for the Violoncello* (London: Musical Bouquet Office, [1851–55]), p. 5.

of the arm should be absolutely rigid, but it should only move in subservience to the lower joint, without becoming a positive agent [...].[20]

Lindley's 'natural play of the wrist' is a more modest requirement than Romberg's more exaggerated supination.

The flexibility of the wrist continues to be described in very similar terms. Examples virtually identical to those already given can be found in, among others, Grützmacher's *Tägliche Übungen* (the original edition and all later revisions), de Swert's method, Becker's revisions of both Dotzauer and Kummer, and Whitehouse's edition of Piatti. There are numerous exercises specifically directed at the right wrist. These include: Kummer's *Violoncelloschule*, exercises nos. 40–47, Lee's studies op. 31, no. 32 'pour l'articulation du poignet droit', and no. 36 'pour donner l'elasticité au poignet', Josef Werner's numerous exercises, and the first study in Popper's *Höhe Schule des Violoncellspiels* (marked in all older editions 'With a very loose wrist, at the nut, lightly staccato'); a loose wrist is clearly implied in many of Popper's *legato* studies.[21] Oskar Brückner's *Scale & Chord Studies for the Violoncello* and the editions of Grützmacher's *Tägliche Übungen* by Willem Welleke and Hugo Becker even contain specific detailed markings for a higher or lower wrist, changing from note to note, and Carl Fuchs distinguishes no less than three wrist heights.[22] There are also many earlier studies which are clearly, though not explicitly, aimed at developing the flexibility of the wrist in string-crossing, by Duport, Dotzauer, Merk, Franchomme, Grützmacher, and others. Sebastian Lee's wrist studies are characterized by combinations of long slurs across three strings with one or two *détaché* semiquavers played at the heel or the tip of the bow. These studies make it clear that flexibility of the wrist was not only important in slurred complex string-crossing, but was also part of the technique of playing short *détaché* notes in any part of the bow.

Thus far, the unanimous view is that the upper arm is largely passive (if not indeed positively restricted), with wrist, hand and fingers as the most active elements in the chain from shoulder to fingertip. However, towards the end of the nineteenth century, a subtle revision of this consensus can be observed. Laurent Junod (1878) sees string crossing as beginning with the arm, not the wrist:

---

[20] Ibid., p. 11. By the 'upper joint' Lindley means the shoulder; his 'lower joint' is the elbow.

[21] Sebastian Lee, *40 Etudes mélodiques et progressives* op. 31 (Mainz: B. Schott's Söhne, [1853]); Josef Werner, trans. anon., *Die Kunst der Bogenführung The Art of Bowing op. 43. Supplement No. VII to the Author's Violoncello-Method* (Heilbronn: C.F. Schmidt, 1894), p. 17ff; David Popper, *Hohe Schule des Violoncellspiels 40 Études op. 73* (Leipzig: F. Hofmeister, 1901–05), no.1. See also nos. 2, 3, 4 and 8.

[22] Oskar Brückner, *Scale & Chord Studies for the Violoncello* Op. 40 (London: Augener, [1895]); Friedrich Grützmacher, ed. Willem Welleke, *Daily Exercises* op. 67 (New York: G. Schirmer, 1909); Carl Fuchs, *Violoncello-Schule Violoncello Method*, 3 vols (Mainz: Schott & Co. Ltd, 2nd edn, 1909), Vol. 1, p. 18.

The pupil should draw the bow very slowly from one end to the other on each note. The right arm must be well opened without any movement from the shoulder. The pupil should accustom himself not to raise his fingers unnecessarily high, especially in passing from one string to another. In order to change the string he should stop the bow for a moment at each extremity, *but without raising it until the movements of the arm and wrist are well regulated.*[23]

Carl Schroeder is less emphatic than his predecessors on the degree of flexibility required of the wrist:

the wrist, while passing to the higher string, makes a slight inclination inwards, and in passing to the lower string, a slight inclination outwards.[24]

On the other hand, Welleke still focuses on the shape of the hand, and by implication, wrist, when he says of scales using all four strings that

[t]he wrist-movement [...] is like that for the arpeggio (gradually raising then lowering), but pausing on each separate string. The hand is *constantly bent downward* [meaning that the wrist is raised] till the C-string is quitted, to enable it to rise three times up to the A-string; correspondingly, in passing back from the A-string, it is *constantly bent upward* [meaning that the wrist is lowered] [...].[25]

Thus, even in 1909, some cellists managed string-crossing primarily with the wrist. At first sight, van der Straeten gives similar advice, saying that the wrist 'must be constantly and gradually altering its relative position to the forearm', and describing how it is lowered during a down-bow.[26] However, unlike Welleke, he also asks for a 'firm wrist' combined with a turn of the forearm for a bigger sound. In general he minimizes the movement of the wrist overall, ascribing to it a more passive role, and avoiding excessive supination of the Romberg/Kummer type:

it must be remembered that the wrist must *never* sink below the level with the forearm; nor should the movements of the wrist be sudden or self-intentional. Their only purpose is to allow the bow to travel in the right direction and to the proper distance; and in order to fulfil their purpose they must *follow* those primary motions, being just sufficient to allow their proper executions, which will be impeded by excess.[27]

---

[23]   Laurent Junod, trans. F. Clayton, *New and Concise Method for the Violoncello* op. 20 (London: Lafleur, 1878), p. 6. Emphasis added.

[24]   Carl Schroeder, *Catechism of Cello Playing* (London: Augener, 1893), p. 32.

[25]   Grützmacher, *Daily Exercises*, p. 9.

[26]   Edmund. van der Straeten, *Technics of Violoncello-Playing* (London: 'The Strad' Office, 1898), pp. 30–31.

[27]   Ibid., p. 36.

If read outside its historical context this advice appears banal, but it differs significantly from earlier practice. Even though for modern cellists it appears inconceivable, both Romberg and Kummer show by unambiguous illustration that the wrist should be lower than the forearm when playing at the tip of the bow. The different approach described by van der Straeten became widespread. Emil Krall went into great detail on the anatomical construction of the arm (drawing, like Becker and Fuchs, on Steinhausen's influential 1903 essay *Die Physiologie der Bogenführung*) and in doing so also totally reversed the previous conventional wisdom.[28] For Krall, the arm was the most free, and the hand the least free, part of the linkage from shoulder to hand. He stresses the '*swing* of the whole arm as a unity' and even says that the upper arm should lead the bow-stroke.[29] In the course of an entire chapter on the wrist, he makes his perspective clear:

> The wrist is only a subordinate joint in that system of levers: the arm. It belongs to that part of the arm which is relatively passive. Its function is to *mediate* between the movements of the arm and those of the bow. If kept in a natural supple condition, it smoothes and polishes awkward and unpractised arm-movements and assists in perfecting them. [...] There is a great difference between a mediating wrist and an active wrist; the first does what the whole mechanism (arm) desires it to do, the latter imposes upon the arm a tyrannical conception of limited, pettish movements. An over-active wrist completely spoils the production of a large and sonorous tone; it is mainly responsible for absence of tone-power. As already indicated: any bowing executed *exclusively* by the wrist will always bear the stamp of artificiality – of restriction; it is neither significant nor convincing, because it is detached from all other functions of the arm. On the other hand, if a player exhibits perfect ease and freedom in what he believes to be a wrist-technique, then he believes what he *sees*, but is ignorant of what *actually happens*! [...] the [wrist] is always supported and accompanied by the *swing* of the arm, and it is due to this and not to the wrist that he is able to execute the technique with ease and grace.[30]

This explanation, depending as it does on distinctions between the 'mediating' and 'active' wrist, and between the player's own perception and 'what *actually happens*', finally resolves the paradox implicit in Raoul's formulation of the leading and following wrist. Alexanian continues in this direction.[31] In slower exercises he keeps the curve of the wrist more or less constant, and in rapid

---

[28]   Friedrich Adolf Steinhausen, *Die Physiologie der Bogenführung auf den Streich-instrumenten* (Leipzig: Breitkopf & Härtel, 1903).

[29]   Emil Krall, *The Art of Tone-Production on the Violoncello* (London: 'The Strad' Office, 1913), p. 18. All emphases as original.

[30]   Ibid., p. 22. Original emphasis.

[31]   Diran Alexanian, trans. Frederick Fairbanks, *Traité théorique et pratique du violoncelle* (Paris: Mathot, 1922), pp. 36ff.

string crossing he concentrates not on the wrist, but the arm, saying that 'these movements of the hand should be as little pronounced as possible'.[32] Even in passages of *détaché* string crossing in semiquavers he seems not to use the wrist to any marked degree.[33] This aspect of his teaching was noted in the *Musical Times*:

> In a down-bow, contrary to current practice, [Alexanian says] the whole of the arm should always be at work.[34]

This suggests that, in England at least, in the years after the First World War, many cellists were still playing in the older manner with less engagement of the upper arm. Alexanian's codification of cello technique was strongly influenced by the practices of Casals, one of whose technical traits was to play with a higher wrist even when at the tip of the bow, with a correspondingly higher elbow, but to move the wrist in general less. This aspect of Casals's playing surprised David Popper when he attended a recital by Casals in Budapest in 1912, which included three of Popper's own pieces. Popper's pupil Stephen De'ak was present:

> During the concert I watched Popper's reaction. His serious appraisal of the performance showed in the expression of his face, and he applauded after each number. But a slight puzzlement veiled the otherwise interested countenance. The striking differences between the prevailing bowing with loose wrist and straight thumb, and Casals' bowing, seemed most obvious when he played at the upper part of the bow without lowering his wrist, and compensated by the gradual pronation and elevation of his arm. But the upper arm position was radically altered when the bow was applied on the 'C' string. It was drawn in close to the body, with the wrist fairly straight.[35]

While Casals was not alone in this use of the wrist, it seems likely that he was more extreme than most other cellists of the period. Indeed, he was to claim many years later that his coupling of a higher wrist with a higher elbow 'caused a *furore* among traditionalists'.[36]

This general change of emphasis with regard to the role of the wrist provides a context for discussion of the only other innovative approach in this field, that of Carl Davidoff and his pupil Carl Fuchs. This concerns the so-called 'Davidoff hinge' and the term 'hand-bowing'.

Davidoff appears to look more at the function of the whole arm than many of his predecessors:

---

[32]   Ibid., p. 74.

[33]   Ibid., p. 81.

[34]   'M.-D. C', *MT*, 1 May 1923, p. 325.

[35]   Steven De'ak, *David Popper* (Neptune, NJ: Paganiniana Publications, 1980), p. 240.

[36]   J.M. Corredor, trans. André Mangeot, *Conversations with Casals* (London: Hutchinson, 1956), p. 25.

Herein rests the greatest difficulty in the use of the bow, because with this combined movement of the upper and lower arm, wrist-movement is mainly necessary.[37]

However, he makes it clear that string-crossing is still almost entirely executed by the wrist:

Crossing with the bow from one string to another occurs, as explained earlier, through a small turn of the hand: the movement to the right brings the bow from a higher to a lower string; in the other direction a turn to the left serves to cross from a lower to a higher string. The transition between the strings is relatively so small, that with a certain pressure of the bow only a small turn suffices, in order to take the bow from one string to another. This very important fact for the experienced player presents so much difficulty to the beginner that he does not have control of the bow, and from this easily arises the risk of unnecessarily touching the lower string.[38]

Davidoff is describing a turn of the wrist in order to change to a neighbouring string, not, for example, the slight stretching of the fingers followed by a simple lifting of the wrist/forearm described by earlier cellists (although Gunn, quoted above, appears to anticipate him). This necessitates an alteration to the angle between string and bow. Davidoff's pupil Carl Fuchs describes this process in much more detail. In the opening sections of his cello method Fuchs describes basic string-crossing:

When passing from a lower to a higher string near the nut, the point of the bow is turned inwards by revolving the wrist slightly to the left [...]. In passing from a higher to a lower string the process is reversed. During these movements the wrist should remain raised.[39]

---

[37] 'Darin besteht die größte Schwierigkeit bei der Bogenführung, weil hierzu kombinierte Bewegungen von Ober- und Unterarm, hauptsächlich aber Handgelenk-Bewegungen notwendig sind.' Carl Yu. Davidoff, *Violoncell-Schule* (Leipzig: Peters, [1888]), p. 2.

[38] 'Der Übergang mit dem Bogen von einer Saite zur anderen geschieht, wie früher erwähnt, durch kleine Drehungen der Hand: die Bewegung nach rechts bringt den Bogen von einer höheren zur tieferen saite; um gekehrt dient eine Drehung nach links zum Übergang von einer tieferen zur höheren Saite. Die Entfernung zwischen den Saiten sind verhältnismäßig so gering, daß bei einem gewissen Druck des Bogens nur eine kleine Drehung genügt, um den Bogen von einer Saite zur anderen zu bringen. Diese für den geübten Spieler sehr wichtige tatsache bietet dem Anfänger so manche Schwierigkeit, da er den Bogen nicht in der Gewalt hat und daher leicht in Gefahr kommt, die Nebensaiten unnötigerweise zu berühren.' Ibid., p. 10.

[39] Fuchs, *Violoncello-Schule*, Vol. 1, p. 7.

In the usual down-bow [...] the wrist gradually sinks as the point of the bow is reached, but if the down-bow precedes the change to a higher string, the wrist [...] must not sink so that when the point of the bow is reached, a *sudden* drop of the wrist and raising of the hand will bring the bow onto the higher string without any movement of the arm.[40]

He elaborates this in Part 2:

Davidoff's 'Bow-turning' (or 'Swinging'). In order to avoid roughness in passing from one string to another when playing slurred notes, Davidoff recommended raising the point of the bow slightly in the down bow and lowering it in the up bow, so that the angle (90 degs.) formed by the strings and bow is increased or decreased by 10–20 deg. respectively. By this means the bow touches the next string at a point slightly further from the bridge, where a softer tone can be produced than near the bridge.[41]

Fuchs gives examples (Example 3.1) from a Dotzauer study and Tchaikovsky's first string quartet op. 11, with instructions for the change in bow angle.[42]

Example 3.1   Carl Fuchs, *Violoncelloschule*, music examples for Davidoff's 'Bow-turning' © 1909 SCHOTT MUSIC, Mainz – Germany. Reproduced by permission. All rights reserved

a. Spitze heben! *Raise point!*
b. Spitze senken! *Lower point!*

He also gives a photograph to illustrate the changed angle of the bow, which appears much greater than his verbal description alone suggests.[43]

---

40   Ibid., p. 8.
41   Ibid., Vol. 2, p. 55.
42   Ibid.
43   Ibid., p. v.

Davidoff's 'bow-turning', and the 'Davidoff hinge', utilize the more or less vertical movement of the hand about the wrist. However, 'hand-bowing', a term apparently unique to Fuchs, uses the more limited sideways rotation of the hand, with little active involvement of the wrist. Both techniques are integral to Fuch's explanation of bowing technique:

> Imagine that the hand is a pendulum to the end of which the bow is pivoted. The wrist itself is the point from which the pendulum is suspended, the hand forming the pendulum. [...] strictly speaking this bowing is produced by the rotation of the forearm about its longitudinal axis. In spite of the fact that the wrist takes very little part in this bowing it is often but wrongly called 'Wrist-bowing'.[44]

He gives some simple exercises in 'hand-bowing' with the wrist at three different heights – high, 'half-raised' and low (Example 3.2). These show that this bowing technique is used at the heel or in the middle of the bow, but not at the tip because the wrist is lowered and cannot therefore suspend the hand. Note that he gives bar 36 of the cello part of Beethoven's ninth symphony as an example of 'hand-bowing' in the middle of the bow, with the wrist half-raised. This example shows that Fuchs played these repeated sextuplets with the bow on the string, and not with a lifted stroke of any kind. Fuchs's illustrations show his mid-bow 'hand-bowing' exercise holding the bow by thumb and index finger alone, with the wrist height he recommends. Using his exercises and photographs, it is possible to reconstruct with reasonable accuracy the type of sound that Fuchs probably expected from his Hallé Orchestra cello section in the opening bars of the 'Choral' symphony – not particularly clear, and not, perhaps, absolutely *pp* either.

Discussion of bow-strokes is often hampered by problems of highly inconsistent symbolic notation and terminology. In some cases, their significations can be almost diametrically opposed to current practice, and this problem becomes greater as we move into the nineteenth century. Robert Crome sets out an apparently simple classification of bow-strokes:

> the principal ways are four. Bowing, which is drawing the Bow backward and forward from every Note, Slurring, which is by drawing the Bow but once for two or any number of Notes; Feathering the Bow, which is done like the Slur, only it must be taken off the String after touching it: The Spring, which last can't be explain'd but by Demonstration.[45]

---

[44] Ibid., Vol. 1, p. 17. Fuchs gives a very similar explanation in his *Violoncello-Werke – Violoncello-Works – Oeuvres pour Violoncelle* (Mainz: B. Schott's Sohne, 1911), p. 2, where he adds that 'hand-bowing in cello-playing is often misnamed wrist-bowing, a name quite justified in violin-playing, where the difference in the position of the hand necessitates a different sort of movement'.

[45] Robert Crome, *The Compleat Tutor for the Violoncello* (London: C. & S. Thompson, [1765?]), p. 11.

Example 3.2   Fuchs, *Violoncelloschule*, 'hand-bowing' exercises with different
               wrist heights © 1909 SCHOTT MUSIC, Mainz – Germany.
               Reproduced by permission. All rights reserved[46]

He sees no need of any subdivision of types of *détaché* bowing – 'drawing the
Bow backward and forward from every Note' suffices – but his approach quickly
becomes inadequate. Baillot, in the Paris Conservatoire method, specifies the part
of the bow and also the resultant sounding note-length (quavers are played as
semiquavers separated by rests). In a moderately fast tempo, quavers should be
played in the middle of the bow, and shortened:

---

[46]   Ibid., p. 18.

> Separate the notes by drawing the bow with vivacity and stopping it suddenly at the end of every note.[47]

In fast tempi Baillot advises playing in the middle or even three-quarters of the way down the bow, but he says that the tip should never be used, 'giving always a dull, hard tone, and being unfit for exercising vibrations in such thick strings as those of the cello'.[48] Baillot uses a vertical dash to indicate a *détaché* with a longer stroke than that implied by a staccato dot.[49] The latter should be played shorter, but still 'sufficiently distant from the bridge to produce a round and agreeable tone', giving a simple example in triplet semiquavers marked with dots.[50] Baillot does not suggest that such a passage should be played with the bow bouncing off the string, although in practice above a certain tempo this is almost inevitable to some degree.

Eley gives examples of what he calls 'staccato' and 'marcato', which he sees as opposites (and which are also notated in the opposite way from Baillot). Staccato, notated by Eley with vertical dashes, 'denotes to play the notes very short which is produced by lifting the Bow up from the string after each note is played'.[51] Marcato, notated by Eley with dots, 'means to give a particular stress to each note, but sustain each note its full value with the Bow on the String'. So Eley's 'marcato' is an on-the-string *détaché*, perhaps similar to the French *grand détaché*, notated with staccato dots that do not imply separation, but rather a stressed *non legato*. Eley's staccato is lifted, but not necessarily bounced, which implies a bow-stroke fairly close to the heel. Eley omits modern *spiccato* entirely, and only uses a fast slurred staccato (both down- and up-bow) in some of his arpeggio exercises, similar to Romberg's two-note arpeggio bowing.

Eley uses articulation marks quite consistently, with dots only used for a group of several notes played within one bow (and therefore with a different meaning from dots on separate notes), and dashes for notes played with separate bows. In this he corresponds to the practice of several other string players: many of the performing editions by Ferdinand David observe the same distinction. Eley does

---

[47]   P. Baillot, J.H. Levasseur, C.-S. Catel and C.-N. Baudiot, *Méthode de violoncelle* (Paris: Janet et Cotelle, 1805), p. 23. Eng. trans. A. Merrick, *Method for the Violoncello* (London: Cocks & Co. [1]).

[48]   Ibid.

[49]   The notational confusion between dots and strokes (*Punkte* and *Striche*) generally in the classical and romantic periods is beyond the scope of this book. See Clive Brown, 'The Notation of Articulation and Phrasing', in *CRPP* pp. 200–258, and 'Dots and strokes in late 18th- and 19th-century music', *Early Music*, 21 (1993), pp. 593–7 and pp. 599–610; Frederick Neumann, 'Dots and strokes in Mozart', *Early Music*, 21 (1993), pp. 429–35; Robert Riggs, 'Mozart's Notation of Staccato Articulation: A New Appraisal', *Journal of Musicology*, 15 (1997), pp. 230–77.

[50]   Baillot et al., *Méthode*, p.123.

[51]   Eley, *Improved Method*, p. 13.

not deal explicitly with multiple-note up-bow staccato, with the bow remaining on the string throughout and stopping between the notes, but some of his exercises could be read in this way.

Crouch, generally paraphrasing the Paris Conservatoire method, departs from it here. For *detaché* passages in moderate tempi, Crouch advises using 'that part of the bow rather approaching the point than the nut', while in fast tempi 'that part of the bow near the centre is preferable', using no more than half an inch of bow per note.[52] Crouch uses the vertical dash to mean a short note, playing a quaver as a semiquaver as in Baillot's example above (which Crouch also uses). However, the staccato dot means, for Crouch, that 'the notes must be played one after the other *without* separating them by a rest'.[53] The bow-stroke is still short and, as in Baillot, should be far enough from the bridge to ensure a full round sound. The inconsistency between Baillot and Crouch underlines the latter's despairing observation about articulation marks (the slur, the dash, and the dot): 'From the several ways in which these signs are placed, proceeds an almost endless variety.'[54]

Duport is less clear than usual when discussing *detaché*. At first, he appears to distinguish only between *detaché* (separate) and *coulé* (slurred). *Détaché* describes groups of quavers or semiquavers played with alternating down- and up- bows, while *coulé* refers to such groups linked together within one bow.[55] The bowing variations he gives, applied to a simple pattern of semiquavers, combine *detaché* and *coulé*, all of which are to be practised starting with an up-bow as well as a down-bow, to acquire 'de la facilité et de l'habileté'. Almost as an afterthought he then notes that:

> There are two types of *detaché*, the first pressed [*appuyé*, i.e., on the string], which one uses when one wishes to produce a firm tone, and the other skipping a little [*un peu sauté*], which one makes use of in light passages. The latter stroke is played three quarters of the way down the bow, towards the tip.[56]

Duport gives no example of the *peu sauté* stroke in the main text of his *Essai*, and his studies contain no passage-work that unambiguously requires it. At first sight this part of the bow is peculiarly unsuitable for a 'skipping' stroke, at least for anything more than one or two notes. Indeed, this passage was silently amended in Lindner's 1864 trilingual edition, which cuts much material on bowing, to read:

---

[52]   Frederick Crouch, *Compleat Treatise*, p. 28.

[53]   Ibid. Emphasis added.

[54]   Ibid.

[55]   Duport, *Essai*, p. 166.

[56]   'Il y a deux sortes de détaché, le premier appuyé dont on se sert quand on veut tirer du son, et l'autre un peu sauté dont on se sert dans les choses de légèreté. Ce dernier s'exécute des trois quarts de l'archet, vers la pointe.' Ibid.

There are two manners of detaching: the first manner, with a firm stroke, is used if a full tone is to be drawn out; the second, with a slight skipping of the bow, is employed for passages, which are to be played with a light, brilliant, style. This latter stroke is played with the *middle* of the bow.[57]

However, it could be that Duport has in mind the faster *détaché* of Baillot, played three-quarters of the way down the bow, with a somewhat lifted stroke. Lindner's emendation might therefore imply that this stroke was out of favour later in the nineteenth century and the more clearly lifted bow-stroke, requiring a mid-bow point of contact, or a little closer to the heel than that, was more normal. However, some caution is required here. There is no shortage of cellists who continue to advocate a mid-bow *détaché* firmly *on* the string. Jules de Swert notes in his so-called 'staccato exercises' that they 'must be played from the middle of the bow, each note of equal length and force'.[58] Kummer does not discuss *spiccato* bowing at all, so when Becker revises him he adds his own explanation, under the heading 'The springing bowstroke and its variations (by the editor)':

Oddly, this type of bowing does not appear in Kummer's school. The editor has already explained in his 'mixed bowing and finger exercises' how this type of stroke is learned. Here the following is mentioned:

a. The spring-bowing (*spiccato*).

The cello bow has its greatest elasticity a little below the middle. (Were its weight not unevenly distributed through the weight of the frog and the increasingly strong curve of the bow, it would be found – like the [archery] bow – exactly in the middle). The bow is placed at this point, with a raised wrist, and with all the hair on the string (at an angle of 90°). The tone production will now be achieved, so that the hand (with the lightly springing participation of the arm) allows a knocking movement of the bow, in a diagonal direction from left to right. This movement combines a mixture of both wrist styles, the sinking and the sideways movements. By the correct use of the finger joints one prevents the bow from wandering from this position. With a slower tempo, a larger arm movement is combined with the hand movement, as required. This decreases, however, in proportion to the tempo, again, so that very rapid consecutive notes can be played with so-called 'standing still' arms. The fingers are always to touch the bow very loosely, in order to make possible the reaction of the 'hinges'. Also one must not overlook lifting the bow off the string from the first note so that it is able to recoil with its own elasticity.[59]

---

[57]   Duport, trans. Lindner, *Essai*, p. 143. Emphasis added.

[58]   Jules de Swert, *Le Mécanisme du Violoncelle* (Berlin: N. Rimrock, [1872]), p. 36.

[59]   'Der Spring-Bogenstrich und dessen Abarten. (Vom Herausgeber.) Merkwürdiger weise figurierten diese Bogenstricharten in der Kummerschen Schule nicht. Der Herausgeber hat in seinen "gemischten Bogen- un Fingerübingen" bereits dargelegt, wie diese Stricharten zu erlernen sind. Hier sei das Folgende erwähnt: a. Der Spring-Bogenstrinch (Spiccato).

This type of *spiccato* bowing, relying on a very flexible wrist movement, may have been used by Popper. Van der Straeten describes how Popper played his own 'Herbstblume' with 'wonderful charm', and played 'the staccato notes in the first bar in a down bow very lightly from the wrist'.[60] Discussing the opening of Offenbach's 'Musette', van der Straeten suggests an easier alternative bowing:

> There is at the beginning of the bar a little staccato figure of two quavers and a dotted crochet. This must be played in a down bow with a neat, sharp forearm movement, and unless the violoncellist can do it lightly and gracefully it would be much better to play the notes separately, using a short *détaché* for the quavers. Of course the effect of the staccato is better, if done well.[61]

Straeten's presumed preferred bowing is as shown in Example 3.3.

Example 3.3   Straeten, *Well-Known Cello Solos*, Offenbach 'Musette', preferred bowing

Seine größte Elastizität besitzt der Cellobogen etwas unterhalb der Mitte. (Wären seine Gewichtsverhältnisse durch die Schwere des Frosches und die nach unten stärker werdende Bogenstange nicht ungleich verteilt, so mußte sie, – wie bei dem Schießbogen – genau in der Mitte zu finden sein.) An dieser Stelle setze man den Bogen, bei hochgehobenem Handgelenk, mit allen Haaren (Winkel von etwa 90°) auf die Saite. Die Tonerzeugung wird nun dadurch bewirkt, da[ss] die Hand (unter leichter federnder Beteiligung des Armes) den Bogen, in diagonaler Richtung von links nach rechts, eine klopfende Bewegung ausüben läßt. Diese Bewegung bildet eine Mischung der beiden Handgelenkarten, der senkrechten und der wagrechten [small diagram of arrows]. Durch den richtigen Gebrauch der Fingerscharniere verhindert man den Bogen aus einer einmal angenommen Lage abzuirren. Bei langsameren Tempo gesellt sich zu der Handbewegung, je nach Bedarf, eine größere Tätigkeit des Armes. Diese nimmt jedoch, in richtigem Verhältnis zur Schnelligkeit des Tempos, wieder ab, sodaß sehr rasche aufeinander folgende Noten mit sog. Stillstehendem Arme gespielt werden könner. Die Finger sollen den Bogen stets sehr locker anfassen, um das Reagieren der "Scharniere" zu ermöglichen. Auch darf nicht übersehen werden, den Bogen von der ersten Note ab auf die Saite aufzuwerfen, damit er vermöge seiner eigenen Elastizität zurückprallt.' Kummer, rev. Becker, *Violoncelloschule*, p. 26.

60   E. van der Straeten, *Well-Known Violoncello Solos: How to Play Them with Understanding, Expression and Effect* (London: William Reeves, [1922]), p. 2, discussing David Popper, 'Herbstblume' op. 50 no. 5, from *Im Walde* (Hamburg: Rahter, [1882]).

61   Straeten, *Well-Known Violoncello Solos*, p. 7, discussing Jaques Offenbach, *Musette. Air de Ballet du 17e Siècle* op. 24 (Berlin: Schlesinger, [1846]).

Beethoven, 'Judas Maccabaeus' Variations, no. 7

The seventh of Beethoven's variations on Handel's 'See, the Conquering Hero comes' (WoO 45) gives some idea of the subtle nuances involved in trying accurately to describe these bow-strokes or interpret their notations. Vaslin uses this variation to show how Baillot played it on the violin.[62] Berlioz described Baillot's performance of this work thus:

> the theme of Handel [...] is of a noble and simple majesty; the variations with which Beethoven took pleasure to ornament it were performed by Baillot with exact refinement and the fire of youth which we know in him.[63]

According to Vaslin, Baillot's bow-stroke corresponded to the last of Vaslin's categories of *détaché*, the triplet quaver 'avec attaque [...] martelé ou piqué' (Figure 3.1).[64] Note that in Vaslin's diagram, every other type of note-length can be played with or without accent, but triplet quavers are only shown as played 'avec attaque'. Vaslin's discussion of *détaché* is chiefly concerned with the quality of sound in short notes, and he is especially interesting given his connection with Baillot, whose playing made a deep impression on Vaslin when he was a student at the Paris Conservatoire; there are many fulsome eulogies of Baillot in *L'art du violoncelle*.

> The rapidity of lively notes forces the restriction of the movement of the right arm. The best part of the bow is found in the middle, because there the hair, having all its elasticity perfectly matching that of the string, can in a circumscribed space obtain an open, rich, albeit short, sound.[65]

Vaslin consistently prefers the middle of the bow for *détaché* passages and for those that combine *détaché* and short slurred groups.

---

[62]   Ludwig van Beethoven, XII *Variations [...] sur un thème de Händel* WoO 45 (Vienna: Artaria, [1797]).

[63]   '[...] le thème Haendel au contraire, est d'une noble et simple majesté, les variations dont Beethoven s'est plu à le broder ont été dites par Baillot avec élégance exacte et ce feu de jeunesse que nous lui connaissons.' Hector Berlioz, *Revue musicale*, 17 February 1835, quoted from Marie-Hélène Coudroy-Saghaï (ed.), *Hector Berlioz: Critique musicale 1823–1863*, 2 vols. (Paris: Buchet/Chastel, 1998), Vol. 2, p. 65.

[64]   Olive Vaslin, *L'art du violoncelle* (Paris: Richault, 1884), pp. 11–12. This diagram is divided across two pages in the original; the two sections are brought together as one for this illustration.

[65]   'Là rapidité des notes vives oblige a restreindre les mouvements du bras droit. La meilleure portion de l'archet se trouve au milieu parceque là le crin ayant toute son élasticité en parfaite analogie avec celle de la corde, c'est là que dans un espace circonscrit l'on peut obtenir le son franc et nourri, quoique bref.' Vaslin, *L'art du violoncelle*, p. 10.

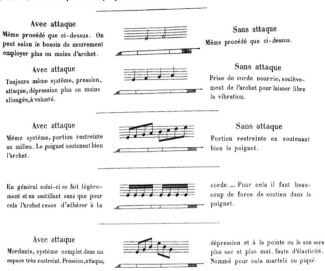

Figure 3.1   Vaslin, *L'art du violoncelle*, bowing diagram

Beethoven's original has neither staccato markings nor slurs, so Baillot's bow-stroke, endorsed nearly half a century later by Vaslin, is in itself unremarkable (Figure 3.2). Edmund van der Straeten also comments on this variation, saying that it requires a 'very short and energetic forearm stroke (the short detached stoke – *petit détaché* [...]) in the middle of the bow', implying a certain degree of separation, but firmly on the string.[66]

It therefore appears that Baillot, Vaslin and van der Straeten used a similar bow-stroke in this variation, more or less corresponding to a modern *martelé*. Other cellists also recommended such a bow-stroke in similar exercises. Such an

---

[66]   E. van der Straeten, *Well-Known Violoncello Solos*, p. 75. Van der Straeten does not mention the use of slurs.

Figure 3.2   Beethoven, *'Judas Maccabaeus' Variations*, no. 7: Baillot's bowing
as given by Vaslin

Example 3.4   Jules de Swert, *Mécanisme, détaché* triplets

exercise in de Swert (Example 3.4) is explicitly marked to be played in the upper
part of the bow and only with the forearm.[67]

Something very like Baillot's full-sound staccato note can be found much later
in the century in Carl Schroeder, who describes:

> The Hammer bowstroke. In this style of bowing, which is played with the wrist,
> between the middle and point of the bow, not quickly and without raising the
> hair from the strings, the attack of the down- and up-stroke must be sharp and
> firm, short and abrupt, yet full and resonant in tone.[68]

Thus far, many players agree that this variation (or music like it) should be played
with a stroke which Vaslin describes as 'biting [...] in a very limited space'.[69]

---

[67]   de Swert, *Mécanisme*, p. 10.

[68]   Carl Schroeder, *Neue grosse theoretisch praktische Violoncell-Schule* op. 34
(Leipzig: J.Schuberth & Co., [1877]), p. 28.

[69]   'Mordante [...] dans une espace très restreint'. Vaslin, *L'art du violoncelle*, p. 12.

However, Grützmacher's edition of this work (Example 3.5) marks the seventh variation with staccato dots throughout, and with more slurs than Baillot.[70]

Example 3.5   Beethoven, ed. Grützmacher, *'Judas Maccabaeus' variations*, no. 7 (extracts)

What these dots mean here is not clear. They need not necessarily imply a bow-stroke that comes off the string, whether lifted, bounced, or thrown. Grützmacher could intend a lifted bow-stroke, similar to *spiccato* but longer, although this would depend on tempo (the theme is marked 'Allegretto', *alla breve*, and this is unchanged for the first nine variations).

In the pedagogical works and performing editions of cellists such as Grützmacher and Romberg, off-string bowing occupies a marginal position, but is not totally rejected. Grützmacher generally limits the use of a *spiccato* bow-stroke in his own compositions to notes shorter than semiquavers, or repeated semiquavers. He indicates it twice in his op. 38 studies, and almost certainly intends *spiccato* in the passage from his edition of Servais's concerto op. 5 shown in Example 3.6.[71]

Example 3.6   Servais, ed. Grützmacher, Concerto op. 5, third movement, *spiccato*

His reluctance to exploit *spiccato* may explain why it is only clearly indicated in his studies and only rarely elsewhere; he appears to be offering it as a technique that he does not himself use, like Romberg. The opposite is the case with Davidoff, whose *Violoncelloschule* does not mention staccato or *spiccato*, even though many of his works, such as *Am Springbrunnen*, require it. Romberg uses *détaché* to

---

[70]   Ludwig van Beethoven, ed. F. Grützmacher, *Zwölf Variationen über ein Thema aud "Judas Maccabaeus" von Händel* (Leipzig: Peters, [1870?]).

[71]   Friedrich Grützmacher, *Technologie des Violoncellspiels* op. 38 (Leipzig: C.F. Peters, (1865]), studies nos. 12 and 20; Adrien-François Servais, ed. F. Grützmacher, Concerto in B minor op. 5 (Leipzig: C.F. Peters, [1896?]).

mean a light off-the-string separated bow-stroke, with the bow held lightly by the thumb, first and third fingers so that it can 'spring well upon the strings' – in other words, the modern *spiccato*.[72] He describes this stroke, but disapproves of it, restricting its use to 'those pieces which are written in a playful style, such as Rondos in 6/8 Time, or Solos for chamber-Music'. It is not appropriate for *forte* passages, or for 'music of a higher order', and indeed it is even old-fashioned:

> This bowing was formerly in great repute with all Artists, who introduced it in passages of every description. It is, however, quite incompatible with a fine broad style of playing, which fully accounts for the inferiority of their compositions. Now-a-days Musical compositions are expected to contain more solidity, both in signification and expression.[73]

Romberg still overcomes his distaste long enough to give an entire variation movement as an exercise for this technique (Example 3.7). Note that this exercise uses *spiccato* in neck and thumb positions, but is almost entirely played on the upper two strings.

Example 3.7   Romberg, *Violoncellschule, spiccato* exercise, opening[74]

3da.

The staccato dots and short slurs that Grützmacher adds to the *Judas Maccabaeus* variation are not unique to him; they are also added by Ferdinand David in his arrangement for violin.[75] In David's case, dots in general do not rule out an on-string bow-stroke, and there are many instances where they appear simply to indicate or confirm the end of a slurred passage. But David also describes a 'springing' ('*hüpfend*') bow-stroke that 'must never entirely leave the strings; try to make the stick vibrate strongly [...] in playing forte use the middle of the bow, in piano the upper half'.[76] His exercise for this stroke uses a simple pattern of repeated semiquavers, one which is given in an almost identical version for the

---

[72]   Bernhard Romberg, *Violoncellschule* (Berlin: Trautwein, [1840]), p. 109.

[73]   Ibid.

[74]   Ibid., p. 120.

[75]   Beethoven, arr. F. David, *Sonaten und Variationen für Pianoforte und Violoncell* (Leipzig: C.F. Peters, [1874].

[76]   'Der Bogen darf die saite nicht ganz verlassen; man suche die Stange in starke Vibration zu bringen [...] beim forte in der Mitte, beim piano etwas mehr nach der obern Hälfte des Bogens zu.' Ferdinand David, *Violin-schule* (Leipzig: Breitkopf & Härtel, [1863]), p. 38.

cello by Carl Schroeder.[77] This bow-stroke was also described several decades earlier by Georg Kastner, who warned that it was not easy:

> The staccato is obtained on the cello by letting the bow fall in a manner such that it jumps bouncing from the strings, *without at the same time leaving them*; this type of expression is very difficult, and is only acquired through long work; the second type of staccato, more accurately called martelé [example of a note with a wedge accent], has still more liveliness and dryness [...].[78]

On the other hand, a passage in triplet quavers from Servais's second concerto is marked 'martelé', with staccato dots (Example 3.8).

Example 3.8   Servais, Concerto no. 2, martelé

Welleke's edition of Grützmacher's *Tägliche Übungen* describes the springing bow-stroke:

> In the middle of the bow (or, rather, a trifle nearer to the nut). To be played with easy and supple arm and wrist.[79]

His exercises suggest that this stroke is used as much in rapid passage-work as in passages of repeated notes. This *hüpfenden* stroke, though probably a little longer than modern *spiccato*, clearly has the potential to overlap with it, and the distinction probably depends more on tempo than any other technical consideration.

If Welleke appears to require something closer to a modern *spiccato* in staccato semiquaver passage-work, Alexanian attempts to clarify the point (in a typically elaborate way). He distinguishes two types of bounced, off-the-string, bow-strokes: '*spiccato*' and '*saltellato*'. His *spiccato* is:

---

[77]   Carl Schroeder, *Tägliche Studien* (Hamburg, [1877]), p. 26.

[78]   'Le Staccato s'obtient sur le Violoncelle en laissant tomber l'archet de manière à ce qu'il bondisse en sautillant sur les cordes, sans toutefois les quitter; ce genre d'expression est très difficile, et ne s'acquiert que par un long travail; la seconde espèce de staccato plus particulièrement appelée Martelé a encore plus de vigueur et de sècheresse; voici une leçon sur ces deux genres de Détaché.' Georg Kastner, *Méthode elementaire de violoncelle* (Paris: E. Froupenas & Cie, [1835]), p. 37.

[79]   Grützmacher, *Daily Exercises*, p. 29.

a fluttering of the bow, light, rapid and dainty [...] the result of the 'launching' of the bow with a continuous adherence of the hairs to the string [...]. In the '*spiccato*', the horizontal movement of the bow should not exceed about half an inch. As for its intermittent elevation above its points of contact with the strings, it could only be given in eighths of an inch. Any exaggeration of the rebound would destroy that aerial lightness that gives the charm to this manner of bowing.[80]

His '*saltellato*' is more consistently off the string, and:

consists in a fairly heavy fall of [the bow hairs] that are at once thrown back to their original position, above the strings [...] it is a '*spiccato*' without any 'finesse' [...] the resulting rebounds are much more clearly defined than in the '*spiccato*', and the acoustic effect is therefore much coarser.[81]

Alexanian's *spiccato* is therefore more akin to earlier players' springing or *hüpfend* stroke, in that the bow remains fairly close to the string.

It is therefore likely that in the seventh *Judas Maccabaeus* variation, the bow-stroke implied by David and Grützmacher is the slightly lifted stroke of David (*hüpfend*) and Kastner (*staccato*), and possibly quite similar to Duport's *un peu sauté*. But the bow-stroke used for this passage by Baillot (*martelé*), Vaslin (*martelé* or *piqué*) and van der Straeten (*petit détaché*), also described by de Swert and Schroeder, and probably used in a similar passage by Servais, is the more firmly on-the-string, mid- to third-quarter bow-stroke. There is evidence to support either type of bow-stroke in nineteenth-century practices, and both have associations with prominent players from the early part of the century. In this case, then, even if using the methodologically insecure model of teacher–pupil transmission, it is not possible to say with any clarity which bow-stroke might have been the more likely one to be used in the first decades of the century. To complicate the matter further, above a certain tempo the distinction begins to dissolve. There is a natural physical tendency for the bow to lift, and keeping it firmly on the string becomes increasingly artificial.

The term 'staccato' is also used much more consistently throughout the nineteenth century to denote, specifically, a group of clearly articulated notes played in one bow, as opposed to any generally short note, or a single note with a dot. There are two distinct types of up-bow staccato: the virtuosic type, often involving many notes in one bow played as fast as possible, and a less abruptly articulated stroke, played slower and with far fewer notes, closer to *portato*. Crome and Hardy describe the 'soft' technique. Crome's 'feather' stroke does not take the bow far from the string:

---

[80]   Alexanian, *Traité théorique et pratique*, p. 203.

[81]   Ibid.

We will now set an Example for slurring and Feathering the Bow; the Slur is known by this semicircle put over the number of Notes it contains, [...] the same sign serves for the Feather, only dotted [...] the difference is this, for the Slur; the Bow is to keep on the String, and for the Feather; it is just taken off the String, but with the same Bow.[82]

Hardy's use of the same term refers to something more like a modern up-bow staccato, with the bow apparently remaining on the string (compare Crome's 'just off the string' above) and stopping between notes:

Feathering the Bow [example showing slur over dots] this character is used to any number of notes, and signifies that they are to be played with one strike of the bow, and generally with an up bow, but not in that smooth stile like unto a slur; as in feathering, there should be a kind of stop, or small distinction between every note, so as each may be plainly articulated.[83]

Crome and Hardy are the only English cellists to use the term 'feathering', and relatively few cellists in general address this 'semi-soft' articulation. Gunn emphasizes that a lifted stroke is needed, but not a short one.[84] Dotzauer also describes an undulating, *portato* bow technique, which he calls '*portamento*', applied over a group of notes rather than during one long note:

The two crotchets [...] are played with (*Portamento*) that is to say, that the bow lightly presses each note, which is effected by the pressure of the index finger, without the hair leaving the string.[85]

Romberg does not specifically discuss the *portato* stroke, but comes close to it when he talks of a generally articulated slur:

when, in a slow movement, notes occur, which are marked to be played together in one Bow, and also marked with dots above, each note must be separated from the other by a short cessation of the bow. In order to give more force to the expression, a slight pressure is also frequently made upon each note. But when notes marked with the slur and dots occur in quick movements, each note will then require but a very little pressure. [...] Slurred notes which are marked with strokes above should be played shorter, and more detached than those marked with dots. This difference however is not marked with sufficient care by many Composers.[86]

---

[82]   Crome, *Compleat Method*, pp.14–15.
[83]   Henry Hardy, *The Violoncello Preceptor* (Oxford: the author, [c.1800]), p. 11.
[84]   Gunn, *Theory and Practice*, 1st edn, [1789], pp. 69–74.
[85]   Dotzauer, *Méthode*, p. 43.
[86]   Romberg, *Complete School*, p. 98.

However, his 'short cessation of the bow' implies something more clearly articulated than Crouch's *ondulé*, 'feathering', or Gunn's slurred staccato – it most resembles Hardy's 'plainly articulated' stroke.

The Paris Conservatoire method scarcely deals with up-bow staccato at all, but includes it by implication in some of its bowing exercises, in both directions (Example 3.9).[87] Apart from exercises like this, it offers the simple advice that the player should adjust the amount of bow to the number of notes.[88]

Example 3.9   Baillot et al., Paris method, up- and down-bow staccato

Duport describes this technique, which he calls staccato or *martelé*, in more detail. He uses the same term for a short group of notes played in this way or a much longer one:

> Here again is an often-used bow-stroke of three and three. Play three with a down-bow and three with an up-bow, but the first three must be slurred, and the next three Staccato.[89]

He then offers an example of more extended up-bow staccato over several two-octave scales, ending with a charming disclaimer:

> On the Martelé, or Staccato. Everyone knows this bowing; I do not think it necessary to show how it is performed. It is entirely a question of *tact* and *addresse*; one arrives at it with much exercise; there are those who grasp it immediately, others who never achieve it perfectly. I am of that number.*
> *Editor's note. All M. Duport's friends know the extent of his modesty.[90]

Duport was certainly not alone in suggesting that it could be a troublesome technique to learn. Crouch describes it as 'extremely difficult on the Violoncello, and but seldom used excepting by the most skilful performers.'[91] Lindley agrees:

---

87   Baillot et al., *Méthode*, p. 25.

88   'Il faut en outre ménager plus au moins l'Archet suivant qu'on a plus ou moins notes à faire [...].' Baillot et al., *Méthode*, p. 16.

89   'Voici encore un coup d'archet de trois en trois très-usité. Tirez trois et poussez trois, mais il faut que les trois premières soient coulées, et els trois dernières Staccato.' Duport, *Essai*, p. 169.

90   Ibid, p. 171.

91   Crouch, *Compleat Treatise*, pp. 34–43.

The Staccato style of bowing is very difficult to a beginner, who too often aims at some object beyond his reach, instead of mastering the easier point which should engage his attention. In Staccato bowing the note is produced by a very slight, short jerk of the wrist, and after practice an incredible number of notes may be struck without reversing the motion of the bow. Such notes have been aptly likened to a 'String of Pearls'. However, the Pupil must make a few notes at first, beginning at the point of the bow, and using as little of it as possible for each note. Some Masters maintain that Staccato passages should be entirely confined to the upper half of the bow, but this can only hold good in [p]hrases of moderate length.[92]

Romberg is as sceptical about the usefulness of an up-bow staccato technique as he is about *spiccato*:

This mode of Bowing, when used for several notes or passages consecutively, is more peculiarly adapted to the Violin; since in playing this Instrument, the bow rests upon the strings, and requires but a slight motion of the hand to produce the staccato. [...] But this is not the case with the Violoncello, where the bow does not rest with its own weight on the strings, and where the staccato cannot be produced with merely a gentle pressure, so that, it must either be made with the arm held stiff, or the bow must be drawn up so tight as to spring off the strings by its own tension, and even then, the Player can never be sure of success. Indeed, as the Violoncellist is so seldom called upon to employ the staccato, it would be a great pity that he should spoil his Bow-hand by practicing it to any extent; and I would rather advise him to abstain from it wholly and entirely. In Quartetts and other compositions (which are not to be considered as solos) passages are marked to be played staccato. The notes of such passages may be played with a short, detached, Bow.[93]

He gives several examples of these bowings, indicating a quasi-*portato* staccato in a few exercises in slow or moderate tempi before it is discussed in the text.[94] But Romberg gives no extended examples of fast up-bow staccato – hardly surprising given his evident reluctance to use the technique – and it is not required for any of his compositions, even the most virtuosic. He refers to his own concerto no. 4 in E minor, but only to advise against his own printed bowing:

This sort of arpeggio, however, can only be made in a quick movement because the bow itself must partly produce the spring. I do not recommend the young

---

92   Lindley, *Hand-book*, p. 11.
93   Romberg, *Complete School*, pp. 109–10.
94   Romberg, *Violoncellschule*, p. 99.

pupil to study this arpeggio, as it is apt to give him a stiff arm, which […] is diametrically opposed to neat playing. It has a much better effect when played in detached notes with the up-bow, where each note occupies but a small portion of the bow, used at about a hand's breadth from the end of it. (This arpeggio occurs in the *rondo alla polacca* in my E minor concerto).[95]

The bowing in pairs of staccato semiquavers involves a different technique from the up-bow staccato used for long scales, as the string-crossing requires in effect a quasi-*jeté* stroke. An almost identical passage appears in Joseph Reinagle's (1762–1825) Quartet in D, given here in its original notation (Example 3.10).[96] Here the context strongly suggests that Reinagle's semiquaver passage begins on a down-bow, unlike Romberg's example above, but the technique is fundamentally the same.

Example 3.10   J. Reinagle String Quartet no. 2, first movement

[Allegro moderato]

Romberg's remarks on this bowing imply that he would perform a passage like the one shown in Example 3.10 with separate bows, beginning with an up-bow, near the tip of the bow. This would of necessity entail an on-string bowing and not a *spiccato* one. His preference here is partly explained by his description of the bowing pattern that he thinks the most difficult of all – it is the one that feels least under his control: '[Variation 6] contains the most difficult of all Bowings because it often takes away from the player, all mastery over the Bow'.[97] Surprisingly, this is not a *spiccato* bowing, but a 'hooked' or 'tucked in' dotted-rhythm bowing (Example 3.11).

Example 3.11   Romberg, *Violoncelloschule*, dotted-rhythm bowing

---

[95]   Ibid., p. 59. Carl Schroeder's edition of this concerto removes Romberg's bowing. Berhard Romberg, ed. Carl Schroeder, *Concerto no. 4* op. 7 (Brunswick: Litolff, [1879]).

[96]   Joseph Reinagle, 'Quartetto II', in *Three Quartetts* (London: the Author, [c.1805]).

[97]   Romberg, *Complete School*, p. 112.

Taking all Romberg's bowing preferences into account, it appears that the bowings he avoids, or towards which he has some antipathy, are all those that require the bow itself to do some of the work and over which the player has less control. Unlike his attitude to vibrato, this would not seem to be due to an unusual hand shape or bow hold. However, it could partly have been influenced by the tightness of his bow. The illustrations included in his *Violoncellschule* show a bow with the stick parallel to the hair. This is not an inaccurate drawing, for Romberg describes it explicitly:

> it should be so tightened that the upper surface of the bow, (reckoning from the nut), may form a straight line with the undersurface of the head.[98]

Romberg also used a light bow, which he thought unsuitable for bounced bow-strokes, advising those who were 'fond of using much staccato' that it would be too light, 'as it will not possess sufficient spring'. Romberg owned two bows of the Tourte design, both stamped with his name, and very similar in length to modern cello bows, with hair lengths of 59.9 cm and 59.7 cm.[99] A bow of this type, tightened to this degree, would indeed be difficult to control in complex staccato bowings.

Here it is interesting to note that the middle section of Piatti's *Capriccio* no. 5 (Example 3.12) appears to have been performed by Piatti entirely *on* the string (modern cellists frequently use something like an up-bow *jeté*, rather like Eley's arpeggio exercises mentioned above).

Example 3.12   Piatti, *Capriccio* no. 5, opening bars and middle section

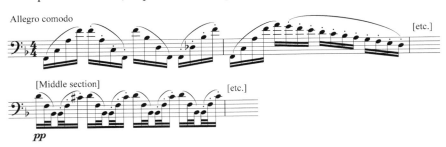

His pupil William Whitehouse commented:

> No. 5 Allegro comodo – quite slow, rather heavy staccato arpeggio, (an 'accommodating' time) to enable the pace of the arpeggios in the second part of

---

98   Ibid., p. 4.

99   So described by Valerie Walden, *One Hundred Years of Violoncello A History of Technique and Performance Practice 1740–1840* (Cambridge: Cambridge University Press, 1998), p. 90 n. 31.

the Caprice to be twice as fast as those in the first part, as written. – The second part to be pianissimo, *the bow remaining on the strings* except for the sixth note of each group, when it should be lifted momentarily. This bowing is best played about the middle of the bow. – The groups should on no account sound like triplets.[100]

However, according to Whitehouse, Piatti's own practice seems to have varied in another passage from *Capriccio* no. 12 (Example 3.13):

the master performed the staccato notes sometimes with a springing bow – (spiccato) and as an alternative – with the bow kept on the string (staccato), but in either case, at the eighth bar, he kept the bow well on the string – at the double bar in C major he somewhat slackened the pace of the movement, keeping the bow also on the string for the staccato [...].[101]

Piatti's tempo alteration and decision to keep the bow on the string at the C major section are both largely necessitated by the artificial harmonics later in the work.

Example 3.13   Piatti, *Capriccio* no. 12, opening bars, and passage in artificial harmonics

However, even allowing for the particular technical challenges posed by this exceptional passage, it seems that Piatti's general preference was to play on the string. The concerto by Molique, written for Piatti and frequently performed by him, contains many passages clearly designed to be played with on-string up-bow staccato, and there are no passages of separately bowed semiquavers (or shorter notes) in this work or in his *Capricci* that absolutely necessitate *spiccato* rather than a degree of *détaché*.[102]

Romberg may have thought the springing bow irrelevant to the requirements of modern music, apart from more or less frivolous pieces, but he was fast becoming out of date. Kummer gives some attention to a fast up-bow staccato, with a basic description of how to obtain it:

---

[100]   Alfredo Piatti, ed. W.E. Whitehouse, *Dodici Capricci* op. 25 (Leipzig: N. Simrock [1874]), p. [2]. Emphasis added.

[101]   Ibid.

[102]   Bernhard Molique, *Concerto* op. 45 (Leipzig: Kistner, [1854]).

By staccato, violinists and cellists understand the pushing of many notes in one bow, whereas the Italians simply call this 'pushed' [*gestossen*]. After the first note, in which the bow is extended in a down-bow to the tip, the right hand returns the bow (without lifting it from the string) in a short and firm up-bow continuously and uses of its length as little as possible for each note. The index finger of the right hand presses the bow-stick a little more than usual. The first and last notes must stay a little less marked.[103]

He gives two exercises, the first of which is very similar to Kreutzer's study no. 4, and second of which is a conventional up-bow staccato scale.[104] Two generations later, Servais's pupil Jules de Swert was to justify the study of up-bow staccato as an essential for any player who wanted to play modern music. In his edition of Romberg's treatise he noted:

The staccato is of great importance in relation to demands that are nowadays made of virtuosi. I know many artists both on the violin and on the cello, who have to avoid modern compositions because they cannot execute a staccato. I advise everyone to study the staccato in the way described above. Admittedly, one will develop it with greater skill than another (each according to his natural talents), but it will not be totally fruitless for anyone.[105]

Hugo Becker elaborates Kummer's explanation, adding that, as described by Kummer, this technique can have physical problems:

Steinhausen tends towards the view shared by the editor [Becker], that the staccato originates solely in the pronation and supination of the forearm. This

---

103 'Unter Staccato verstehen Geiger und Cellisten das Abstoßen mehrerer Noten auf einen Bogenstrich, während das dem Italienischen entnommene Wort schlechthin "gestoßen" heißt. Nach dem ersten Tone, bei welchem der Bogen im Herunterstrich bis an die Spitze auszuziehen ist, rückt die rechte Hand den Bogen (ohne ihn von den Saiten zu heben) in hinaufstrich kurz und kräftig fort und verbraucht von seiner Länge so wenig als möglich bei jedem Ton. Der Zeigefinger de rechten Hand drückt dabei die Bogenstange etwas mehr als gewöhnlich. Die erste und letzte Note müssen stets ein wenig markiert werden.' F.A. Kummer, rev. Becker, *Violoncelloschule*, p. 25.

104 Kummer, *Violoncelloschule* op. 60 (Leipzig: Hofmeister, [1839]), p. 109. Rudolphe Kreutzer, *40 Etudes ou Caprices* (Paris: Conservatoire de Musique, [1796]). Dehn's cello transcription of Kreutzer (Leipzig: Breitkopf & Härtel, [1831]) had already appeared.

105 'Das Staccato ist in Bezug, auf die Antsprüche die man heutzutage an Virtuosen macht, von grosser Wichtigkeit. Ich kenne viele Künstler sowohl auf der Geige auf dem Violoncell, die auf manche moderne Composition verzichten müssen, weil sie kein Staccato machen können. Ich rathe also Jedem das Staccato nach der oben beschiebenen Weise zu studiren. Der Eine wird es freilich auf grösserer Fertigkeit bringen wie der Andere, (jedem seiner natürlichen Anlage gemäss) aber ganz fruchtlos wird er für Keinen sein.' Bernhard Romberg, rev. Jules de Swert and Heinrich Grünfeld, *Violoncelloschule* (Berlin: E. Bote & G. Bock, [1888]), p. 115.

would be a similar movement to that of the left forearm in vibrato […]. In many players, very fast staccato passages are produced through a convulsive stiffening of the muscles, with a so-called stiff arm. However, this staccato production has the disadvantage that it is usually only maintained at a particular tempo.[106]

Becker's additional advice on up-bow staccato clearly implies a much more active wrist than any earlier treatment of the subject by a cellist. Indeed, de Swert had actually rejected this in the context of an extreme up-bow staccato over four octaves, acquired, according to him, over a period of two years: 'One is not to study the above staccato with the wrist'.[107] Stiffening of the arm was a recognized problem with up-bow staccato. Junod warned that:

To execute the staccato well it must be commenced slowly at first, until equality of tone is acquired. Rigidity of execution must be avoided, the first finger only slightly pressing the stick of the bow, which is stopped at each note, as little of it as possible being used. The staccato is an affair of skill and touch [*tact*]. It is acquired after much labour combined with great care.[108]

Jules de Swert was also concerned about stiffness:

By staccato is meant several detached notes which are played in one bow. In playing the first note draw the bow from the nut right down to the point and give a short strong pressure for each note in the up-bow, without lifting it from the strings. Hold the bow a little firmer than usual, but avoid stiffness. Play at first slowly, use as little of the length of the bow as possible, and stop after each note.[109]

The only nineteenth-century cellist who appears to have embraced a wide range of bowing techniques including *spiccato* and up- and down-bow staccato is Adrien-François Servais. There are many examples of extreme up-bow staccato in Servais such as shown in Example 3.14.[110]

---

[106]   'Steinhausen ist der Ansicht, zu der auch Herausgeber neigt, daß das Staccato lediglich aus Pronation und Supination des Vorderarms entsteht. Dies wäre eine dem Vibrato des linken Vorderarms ähnliche Bewegung […]. Sehr rache Staccatopassagen werden von vielen Spielern durch krampfhaftes feststellen der Armmuskeln, mit sogenannten steifem Arm, hervorgebracht. Diese Stacaatoproduktion hat aber den Nachteil, daß sie meistens nur auf ein bestimmtes Tempo eingestellt ist.' Kummer, rev. Becker, *Violoncelloschule*, p. 25.

[107]   'Man soll das Staccato oben nicht, mit dem Handgelenk studieren'. Romberg, ed. de Swert, *Violoncelloschule*, p. 115.

[108]   L. Junod, *New and Concise Method*, p. 58.

[109]   Romberg, rev. de Swert, *Violoncelloschule*, p. 86.

[110]   Servais, *Fantaisie burlesque sur le carnaval de Venise*, autograph MS, Brussels Royal Conservatoire MS. 45.106, p. 76. This version differs in many respects from the published version (*Fantaisie burlesque (ou le Carnaval de Venise)* (Mainz: B. Schotts Söhne, [1849]).

Example 3.14   Servais, *Fantaisie burlesque*, up-bow staccato

Just as frequently, he uses what would appear to be a 'heavier' version of this technique in slow tempi (Example 3.15).

Example 3.15   Servais, *Concerto militaire, Andante religioso*, up-bow accents

One work in particular constitutes a compendium of bowing effects (*jeté*, up- and down-bow staccato), unequalled by any other cellist-composer in this period – the *Fantaisie 'Le Desir'*, a set of variations on Schubert's 'Sehnsucht' waltz (Example 3.16).[111] Servais is also unique in his predilection for effects played at the heel of the bow. This is indicated in many of his compositions; Examples 3.17 and 3.18 are representative. However, Servais's evident interest in extreme bowing effects was not to become part of the cello's technical repertoire. Neither composers nor cellists pursued this kind of writing, which is not found in any of the modern cello canon. Even Popper, who, like Servais, was frequently called the 'Paganini of the cello', did not explore complex up-bow staccato, *spiccato* or mixtures of the two in anything like this way in his own compositions, although his studies do examine some of these techniques individually and at some length. Indeed, Servais's sophisticated bowing technique does not merely emulate that of his contemporary, the violinist Vieuxtemps; it sometimes exceeds it in virtuosity. Vieuxtemps's violin concertos share a number of Servais's techniques, in particular where complex passages in double-stops are concerned. Vieuxtemps frequently uses staccato and *spiccato* bowings, and marks many semiquaver passages to be played *au talon*, but his own cello concerto uses these techniques vary sparingly.[112] On the other hand, in the duos written by Servais and Vieuxtemps together, the

———————————

[111]   Servais, *Fantaisie et Variations brillantes sur la Valse de Schubert intitulée : le Désir (Sehnsuchts-Walzer)* (Mainz: B. Schott's Söhne, [1844]). The contemporaneous MS copy by Ulysse Claes (Brussels Royal Conservatoire MS. 45.106, p. 7) is entitled 'Hommage à Beethoven', as apparently Servais originally thought he was the composer of the theme. This work was recorded by Heinrich Kruse (1866–192?) in 1915 with numerous small changes. *The Recorded Cello*, Vol. 2.

[112]   Henri Vieuxtemps, *Concerto pour violoncelle* op. 46 (Mainz: B. Schott's Söhne, [1877]).

Example 3.16   Servais, *Fantaisie 'Le desir'*, mixed bowings

Example 3.17   Servais, *Souvenir d'Anvers*[113]

p scherzando   [etc. for 16 bars]

Example 3.18   Servais, *Duo sur une mélodie de Dalayrac*, variation 2[114]

solo parts are equally challenging, suggesting that Servais's tendency was to write violinistically for the cello.[115]

As Dotzauer observed, it is difficult to write about cello bowing because of the 'amount of small *nuances* which, essential in themselves, are denied a verbal explanation'.[116] However, the over-riding principles of bow hold as described in the nineteenth and early twentieth centuries – playing with a raised wrist, a lowered right elbow and an virtually inactive upper arm – should suggest to the player what 'little *nuances*' are possible. It need hardly be added that the canonic cello studies for modern conservatoire students, such as the exercises by Duport, Franchomme, Grützmacher, Piatti, and Popper, take on a very different character if one attempts to play them with this conformation of the bow arm. An analysis of the action of the bow arm in terms of its active and passive elements, and an awareness of how perceptions changed in this respect, also offers a way of deciding on which practices the player wishes to emulate. As with almost every other element of the cello technique in the nineteenth century, there is no 'practice'; there is a variety of practices co-existing at the same time, as well as a gradual overall change in these practices. For a cellist minded to play historically, these technical fundamentals – posture, bow hold, the shape of the hands and arms (especially the supinated wrist when playing at the tip of the bow, and the consistently low position of both elbows), basic fingering patterns, bowing – should come before questions of expression. Attempting to recapture older expressive techniques, while retaining

---

[113]   Servais, *Souvenir d'Anvers* (Mainz: B. Schott's Söhne, [1844]), p. 29.

[114]   Servais, *Duo sur une mélodie de Dalayrac pour deux violoncelles* op. posth. (Mainz: Schott's Söhne, [1876]).

[115]   See, for example, Henri Vieuxtemps and Adrien-François Servais, *Duo brillant* op. 39 (Mainz: B. Schott's Söhne, [1864]).

[116]   'la quantité de petits nuances qui, essentielles en leur mêmes, se refusent á une explication verbale'. Dotzauer, *Violonzellschule*, p. 6.

a modern posture, amounts to putting the cart before the horse, at least if also claiming to be historically informed. Indeed, string players in general who adopt some period practices almost unanimously avoid the recreation of period posture. It is not hard to understand why. Some postures, such as Romberg's left hand, are extremely difficult to maintain; others, such as the apparently excessive supination of the wrist when playing at the tip of the bow, are (at least to the writer) physically painful. Clive Brown's fascinating discussion of nineteenth-century violin posture shows that this issue is at least as pertinent for violinists.[117] As far as the cello is concerned, the effect of these postural traits on tone production is surely clear: they all point in the direction of reduced tonal projection.

---

[117] Clive Brown, 'The physical parameters of 19th and 20th century violin playing' (updated 2013): http://chase.leeds.ac.uk/article/physical-parameters-of-19th-and-early-20th-century-violin-playing-clive-brown/ [accessed July 2012].

Chapter 4
Playing with Expression – Portamento

In this and the following chapters, 'portamento' denotes any audible connection between notes, and 'vibrato' is taken to mean a regular oscillation of the left hand, used either occasionally or continuously, and denotes any such embellishment however named elsewhere.[1] These are the two most frequently discussed expressive techniques used by string players, but they have quite contrasting statuses in modern performance. There are more generally applicable expressive techniques, such as embellishment, or the use of *tempo rubato*, but they do not have a specific manifestation unique to the cello or even to instruments of the violin family in general, and will therefore not be discussed here. Earlier in the nineteenth century, cello tutors often included merely routine instructions in the realization of ornaments that are of no intrinsic interest, and nineteenth-century cellists are completely silent on the topic of *rubato*. No concert review of a cellist examined to date mentions or even alludes to the term; Becker is the first cello teacher to discuss it.[2] It is of course entirely plausible that cellists would have followed the examples of violinists or pianists in this respect, but that does not provide grounds for a study of *rubato* concentrating specifically on the cello.[3]

Portamento is still viewed with some suspicion in historically informed circles, while the lack of vibrato is almost a shibboleth of modern historical performance practice. What is more, neither portamento nor vibrato are theorized by cellists to anything like the degree found in at least some violin methods. The detailed explanations found in earlier nineteenth-century violin treatises, such as those by Baillot, Spohr, Bériot or David, have no real equivalents in the cello repertoire until the second decade of the twentieth century. No cellist goes into as much taxonomic detail as Bériot does for the violin, with his gradations of *ports-de-voix*, '*vif*', '*doux*' and '*trainé*'.[4] While one could reasonably assume cellists imitated violinists in the technique and application of vibrato and portamento, this *a priori*

---

[1] In essence this follows David Milsom, *Theory and Practice in Late Nineteenth-Century Violin Performance* (Aldershot: Ashgate, 2003), pp. 75–6 (portamento) and pp. 111–12 (vibrato). The different historical terminologies (and the use of the term by singers, are elucidated in Brown, *CRPP*, pp. 517–21 (vibrato) and pp. 558–9 (portamento).

[2] Hugo Becker and Dago Rynar, 'Vom Rubato', in *Mechanik und Äesthetik de Violoncellspiels* (Vienna and Leipzig: Universal-Edition, 1929), pp. 169–73.

[3] The most recent detailed examination of *rubato* is Richard Hudson, *Stolen Time: The History of Tempo Rubato* (Oxford: Clarendon Press, 1994), which does not approach the subject from the point of view of individual instrumental techniques.

[4] Charles de Bériot, *Méthode de violon* (Mainz: B. Schott fils, 1858), p. 237.

assumption should not go unquestioned, if for no other reason than that there are significant technical differences between the two instruments. Vibrato on the violin is a fundamentally different physical technique; portamento is 'enforced' on the cello far more than on the violin.

Daniel Leech-Wilkinson's assertion, in the context of singing, that portamento 'can be suppressed at will', does not quite fit the physical realities of large string instruments.[5] Unlike the violin, playing the cello necessitates frequent shifting of the left hand. In its normal configuration, the fingers are only a semitone apart, and even in extension the hand conventionally only covers a major third in the lower positions. There are many instances in the baroque repertoire of passage-work requiring a stretch of a fourth in order to play octaves in first position, and there are also a few examples in Duport and Baudiot, as well as one passage in the third, *adagio*, movement of Beethoven's String Trio op. 3. But this is the limit for normal-sized hands; only in the twentieth century is there an attempt to develop a larger extension or '*grosse Spannung*'.[6] The discussion of scale fingerings in Chapter 2 showed that cellists frequently overcame this fundamental physical obstacle by the simple expedient of shifting with the same finger, typically the first or fourth in a diatonic scale, or with almost any finger in a chromatic scale. Clearly, if the passage in question uses intervals larger than a tone, then, unless the piece remains wholly in first position, some shifting is inevitable. There are therefore, on the cello far more than on the violin, 'forced' as well as discretionary or 'unforced' shifts. This complicates the discussion of portamento, as some fingerings unavoidably 'slide' unless the player employs a degree of sophistication (taken for granted by modern players, but largely unexplained in the nineteenth century) in the action of both left hand and bow. Some cellists may have shifted audibly as a matter of course, while others were concerned only to shift audibly when musically appropriate. Some cellists suggested quite simple ways to minimize the effect, but in other cases they designed fingerings specifically to create portamento opportunities.

Cello methods of the late eighteenth/early nineteenth centuries, even the most technically advanced treatises such as those by Azaïs, Raoul or Bréval, more or less ignore portamento. The material offered to the student generally does not raise the issue as it uses very little sustained *cantabile* and a great deal of *detaché* or mixed slurred/*detaché* bowing in fast tempi.[7] Baillot introduces portamento in the context of an explanation of the *appoggiatura*:

---

[5]   Daniel Leech-Wilkinson, 'Portamento and Musical Meaning', *Journal of Musicological Research*, 25 (2006), p. 237 n. 9.

[6]   So termed by Joachim Stutchewsky (1891–1992), in his *Violoncell-Technik*, Vol. 1 (London: Schott, n.d.).

[7]   See, for example, Pierre-Hyacinthe Azaïs, *Méthode de basse* (Paris: Bignon, [c.1775]); Jean Marie Raoul, *Méthode de violoncelle* (Paris: Pleyel, [c.1797]); J.B. Bréval, *Traité du Violoncelle* (Paris: Imbault, [1804]).

Composers sometimes employ the small note to indicate the *portamento*, or *porte-de-voix*. [a music example shows this notation] The appoggiatura should never be used on a note commencing a melody nor on any notes whatsoever preceded immediately by rests.[8]

He includes portamento with his discussion of appoggiatura because both are notated with additional small notes. This implies that his prohibition on the use of the appoggiatura at the start of a melody applies equally to portamento; this limitation was not observed by some later cellists.

Duport's *Essai* offers a more detailed discussion of the topic, albeit a largely negative one:

> You may think it extraordinary that in scales I have avoided with great care making two notes with the same finger, as is found in all published methods until now. In my opinion this custom is a vice, in that it produces a bad effect. Everyone knows that it is the touch [*tact*] of the fingers that makes good articulation (*perlé*), and certainly, it is impossible to have this touch when one slides with one finger from one semitone to another, since if the bow does not seize the moment when the finger has slid to attack the string, one hears something very unpleasant. One can, it is true, play two notes with the same finger, quite slowly; one can shift over even an interval of a third, fourth, fifth, etc., sliding firmly with the same finger, and this produces a very good effect, called portamento (*porter le son*). [Music examples showing slides between first and fourth position] These slides, if I may explain myself thus, are made more or less quickly, according to the expression required by the melody, but at speed (of which clarity constitutes a large part of merit), notes with the same finger are, in my opinion, insupportable, in that they oppose this clarity. Playing at sight, if one is taken by surprise, not having foreseen the best position, one would be better, without doubt, to play two notes with the same finger, rather than not to play them at all, but in a prepared solo it is well to avoid them.[9]

---

[8]　P. Baillot, J.H. Levasseur, C.-S. Catel and C.-N. Baudiot, *Méthode de violoncelle* (Paris: Janet et Cotelle, 1805), p. 20.

[9]　'On trouvera peut-être extraordinaire que j'aie évité avec le plus grand soin, dans les Gammes de faire deux notes du même doigt, comme on le trouve dans tous les livres de principes qui ont étés publiés jusqu'ici. Mon opinion est que cette manière est vicieuse, en ce qu'elle produit un mauvais effet. Tout le monde sait que c'est le tact des doigts qui fait le perlé, et certes, il ne peut y avoir de tact, quand on glisse un doigt d'un demi-ton a l'autre, car si l'archet ne saisit pas bien l'instant ou le doigt a glissé, pour attaquer la corde, on entend quelque chose de très-désagréable. On peut faire, il est vrai, deux notes du même doigt, un peu lentement: on passe même d'un intervalle de tierce, de quarte, de quinte, &c en glissant fortement le même doigt, et ceci produit un très-bon effet, cela s'appelle porter le son. [*example*] Ces glissades, si j'ose m'exprimer ainsi, se font plus ou moins rapidement, suivant l'expression qu'exige la mélodie, mais dans la vitesse, dont la netteté fait une grande partie du mérite, les notes du même doigt sont, à mon avis, insoutenables,

Later, he makes an exception, allowing some same-finger shifting in fast *detaché* and in slurred passage-work. Nonetheless, for Duport, same-finger shifting is generally a necessary evil for use in an emergency, or when there is simply no alternative. The above quotation includes his only example of portamento, and the detailed fingering he gives in the 21 studies that comprise 'Titre XIX' of the *Essai* excludes almost any possibility of using it, even in slow tempi.[10]

Baudiot is scarcely more forthcoming.[11] In the short section of his *Méthode* devoted to the fingering of expressive melodies, he looks at two fingerings that make 'a good effect'. The first is used when the same note is repeated with different fingers within the same bow (Example 4.1).

Example 4.1   Baudiot, *Méthode*, finger substitution exercise

These shifts are however clearly not meant to be 'scooped' – a new finger is substituted so that the note is only lightly articulated.[12] The second type of shift is simply 'made with a single finger between two different notes ascending or descending, sliding the hand'. Baudiot gives no real indication as to how quickly, slowly, when, or how often, such portamenti should be applied, and gives no further examples.

Dotzauer's 1824 cello method gives more detailed shifting exercises, with same-finger and different-finger shifts (Example 4.2), both within one bow and combined with a change of bow. Dotzauer's first example strongly resembles that given by Duport.[13]

Example 4.2   Dotzauer, *Violonzellschule*, portamento exercises

---

en ce qu'elles s'opposent à cette netteté. En jouant à livre ouvert, si l'on se trouve surpris, n'ayant pas prévu la meilleure position, on sera mieux, sans contredit, de faire deux notes du même doigt, que de ne pas les faire du tout; mais dans un SOLO étudié, on sera très-bien de les éviter.' Jean-Louis Duport, *Essai sur le doigté du violoncelle* (Paris: Imbault, [1806]), pp. 17–18.

    [10]   Duport, 'Titre XIX', in *Essai,* pp. 176–267.

    [11]   Charles Baudiot, *Méthode de violoncelle* (Paris: Pleyel et fils aîné, 1826), pp. 17–18.

    [12]   Spohr describes the same technique, with an almost identical exercise. Louis Spohr, *Violinschule* (Vienna: Haslinger, [1833]), p. 175.

    [13]   J.J.F. Dotzauer, *Méthode de Violoncelle. Violonzell-Schule* (Mainz: B. Schott fils, [1825]), pp. 38–9. Inconsistent key-signatures and accidentals have been silently corrected here.

Overall, however, Dotzauer, though more enthusiastic than Duport, is still very restrained on the subject. For him, portamento is primarily a technical device, an aid to staying in tune when shifting to difficult notes:

> The *glissement* gives the artist the means to grasp and progress with more accuracy from one note to another, in awkward passages; but this means, unless applied with taste, rarely makes a good effect. It is obvious that one would not wish to use it in a tutti, since ornaments in general only have their place in a concerto or a solo, which allows the artist to give way to his feeling.[14]

Romberg is more positive:

> The expression *Portamento di voce* (the sustaining and combining of notes) is applicable in the same manner to Instrumental, as to Vocal Music, and signifies the gliding from one note to another, by which means, the most strongly accented notes of the air are blended together with those which precede them, and an agreeable effect produced.[15]

In the demonstration exercise following this observation Romberg specifically points out that a grace note indicates portamento: 'the blending is marked by a small note' ['dies Hinüberzeihen vermittelst einer kleinen Note angegeben ist'].[16] However, in practice, he does not restrict portamento to this particular notation: it is strongly implied by his fingerings elsewhere. Although Romberg does not provide specific exercises for shifting, there are many small examples throughout his *Violoncellschule*, particularly of multiple unforced same-finger shifts, such as those from his 'piece in the style of a concertino' (Example 4.3).[17]

Like Dotzauer, Romberg is fond of the combination of a turn followed by a shift up to the octave harmonic, a feature of another Romberg ornamentation

---

[14]   'Le glissement facilite a l'artiste le moyen de saisir et faire succéder, avec plus de justesse, un ton a un autre ton, dans des passages embarrassans; mais ce moyen, quoiqu' appliquer avec goût, fait rarement un bel effet. Il est évident qu'on n'ose pas s'en servir dans le tutti, puisque les agremens, en général, ne sont à leur place que dans un concert ou dans un solo, qui permet à l'artiste de céder à son sentiment.' Ibid.

[15]   'Die Bennenung (das Tragen des Stimme), portamento di voce, wird bei der Instrumental-Musik eben so angewandt, als bei der Vocal-Musik, und bedeutet das Hinubersiehen eines Tones zu einem andern, durch welches die am starksten betonte Note de Gesanges mit der vorhergegangenen zusammen gezogen wird, und dadurch mehr Anmuth erhalt....' Bernhard Romberg, trans. anon., *A Complete Theoretical and Practical School for the Violoncello* (London: T. Boosey & Co., [1840]), p. 87. *Violoncellschule,* (Berlin: Trautwein, [1840]), p. 85.

[16]   Ibid., p. 87.

[17]   Ibid., p. 100.

Example 4.3   Romberg, *Violoncellschule*, same-finger shifts

exercise.[18] However, Romberg was exceptional among cello teachers in the earlier nineteenth century in his relative enthusiasm for portamento. He may simply have particularly liked its effect, but his taste may also have been influenced by his idiosyncratic violinistic left hand shape, which would have made it harder to avoid audible sliding.

Friedrich Kummer was much more cautious about portamento:

> There is another bad habit against which the young player should be equally cautioned: – that is, frequently – in some cases continually – gliding the finger along the String from one note to another in intervals of thirds, or fourths; for both the ear and feeling run a great risk of being spoiled by this habit so that by degrees, even the most exaggerated expression of this sort will appear tasteful to the player; whilst to an unvitiated ear it will give no other effect than that of continual moaning and wailing.[19]

While he deplores its unthinking overuse, he gives no suggestions as to how to minimize its effect. Techniques for concealing shifts, such as the subtle manipulation of bow pressure and speed, relaxation of the pressure of the shifting finger, or simply by shifting as quickly as possible, are only described much later in the nineteenth century. Davidoff may be the first to examine such techniques of minimizing audible shifting. He begins with simple shifts from first to fourth position on the same string, where he demonstrates his fundamental principles in some detail:

> The shift from one position to another is made possible by the sliding of the thumb on the neck (i.e. of the instrument); the finger has its own role to undertake; it is very simple, if the first note of the new position is to be held by the same finger as the last of the foregoing position [example]. Here the thumb slides down the neck and the finger down the string quickly and easily from one position to another. It is a harder exercise if the first note of the following position is to be held by another finger than the last note of the previous position. One can in this

---

¹⁸   Ibid., p. 94.

¹⁹   F.A. Kummer, trans. anon., *Violoncello School* op. 60 (London: Ewer and Co., [1850?]), p. 27.

case (with few exceptions) establish a basic rule, that the finger already lying on the string slides into the new position without leaving it, and at its destination either stays still or is quickly lifted up (whether that following position begins with a higher or lower finger), and where the new position is reached the latter finger drops in place, in but a moment. – If two fingers are replaced in a change of position, one must also let one finger slide and the other drop – to be precise, following the above-established rule, drop the beginning finger of the new position. The opposite case is not absolutely to be rejected; now and then, the player can achieve a glissando in this way. The learner is nonetheless advised initially not to depart from this rule; he thus achieves precision in playing and avoids many needless unattractive-sounding glissandos.[20]

Davidoff is the first cellist clearly to describe what Flesch calls the 'B-shift', where the slide is made with the '*b*eginning' finger (the alternative is the 'L-shift', sliding on the arriving or '*l*ast' finger). Although Flesch used this terminology, the distinction originates much earlier in Spohr.[21] Cello methods that discuss portamento in the nineteenth century concentrate on the B-shift, although in practice the L-shift was often used, as will be shown below – Davidoff himself acknowledges its occasional usefulness. Davidoff's principles also apply in the case of a shift involving a string-crossing ('the established rules remain similar,

---

[20] 'Der Übergang von einer Position zur andern wird durch in Gleiten des Daumens am Halse ermöglicht; die Finger haben dabei ihre eigene Rolle durchzuführen; sie ist sehr einfach, wenn der erste Ton der neuen Position mit demselben Finger zu greifen ist wie der letzte der vorhergehenden Position, z. B. [*music example*]. Hier gleiten Daumen am Halse und Finger auf sen Saiten schnell und leicht von einer Position in die andere. Schwieriger wird die Aufgabe, wenn der der erste Ton der folgenden Position mit einem andern Finger zu greifen ist wie der letzte Ton der vorhergehenden Position. Man könnte für diese Falle (mit wenigen Ausnaen) als Grundregel feststellen, daß der Finger, der schon auf der Saite liegt, ohne sie zu verlassen, in die neue Position gleitet, und auf dem erreichten Platze entweder liegen bleibt oder schnell aufgehoben wird, je nachdem die folgende Position mit einem höhern oder tiefern Finger beginnt, daß dieser letztere Finger aber in dem Augenblick, wo die neue Position erreicht ist, auf seinen Platz fällt. – Man hätte also, wenn sich zwei Finger beim Positionswechsel ablösen, den einen gleiten und den andernfallen zu lassen, und zwar müßte nach der oben aufgestellten Regel der neue Position beginnende Finger fallen. Der umgekehrte Fall ist nicht absolut zu verwerfen; zuweilen kann der Spieler dadurch ein ausdrucksvolles Glissando erzielen. Dem Schüler ist aber anzuraten, anfangs nicht von der gegebenen Regel abzuweichen; er erreicht dadurch Präzision im Spiel und vermeidet viel unnütze und unschön klingende Glissandos.' Carl Yu. Davidoff, *Violoncell-Schule* (Leipzig: Peters, [1888]), p. 32.
[21] Carl Flesch, trans. Frederick Martens, *The Art of Violin Playing*, 2 vols. (New York: C. Fischer, 1930), Vol. 1, p. 30. Spohr, *Violinschule*, p. 120.

whether the new position is on the same or on another string')[22] and to longer shifts going beyond fourth position:

> In crossing from lower to higher positions, the greatest exception to the rule concerning the sliding and the falling fingers is made; such an exception must be made with the fourth finger, since this finger is not allowed to arrive in higher positions at all. A sliding following finger is at times of even more beautiful effect, namely if it, as in the case of experienced players, begins not immediately, but if the finger be, so to say, replaced. […] A shift like that from one position to another must occur so skilfully, that nothing is heard of the picking up or the replacing […].[23]

Davidoff goes on to warn beginners of a tendency to smudge the note immediately preceding a long shift (a sixth or more). He clearly sees portamento as something only to be used occasionally, and his emphasis is very much on the acquisition of a shifting technique that minimizes the audibility of the shift, especially for less advanced players. The effect of his detailed attention to almost every permutation of fingerings means that his example study for shifts into higher positions is an exercise in the avoidance of audible sliding, not a demonstration of portamento possibilities (Example 4.4).[24]

It may be significant that when both Davidoff and Grützmacher arranged various works of Chopin for the cello, Grützmacher's version used copious

---

22   'Die aufgestellten Regeln bleiben die gleichen, ob nun die neue Position auf derselben oder auf einer andern Saite sich befindet'. Davidoff, *Violoncell-schule*, p. 35.

23   'Bei den Übergängen von den tieferen in die höheren Positionen warden die meisten Abweichungen von der Regel bezüglich des gleitenden und fallenden Fingers gemacht; solche Abweichungen müssen beim vierten Finger sogar notwendig stattfinden, da dieser Finger gar nicht in die höheren Positionen gelangen darf. Ein gleitender folgender Finger ist hier sogar zuweilen von schöner Wirkung, namentlich wenn er, wie beim geübten Spieler, nicht unmittelbar beginnt, sondern wenn die Finger sich sozusagen ablösen. [..] Ein derartiger Übergang aus einer Position in die andere muß aber so gewandt geschehen, daß von dem Aufheben und dem Ablösen nichts gehört wird [..] Noch auf einen Umstand – der dem Anfänger so manche Schwierigkeit bietet – müß hier aufmerksam gemacht werden: auf das Verwischen der Töne, die den Ausgangspunkt eines Überganges bilden, namentlich, wen das Intervall der aufeinanderfolgenden Töne ein größeres (Sexte, Septime, Oktave etc.) ist. In folgenden Figur z. B.[music example] geraten die mit NB.versehenen Töne nur zu häufig verwischt oder undeutlich: der Anfänger hat dabei nur die folgenden Töne, das Treffen der weit gelegenen Intervalle im Auge; er beginnt mit dem Übergang zu zeitig, noch ehe die betreffenden Töne deutlich gegriffen sind. – Es ist daher dem Anfänger sehr anzuraten, auf solche Töne mehr Gewicht zu legen, nicht eher an den Übergang zu denken, bis der betreffende Ton klar zur Geltung gekommen, i sogar eine etwas größere Dauer zu geben, als i zukommt.' Ibid., p. 70.

24   Ibid., p. 72.

Example 4.4   Davidoff, *Violoncellschule*, shifting exercise

portamento markings, while Davidoff not only gave no explicit indications for its use, but included fewer fingerings that could even imply it.[25]

Carl Schroeder had similar reservations to many of the cellists already quoted, and echoed Kummer in particular:

> Sliding from one position to another must be done with ease and certainty, much practice being necessary to attain this. Passing from the third or fourth position to the higher ones causes special difficulty [...] If the notes of the different positions are not bound together by means of legato signs, this sliding of the finger must take place so rapidly that no notes are noticed between. If the notes are bound together to be played in one bow, then the slide or portamento will be audible. The player must beware lest the portamento from one tone to the other becomes exaggerated, and that the entire enharmonic scale lying between is not heard. All 'whining' must be avoided, and the note adjoining that to which the finger is sliding should not be heard.[26]

Schroeder returns to this theme, describing the widespread fault of 'whining' as 'a mawkish drawling from one note to another'.[27] In his editions of baroque sonatas, fingerings clearly implying portamento are extremely rare.[28] His version of Bach's G major suite (with piano accompaniment) almost entirely avoids even an implied portamento – the few same-finger shifts in the Sarabande are so short as to be inconsequential and are certainly not primarily expressive gestures.[29]

---

[25]   Frédéric Chopin, arr. C. Davidoff, *Mazurkas von F. Chopin* (Leipzig: Breitkopf & Härtel [1874]); Chopin, arr. F. Grützmacher, *Ausgewählte Kompositionen von Fr. Chopin* (Leipzig: C.F. Peters [1880]).

[26]   Carl Schroeder, (trans. J. Matthews), *Catechism of Violoncello Playing* (London: Augener & Co., 1893), pp. 37–9.

[27]   Ibid., p. 73.

[28]   An exception occurs in his edition of a sonata attributed to Grazioli, where two same-finger shifts are indicated with an upward dotted-rhythm pattern, which is itself strongly suggestive of portamento. G.B. Grazioli, ed. C. Schroeder, *Classical Violoncello Music Book XII. Sonate von G. B.Grazioli* (London: Augener Ltd., n.d.), vc pt, p. 5.

[29]   J.S. Bach, ed. C. Schroeder, *Classical Violoncello Music Book I. J.S. Bach, Sonate I* (London: Augener Ltd., n.d.).

Josef Werner adopts a more systematic approach.[30] A group of exercises on unisons begins with simple shifts from a note to the same note on the neighbouring string. This idea is extended to playing four such notes (a very fast version of this technique on the violin is used in Bazzini's *La ronde des lutins*, played with almost no audible shift by Jan Kubelík in his 1903 recording.).[31] After this, Werner returns to the two-string version, but this time using the thumb and third finger for double-stopped unisons. The whole exercise is intended to produce 'perfect equality of tone', which must be achieved with each fingering. It shows a way to practise shifting while avoiding audible sliding, and is one of the earliest exercises of its kind. Although many of these fingerings are associated by Grützmacher with an expressive portamento, this is not at all Werner's intention. Nonetheless, Werner is not above using dramatic downward portamento; the ninth of his *10 Etuden* includes a downward two-octave gliss. (d′′′–d′) followed in the next bar by a further downward octave *gliss.* (d′–D).[32]

Carl Fuchs advises an 'inaudible change of position during the change of bow' when shifting in Meinhard's *Konzertstück*.[33] This is one of the earliest examples of advice on how to conceal shifts within a change of bow, a point developed considerably by Alexanian. Fuchs also repeats his teacher Davidoff's advice concerning longer shifts, but more emphatically:

> In case it is impossible to employ an auxiliary note in changing position, Davidoff recommended this: Play the last note in the old position very clearly, giving it its full value and then change position very quickly so that the ugly sliding is heard as little as possible.[34]

Van der Straeten also takes a conservative view of portamento, frequently rejecting fingerings in the standard repertoire that encourage an unpleasant sliding effect. Remarks such as these pervade his discussion of 'well-known solos': Van der Straeten also takes a conservative view of portamento, frequently rejecting

---

[30]   Josef Werner, trans. anon., *Die Kunst der Bogenführung. The Art of Bowing. op. 43. Supplement No. VII to the Author's Violoncello-Method* (Heilbronn: C.F. Scidt, 4th edn, 1894), p. 32.

[31]   Bazzini, *La ronde des lutins,* Jan Kubelík (vn), un-named pianist (Gramophone & Typewriter Co., matrix 408c, catalogue no. 07901, 1903; reissued *The Great Violinists Volume 1*, EMI: V Treasury, EX 7 61062 1, 1988).

[32]   Werner, *Kunst der Bogenführung*, study no. 9, p. 21.

[33]   Adolphe Meinhard, *Konzertstück*, in Carl Fuchs (ed.), *Violoncello-Werke – Violoncello-Works – Oeuvres pour Violoncelle* (Mainz: B. Schott's Sohne, 1911), p. 2.

[34]   'Wenn man bei Lagenwechsel keine Hilfsnote anwenden kann, empfahl Davidoff, die letzte Note in der altere Lage möglichst deutlich und verkürzt zu spielen und dann die Lage sehr schnell zu wechseln, sodass das hässliche Gleiten so wenig wie möglich zu hören ist.' Carl Fuchs, *Violoncello-Schule Violoncello Method Part II* (Mainz and Leipzig: B Schott's Söhne, 1909), p. 50.

fingerings in the standard repertoire that encourage an unpleasant sliding effect. Remarks such as these pervade his discussion of 'well-known solos':

> At this point glide up with the first finger until the third can be dropped onto the B in the tenor clef, avoiding any whining effect in the gliding.[35]

> Never change your bow or commence a new stroke before the respective finger of the left hand is firmly placed on the note to be played, to avoid any gliding to it where it is not used intentionally, and for a particular effect.[36]

> In bar six you find the second finger gliding from [d′ to f′]. If you cannot do that with sufficient skill and delicacy to avoid a disagreeable whining effect, it will be better to set the fourth on F [...].[37]

Van der Straeten shares Davidoff's emphasis on the finger being firmly in place before a change of bow, but his general concerns can be found over a century earlier in Duport. Nonetheless, although he appears to be one of the most cautious writers on the subject, he also suggests an extreme use of same-finger portamento in Schumann, discussed below.

The most detailed modern account of portamento is Alexanian's. This is the first cello treatise that gives any really detailed instruction on the avoidance of audible sliding other than simply recommending fast shifting, and is also the first to make explicit the distinction between forced and unforced shifts.

> Certain musical effects require an absolute unity of the quality of sound. This unity can be obtained only by the use of the same string, and it often happens that the hand changes its position [...] several times during the execution of notes that could be played, by a change of strings, [in one position]. [...] These changes of [position] are, to a certain extent, subservient to the fingering; the inverse is also often the case. Here, the art of the performer consists in hiding the disadvantages of an awkward fingering, made necessary by a musical[ly] important change of [position], or else in causing to pass unobserved a change of [position] imposed by technical necessity [...] not coinciding either with an accent or a 'breath'.[38]

Alexanian normally uses the B-shift, but adds that this shift 'should always be preceded by an extension, tending to bring the finger that is to play nearer to

---

[35]   E. van der Straeten, *Well-Known Violoncello Solos How to Play Them with Understanding, Expression and Effect* (London: William Reeves, [1922]), p. 117.

[36]   Ibid., p. 105.

[37]   Ibid., p. 46.

[38]   Diran Alexanian, trans. Frederick Fairbanks, *Traité théorique et pratique du violoncelle* (Paris: Mathot, 1922 [written 1910–13]), p. 50. Alexanian's French and Fairbanks's translation are both highly idiosyncratic; bracketed emendations here are for clarity.

its goal' and that the arriving finger should actually 'strike' (*percuter*) its note.[39] Portamento with one finger where the shift crosses two strings involves a subtle transfer from one string to the other.

> In this case we must execute the 'portamento' on the string to which we are proceeding, but without allowing the initial note of the slide on this string to be heard. [...] the putting in motion of the hand should coincide with the change of string. [...] In the case of a change of [bow], the 'portamento' (rising or falling) should be made on the initial string and stroke [...] with an imperceptible interruption of the sound, towards the end of the slide.[40]

Cross-string portamento with different fingers is minimized by extending the hand, sliding on the initial finger and string, and striking the arrival note. Alexanian adds here that in scales the extension of the hand before the shift enables the smooth linking of positions and the complete avoidance of portamento.[41] Alexanian advocates the A-shift when shifting upwards across two strings, from a higher-numbered finger to a lower, either within one bow or with a change of bow.[42] He also points out cases where portamento should not be heard at all, and gives an example very similar to that from Baudiot (see Example 4.1), saying that:

> In the following example the 'portamento' would make a deplorable effect unless executed so rapidly that it could not be heard.[43]

Where much larger intervals are concerned, across several strings, and with a change of bow, Alexanian shifts exactly at the moment when the bow is moving to the other string and the new finger is ready – in these examples the shift is from a lower-numbered finger to a higher. A portamento at such places is an exception, and 'should be used very parsimoniously, and only in case a musical necessity demands it'.[44] His examples clearly allude to the opening of Beethoven's Cello Sonata in A op. 69 (on one string) and to a passage near the end of the first movement of Brahms's Sonata in E minor op. 38 (on two). Although Alexanian was Grützmacher's pupil and praised 'this marvellous pedagogue['s] [...] fine logic and gift of research', he is clearly much more restrained compared with his teacher's generous portamenti across three or four strings and as many positions.[45] Indeed, notwithstanding Alexanian's quasi-scientific, modernist, presentation,

---

[39]   Ibid., p. 52.
[40]   Ibid., p. 55.
[41]   Ibid.
[42]   Ibid., p. 56.
[43]   Ibid.
[44]   Ibid., p. 57.
[45]   Ibid., p. 174.

he has much in common with Joachim, who himself is content to quote Spohr verbatim on portamento, and who also uses an example very similar to Baudiot's.

In pedagogical works for the cello, portamento is therefore generally treated with caution if not actual suspicion throughout the nineteenth century. However, there are several explanations of the physical movements required to execute portamento – it is in fact *taught,* something to bear in mind later in the context of vibrato. Portamento, therefore, is offered as a valid expressive device, and differences of emphasis mainly reflect differing views as to how much should be used, and where. However, pedagogical theory is often at odds with the actual practice. This chapter will examine practice as evidenced in printed sources (often edited by the same cellists), while evidence from recordings will be considered in Chapter 6. Evidence for the use of portamento in the eighteenth century is sketchy at best, although there is a reference to unsatisfactory portamento in a review of a concert given in 1787 by Madam Mara, whose husband was a cellist:

> The violoncello of Mr. Mara is by no means an object of admiration; his *portamento,* as Dr. Burney would say, is embarrassed and ungraceful, and he is deficient both in tone and in the articulation of passages which require a dexterous management of the bow.[46]

This tantalizing reference to portamento might suggest that its use may have been more frequent than any cello methods from the period might suggest, although it would appear that the term was not yet in widespread use in London – the reference to the scholar Burney suggests that it may have been seen by at least some as a learned, academic term. From the nineteenth century onwards there is rather more evidence of the use of portamento in ways that put its theoretical exposition in a different light.

Notwithstanding the numerous reservations already outlined, there are many examples of same-finger shifts in all types of nineteenth-century cello compositions. Dotzauer, cautious about portamento in theory, is somewhat more liberal in practice. There are two examples in his Bach edition. In the G major Menuet and the D minor Sarabande, Dotzauer shows his fondness for the higher reaches of the D string, which he describes as 'mellow' [*moelleux*] – he frequently uses portamento in this particular context.[47] It also occurs more prominently in his op. 70 exercises.[48] The moderately taxing cello part of Dotzauer's String Trio

---

[46]   Anon., 'The Mara Concert', *Gazeteer and New Daily Advertiser*, 24 February 1787, p. 2.

[47]   J.S. Bach, ed. J.J.F. Dotzauer, *Six Solos ou Etudes pour le Violoncelle* (Leipzig: Breitkopf & Härtel, [1826]). The complete text is available at http://chase.leeds.ac.uk/view/pdf/99/1/ [accessed July 2012].

[48]   J.J.F. Dotzauer, *Twelve Exercises op. 70. Wessel & Co's Collection of Studies by I.I.F. Dotzauer. Book 4* (London: Ashdown & Parry (Successors to Wessel & Co.), n.d.), no. 1, p. 1 and no. 12, p. 19.

op. 52 is fingered in some detail throughout, and the fourth of its six movements opens thus (Example 4.5).[49]

Example 4.5 Dotzauer, String Trio op. 52

The repeated first finger markings on the semiquavers are not unusual. In a surprising number of cases, cellists indicate that more than two notes (sometimes many more) are to be played with the same finger successively. Examples, sometimes over intervals as large as a seventh, can be found in Stiastny's Concerto op. 7, the second of Wolff and Batta's *Duos Concertants*, or the *adagio* section from Joseph Merk's *Variations sur un air tirolien*.[50] Neither is this confined to what might now be seen as minor works. Josef Werner's detailed fingerings for Beethoven's Cello Sonata in A major op. 69 include the unaccompanied opening bars, with a fourth-finger shift followed by three successive first-finger notes (Example 4.6).[51]

Example 4.6 Beethoven, Sonata in A op. 69, Werner's fingering

Werner's *40 Studies* generally avoid portamento, as they are chiefly concerned with agility, but no. 37 contains several implied fourth-finger portamenti, and a manufactured fingering of the Grützmacher type (discussed later).[52] The works of Servais, in their first and in the later editions prepared by his pupil Edmund de Munck, offer a particularly rich source for this technique. Munck's edition of Servais's *Concerto militaire* indicates serial same-finger shifts in the *Andante*

[49] J.J.F. Dotzauer, *Grand Trio pour Violon, Alto & Violoncelle* op. 52 (Hamburg: Jean Aug. Böe, n.d.), vc pt, p. 7.

[50] J. Stiastny, *Concert pour Violoncelle* op. 7 (Bonn: N. Simrock, [1817]); E. Wolff and A. Batta, *Les intimes Deux Duos Concertants. No. 2. Fantaisie dramatique* op. 49 (Mainz, Anvers and Brussels: chez les fils de B. Schott, [1844?]), vc pt, p. 1; Joseph Merk, *Variations sur un air tirolien* op. 18 (Brunswick: G.M. Meyer jr, and London: J.J. Ewer & Co., [1836]), vc pt, p. 6. Merk was the cellist in the Schuppanzigh quartet, closely associated with Beethoven.

[51] Josef Werner, *Die Kunst der Bogenführung* (Heilbronn: Schmidt, [1894]), p. 43.

[52] Josef Werner, *40 Studies* op. 46, Book II (London: Augener, [1897]) pp. 68–9.

religioso movement that are clearly solely for expressive purposes, and there are examples of same-finger shifts in the first and third movements as well.[53] Servais's arrangement of Chopin's *Nocturne* op. 9 no. 2 (arranged for cello by Alfred Moffat, David Popper, and W.H. Squire, among others) contains some of the most remarkable fingerings of this type from the period. In Example 4.7, the first finger is used for seven consecutive notes in bar 4 (and the equivalent passage in bar 8, which includes a downward portamento indication).[54] Within this short piece there are many other passages fingered in this way, and these fingerings are also found in the manuscript copy of the work prepared by Ulysse Claes (a close friend of Servais) held at the Brussels Conservatoire.[55] In fact, this was something of a Servais speciality, found in many of his works. This example, from his *Andante cantabile* on a theme by Balfe, is representative (Example 4.8).[56]

Example 4.7   Chopin, arr. Servais, *Nocturne*, opening bars

[*espress., dolce, cresc.*]

Example 4.8   Servais, *Andante cantabile*

Edmund van der Straeten may have warned repeatedly against 'whining', but he himself suggests an extreme example of successive same-finger shifts. In the opening bars of the second of Schumann's *Stücke im Volkston* (Example 4.9), he indicates that the first five notes are all to be played with the second finger, something that even Grützmacher avoids (although in the latter's edition he does remain on the D string for almost the whole of the first section of the piece).[57]

Some portamenti occur in the context of a particularly extended passage played on one string (normally D or G). In such cases, the passage can cover more than

---

[53]   Adrien-François Servais, rev. E. de Munck, *Concerto militaire* op. 18 (Mainz: B. Schott's Söhne, n.d.) p. 6.

[54]   F. Chopin, arr. F. Servais, *Nocturne de Chopin* (Mainz: B. Schott's Söhne, [1863]).

[55]   Brussels Royal Conservatoire, MS. 45.106(a).11, pp. 101–3.

[56]   Adrien-François Servais, *Concerto militaire* op. 18 (Mainz, Brussels and London: B. Schott fils, [1860]); Servais, *Andante cantabile et Mazurka sur un air de Balfe* op. 7 (Mainz: B. Schott fils, [1849]).

[57]   E. van der Straeten, *Well-Known Violoncello Solos*, p. 154; R. Schumann, ed. F. Grützmacher, *Stücke im Volkston* op. 102 no. 2 (Leipzig: C.F. Peters, [1874]).

Example 4.9   Schumann, *Stücke im Volkston* op. 102 no. 2, van der Straeten's fingering above, Grützmacher's below

an octave, going beyond the octave harmonic often used as a convenient upper limit for a phrase or ornamental gesture. However, there is a clear preference for portamento on the D string rather than the G. This is almost certainly due to the G string's metal windings, which were noticeably rougher than twentieth-century flat-wound strings. Until the early twentieth century these were not flat-wound, but round- (or wire-) wound: extended shifting on these strings produces string noise similar to that of a guitar. There are many exercises on the D and G strings, but the earlier examples are not presented as primarily expressive studies. Raoul uses both these strings, but his detailed fingering largely eliminates any opportunities for portamento.[58] Kummer's G-string study op. 44 no. 7, with a mostly stepwise melodic line, has many fewer such opportunities, compared with his D-string study op. 44 no. 4, which opens with a series of third-finger shifts.[59] The extended G-string passage in Louis Hegyesi's (1853–94) 'Liebesschmerz' almost discourages portamento, given its detailed articulation (Example 4.10).[60] Kummer does, however, explore its expressive potential in his *Pièce fantastique* op. 36, entirely played on the G string, with some Servais-like series of same-finger shifts (Example 4.11).[61]

Grützmacher's Concerto op. 10 contains another example of extended expressive writing on the G string, at the transition to the second movement, and the implied G-string octave portamenti in Grützmacher's arrangement of Spohr's eighth violin concerto, 'in modo di scena cantante', are even more dramatic (Example 4.12).[62]

It is in Friedrich Grützmacher's editions of eighteenth- and nineteenth-century cello compositions that we find portamento notated on a scale unparalleled in any other cello repertoire, if not indeed string music generally. It pervades his work, whether in his performing edition of the Bach cello suites and viola da gamba sonatas, his editions of works by Romberg, or of Mendelssohn's cello sonatas. Particularly striking are his downward portamenti, rarely indicated or even implied elsewhere. For Grützmacher, portamento is not confined to legato notes

[58]   Jean Marie Raoul, *Méthode de Violoncelle* (Paris: Pleyel, [c.1797]), p. 79.

[59]   F.A. Kummer, *8 Grandes Etudes* op. 44 (Dresden: Meser, [1838]).

[60]   Louis Hegyesi, 'Liebesschmerz', *Romanze* op. 4, (Mainz: B. Schott fils, [1877]).

[61]   Friedrich Kummer, *Pièce fantastique* op. 36 (Leipzig: Fr. Hofmeister, [1840?]).

[62]   Friedrich Grützmacher, *Concerto en la mineur* op. 10 (Leipzig: Hofmeister, [1854]); Louis Spohr, arr. F. Grützmacher, *Concerto in modo di scena cantante* (Leipzig: C.F. Peters, [1854]), vc pt, p. 4.

Example 4.10   Hegyesi, 'Liebesschmerz' – this passage is immediately repeated
                with some alterations, but remaining on the G string

Example 4.11   Kummer, *Pièce fantastique*

Example 4.12   Spohr, arr. Grützmacher, Concerto no. 8

in the middle of a melodic phrase. He can apply a portamento to a note preceded
by a rest, by a staccato note, or by a note on another string (sometimes an open
string) – in other words, even where there is no *legato* context, and thus on a far
wider scale than, for example, Baillot. In his arrangement of Chopin's C♯ minor
Waltz op. 64 no. 2 (in C minor) he even makes a glissando between double stopped
sixths into a feature of the opening motif.[63] But it is his edition of Mendelssohn's
cello sonatas that is particularly rich in examples, some of which are quite startling
to modern eyes.[64]

Of the two sonatas, the first, op. 45 in B♭, has the greater quantity of portamento
markings. This is unsurprising given its more lyrical, less energetic, character,
although there is one remarkable example of portamento in the Sonata in D op. 58,
discussed below. This passage from the third movement shows many different
applications of portamento within a few lines of music (Example 4.13).

---

63   Chopin, *Ausgewählte Kompositionen*.

64   Felix Mendelssohn-Bartholdy, ed. Friedrich Grützmacher, *Felix Mendelssohn
Bartholdys Sämmtliche Werke. Compositionen für Violoncell und Pianoforte* (Leipzig:
C.F. Peters, [1878]). Full text available on-line at the CHASE project, http://chase.leeds.
ac.uk/view/pdf/965/1/ [accessed July 2012].

Example 4.13   Mendelssohn, ed. Grützmacher, Sonata in B♭, third movement

Here we can see one-string fingering with some implied portamento (bars 4ff of the example), portamento to the first note of a phrase (bar 8), same-finger shifts (bars 3 and 17), portamento from an open string to a harmonic (bar 20), and the use of same-string fingering to vary a repeated phrase (compare bar 1 with bar 3). Each of these devices is used frequently throughout the sonata. There are several examples of Grützmacher using the presence or absence of portamento to vary a repetition, which show that it was used frequently, but not necessarily unthinkingly. In the example given, the quality of the two *sforzandi* in bars 2 and 4 changes: the first, coming after the open A, is more dramatic than the second, which is approached from a fourth-finger shift and is therefore more melodic in character. Such fingerings create subtle nuances within a single overall dynamic level. On the other hand, it is hard to see the expressive justification for a portamento marking connecting two notes that constitute a simple bass line, as at the end of the example. Grützmacher often uses portamento to approach a harmonic, an expressive device also used by Dotzauer and Romberg. He can approach a harmonic at the very beginning of a phrase in this way, or within a phrase, as in the second movement (Example 4.14).

Portamento from an open string to the octave harmonic, requiring the sliding finger to be applied seamlessly to the open string (as in the last two bars of Example 4.13) is more unusual. Grützmacher uses this occasionally elsewhere, as in his arrangement of Schumann's second Violin Sonata op. 121.[65] Downward portamento can be used over relatively large intervals like the descending sixths in the first movement of the B♭ sonata, but for the most extreme example of this we must look not in Grützmacher's Mendelssohn, but in his arrangement of the Serenade from the op. 3 String Quartet attributed to Haydn (Example 4.15).[66]

There are several examples of portamento applied to notes preceded by rests, or occurring between changes of bow, especially in the passage from the end of the third movement shown in Example 4.16.

---

[65]   R. Schumann, arr. F. Grützmacher, *Zweite grosse Sonate* op. 121 (Leipzig: Breitkopf & Härtel, [1874]).

[66]   F. Grützmacher (ed.), 'Serenade von J. Haydn', in *Transcriptionen classische Musikstücke* op. 60 no. 2, (Leipzig: Kahnt, 1868).

Example 4.14   Mendelssohn, ed. Grützmacher, Sonata in B♭, second movement

Example 4.15   Haydn (attr.) arr. Grützmacher, 'Serenade', end of first section

Example 4.16   Mendelssohn, ed. Grützmacher, Sonata in B♭, third movement

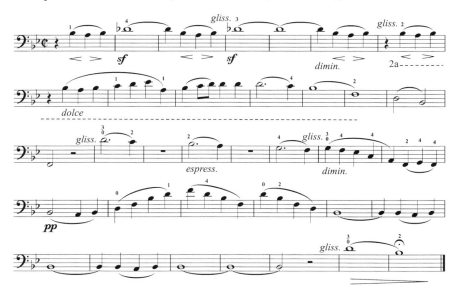

In spite of his use of portamento to create variations in repeated passages, Grützmacher is also not afraid of tiring the listener's ear with repeated portamenti, as the remarkable passage from the third movement of the D major sonata shown in Example 4.17 illustrates.

Passages such those cited here offer unusually detailed examples of Grützmacher's approach to the editing of musical texts. In particular, we can gather a great deal of information about the frequency of his use of portamento, the wide

Example 4.17   Mendelssohn, ed. Grützmacher, Sonata in D, third movement

range of its applications, and his use of portamento over small as well as large intervals. But the remarkable visual appearance of such editions is one thing, and their practical execution is another. We know next to nothing of how Grützmacher performed in general, in these or other works. Contemporary reviews, as is so often the case, give very few details. He was praised for his technique, that of the left hand in particular, and his strong playing, although his tone quality was sometimes found wanting in comparison with Kummer – his teacher Drechsler had been criticized in similar terms. In 1866, in advance of his first visit to London, he was compared to Alfredo Piatti:

> Of this gentleman [Grützmacher] a private letter from a good authority says: 'He is a magnificent player, and possesses a power and certainty of execution quite extraordinary. His style is much stronger and broader than Piatti's but not so sweet and sympathetic and lovely. But he is undeniably a great artist and an accomplished musician, witness many compositions both for the orchestra and his own instrument.'[67]

Grützmacher's type of edition was seriously criticized on one occasion when Piatti played his version of a gamba sonata attributed to Handel:

> Handel's sonata, written for the viol da gamba and cembalo originally, was arranged for piano and violoncello by Herr Grützmacher, a famous violoncellist. The writer of the analytical book states that 'none of the marks of expression indicated by Herr Grützmacher is reproduced in this cursory analysis, as none of them is Handel's own. It is curious that such matters cannot be left to the judgment, taste, and feeling of the executive artists themselves, instead of being dictated, as is too much the fashion now-a-days, by special individuals.' We quite agree with the analyst; the Athenaeum has always contended for the right of artists to have a free and independent interpretation, just as the conductor has the privilege of reading a score, and having it executed according to his views of a composer's intentions.[68]

Grützmacher himself appears to have claimed that when making his editions, he was following the composer's intentions. Having apparently had a proposed edition turned down by Peters, he wrote thus:

---

[67]   *The Reader*, 7 (1866), p. 452.

[68]   Anon., 'Concerts', *Athenaeum*, 2520, 12 February 1876, p. 240.

I could not have a more unhappy surprise than that contained in your letter. ... A work which has been done on my part with the greatest care and love you regard as a failure? ... Some great masters like Schumann and Mendelssohn have never taken the time to notate all the indications and nuances necessary, down to the smallest detail. ... My main purpose has been to reflect and to determine what these masters might have been thinking, and to set down all that they, themselves, could have indicated. ... Regarding this activity, and relying on my long musical experiences, I feel I have more right than all the others to do this work. I have the approval of many renowned composers, but naturally, Schumann and Mendelssohn can no longer give theirs to me. ... I do not fear the opinion they could have had because when one has had – as I – the opportunity to play all types of music often, there is not a doubt that he is capable of doing this kind of editing. ... Schumann had no practical sense, so it is indispensible not to correct but to complete the nuances. ... Who could possibly see anything in my work but a great deal of care and love, since it cannot be thought that it is done from a lack of knowledge. That would indeed be censurable. ... PS My concert version of the Bach Suites, which you likewise mention, cannot also be a subject of reproach since, in editing them, I not only tried to follow the same intentions of which I have just spoken but I succeeded at it. I have reaped much success in presenting this edition in concert, something that would have been impossible with the bare original in its primitive state.[69]

The title page of Grützmacher's Mendelssohn edition bears the statement, 'exactly marked in the tradition of the composer' ('nach der Tradition des Componisten genau bezeichnet'), ostensibly implying that this degree of portamento was in some sense authorized by the composer himself. Almost identical claims are made in some other Peters publications from the later nineteenth century such as David and Hermann's editions of Spohr.[70] They form part of a tradition of such publishers' claims going back at least to the beginning of the nineteenth century. Typically, in the later eighteenth and early nineteenth centuries, the publisher emphasizes the novelty of the work, its technical accessibility, some form of direct contact with the composer (if still alive or only recently deceased), the textual correctness of the edition, or the approval of the work by other 'masters'. Later in the nineteenth century, such claims take on a more historically-orientated character, asserting a

---

[69] F. Grützmacher, letter to Peters, 17th September 1884, as quoted in Dmitry Markevitch, trans. Florence W. Seder, *Cello Story* (New Jersey: Alfred Publishing Company, 1984), pp. 62–3. All ellipses as in Markevitch's version. A facsimile of this letter is included in Ludolf Lutzen, *Die Violoncell-Transkriptionen Friedrich Grützmachers. Untersuchungen zur Transkription in Sicht und Handhabung der 2. Hälfte des 19. Jahrhunderts*, Kölner Beiträge zur Musikforschung, Vol. 79 (Regensburg: G. Bosse, 1974), pp. 225–8. My thanks to Kate Haynes for drawing my attention to this source.

[70] L. Spohr, ed. F. Hermann, *Salonstücke* op. 135 (Leipzig: C.F. Peters, [1885]); Spohr, ed. F. David and F. Hermann, *Concerto no. 11* op. 70 (Leipzig: C.F. Peters, [1878]).

connection with the tradition of the composer (if dead for some time), a pedagogical tradition, or a tradition of performance practice.[71] David could claim direct contact with Spohr, and could therefore plausibly state in another edition that he strictly followed that composer's intentions.[72] But Grützmacher's connection with Mendelssohn is necessarily more indirect, principally through the composer's friends and colleagues David and Rietz, who were instrumental in his moves to the Leipzig Gewandhaus and the Dresden Staatskapelle respectively. A claim to be following a tradition is not the same thing as a claim to know the composer's intentions directly from the source. In the case of the Mendelssohn cello sonatas, it is hard to argue for the existence of a coherent performing tradition, in the sense of something carefully transmitted from teacher to pupil, as distinct from the mere fact of their frequent performance.[73]

But his equally remarkable edition of the Schumann concerto may have a stronger connection with the composer himself, even if this was not used as a marketing aid.[74] Grützmacher performed chamber music several times with Clara Schumann in the years after Robert Schumann's death and played the concerto quite often in the late 1860s, more so than the Mendelssohn sonatas. Although Robert Bockmühl assisted Schumann in its composition (and Carl Ripfel was also involved), neither of these cellists provided any information about its performance, though some aspects of their performing styles can be glimpsed in Bockmühl's other editions and in Ripfel's few compositions.[75] Grützmacher's is therefore the first performing edition of this work, and given that it dates from less than a decade after the 1860 première and is prepared by a cellist who gave many of its earliest performances and performed with Clara Schumann, it carries undeniable significance. It contains several distinctive markings, of which Example 4.18 is probably the most surprising for modern cellists, who are accustomed to playing

---

[71]   See, for example, Jean-Delphin Alard's series of edited violin works, *Les maîtres classiques du violon* (Paris: E. Gérard, and Mainz: Schott, 1862–83), whose title pages claimed to offer 'le style, le phrasé, l'expression, les doigtés, et les coups d'archet propres à l'interprétation traditionnelle de ces œuvres' [the style, phrasing, expression, fingering, and bowing appropriate to the traditional interpretation of these works].

[72]   The title page reads 'strictement d'après les Intentions de l'Auteur'. L. Spohr, ed. F. David, *Concertos nos. 2, 7 and 8* (Leipzig: C.F. Peters, [1861]).

[73]   In 1902, J. Matthews (the translator of Schroeder's *Cellist's Handbook*) claimed they were superior to Beethoven's cello sonatas. J. Matthews, *The Violin Music of Beethoven* (London: 'The Strad' Office, 1902), p. 93.

[74]   F. Grützmacher (ed.), *Robert Schumann's Samtliche Werke. Konzert op. 129 für Violoncell und Pianoforte herausgegeben von Fr. Grützmacher* (Leipzig: Peters, [1887]). The complete cello part is available at http://chase.leeds.ac.uk/view/pdf/1439/1/#page [accessed July 2012].

[75]   This is discussed at length in Bernhard R. Appel (ed.), *Schumann Forschungen: Robert Schumann, das Violoncello und die Cellisten seiner Zeit* (Mainz: Schott, 2007).

the second note with no suggestion of a slide and who would never consider using the fourth finger in the way notated here.

Example 4.18 Schumann Cello Concerto, ed. Grützmacher, first movement (bowing as original)

It may well be that Grützmacher was at least in part notating a widespread practice. This would in turn suggest that what is exceptional is the degree of notation rather than that of actual performance. But, if we allow the possibility that his notation reflects at least some personal idiosyncrasy of performing style, Grützmacher may still have used portamento significantly more often, and in many more different ways, than his Dresden predecessors Romberg, Dotzauer, or Kummer. A third possibility cannot be discounted: that, in spite of the extremely detailed appearance of his editions, Grützmacher's execution may have been considerably more restrained in performance.

While recordings show that Grützmacher's range of portamenti was still exploited in the early twentieth century (discussed in a later chapter), this was not unanimously the case. Carl Schroeder's restrained attitude to portamento has already been mentioned. In Schroeder's and Grützmacher's editions of Romberg's sixth concerto, there are places where both agree on a fingering but Grützmacher adds a *gliss.* marking. These are ambiguous: Grützmacher could either be making explicit a portamento implied by Schroeder, or adding one where Schroeder made so such assumption. But there are other examples that do not allow this interpretation, such as Grützmacher's descending *glissandi* from high harmonics to low stopped notes, which create particular technical difficulties.[76] Comparison with David Popper's violin transcription of the Mendelssohn sonatas shows that in general Popper also indicates fewer portamenti than Grützmacher (his text is clearly derived from Grützmacher's).[77] However, Popper does not avoid the more extreme or dramatic portamenti, but rather reduces their quantity in general, across the board. Where Grützmacher repeats a phrase on a different string (usually moving from the A string to the D string, and with the possibility of portamento on the latter), Popper prefers more consistency, remaining on the same string for the repetition. On the other hand, much in Popper agrees exactly with Grützmacher,

[76] B. Romberg, ed. Carl Schroeder, *Concerto no. 6* op. 48 (Brunswick: Litolff, [1879]); Romberg, ed. F. Grützmacher (Leipzig: C.F. Peters, [1881]).

[77] Felix Mendelssohn-Bartholdy, ed. David Popper, *Compositionen für Violoncello und Pianoforte* (Vienna: Universal Edition, [c.1901–04?]). Full text available at http://chase.leeds.ac.uk/view/pdf/962/2/#page [accessed July 2012].

and he keeps many of the portamenti in the second movement of the B♭ sonata. Popper indicates portamento explicitly very rarely in his own works. There is one example in his *Requiem* for three cellos and piano involving a sequence of same-finger shifts and a *glissando* marking over a change of bow; in his salon piece 'Wie einst in schöner'n Tagen' he creates a fingering solely to enable an A-string portamento.[78] In pieces like *Zur Guitarre*, or 'Reigen' from *Im Walde*, he indicates much shorter portamenti.[79] Evidence from Popper's own compositions and from his Mendelssohn edition suggests, therefore, that he may have used portamento less frequently than Grützmacher, but in a more highly nuanced way (a similar distinction is observable with W.H. Squire's and Beatrice Harrison's performances of the Elgar Cello Concerto, discussed in Chapter 6).

Portamento, then, was a normal part of the cellist's expressive repertoire throughout the nineteenth century, and was probably used increasingly through that period. Grützmacher and Popper would contrive fingerings to create portamento opportunities, but in other cases the picture is not so clear – at least in the cases of Davidoff or Schroeder there are grounds for suggesting that they were more restrained. The increasingly strong warnings about the 'abuse' of portamento in the later nineteenth century can of course be read as an indication of its increasing prevalence. But, though this is a traditional historiographical move in this field, it is questionable, since a negative instruction does not automatically mean that the unwanted action is in fact already widespread. In the pre-recording era the available evidence for its universal use as an expressive melodic enhancement is not unequivocal. In particular, in the case of printed fingerings for different-finger shifts on the same string, it cannot be automatically assumed that some type of portamento is implied by default. Every notated example offered in this chapter can be executed with a very wide range of intensity or refinement, with both the left hand and the bow, matters on which written sources are to all intents and purposes literally and metaphorically silent. The range of notational practices may – or may not – correspond to the range of performing practices, and any attempt to infer the latter from the former in the absence of any significant body of aural evidence is therefore insecure. Those who wish to recreate nineteenth-century portamento need to decide whether the historical models they choose to follow represent a personal idiosyncrasy, a consensus view, or a style extrapolated from a variety of sources. Chapter 6 will continue this discussion in the context of early twentieth-century recordings and printed sources, but in the meantime we will examine the use of vibrato.

---

[78] David Popper, 'Wie einst in schöner'n Tagen', *Drei Stücke* op. 64 no. 1 (Leipzig: Breitkopf & Härtel, [1892]); Popper, *Requiem. Adagio für 3 Celli* op. 66 (Hamburg: Rahter, [1892]).

[79] David Popper, *Zur Guitarre* op. 54 (Hamburg: Rahter, [1886]); Popper, 'Reigen', *Im Walde* op. 50 no. 4 (Hamburg: Rahter, [1882]).

Chapter 5
Playing with Expression – Vibrato

Nineteenth-century cello methods discuss vibrato far less often, and less systematically, than do those for the violin. Spohr's study for the use of vibrato on accented tones or expressive notes distinguishes four types of vibrato: intense and fast, slower and less intense, increasing in intensity through the note, and decreasing in intensity.[1] These are included in his annotations to the solo parts of Rode's seventh concerto and Spohr's own ninth concerto, and in some of the extended practice pieces in his *Violinschule*.[2] Some of Spohr's late works, such as the violin duos opp. 148, 150 and 153, include standardized vibrato markings in the form of short wavy lines quite distinct in appearance from mordents. Ferdinand David adopts Spohr's distinctions of speeds of vibrato and makes it clear that in quieter dynamics the vibrato is slower, becoming faster as the dynamic level rises.[3] Baudiot and Bériot discuss it, although their predominant concern is to warn against anything more than its most sparing use. Luis Alonso's eccentric classification of five types of vibrato (with the finger, the wrist, the arm, by sympathetic resonance, and with the bow), most of which are deprecated, is based on different physical techniques rather than on variations of speed or amplitude.[4] Spohr's fundamental vibrato principle is the standard consensus view, reinforced by later violinists in the nineteenth century:

> This movement must not be too strong and the deviation from the purity of the note should scarcely be perceptible to the ear.[5]

The width remains narrow, so that the only significantly variable element is speed.

But hardly any cello method mentions vibrato before Dotzauer, even Duport's *Essai*, which is mostly concerned with the technique of the left hand. It probably occurs for the first time in the cello literature in Joseph Alexander's *Anleitung*

---

[1]   Louis Spohr, *Violinschule* (Vienna: Haslinger, 1833), pp. 175–6.

[2]   Ibid., pp. 198–244.

[3]   Ferdinand David, *Violin-schule* (Leipzig: Breitkopf & Härtel, [1863]), p. 43. Some very interesting examples of David's hand-written vibrato markings are discussed by Clive Brown on the CHASE website: see http://chase.leeds.ac.uk/article/ferdinand-david-as-editor-clive-brown/ [last accessed November 2013].

[4]   Luis Alonso, *Le virtuose moderne* (Paris: Ch. Nicosias et Cie, [c.1880]), p. iv, cited in Brown, *CRPP*, p. 536.

[5]   'Diese Bewegung darf aber nicht zu stark seyn und das Abweichen von der Reinheit des Tons dem Ohre kaum bemwerklich werden'. Spohr, *Violinschule*, p. 175, in Brown, *CRPP*, p. 550.

zum Violoncellospiel (c.1802), notated as a series of dots over a minim, whose execution is described in these rather minimal terms:

> The vibrato [Bebung], where one can, through a fast back-and-forth rolling of the finger pressing on the string, alternately change the pitch from strong to weak, from high to low.[6]

The cellist John Gunn's flute treatise of 1797 discusses vibrato, but only as an old-fashioned absurdity.[7] A contemporary reviewer of this work particularly praised Gunn's remarks on musical expression in general, which may suggest some implicit agreement on this topic.[8] (However, vibrato was being recommended 50 years later as 'worthy every attention' in Nicholson's flute tutor, anonymously revised for the eight-keyed flute).[9] Dotzauer gives the topic cursory treatment:

> In long sustained notes one sometimes (especially Italian professors) makes use of a type of vibration (*tremolo*) or trembling, which is effected by leaning the finger on the string from one side to the other, with little speed. Other artists try to produce the same effect by a movement of the wrist which is called *ondulé* and which is indicated by this sign [wavy line].
>
> This is made up by several *sons filés*, of which one makes the *forte* felt at the beginning of each beat or half-beat.[10]

The German text of Dotzauer omits the reference to Italian players – puzzling, as Dotzauer, a sometime teacher at the Naples Conservatoire, was presumably well placed to make this comment – but it also makes it clear that the alternative wrist vibrato is produced by the bow ('many seek to bring this about through the bow').[11]

---

6   'Die *Bebung* (*tremolo*) wo man durch schnelles Hin- und Herwälzen des die Saite niederdrückenden Fingers Stärke und Schwäche, Höhe und Tiefe des Tones hintereinander abwechseln lässt.' Joseph Alexander, *Anleitung des Violoncellspiel* (Leipzig: Breitkopf & Härtel, [c.1802]), p. 25.

7   John Gunn, Chapter 6, 'Of Shakes, and other Graces', in *The Art of Playing the German-Flute* (London: the Author, [1793]).

8   Anon., *Monthly Review*, 12 (1793), pp. 376–81 (p. 380).

9   Anon, *Nicholson's Flute Preceptor* (London: Davidson. [1845]), p. 25.

10   'Dans des sons longtems soutenus on se sert quelquefois (surtout des professeurs italiens) d'une espèce de vibration (Tremolo) ou tremblement, qu'on effectue en inclinant le doigt posé sur la corde avec peu de vitesse d'un côté et de l'autre. D'autres artistes tâchent de produire le même effet par un mouvement du poignet qu'on appelle ondulé et qui s'indique par ce signe [music example]. Ce qui est un composé de plusieurs sons filés, dont on fait sentir le Forté au commencement de chaque tems ou demi-tems.' J.J.F. Dotzauer, *Méthode de violoncelle Violonzell-Schule* (Mainz: B. Schott fils, [1825]), p. 47.

11   'und manche suchen dieses durch den Bogen zu bewircken welches ungefähr so zu bezeichnen wäre'. Ibid.

Both of these vibrato techniques produce a slow vibrato. There is also a difference in nuance between the French and German parallel texts here: in the French, 'some other' (*d'autres*) players use a bow-vibrato, but in the German, 'some' or 'many' (*manche*) do so. The final sentence quoted concerning the *forte* at the beginning of the beat is only found in the French text.[12]

Dotzauer, however, was evidently not representative. An extremely favourable review of Josef Merk (1795–1852) in 1825 criticized vibrato as widely practised at that time:

> Then followed an Adagio and Rondeau for cello, composed and played by Herr Prof. Merk, performed with execution and skill of the character suggested above. However, the too-frequent vibrating accentuation of the note is a habit of string players that is not wholly to be praised. One often longs for a pure sustained note, which makes an effect through calmness and fullness. Something as anomalous as the vibrating of notes must only be used rarely and with reason.[13]

It is not absolutely clear whether the reviewer means left-hand or bow vibrato (this question often arises in the earlier nineteenth century). The narrow width of left-hand vibrato meant that it was not primarily perceived as a real fluctuation of pitch. The reviewer contrasts 'bebende Accentuiren' with a 'rein ausgehaltenen Ton', which could imply a bowed effect – 'accentuation' is perhaps more easily associated with this technique. This would place Merk among the 'some' or 'many' in Dotzauer's German text. On the other hand, very few cellists describe bow-vibrato at this time. Apart from Dotzauer, it is only briefly mentioned by Crouch, paraphrasing the Paris Conservatoire method, who also uses it at the beginning of each beat or half-beat of a long note:

> There is another species of bowing, called Undulating. It is a compound of several notes each being soft increased and diminished or to which may be given the forte, at the commencement of each beat, or half beat in the bar.[14]

---

[12] A French-only edition of Dotzauer translated by Minche was published c.1830. The French text is identical with that in the earlier bilingual editions, also presumably prepared by Minche, who therefore may well have been responsible for these and other variants. Dotzauer, trans. G. Minche, *Méthode de violoncelle* (Paris: Richault, [c.1830]).

[13] 'Dann folgte Adagio und Rondeau für Cello, komponirt und gespielt von Herrn. Prof. Merk, mit Vortrag und Fertigkeit in dem oben angedeuteten Karakter ausgeführt. Das zu häufige bebende Accentuiren der Töne ist indess eine Sitte der Streichinstrumentisten, die nicht ganz zu loben ist. Man sehnt sich oft nach einem rein ausgehaltenen Ton, der durch die Ruhe und Fülle seiner selbst wirkt. Etwas so anomalisches, als das Beben des Tones, muss nur selten und mit Grund angewandt werden.' *BAmZ*, 2 (1825), p. 170.

[14] Frederick Crouch, *Compleat Treatise on the Violoncello* (London: Chappell & Co., 1826), p. 43. The equivalent passage, with the same music example, is in Baillot et al., *Méthode de violoncelle* (Paris: Janet et Cotelle, [18054]), p. 28.

Dotzauer is the only cellist to describe another technique, which he calls the *'Pochen'* (Fr., *tintement*), which translates into English as beating, knocking or pounding. He includes this in a discussion of resonant effects in general, such as the doubling of an open string for extra volume in orchestral playing, but the *Pochen* is a much more refined effect. It is obtained when holding a stopped note an octave above an open string or in unison with it, but without actually playing it. The open string will naturally resonate sympathetically with the stopped note, but this can be interrupted by touching it with a free finger:

> In order to be better convinced of the truth of this phenomenon, one only has to strike the open string lightly with the index finger, while making the other note vibrate with the bow, and one hears a beating occasioned by the resonance of the string, which the finger, in striking it, prevents from freely vibrating.[15]

Earlier in the treatise, Dotzauer mentions this in the context of ornamentation (portamento and vibrato) as a topic for later explanation:

> Sometimes, in very sustained notes, one can use an ornament which results from the vibrations of sounds [*Pochen*] and which will be explained in an article below.[16]

However, he warns that:

> Although these experiments cannot be rejected absolutely, good taste dictates that they should only be used rarely; moreover, it is quite separate from the art of drawing a good, clear, round, sweet sound.[17]

Dotzauer may partly be offering the *Pochen* as a form of embellishment (as did some violinists), but also partly as empirical acoustical proof that the open string does indeed vibrate sympathetically in this way.[18] At all events, the effect is not described by any other cellist.

---

[15] 'Will man sich noch besser von dieser Wahrheit überzeugen, so tupfe man während dem angeben eines Ton's mit dem ersten Finger auf die leere Saite, und man wird ein Pochen verneen welches von der Hemmung des Mitklang's durch den Finger entstehet. // Pour se persuader de la réalité de ce phénomene, on n'a qu'à frapper légèrementdu premier doigt sur la corde à vide, pendant que que l'on fait vibrer l'autre par l'archet, et on entrendra un tintement occasioné par la résonance de la corde, que le doigt en Frappant dessus empèche de vibrer librement.' Dotzauer, *Violonzell-Schule* (1824), p. 52.

[16] 'Viele bedienen sich bey langen Tönen, wo es möglich ist des Pochens, welches vom Mitklingen der Töne herrührt wie in 12ten Abschnitt zurschen ist. // On peut quelques fois dans des sons très longtems soutenus employer un grément qui resulte de la vibration des tons et qui sera expliqué plus bas à l'article'. Ibid., p. 47.

[17] Ibid.

[18] Versions of this technique are described by Luis Alonso (c.1880) and Hermann Schröder (1887). Brown, *CRPP*, p. 537.

Romberg, who was relatively enthusiastic about portamento, is rather more cautious about vibrato:

> The close shake, or Tremolo, is produced by a rapid lateral motion of the finger when pressed on the string. When used with moderation, and executed with great power of bow, it gives fire and animation to the Tone, but it should be made only at the beginning of the note, and ought not to be continued throughout its whole duration. Formerly the close shake was in such repute, that it was applied indiscriminately to every note of whatever duration. This produced a most disagreeable and whining effect, and we cannot be too thankful that an improved taste has at length exploded the abuse of this embellishment.[19]

The anonymous English translator weakens the pungency of Romberg's expression here; 'Jammer-musik' could more vividly be rendered as 'misery-music'. More remarkably, the whole sentence where this word occurs ('In früherer Zeit ... eine wahre Jammer-Musik daraus') is omitted entirely from the French translation, which might suggest a slightly greater tolerance for vibrato in France.[20]

In the annotations to his studies and exercises, Romberg goes into a little more detail:

> The 2nd finger will be found the best in making the close-shake, for which reason I have marked it to be used upon the first note of the following exercise, where the passing-shake [mordent] must be made with the third. The third finger [...] is not so well adapted to the close-shake. The close-shake should never be held on through the whole duration of the note, otherwise it will fail in its object, which is, to add power to the tone; and should never exceed in time the third part of the value of the note.[21]

---

[19] 'Das Beben (tremolo) wird hervorgebracht, indem man den Finger, mit dem man einen Ton genommen hat, mehrere Male in sehr geschwindem Zeitmaass vor und rückwärts biegt. Selten angebracht, und mit vieler Kraft des Bogens ausgeführt, gibt es dem Tone Feuer und leben; es muss aber nur im Anfange der Note, und nicht durch die ganze Dauer derselben gemacht werden. In früherer Zeit konnte niemand einen Ton, wenn auch von noch so wenig Dauer, aushalten, ohne beständig mit dem Finger zu beben, und es wurde eine wahre Jammer-Musik daraus'.' Bernhard Romberg, trans. anon., *Complete Theoretical and Practical School for the Violoncello* (London: T. Boosey & Co., [1840]), p. 85. 'Close shake' is almost a standard English term for vibrato; it is used in Christopher Simpson's *The Division-Viol* (1665), and it survived well into the 20th century – the writer's father, the violinist William Kennaway (1913–86), frequently used the term following the practice of his Edinburgh teacher James Winram. See Winram, *Violin Playing and Violin Adjustment* (Edinburgh: William Blackwood & Sons, 1908), *passim*.

[20] Bernhard Romberg, trans. anon., *Méthode de violoncelle* (Paris: Henry Lemoine, [1840]), p. 84.

[21] Ibid., p. 90.

Example 5.1   Romberg, *Violoncellschule*, vibrato exercise

Example 5.2   Romberg, *Concertino* (first movement), vibrato markings

In fact, the vibrato markings in bars 1 and 3 are the only ones in the 65 bars of the exercise (Example 5.1 – the shorter markings in bars 2 and 4 indicate mordents, not vibrato). Elsewhere in his *Violoncellschule* Romberg only indicates vibrato in one passage (Example 5.2).[22]

His few vibrato examples use only the second finger, and his approach is very limited. For Romberg, vibrato is used only with the strongest finger, for just the first third of the duration of long notes. It is not combined with any other ornament – neither with an ornament beginning with a longer note with decorative notes such as a turn or *Doppelschlag* at the end, nor with a short *messa di voce* double hairpin. Romberg is much more interested in the execution of ornaments like the appoggiatura or trill. His lack of attention to vibrato is partly because he dislikes its excessive use, but it may also be a physical consequence of his violinistic left hand. Although this may have encouraged portamento, as suggested in the previous chapter, it would also have made vibrato particularly difficult with any other finger than the second. This is obviously a severe limitation in terms of later technique, but it would appear to be consistent with Romberg's general aesthetic position. Indeed, one could even argue that Romberg is trying to make a virtue out of necessity by defining the aesthetic limits of vibrato in terms that match his own idiosyncratic physical limitations.[23] In this connection it is striking that Romberg's second cello concerto features a number of themes where the note most apt for vibrato is played with the second finger (see Chapter 8, Example 8.5).

---

22   Ibid., p. 101.

23   David Watkins takes the slightly different view that Romberg's vibrato would have been even more restricted than his own advice would suggest, because of his extremely slanted left hand. David Watkins, 'Beethoven's Sonatas for Cello and Piano' in Robin Stowell (ed.), *Performing Beethoven* (London: Cambridge University Press, 1994), pp. 89–116 (p. 111).

One of the earliest cello vibrato indications discovered to date in a musical work as opposed to a study, exercise, or instruction book occurs in François Hainl's 1842 *Fantasia* on themes from *Guillaume Tell* (Example 5.3).[24]

Example 5.3   Hainl, *Fantasia*, vibrato marking

It is clearly used here as an intensifying device, at the end of a highly operatic *adagio* section in the remote key of E major (the previous section is in two halves, in G major and B major/G♯ minor respectively, and the following section is in C). Indeed, this entire section is unusual in that operatic transcriptions for the cello do not generally strive after vocal effects, paradoxical though this may seem. Hainl's use of a repeated accent sign for the vibrated notes recalls Hamilton's notation for the 'vibration or close shake', in which vibrato is represented by a wavy line or by repeated accents.[25]

Hainl's and Hamilton's notation may cast some light on the vibrato practice of Adrien-François Servais (1807–66). The evidence for Servais's use of vibrato is patchy. The sole written source for Servais's vibrato is a review by Pavel Makarov in 1866, the year of Servais's death:

> Servais's [...] lilt is so full of the unending sugary vibrato that one would, no doubt, like to cleanse one's ears with full and clear sounds, as one would like to have some plain water after eating candies.[26]

Other evidence for this is less explicit. While Servais does not explicitly notate vibrato (the word does not appear in any of his music, printed or in manuscript, and he never uses a wavy line to mean vibrato), many pieces include passages of notes marked with repeated accents (sometimes with separate bows, sometimes under a slur), and he also frequently adds markings that imply some vivid, if generic, form of heightened expression, such as *avec abandon*, *avec passion*, or *avec âme et passion*. An example from his *Grande fantaisie* on themes from Lestocq is representative of many (Example 5.4).[27]

---

[24]   François Georges Hainl, *Fantaisie sur des motifs de Guillaume Tell* op. 8 (Mainz: B. Schott fils, [1842]), vc pt, p. 3.

[25]   Brown, *CRPP*, p. 551, citing James Alexander Hamilton, *Dictionary [...] of Musical Terms* (London: R. Cocks and Co., 1837), p. 88.

[26]   Quoted in Lev Ginsburg, *History of the Violoncello* (Neptune City, NJ: Paganiniana Publications, 1983), citing P. Makarov, 'St. Petersburg Concerts', *Muzikalniy tsvet* (1866), no. 6.

[27]   Adrien-François Servais, *Grande fantaisie sur des motifs de l'opéra Lestocq* (Mainz: B. Schott fils, [1852]). Many other examples can be found in such works as his

Example 5.4   Servais, *Grande fantaisie sur [...] Lestocq*

It is possible that Servais himself even parodied his own expressive excess. In the autograph MS of his *Fantaisie burlesque* (variations on the popular *Carnaval de Venise*) Servais included the marking '*dol. et fausse expression*' ('dolce and false expression') (Figure 5.1). This marking does not appear in the published version.

Figure 5.1   Servais, *Fantaisie burlesque*: MS version[28]

Servais does use a series of repeated accents in other contexts that need not imply vibrato. In particular there are several cases where it seems closer to a heavy *portato* effect, made with the bow and not the left hand. Examples of the accent-mark notation combined with a slur could certainly imply the former at least as strongly as the latter. While the position is therefore ambiguous, it seems possible that in certain circumstances repeated accentuation was combined with vibrato for additional expressive effect.

Dotzauer and Romberg respectively locate vibrato in Italy and in the past. The first cellist to write positively and in some detail about vibrato is Friedrich Kummer (1797–1879). Kummer treats both portamento and vibrato under the heading of 'Ton und Vortrag', tone and expression, rather than 'Verzierungen', or ornaments:

> One can also occasionally give a note more expression and gloss by a certain trembling, which is produced if one puts the finger firmly on the string and lets

---

Fra Diavolo 2me. Grand Duo Brillant (Mainz: B. Schott fils, [1853]), the *Fantaisie la Romantique*, Brussels Royal Conservatoire MS 45.106, or the *Fantaisie burlesque sur le carnaval de Venise,* Brussels Royal Conservatoire MS 45.106, published as *Fantaisie burlesque (ou le Carnaval de Venise)* (Mainz: B. Schotts Söhne, [1852]).

[28]   Servais, *Fantaisie burlesque*, MS p. 77. Servais tended to add puns (in Flemish) and jokes to his MSS. My thanks to the library of the Conservatoire royal/Koninklijk Conservatorium, Brussels for permission to reproduce this source.

the hand make a trembling movement, whereby, in order to be able to perform the same more freely, the thumb lies very loosely on the neck of the instrument.[29]

Examples in his exercises and studies show that Kummer could play with vibrato on any finger, although he appears to favour the third. From his notation we can begin to infer some general principles concerning Kummer's use of vibrato. He uses vibrato on metrically strong beats, on weak beats when combined with agogic lengthening, on diatonic notes much more often than chromatic ones (notes that are already chromatically expressive do not normally have vibrato as well), on longer rather than shorter notes (although by no means every long note), and never uses it on harmonics (see the discussion of consistency, below). His exercise no. 77 (Example 5.5) uses vibrato much more on the second, third and fourth fingers. His study on the D string op. 44 no. 4 marks vibrato at several points, including f♯′ and b′, high on the D string, played with consecutive third fingers (Example 5.6).

Example 5.5   Kummer, *Violoncellschule*, study no. 77, opening bars ('G.B.' means whole bow [abbr., *Ganz Bogen*])

Example 5.6   Kummer, study op. 44 no. 4, opening bars (D string throughout)

Reviews of some of Kummer's compositions sometimes appear to see them as potential sites for tasteless vibrato, although his own performances are not criticised in these terms. His *Variations brillantes* on *La sonnambula* op. 16 provoked this reaction:

> Elvin's Arioso […], depicting his pangs of love and unpleasant convulsions of the heart, which follows, gives the player the most beautiful opportunities for

[29]   'Man kann auch zuweilen einem Tone mehr Ausdruck und Glanz durch eine gewisse Bebung geben, die hervorgebracht wird, wenn man den Finger fest auf die Saite setzt und die Hand eine zitternde Bewegung machen läßt, wobei man, um dieselbe freier ausführen zu können, den Daumen ganz locker an den Hals des Instruments legt. Ausgedrückt wird diese Bebung durch das Zeichen.' F.A. Kummer, *Violoncelloschule* (Leipzig: Hofmeister, [1839]), p. 45.

producing sufficient whimpering and dreadful sobbing by means of the now so popular *vibrando* (tremolando), and thus makes it so much easier for him to move his audience.[30]

Kummer's *Elegie*, considered simply as a piece of music in itself, was seen as opposed to the popular taste for emotional extravagance:

> Herr Kummer [...] has avoided that whining note of insipid salon-sentimentality; [...] the predominant expression of mourning and pain almost consistently retains a manly composure, healthy, noble, in complete contrast to certain fashionable compositions of this genre, whose sickly affectation and revolting effeminate coquettishness of feeling often cause positive physical discomfort, leaving [anyone with] a strong, pure temperament the most disagreeable feelings.[31]

This piece's masculine character presumably rendered vibrato inappropriate (the perceived gender identity of the cello is discussed in Chapter 7). Kummer's *Air et Danse suédois nationaux* contains a rare verbal indication of vibrato (Example 5.7). A similar vibrato marking over a long note occurs in the third of Auguste Lübeck's (1838–1904) preludes based on Chopin's op. 28.[32]

Example 5.7   Kummer, *Swedish Air and Dance*, vc pt, p. 5

---

[30] 'folgt Elvin's, seinen Liebesjammer und widrigen Herzenszwang aushauchendes Arioso [...] das dem Spieler die schönste Gelegenheit zu hinlänglichem, mittelst des jetzt so beliebten Vibrando (Tremolando) zu bewerkstelligenden Wimmern und erkschlecklichen Schluchzen an die Hand gibt, und so die allgemeine Ruhrung seines Auditoriums wesentlich erleichtert.' *AmZ*, 47 (1845), p. 536. While there is a theoretical possibility that the reviewer is describing bow-vibrato, Kummer never describes this technique and it is much more likely that left-hand vibrato is the emotionally affecting device.

[31] 'Was uns besonders darin angesprochen, ist, dass Herr Kummer, mit Ausname einiger wenigen Stellen, jenen weinerlichen Ton fader Salonsentimentalität vermieden hat, dass der in der Elegie vorherrschende Ausdruck der Trauer und des Schmerz fast durchgehends ein männlich gefasster, edler und gesunder bleibt, ganz im Widerspruche mit gewissen dieser Galtung angehörigen Modecomposition, deren krankhafte Affectation und widerlich weibische Gefühlscoquetterie oft förmliches physisches Unwohlsein verinsachen, und wovon eine kräftige, unverdorbene Natur sich nur auf's Unerquicklichtest berührt fühlen kann.' Anon., 'Recensionen', *AmZ*, 47 (1845), p. 536.

[32] Friedrich Kummer, *Air et Danse suédois nationaux* (Hanover: Bacann, [1851]); Auguste Louis Lübeck, *Vier Praeludien aus Op. 28 von Fr. Chopin* (Berlin: C.A. Challier & Co., [1885]), no. 3 (Chopin's op. 28 no. 2).

Example 5.8   Romberg, ed. Grützmacher, *Duo* no. 1, third movement

Grützmacher, so assiduous in marking portamento, indicates vibrato only once. This occurs in his edition of Romberg's *Duos* op. 9, in a passage also featuring a succession of small-scale *messa di voce* pairs of hairpins (Example 5.8).[33] In the light of Romberg's own views on vibrato it seems that this marking almost certainly reflects Grützmacher's own performance practice. As was mentioned in the previous chapter, almost all Grützmacher's editions of Romberg were annotated in detail for teaching purposes. The title page of his edition of it is typical, in what claims to be a 'new, exactly marked edition for use in teaching'.[34] Similar claims were made, both in more technically advanced works such as Romberg's concerti, and in Grützmacher's own studies, especially the more basic collections.[35] The Romberg *Duos* are particularly heavily annotated, so it may be that his edition includes some material that might otherwise have been omitted as obvious. This is apparent even in this small example, where the f♯' in bar 1 in the second cello part carries a fingering, an articulation mark, a down-bow marking, a dynamic level, hairpins *and* the vibrato marking.

Grützmacher uses this marking over a single note quite frequently, and it may imply an effect of vibrato as well as of dynamic. Just as he can use portamento repeatedly within a few bars, so he can use the *messa di voce* equally frequently, as his version of Chopin's waltz op. 64 no. 1 in D♭, transposed to A♭, shows (Example 5.9). Within the given tempo, it is likely that this marking implies a vibrato at least as much as a dynamic effect.

The connection between the *messa di voce* and vibrato seems to apply in the violin literature. Brown provides examples from Baudiot, Campagnoli, Rode, and Joachim, and concludes that:

---

[33]   Bernhard Romberg, ed. Friedrich Grützmacher, *Duo no. 1* from *Drei Duos* op. 9 (Leipzig: Breitkopf & Härtel, [1890]).

[34]   'Neue, zum Gebrauch beim Unterrichte genau bezeichnete Ausgabe.' Ibid.

[35]   See, for example, Friedrich Grützmacher, *12 Violoncell-Etuden für den ersten Unterricht* op. 72 (Leipzig: Peters, [1896]).

Example 5.9   Chopin, arr. Grützmacher, *Waltz* in op. 64 no. 1 ('Minute'), B section

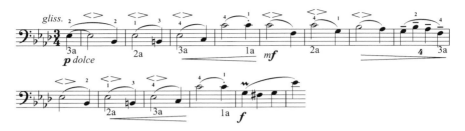

Example 5.10   Romberg, ed. Grützmacher, *Divertimento über schwedische Lieder* op. 42

in the music of [Zelter, Mendelssohn, Schumann and Brahms] it seems probable that, whatever else it might be intended to convey, the sign generally implied a vibrato […] there are certainly instances where […] it could hardly mean anything but vibrato combined with a gentle accent (possibly with an agogic element).[36]

However, a *messa di voce* can be placed on a note where vibrato is unrealistic, such as an open string or a natural harmonic. This can create ambiguity, as several instances in Grützmacher show. He frequently adds *messa* markings to natural harmonics (Example 5.10), but these are unlikely to imply vibrato; vibrato on a natural harmonic, though not in fact impractical, simply does not seem to have been seen as a possibility at this time. Only in 1923 did the cellist Hans Kindler (1892–1949) even suggest using vibrato on artificial harmonics, which is if anything more feasible: 'why should artificial harmonics on the cello mostly sound glassy? Why not give them the benefit of a slight *vibrato* to keep the tone "alive"?'[37]

Examples of the *messa di voce* on stopped notes abound in Grützmacher's editions, and these are equally unproblematic in the sense that vibrato is always

36   Brown, *CRPP*, p. 552.

37   Hans Kindler, quoted in Frederick H. Martens, *String Mastery Talks with Master Violinists, Viola Players and Violoncellists* (New York: Frederick A. Stokes Company, 2nd edn 1923), p. 260. Note however, that Fritz Rau allows the possibility of vibrato on natural harmonics at this time: 'Außerdem kann man aber auch einen flageoletton vibrieren' ['Aternatively one can also vibrate a harmonic']. Fritz Rau, *Das Vibrato auf der Violine* (Leipzig: C.F. Kahnt, 1922), p. 50.

Example 5.11 Romberg, ed. Grützmacher, *Divertimento über westfälische Lieder* op. 65

Example 5.12 Romberg, ed. Grützmacher, *Concerto no. 9* op. 56, first movement

an option. However, in another example, Grützmacher could plausibly intend a contrast between a *forte* harmonic without a *messa di voce* vibrato, and a quieter stopped note with vibrato (Example 5.11).[38]

But where a melodic sequence is marked with dynamic swells on equivalent notes in the sequence, only some of which fall on harmonics, there is a problem of consistency – either vibrato is used on harmonics, or none is used even on stopped notes (Example 5.12).[39]

In Example 5.12, the swells indicated on the minims (bars 1 and 3 in the extract) suggest consistency of treatment, but the first is an harmonic. Given the gradually intensifying expression, playing this *senza* vibrato is musically justifiable, with a possible vibrato on the b'♭ in bar 5 (and similar notes as the sequence continues to rise). A similar issue arises in Joachim and Moser's *Violinschule*, where in a *Musette* by Leclair Joachim indicates a *messa di voce* on both harmonics and stopped notes.[40] In spite of Joachim's lengthy treatment of vibrato elsewhere in the *Violinschule* (almost entirely based on Spohr, but with additional warnings about excess), he does not address this specific point, although it is again most likely that in this particular case no vibrato is intended.

As far as the cello is concerned, it is hard to make a clear case for any fixed or consistent relationship between the *messa di voce* marking and vibrato. Combining the two is clearly historically admissible, especially in the wider context of restrained vibrato use, but passages that use the *messa di voce* with harmonics are unlikely to imply vibrato. However, in sequential passages that use the *messa*

---

[38] Romberg, ed. F. Grützmacher, *Divertimento über westfälische Lieder* op. 65 (Leipzig: Peters, [n.d.]).

[39] Romberg, ed. F. Grützmacher, *Concert no. 9* op. 56 (Leipzig: Peters, [1883]).

[40] J. Joachim and A. Moser, trans. Alfred Moffat, *Violinschule* (Berlin: N. Simrock, 1905), pp. 97–8.

sometimes with and sometimes without a harmonic, consistency would exclude vibrato. In the nineteenth century such consistency may well be anachronistic, but only a large-scale study of nineteenth-century performing editions for specific examples would clarify this point. It need hardly be stated here that in practice, any discerning modern performer would be immediately aware of nuances that could be applied to such passages, which would be far more refined than notation allows.

Actual instruction in the physical means of producing vibrato on the cello is even rarer than indications for its use, and only begins to appear in any detail in cello pedagogy later in the century. The next cellist to offer this after Kummer is Carl Schroeder in 1893:

> The close shake is a trembling of a note arising from the unequal intonation of the string played upon. It is produced by setting a finger upon a string, and then giving it and the wrist also a trembling motion, so that the pitch slightly rises and falls. The unemployed fingers must be lifted. A special sign for the close shake is not in general use, its employment being left to the player's taste. Sometimes the indication 'vibrato' is met with.[41]

Nearly two decades later still, William Whitehouse described a rather different version of vibrato, adding this topic among others to his edition of his teacher Piatti's cello method:

> This term, though rarely written in music, is essentially a feature of artistic interpretation. The use of it vitalizes the tone and increases the power of expression. It consists of a wide movement of the left hand (not a trembling motion) and should be acquired by practicing (preferably with the 2nd finger) a slow semi-circular movement coming from the wrist. By this means the finger will alternately sharpen and flatten the note, thereby creating 'vibrato'. Joachim termed it pulsation.[42]

Whitehouse's wide, non-trembling vibrato, was almost certainly on the slow side (not just practised slowly). His edition of Piatti's *Capricci* op. 25, 'with notes on the Master's Rendering of each Capriccio', includes this note on *Capriccio* no. 2:

> Observe the little accents > by slightly swelling on the notes thus marked – with perhaps a little vibrato.[43]

---

[41] Carl Schroeder, trans. J. Matthews, *Catechism of Cello Playing* (London: Augener & Co., 1893), p. 67.

[42] Alfredo Piatti, ed. W.E. Whitehouse and R.V. Tabb, *Violoncello Method* (London: Augener, 1911), Vol. 2, p. 48.

[43] A. Piatti, ed. W.E. Whitehouse, *Dodici Capricci* op. 25 (Leipzig: N. Simrock, [1874]), p. 2.

Evidence for Piatti's very occasional use of vibrato comes from several sources, which disagree on the effect of his playing. He touched on vibrato in his own edition of Kummer's method, which retains Kummer's examples and notation.[44] At several points, Kummer had recommended the learner to follow the example of good singers in the *messa di voce* and vibrato. But Piatti disagreed in a footnote which referred to both topics:

> Since this method was composed, things have changed, and I think the student would do better to imitate the phrasing of a good instrument-player.[45]

Piatti's restrained vibrato was praised by Hanslick:

> His performance of Schubert's *Litanei*, for example, has a real depth of tender feeling without any of that sickly sweetness which is so generally heard on the cello. […] We found it just as invigorating in the *adagio* not to encounter that ongoing *vibrato* which so many cellists take as being the same as 'feeling'.[46]

Hanslick's praise is not simply a consequence of his general rejection of the emotional effect of music as having anything to do with its aesthetic value (a position he advocates throughout *Vom Musikalisch-Schönen*, and with increasing emphasis in its later editions – see Chapter 7).[47] Hugo Becker referred to Piatti's 'discreet' vibrato in the context of a diatribe against its misuse (discussed below).[48] Three other witnesses confirm it. Piatti's pupil Harold Gorst (1868–1950) relates this anecdote dating from c.1892–93, which shows that Piatti at around the age of 70 favoured temperance rather than total abstinence:

---

[44]   F.A. Kummer, rev. A. Piatti, *Violoncello School for Preliminary Instruction* (Leipzig: Friedrich Hofmeister, 1877).

[45]   Kummer, rev. A. Piatti, *Violoncello school for preliminary instruction* (Leipzig: Friedrich Hofmeister, 1877) p. 30 n.

[46]   'Innig und tief empfunden, wie z. B.sein Vortrag der Schubert'schen "Litanei" war, hatte er doch nichts von jener anwiderdern Süsslichkeit, welche gerade auf dem Violoncell so allgemein vertreten ist. […] Ebensosehr hat uns erquidt, im adagio nicht jenem fortwährenden Vibriren zu begegnen, das bei zahllosen Cellisten mit "Gefühl" identisch ist.' Eduard Hanslick, *Geschichte des Concertwesens in Wien*, Vol. 2 (Vienna: Wilhelm Braumüller, 1870), p. 162. English translation from Annalisa Barzanò and Christian Bellisario, trans. Clarice Zdanski, *Signor Piatti – Cellist, Composer, Avantgardist* (Kronberg: Kronberg Academy Verlag, 2001), p. 240.

[47]   'Music may, undoubtedly, awaken feelings of great joy or intense sorrow; but might not the same or a still greater effect be produced by the news that we have won first prize in the lottery, or by the dangerous illness of a friend?' Eduard Hanslick, trans. Gustav Cohen, *On the Beautiful in Music* (New York: Da Capo Press, 1974; repr. of 7th edn 1885, English version 1891), p. 11.

[48]   Hugo Becker and Dago Rynar, *Mechanik und Aesthetik des Violoncellspiels* (Vienna and Leipzig: Universal-Edition, 1929), p. 202.

After a period of nearly four years' study [with Julius Klengel], I left Leipzig and settled in London. One day I bethought myself of applying to Signor Piatti, whose kindness to young players was notorious, for advice and guidance. […] He was then a very old man […] but it was marvellous to witness the strength and agility of his fingers, and the almost cast-iron precision of his still faultless intonation. When I first played something to him, at his request, with all the fervent *vibrato* of youth, he laid a kindly hand on my shoulder, and remarked gently: 'My dear friend, we cannot *always* be in a passion'.[49]

Horace Fellowes also remembered Piatti's performance of the opening of Beethoven's quartet op. 59 no. 1:

Piatti was a very fine artist of the traditional classical school, an ideal player of chamber music. As was the custom until after his time, he used to hold his instrument between his knees without any peg to support it. Nor had it then become the custom to use the left arm and wrist in the manner of modern 'cellists to produce a tremolo or vibrato effect. The opening phrase of the first Razoumowsky quartet, as played by Piatti with a splendid dignity of style, is a thing to remember.[50]

In 1954 the amateur cellist Stanley Rigby recalled his teenage concert-going years in Manchester in the 1870s and 1880s:

Piatti was a regular visitor. A young cellist once asked me what Piatti played with the orchestra. I remember that in the second half he would play a Locatelli or Sammartini sonata with Hallé, but what he played in the first I couldn't for my life recall. There was not much for him. The Haydn had not been unearthed, Dvorak had not written his concerto, and Tchaikovsky's [Rococo] variations had not reached the West. No one since has played like Piatti. It was beautiful playing but, like Hallé's piano playing, cold. He used 'vibrato' very sparingly. He disdained the use of a peg, and all his long life he nursed his cello between his knees.[51]

Piatti's austere classicism, an impression reinforced by his appearance in photographs, did include an element of vibrato, but used with great restraint. His

---

[49]   Harold Gorst, 'Masters of the Cello', *The Cremona*, 1 (1904), p. 32. Since he began his studies with Klengel in 1877–88, this anecdote probably dates from c.1892–93.

[50]   E.H. Fellowes, *Memoirs of an Amateur Musician* (London: Methuen & Co. Ltd., 1946), pp. 18–19.

[51]   Stanley Rigby, 'Memories', *Music & Letters*, 35 (1954), p. 140. F.A. Gevaert's edition of Haydn's D major concerto (Hob.VIIb/2) was not published until 1890; Klengel gave its UK première in 1887. For a wider discussion, see George Kennaway, 'Haydn's(?) Cello Concertos 1860–1930: editions, performance, reception', *Nineteenth-Century Music Review*, 9 (2012), pp. 177–211.

warning about imitating singers may well reflect an increasing tendency for singers to use what was seen at the time as excessive vibrato, something criticized in the pages of almost every musical journal in the later nineteenth century. This may lie behind the comments made by the leader of the Royal Opera House orchestra, G.H. Betjemann, when judging a music competition in 1896:

> Mr. G. H. Betjemann spoke of the pernicious excessive use of the vibrato in the violoncello competition; it was a burlesque of the human voice. Some of the competitors' hands while playing were shaking as though with the palsy. All good players used the vibrato, and there was a judicious use of it, but he objected to the use of it on every note.[52]

In the twentieth century, a new quasi-scientific approach to vibrato appears in the work of Diran Alexanian. Alexanian's attitude is an interesting combination of older and newer ideas. On the one hand, his vibrato is still very narrow. It 'should not fill up the interval between two enharmonic notes', and is compared to a trill 'an eighth of a tone, at the maximum, apart'.[53] This is considerably narrower than the vibrato widths found by later scientific investigators such as Seashore (discussed in Chapter 6), and is restricted even compared with the narrow vibrato recommended by Spohr. But Alexanian's vibrato is continuous, albeit subtly modified with regard to pitch, dynamic and tone quality. He suggests that vibrato was discouraged in the past because it led to poor intonation. Normally, Alexanian's vibrato went from the main note to a point slightly below it, and was faster in louder dynamics, or in dynamic nuances such as the reinforcement of a small *messa di voce*.[54] In some circumstances, however, it could go above the note:

> Every note attracted by another note, should be played vibrato in the interval that separates it from the note by which it is attracted.[55]

Thus, a D♭ might vibrate below the note, towards C, but a C♯ could vibrate upwards, towards D. This 'attraction' is analogous to Casals's 'expressive intonation', in which leading notes and major thirds are sharpened and minor sevenths and perfect fourths flattened, adjusting them in the direction in which they are conventionally resolved.[56]

---

[52]   *Musical Herald*, 1 May 1896, p. 140. He may be recalling Leopold Mozart's description of violinists 'afflicted with the palsy'. Leopold Mozart, trans. Editha Knocker, *Treatise on the Fundamental Principles of Violin Playing* (Oxford: Oxford University Press, 2nd edn, 1951), p. 203.

[53]   Dinan Alexanian, trans. Frederick Fairbanks, *Traité théoretique et pratique du violoncelle* (Paris: A.Z. Mathot, 1922), p. 97.

[54]   Ibid.

[55]   Ibid.

[56]   See J. Ma. Corredor, trans. André Mangeot, *Conversations with Casals* (London: Hutchinson, 1956), pp. 196–8; Lillian Littlehales, *Pablo Casals* (New York: W.W. Norton

The direction of Alexanian's vibrato seems to depend less on the harmonic function of the note than on its enharmonic spelling, though for all practical purposes he and Casals would agree. Alexanian's vibrato is also modified before and after an open string, so as not to 'destroy the continuity of sound colour'.[57] Disentangling what is new in Alexanian's theory of vibrato is not easy. Its narrowness is consistent with general nineteenth-century practice. If used to reinforce a small-scale *messa di voce*, it fits with mid-nineteenth-century practice. However, in that it is continuous, it is more 'modern', as recordings show. Indeed, in 1915, Alexanian is actually ahead of his time in teaching a constant subtle modification of vibrato in relation to other factors such as pitch-context, the presence of open strings, and changes in dynamics. Such subtle variation is not particularly evident in general in early recordings, apart from those of Casals himself.

The last treatment of vibrato by a cellist considered here is that by Hugo Becker.[58] Becker is the most forthright of cellists about the distinction between the vibrato of high art and the debased 'popular' version so widely heard, and he makes explicit the hidden sexual dimension that appears in the metaphors of diseased excess so frequently employed by critics from the later nineteenth century onwards.[59] Unlike Alexanian, Becker is most concerned to make the point that vibrato should above all be flexible, sometimes faster, sometimes slower, and sometimes quite absent:

> The intensity and speed of vibrato should be determined and used only in agreement with the respective *Affekt*. Every person of finer feeling will probably have to admit on closer consideration that, for the portrayal of profound, noble feelings, the rapid, lascivious, so-called 'coffee-house vibrato' is inappropriate, although, in a more refined [art] form, it is indispensable in the expression of eroticism! Just as in dynamics, forte and piano alone are insufficient, so just as little can we be content with only one style of vibrato.[60]

& Company, 1929; 2nd edn 1948), pp. 132–40; David Blum, *Casals and the Art of Interpretation* (Berkeley: University of California Press, 1977), *passim*. For a scientific analysis see Peter Johnson, '"Expressive Intonation" in String Performance: Problems of Analysis and Interpretation', in Jane W. Davidson and Hubert Eiholzer (eds), *The String Practitioner* (Aldershot: Ashgate, 2004), pp. 79–90.

[57]   Ibid.

[58]   Hugo Becker and Dago Rynar, 'Das Wesen des Vibrato', in *Mechanik und Aesthetik des Violoncellspiels* (Vienna: Universal-Edition, 1929), pp. 199–202.

[59]   This is discussed further in George Kennaway, 'Do as some said, or as most did? – a Foucauldian experiment with nineteenth–century HIP', *Current Musicology*, 92 (2011), pp. 7–29.

[60]   'Intensität und Schnelligkeitsgrad des Vibrato sollten daher nur in Übereinstimmung mit dem jeweiligen Affekt bestimmt und angewendet werden. Jeder feiner empfindende mensch wird wohl bei näherer Überlegung zugeben müssen, daß zur schilderung tiefer, edler Gefühle das rasche, lüsterne, sogenannte "Cafehaus-Vibrato" nicht das geeignete Mittel sein kann, wenn wir auch auf dieses, jedoch in veredelter Form, nicht verzichten können, sobald es sich darum handelt, Eros zu Worte kommen zu lassen! So wenig wir

The cellist's addiction to vibrato is even seen as analogous to alcohol addiction:

> The inclination to play each cantilena with overflowing feeling is widespread. Because of this, Hanslick called the cello the instrument of melancholy and sentimentality. However, unmotivated, exaggerated sentiment has a ridiculous effect, because it creates an excess of expression. Just as the drinker cannot see a full glass without emptying it, so no cantilena can appear before the cellist without him becoming sentimental.[61]

This sentimentality is seen by Becker as an expression of enervated hypersensitivity:

> Also in the performance of Bach's music vibrato should only be used discreetly. But how is it ordered nowadays? The whining, effeminate Bach playing of many over-sensitive cellists often has an intolerable effect. Serious classical music cannot bear any erotic vibrato; it needs a feeling for style, nobility and dignity, without any loss of warmth. It is a sign of the weakness of a performing artist if his means of expression in vibrato are exhausted.[62]

Becker does not know why vibrato is so abused, but partly puts it down to the influence of 'coffee-house' playing on performers, a topic that pervades his entire treatment of the subject. He cannot see a historical context for it, but points out that that Piatti and Sivori were both restrained in their use of vibrato (a very different account of Sivori's performing style is discussed in Chapter 8).

> It would be difficult to determine when vibrato became normalized. It is certain that the old classical schools of Italy and Germany abhorred the plentiful use of vibrato. The only pupil of Paganini, Sivori (1815–94), who had a wonderful

---

in der Dynamik mit Forte und Piano allein ausreichen, sondern jegliche verfügbare Kraftschattierung anwenden, ebensowenig können wir uns mit einer einzigen Vibratoart begnügen'. Becker and Rynar, *Mechanik*, p. 199.

[61] 'Die Neigung, jede Kantilene mit überfließendem gefühl zu spielen, ist allgemein verbreitet. Hanslick nannte daher das Cello das Instrument der Schwermut und Sentimentalität. Unmotiviertes, übertreibenes Sentiment wirkt aber lächerlich, weil es ein Zuviel an Ausdruck schafft. Wie der Trinker kein volles Glas sehen kann,ohne es zu leeren, so scheint der Cellist keine Kantilene vortragen zu können, ohne sentimental zu werden'. Ibid.

[62] 'Auch beim Vortrag Bachser Musik sollte das Vibrato nur diskret angewandt werden. Wie ist es heutzutage aber damit bestellt? Das winselnde, effeminierte Bachspiel manches überempfinlichen Cellisten wirkt oft unerträglich. Ernste, klaßiche Musik verträgt kein erotisches Vibrato; sie verlangt Stilgefühl, Vorneheit und Würde, ohne dadurch etwa an Wärme einzubüßen. Es ist ein Zeichen der Schwäche des vortragenden Künstlers, wenn sich seine Ausdrucksmittel im Vibrato erschöpfen. Vielleicht lohnt es sich, eine Betrachtung darüber anzustellen, wie dieses übertriebene Vibratospiel entstand.' Ibid., p. 201.

tone, tended not to use vibrato at all. Alfredo Piatti, the greatest cellist of Italian blood, used vibrato seldom, and only in a very discreet manner.[63]

Becker's language on the evils of excessive vibrato is the most extreme of any cellist cited here. His only surviving recording, of his own *Minuet*, is, unfortunately, not especially suitable for examining his vibrato in practice, since the piece is predominantly lively in character with few opportunities for emotional expression.[64] In the slower central section he does use a narrow vibrato with considerable subtle variation, increasing in intensity with the shape of a phrase but also virtually disappearing when not required.

There is an important distinction to observe when considering the diametrically opposed status of the evidence for the use of portamento as opposed to vibrato. In the case of portamento, its techniques and instructions for its use in the nineteenth century are amply demonstrated (even if more refined techniques are rarely discussed). There is basic evidence for its use throughout the pedagogical literature, in fingerings provided for performing editions, and in early twentieth-century recordings. But with vibrato the position is more complex. Were one to confine one's attention solely to cello-related evidence from pedagogical material or printed music, as has been done so far here, then one could argue, on this strictly limited basis, that it was seldom used by solo cellists in the nineteenth century other than as a very occasional ornament. It is rarely mentioned in cello methods, even more rarely indicated in printed music (even in otherwise highly detailed performing editions), and almost never referred to by concert reviewers other than unfavourably. Although there were those at the time who claimed that its use was widespread, they might have genuinely perceived it as more widespread than it really was, or have deliberately exaggerated for polemic effect. The accuracy of such claims in the nineteenth century is therefore at least open to question. Were it not for early recordings, which provide much evidence for the use of vibrato in the earliest years of the twentieth century, it would be hard to argue for more than its strictly limited use on the cello. The evidence of these recordings suggests a very different practice from that inferred from written sources, and some of these will be now be considered in Chapter 6.

---

[63]   'Wann das Vibrato sich einbürgerte, wird sich wohl schwer feststellen lassen. Sicher ist, daß die alten klassischen Schulen in Italien und Frankreich einem reichlich angewandten Vibrato abhold waren. Der einzige Paganini-Schüler: Sivori (1815 bis 1894), der einem wundervollen Ton hatte, pflegte überhaupt nicht zu vibrieren. Alfredo Piatti, der größte Violoncellist italienischen Gebüts, wandte das Vibrato selten und nur in sehr dezenter Weise an ...'. Ibid., p. 202. Becker adds in a footnote that his long-term quartet colleague Hugo Heermann remarked that Sivori's tone was the finest he ever heard: 'mein langjähriger Quartett-Genosse Hugo Heermann bezeichnete sivoris Ton sogar als den schönsten, den er je gehört habe'. Ibid., n. 24.

[64]   Hugo Becker (vc), un-named pianist, *Minuet* op. 3 no. 3 (*The Recorded Cello*, Vol. 2; original recording c.1908).

Chapter 6
Vibrato and Portamento in Early Cello Recordings

[V]ibrato is, to the listener, the most striking development in string-playing during the early twentieth century, and it is also *the element which is most clearly audible* even in recordings from the earliest years of the century.[1]

The previous chapters on portamento and vibrato stopped short of considering the evidence of early recordings. Some of this evidence will be assessed here, in largely qualitative terms. However, *pace* Robert Philip, the perception of vibrato in old recordings is not quite as straightforward as it might appear. While the simple presence or absence of vibrato is generally not in question in a given recording (although even here in some cases it is so narrow that it is barely noticeable as a fluctuation in pitch), even modern comparisons of the same recordings can produce different assessments.

[…] the dim sound-world of the early acoustic recording, and the often distracting quantity of surface noise, make it hard to detect the sought-after traits. Accordingly, the comments made relate, inevitably, to the analyst's own powers of observation […] the results are subjective […][2]

In recent years there have been several empirical studies relevant to the use of sound recordings as source material for the study of early twentieth-century performance practice. They suggest that some caution needs to be employed, but also indicate possible future directions for research.

Some of this research can be misrepresented. For instance, David Hurwitz suggested (relying on a conference paper by Dorottya Fabian and Emery Schubert) that older recording technology in itself obscures the amount of vibrato used.[3] In the course of a lengthy polemic opposing the use of less vibrato in historically

---

[1]   Robert Philip, *Early Recordings and Musical Style Changing Tastes Instrumental Performance 1900–1950* (Cambridge: Cambridge University Press, 1992), p. 99. Emphasis added.

[2]   David Milsom, *Theory and Practice in Late Nineteenth-Century Violin Playing* (Aldershot: Ashgate, 2003), p. 9.

[3]   Dorottya Fabian and Emery Schubert, 'Is there only one way of being expressive in musical performance? – Lessons From listeners' reactions to performances of J.S. Bach's music', in C. Stevens, D. Burnham, G. McPherson, E. Schubert and J. Renwick (eds),

informed performance, he interpreted this study as showing that expert listeners perceive much less vibrato in modern recordings that are acoustically altered to appear much older:

> In a 2002 study carried out at The University of New South Wales, Australia, two recordings of Bach's solo violin music were auditioned by a group of 32 listeners, 20 second year Bachelor of Music students, and 12 period performance specialists. The first recording was Menuhin's, dating from ca.1934, the second was Sergio Luca's 'authentic' 1977 version. The purpose of the study, ostensibly, was to determine if Baroque performance practice would be found equally (or more) expressive in Baroque music. [...] In order to equalize sonic considerations, a second, filtered version of Luca's performance was also auditioned by the panel, with its sound characteristics altered to match those of the 1934 Menuhin recording. The process measurably impaired the listeners' ability to detect vibrato, to a degree that Luca's rendition, initially perceived as using a moderate amount of vibrato, was now perceived as 'lacking' vibrato.[4]

In fact, although the filtered Luca recording was indeed perceived as using less vibrato, Fabian and Schubert themselves qualified this finding by pointing out that 'if the vibrato is prominent its perception is not hindered by early sound recording technology'.[5] Within the measurement scale used by Fabian to grade responses to various aspects of performance such as 'legato' or 'vibrato', the difference between the artificially aged Luca performance and the unmodified version was not quite as dramatic as Hurwitz thinks. In addition, many other perceptions of these two recordings varied considerably as well. Almost every expressive category was heard as much less present in the modified recording, with the exception of 'legato', 'measured', and 'straightness', which all scored slightly higher.[6] This suggests that the responses to the artificially aged recording were in fact much more complex. It is also possible that, given the level of musical knowledge of the experimental subjects, they may have brought prior assumptions to bear – if strongly influenced by their existing knowledge, they could have been predisposed to expect less vibrato in what was perceived as an 'old' recording. This does not invalidate the

---

Proceedings of the 7th International Conference on Music Perception and Cognition, Sydney, 2002 (Adelaide: Causal Productions, 2002), pp. 112–15 [CD-ROM only].

[4]   David Hurwitz, 'Orchestral vibrato', http://www.classicstoday.com/features/Classics Today-Vibrato-part1.pdf;   http://www.classicstoday.com/features/ClassicsToday-Vibrato-part2.pdf (commenced 2007, continually revised), Part 2, p. 62 [accessed July 2012]. Sergio Luca's recording was the first made using a baroque violin. For an equally provocative but better presented argument, addressing the specific question of orchestral vibrato, see Hurwitz's article 'So klingt Wien: Conductors, Orchestras, and Vibrato in the Nineteenth and Early Twentieth Centuries', *Music & Letters*, 93 (2012) pp. 29–60.

[5]   Fabian and Schubert, 'Is there only one way ...?', p. 115.

[6]   Ibid, p. 112.

Fabian and Schubert study, which itself makes carefully circumscribed claims, but it does not bear out Hurwitz's extreme interpretation.[7]

Another paper suggests that the visual effect of vibrato in a live, as opposed to a recorded, performance, contributes significantly to its perception. In Robert Gillespie's 1997 study of the evaluation of vibrato in violinists and violists (beginners and advanced players), it was found that teachers may have to 'occasionally listen to their students' vibrato without watching them since visual clues may inadvertently influence their evaluation of student achievement'.[8] The vibrato of inexperienced players, and the pitch stability of experienced players, were both rated 'significantly higher' when they could be seen as well as heard.[9] While this study mainly concerned the teaching process, it clearly has implications for the study of recordings as an indicator of practice in the pre-recording era. It could be, for instance, that at a time when vibrato was always seen as well as heard, its overall effect on the listener/viewer was more vivid and it was experienced as a proportionately more obvious nuance. The visual aspect of vibrato played no part in the psychologist Carl Seashore's early ground-breaking work on the subject, which was entirely confined to acousmatic sound:

> we find that everything in the way of musical expression that the singer conveys to the listener is conveyed in terms of the sound wave: when we eliminate sight and other senses which are merely accessory, there is only one avenue that can convey the musical message and that is the sound wave [...] For this purpose phonograph records are of inestimable value because they produce the vibrato faithfully [...] .[10]

In the same publication, Scott Reger implicitly agreed: 'In a musical situation the auditor *hears* the vibrato as a whole. His attention may not be centered on the vibrato at all unless he is attracted by an especially beautiful or unpleasant effect [...] .'[11] Seashore himself, while writing frequently of the 'gross normal illusions' that affected the aural perception even of expert listeners ('the vibrato is not heard even by the best musician as it really is'), did not apparently ever consider the

---

[7]   Fabian does not address questions of vibrato at all in her study of post-war Bach performance. Dorrotya Fabian, *Bach Performance Practice, 1945–1975* (Aldershot: Ashgate, 2003).

[8]   Robert Gillespie, 'Ratings of violin and viola vibrato performance in audio-only and audiovisual presentations', *Journal of Research in Music Education*, 45 (1997), p. 212.

[9]   Ibid., p. 218.

[10]   Carl Seashore, 'Measurements on the expression of emotion in music', *Proceedings of the National Academy of Sciences*, 9 (1923), pp. 323–4.

[11]   Scott Reger, 'The String Instrument Vibrato', in Carl Seashore (ed.), *The Vibrato* (Iowa: University of Iowa, 1932), p. 340. My emphasis.

effect of being able to see as well as hear vibrato.[12] However, his 'illusions' are relevant. According to Seashore, listeners generally:

- underestimate the width of vibrato by up to 75 per cent;
- confuse or equate vibrato with fluctuating sound intensity;
- hear successive periodicities as a single tone; and
- tend to identify a specific pitch even when the vibrato is as wide as a semitone.

According to Seashore, if the hearer heard the vibrato without the benefit of these illusions, it would be 'utterly intolerable'.[13] Seashore's experiments were conducted entirely with recordings and made no attempt to recreate the conditions of live performance. His conclusions could be interpreted more narrowly as showing how people listened to recordings rather than live performances, and in this sense could point in the same direction as Gillespie's study: listeners are aware of, and criticize, vibrato more when they have nothing to look at. However, it also resonates with an implication of the Fabian/Schubert study, that listeners may hear less vibrato when the sound quality is degraded. Another study suggests that the perception of vibrato in opera singers is not clearly related to its empirical acoustic measurement, and agrees with Seashore that listeners do not make fine distinctions about vibrato unless it is obtrusive.[14] While there is clearly little visible physical movement in a singer's vibrato, the 'wobble' of a bad technique can often involve a visible jaw movement.

These studies point in suggestive directions, such as reversing the Fabian technique of artificially ageing a modern recording, so as to compare perceptions of vibrato in old recordings with the same recordings digitally restored to remove surface noise. It seems at least plausible that, in the pre-recording era, what would now appear to be a narrow vibrato on a string instrument could have been perceived at the time as being more vivid, if its visual aspect were included. Mark Katz has argued that the recording process in itself encouraged a more easily heard, wider, continuous vibrato, possibly to compensate for the lack of a visual cue.[15] However, this is unlikely to be the sole explanation for the overall increase of vibrato during the first decades of the twentieth century. In any case, the chronology of early

---

[12]   Carl Seashore, 'Introduction', in Seashore (ed.), *Vibrato.*, p. 10 (reprinted from Seashore, 'The Natural History of the Vibrato', *Proceedings of the National Academy of Sciences*, 17 (1931), p. 626.

[13]   Ibid.

[14]   Patricia Howes, Jean Callaghan, Pamela Davis, et al., 'The relationship between measured vibrato characteristics and perception in Western operatic singing', *Journal of Voice*, 18 (2004), pp. 216–30.

[15]   Mark Katz, 'Aesthetics out of exigency: Violin vibrato and the phonograph', in *Capturing Sound: How Technology has Changed Music* (Berkeley: University of California Press, 2004), pp. 85–98. Some of Katz's other views are considered later.

recording is against him. Many cellists were using continuous vibrato well before the recording process could have significantly influenced performance (some examples are given below).[16]

In the period 1900–1930, recordings show a general overall trend towards the wider, ubiquitous vibrato that has been seen as a characteristic of modern string playing since the 1930s, when Tiffin and Seashore declared that 'at present nearly all string instrumental players use the vibrato'.[17] The reservations implied by the previously cited studies should be borne in mind throughout the following discussion.

With two exceptions, all the pre-1930 cello recordings in the Pearl anthology, in repertoire that would allow it (not, for instance, *moto perpetuo* showpieces such as Popper's *Elfentanz*), use constant vibrato. The two exceptions are William Whitehouse's *obbligato* in 'Sing me to sleep' (c.1907) and Heinrich Grünfeld's recording of Boccherini's *Minuet* (c.1927).[18] Whitehouse uses very little vibrato in general, other than at moments of particular expressive intensity. Grünfeld uses almost no vibrato, but the piece offers fewer opportunities for it. Two of Servais's pupils, Auguste van Biene and Josef Hollmann, made recordings. Van Biene's vibrato is unexceptional, unlike his portamento. It is quite narrow, almost continuous, and perhaps a little slower than that of his contemporaries.[19] Contributing factors could include van Biene's age and the particular requirements of his theatrical career, but it is quite similar to that of Hollmann, whose recording of Schumann's 'Träumerei' will be discussed later.[20]

Cellists recorded in the 1920s who use a narrower vibrato include Beatrice Harrison (1892–1965), Peter Muscant (1900–c.1988), Julius Klengel (1859–1933), Paul Grümmer (1879–1965) and Friedrich Buxbaum (1869–1948). These dates show that a narrower vibrato is used at this time by cellists whether in their 20s or in their 60s. It is not especially associated with older players. By contrast,

---

[16] Daniel Leech-Wilkinson pursues the weaknesses in Katz's thesis at greater length in *The Changing Sound of Music: Approaches to Studying Recorded Musical Performances*, published online only (London: Royal Holloway University, [2009]), http://www.charm. kcl.ac.uk/studies/chapters/intro.html, pp. 108–9 [accessed July 2012].

[17] Joseph Tiffin and Harold Seashore, 'Summary of established facts in experimental studies on the vibrato up to 1932', in Carl Seashore (ed.), *Vibrato*, p. 351.

[18] Edwin Greene, 'Sing me to sleep', William Whitehouse (vc), un-named pianist (Gramophone Company cat. no. 02090, matrix no. 1861f, 1907; *The Recorded Cello*, Vol. 1). Luigi Boccherini, *Minuet*, Heinrich Grünfeld (vc), un-named pianist (Electrola, cat. EG 724, c.1927; reissued *The Recorded Cello*, Vol. 2).

[19] Auguste van Biene, 'The Broken Melody' and 'Kol Nidri' [sic], van Biene (vc), un-named pianist (Zonophone, mat. Z-047851, cat. A60, c.1908?).

[20] See George Kennaway, 'The phenomenon of the cellist Auguste van Biene: From the Charing Cross Road to Brighton via Broadway', in M. Hewitt and R. Cowgill (eds), *Victorian Soundscapes Revisited*. Leeds Working Papers in Victorian Studies 9 (Leeds: LCVS and LUCEM, 2007), pp. 67–82.

Hermann Sandby's (1881–1965) vibrato is particularly wide in his recording of Sibelius's *Valse triste*, composed in 1903.[21] This undated recording was probably made before 1930, as after this date Sandby concentrated on composition.[22] His recording of the 'Berceuse' from *Jocelyn* shows a narrower, faster vibrato than is used in the Sibelius.[23] Victor Sorlin's (1878–1912) recordings of the popular favourites 'Evening Star' (from Wagner's *Tannhäuser*) and selections from *Madama Butterfly* also use vibrato differently. It is continuous in both cases, but in the Wagner the vibrato is slower and wider than in the Puccini.[24] Younger cellists such as Boris Hambourg (1885–1984), Maurice Maréchal (1892–1964) and Lauri Kennedy (1898–1985), recorded in the 1910s and 1920s, tend towards a constant, wider vibrato, but this is not by any means exclusive to younger players. The Estonian cellist August Karjus (1906–70) recorded in 1939 uses a fast, narrow, continuous vibrato, including a resonant sympathetic vibrato on the open G string as well.[25] This simple qualitative comparison shows that there is very little correlation between a player's age or 'school' and the type of vibrato they use – continuous/occasional, fast/slow, wide/narrow. If by the 1930s a more uniform picture emerges, it is therefore unlikely to be the result either of age or of the influence of a 'school'.

With portamento, differences between individual players are primarily a question of degree. Heinrich Grünfeld's (1855–1931) 1905 recording of Handel's *Largo* is interesting in that many of the portamenti he employs are similar to Grützmacher's – sliding to the first note of a phrase (sometimes across phrase boundaries), sliding to a high position on the D string, sliding both up and down.[26] Alexander Wierzbilowicz (1850–1911), in a 1904 recording of his teacher Davidoff's *Romance sans paroles*, frequently uses upward portamento, and

---

[21]   Sibelius, 'Valse triste' op. 44, Herman Sandby (vc), un-named pianist (Columbia, matrix WC 34, no. J20, n.d.; *The Recorded Cello*, Vol 1, CD 1).

[22]   The piece itself dates from 1903–04; this is possibly Sandby's own arrangement. See Claus Røllum-Larsen, *Impulser i Københavns koncertrepertoire 1900–1935* (Copenhagen: University of Copenhagen, Museum Tusculanum Press, 2002), Vol. 1, p. 201.

[23]   Benjamin Godard, 'Berceuse' from *Jocelyn*, Herman Sandby (vc), un-named pianist (Edison Blue Amberol no. 28220, [1915]). Online, URL: http://cylinders.library. ucsb.edu, cylinder no. 0544 [accessed July 2012].

[24]   Richard Wagner, 'Evening Star' ['O du mein holder Abendstern'] from *Tannhäuser*, Victor Sorlin (vc), un-named orchestra (Columbia Phonograph Company no. 1049 [1909]); http://cylinders.library.ucsb.edu, cylinder no. 6624. Puccini, *Madama Butterfly* (selections), Victor Sorlin (vc), un-named orchestra (Edison Amberol no. 818 [1911]); http://cylinders. library.ucsb.edu, cylinder no. 2084 [accessed July 2012].

[25]   Kadri Steinbach and Urve Lippus (eds), *Estonian Sound Recordings 1939* (Tallinn: Estonian Academy of Music and Theatre, 2009): CDs nos. 8 and 9. For a discussion of this interesting collection of recordings, see George Kennaway's review in *Fontes Artis Musicae*, 58 (2011), pp. 74–6.

[26]   George Frideric Handel, 'Largo' (*Serse*), Heinrich Grünfeld (vc), un-named pianist (Gramophone Concert Record G.C., matrix no. 19h, catalogue no. 47875x, Berlin, 1905).

somewhat less downward. His sliding is normally quite fast on wider intervals, and much slower and sometimes quite exaggerated on smaller ones, especially in the final bar of the piece.[27] William Whitehouse (1859–1935) uses frequent 'scooping' D string portamenti, and some downward portamenti, in his 1907 recording of the cello *obbligato* to 'Sing me to sleep' with the tenor Edward Lloyd.[28] Hugo Becker (1864–1941), in his own *Gavotte*, uses portamento, but this is a special, almost flirtatious, effect written into the piece and cannot be used as the basis for a generalization about his performing style.[29] The recordings by Hans Kronold (1871–1922), from 1905 to1913, of popular favourites such as *The Swan*, Handel's *Largo* and many others, all use considerable portamento within the phrase.[30] Indeed, Kronold uses portamento so often that its occasional absence over such tempting intervals as upward sixths comes almost as a surprise. His version of Chopin's *Nocturne* op. 9 no. 2 appears to use some of Servais's fingerings (see Chapter 4), although the recording quality is particularly poor.[31] What is clear, however, is that Kronold, like van Biene but unlike Wierzbilowicz, is quite prepared to slow down in order to accommodate portamento when it covers a wide interval.

The portamento of Auguste van Biene (1849–1913) is probably the most extreme of any cellist of the period, and the popularity of his signature piece *The Broken Melody* means that several recordings can be compared. These include his own and those by W.H. Squire (1871–1963), John Barbirolli (1899–1970), Beatrice Harrison (1892–1965), and Cedric Sharpe (1891–1978).[32] Van Biene's own recordings feature an almost continuous slow portamento, even across

---

[27]   Carl Davidoff, *Romance sans paroles*, Alexander Wierzbilowicz (vc), un-named pianist (Gramophone & Typewriter Co., matrix no. 201z, cat. no. 27886, 1904; reissued *The Recorded Cello*, Vol. 1).

[28]   Edwin Greene, 'Sing me to sleep', William Whitehouse (vc), un-named pianist.

[29]   Hugo Becker, *Gavotte*, Hugo Becker (vc), un-named pianist (Gramophone Company, cat. no. 048013, c.1908; reissued *The Recorded Cello*, Vol. 2). This is also true of Casals's 1925 recording of Hillemacher's *Gavotte tendre* (*Casals Encores and Transcriptions*, Vol. 1, Naxos 8.110972, track 2).

[30]   Handel, *Largo*, Hans Kronold (vc), un-named pianist (Edison Gold Moulded Record: 9987, 1908).

[31]   Chopin, *Nocturne*: Hans Kronold (vc), un-named pianist (Edison Gold Moulded Record 9637, [1907]), online at University of California, Santa Barbara Cylinder Preservation and Digitization Project, URL: http://cylinders.library.ucsb.edu [accessed July 2012].

[32]   Auguste van Biene, 'The Broken Melody': Auguste van Biene (vc), un-named pianist (Zonophone, mat. Z-047851, cat. A60, c.1908); Auguste van Biene (vc), un-named pianist (Edison Bell, mat. 3443, cat. 3355, 1912; reissued *The Recorded Cello*, Vol. 2); John Barbirolli (vc), Rose Barbirolli (pf) (Edison Bell, mat. 298k, cat. 2148, 1911; reissued *The Recorded Cello*, Vol. 2); Cedric Sharpe (vc) (HMV, cat. D436, mat. 07884, 1920); W.H. Squire (vc), un-named pianist (Columbia, mat. 3353, cat. L2127, 1928); Beatrice Harrison (vc), Margaret Harrison (pf) (HMV, matrix Cc14160-2, cat. C1626, 1929) (reissued *The Harrison Sisters: An English Music Heritage*, Harrison Sisters' Trust, Claremont GSE78/50/47).

intervals of a tenth played on one string, where, like Kronold, he will slow down in order to incorporate a particularly long slide. W.H. Squire uses nearly as much, and more than his own published edition of *The Broken Melody* indicates. John Barbirolli's 1911 recording has less portamento than van Biene's (in particular, he omits the downward glissando between the first two notes), though it is still prominent. In 1929 Beatrice Harrison uses much less portamento, and tends to release bow pressure at the same time. The opening downward portamento is treated lightly, and her upward portamento in this piece is often combined with a *diminuendo*. Compared with some other cellists, she is quite restrained, but not enough, in 1928, for the *Times*:

> Miss Beatrice Harrison [...] showed in all that the good opinions she has won abroad in recent tours are merited, for her playing, which was always highly finished, has now a greater breadth and power, The control of her bow, for instance, is ample to meet every demand of tone and dynamics with perfect evenness. But there is one mannerism which wants watching – excessive *portamento*.[33]

At around the same time, Joseph Hollmann's portamento was seen as old-fashioned and excessive:

> his intonation is sometimes a bit sketchy, and he has a greater fondness for the portamento than is nowadays generally admired.[34]

Hollmann did indeed tend towards a higher than average frequency of portamento, and a noticeable amount of vibrato, as his recording of Saint-Saëns' *Le cygne* shows.[35] In the 1920s, Cedric Sharpe used portamento mainly on shorter intervals, and though he used W.H. Squire's edition of *The Broken Melody* (significantly different in many respects from van Biene's own), he did not adopt Squire's notated portamenti. There is a sense in the 1920s that portamento is less in demand (similar criticisms of W.H. Squire are cited below). Nonetheless it is still very much present, and the clearer movement away from portamento was not to take place until the 1930s or even after the Second World War.[36] In this historical context, Piatigorsky's complete avoidance of portamento in the opening bars of his 1934 recording of the Schumann cello concerto is very striking – Casals's 1926

---

[33]   *Times*, 3 February 1928. Several other reviews from the 1920s refer to her performance mannerisms.

[34]   Richard Aldrich, 'The Philharmonic Society', *New York Times*, 10 November 1922.

[35]   Saint-Saens, *Le cygne*, Joseph Hollmann (vc), un-named pianist (Victor Record, Victor Talking Machine Co., Camden NJ, matrix no. 64046, 1906).

[36]   For a novel interpretation of the steep decline in the use of portamento from the mid-1940s onwards, in terms of its associations with motherhood and nostalgia, see Daniel Leech-Wilkinson, 'Portamento and musical meaning', *Journal of Musicological Research*, 25 (2006), pp. 233–61.

recording of his own transcription of Fauré's *Après un rêve*, opening with a similar rising fourth, uses considerable portamento.[37]

In the context of these recordings, one could suggest that the types of portamento notated by Grützmacher were still in use in at least the first decade of the twentieth century. But a range of practices is demonstrated that probably indicates a comparable range in the pre-recording period. Recordings also suggest that a more pervasive and intense portamento may be associated more with 'lighter' repertoire, but given a general lack of early recordings of 'serious' cello works, this point is hard to establish. The question of the influence of 'high art' performance on the 'popular' – or *vice versa* – is not at all clear. Piatti's restrained style clearly did not influence Auguste van Biene, even though they were colleagues.

In this respect, W. H. Squire's performances are particularly interesting. Before considering Squire's practice in recordings, and his recording of the Elgar cello concerto in particular, it will be useful to contextualize this in the light of his own performing editions. His *Fourth Violoncello Album* (1913) includes short pieces by Haydn, Bach, Chopin and Schumann ('Abendlied').[38] All the slower pieces are liberally marked with portamento (Examples 6.1 and 6.2).

Example 6.1   Haydn, Concerto in D, second movement, ed. Squire

Davidoff's portamenti in 'Abendlied' are quite similar to Squire's, but Squire's tempo indication is significantly slower, suggesting that his portamento would have been more pronounced.[39] Popper, on the other hand, is closer to Squire.[40] Like Becker and Casals, Squire sees a gavotte (in this case from Bach's D major Suite) as an occasion for an amusing portamento effect, which is applied to the opening phrase throughout the piece (Example 6.3).[41]

[37]   Schumann, *Cello Concerto* op. 129, Gregor Piatigorsky (vc), John Barbirolli (cond), London Philharmonic Orchestra (His Master's Voice, mat. B 6931-1, 6933-1, 6934-2, 6935-1, 6935-2, cat. DB 2244, 1934; reissued Naxos Historical, 8.111069, 2005); Fauré, *Après un rêve*, Pablo Casals (vc), Nikolai Mednikoff (pf) (Victor, mat. BE-31972-12, cat. 1083; Naxos Historical, *Casals Encores and Transcriptions*, Vol. 1, 8.110972, 2003).

[38]   W.H. Squire (ed.), *Fourth Violoncello Album* (London: Joseph Williams Limited, 1913).

[39]   R. Schumann, arr. Carl Davidoff, 'Abendlied' op. 85 no. 12 (Leipzig: Rahter, [1887]).

[40]   R. Schumann, arr. David Popper, 'Abendlied' op. 85 no. 12 (Offenbach: Johann André, 1896).

[41]   J.S. Bach, *Gavotte in D*, in W.H. Squire (ed.), *Second Violoncello Album* (London: Joseph Williams Limited, 1902), pp. 6–10.

Example 6.2   Schumann, 'Abendlied', arr. Squire, Davidoff, and Popper

Example 6.3   Bach, arr. Squire, Suite no. 6 in D, Gavotte

A similar effect occurs in Squire's recording of Dunkler's comical *Humoreske (Chanson à boire),* with much use of extravagant upward portamento over an octave or more to a high harmonic.[42] In Handel's *Largo* Squire uses portamento as a 'scoop' to a note on a lower string (whether of the same pitch or not), as

---

[42]   Handel, *Largo*, and Dunkler, *Humoreske (Chanson à boire)*, W. H. Squire (vc), Hamilton Harty (pf) (Columbia matrices 75851 and 75499, cat. no. L1201, 1928).

an approach to a harmonic, and in both directions. This recording was criticized specifically on these grounds when it was re-issued in 1928:

> A re-recording is of W. H. Squire playing Handel's 'Largo' and his own arrangement of Dunkler's Humoresque. It is late in the day to complain, but I cannot resist a grouse over some very un-Handelian harmonic weaknesses in the accompaniment. Moreover, Mr. Squire is over-fond of *portamento*. The humour in the Dunkler piece is of a very obvious type, and the musical interest is of the slightest.[43]

In Popper's 'Entrance to the Forest' Squire uses downward portamento liberally, often following it immediately with an upward slide.[44] However, it appears from a 1925 review that Squire may have altered his portamento style according to repertoire. Comparing his Brahms piano trio in E♭ op. 40, recorded with Arthur Catterall (vn) and William Murdoch (pf), with two sentimental cello pieces, 'Discus' observed:

> Mr. Squire is apparently a kind of musical Dr. Jekyll and Mr. Hyde. We heard Dr. Jekyll in the Brahms; here is Mr. Hyde in a couple of solos – a 'Hebridean Cattle Croon' and 'Home, sweet home'. The latter is about as sickly an affair as can be. I thought I knew all that the cello can do in the way of expressing nostalgia, but Mr. Squire manages to squeeze out a bit more, aided by lots of *portamento* and a very slow *tempo*. I hope next time there is solo recording to be done the player will be Dr. Jekyll.[45]

Such a distinction of performing style can also be heard in Squire's recordings of the Brahms Clarinet Trio op. 114 and his own *Meditation in C*. Both performances use the same type of heavy portamento, but compared with the *Meditation* the Brahms is fairly restrained.[46] Like Grützmacher, Squire seems to have had no inhibitions about repeated 'scooping' portamenti, as his arrangement of Bach's so-called 'Slumber Song' and of Schubert's 'Weigenlied' show (Examples 6.4 and 6.5).[47]

---

[43]   'Discus', 'Gramophone Notes', *MT*, 69 (1928), p. 813. The re-recording was on Columbia L2128.

[44]   David Popper, *Im Walde* op. 50 no. 1, 'Entrance to the Forest', W. H. Squire (vc), un-named pianist (Columbia, matrix no. AX 85, cat. no. L1497).

[45]   'Discus', *MT*, 66 (1925), p. 135.

[46]   Brahms, *Clarinet Trio in A minor* op. 114, Haydn Draper (cl), Sir Hamilton Harty (pf), W.H. Squire (vc) (Columbia, L 1609, 1925); W.H. Squire, *Meditation in C*, W.H. Squire (vc), un-named pianist (Columbia, L 1513, c.1928), reissued *Cello 2: The Definitive Collection of the 19th Century's Greatest Virtuosos* (Ongen Music, B0046PO87Q, 2010).

[47]   J.S. Bach, 'Schlafe, mein Liebster' (*Weihnacht-Oratorium*, pt. 2, no. 19), arr. W.H. Squire as 'Slumber Song', in *Transcriptions of Standard Vocal Works* (misc. eds), 2nd Series, no. 30 (London: Augener, 1906). F. Schubert, 'Weigenlied', arr. W. H. Squire, in ibid.

Example 6.4   Bach, arr. Squire, 'Slumber Song', conclusion

Example 6.5   Schubert, ed. Squire, 'Weigenlied'

Squire and Harrison: Elgar Cello Concerto

Squire's recording of the Elgar concerto uses portamento frequently, especially in the slow movement, and the slow section of the last movement. In 1931 this was seen as tasteless solution to a technical problem:

> We regret that work in popular spheres paid its toll on Mr. Squire's playing, and he makes too free a use of *portamento*, due, maybe, to the enormous leaps required of the soloist […] One wishes that Albert Sammons was a 'cellist as well as a violinist.[48]

As with *The Broken Melody*, it is possible to compare his practice with Beatrice Harrison's (Examples 6.6 and 6.7).[49]

Beatrice Harrison's Elgar is demonstrably more restrained than Squire's, as her portamenti in the slow movement show (in the following examples those marked with an asterisk are noticeably lighter in character). Squire and Harrison's portamenti differ considerably in terms of nuance and quantity, but this in turn is a consequence of Squire's much slower tempo. Elgar's metronome mark for the slow movement is ♪ = 50, suggesting an overall timing of around 3'36". Harrison, with Elgar conducting, is reasonably close to this as 4'1" (♪ = 45), but Squire is considerably slower, taking 4'43" (♪ = 38). For the whole concerto, Squire (27'36") is more than two minutes longer than Harrison (25'11"). The difference is almost entirely due to Squire's tempi in the slower music.

---

[48]   Anon., 'On the Records', *Musical Mirror and Fanfare*, 11 (1931), p. 25.

[49]   Elgar, *Cello Concerto in E minor* op. 85: W. H. Squire (vc), Sir Hamilton Harty (cond), Hallé Orchestra (Columbia DX117-120, 1930; LP transfer, Imprimatur IMP1, 1981); Beatrice Harrison (vc), Edward Elgar (cond), New Symphony Orchestra (His Master's Voice, D1507-1509, 1928; CD transfer, Naxos 8.111260, 2007).

Example 6.6 Elgar, Cello Concerto, third movement, with Squire's and Harrison's portamenti (Harrison's shown as dotted lines, and particularly delicate examples marked with an asterisk)

Example 6.7   Elgar, Cello Concerto, finale (conclusion), with Squire's and
               Harrison's portamenti

In the last movement, from three bars before rehearsal figure 67 to the end
(Example 6.7), Squire takes 4'08″ while Harrison takes 3'33″. Here, even more than
in the slow movement, Harrison's portamento is more nuanced than Squire's, and
sometimes so subtle that a simple qualitative transcription is difficult. It may be
that she links notes without shifting the hand, producing a 'pseudo-portamento'
effect by releasing or placing a finger slightly 'off-centre'. Harrison's 'non-shifting'
portamento may represent a more modern, less intense approach, than Squire's. This
passage in Harrison's recording attracted special praise in one review:

> Beatrice Harrison's solo work might well prove to be the greatest cello playing
> yet brought into the gramophone. [...] one of the great moments in modern
> music is that final 20- or 30-bar *pianissimo* which comes near the end of the last

movement, with the cello fading into silence upon a note of medium elevation; the present performance arrives there at its climax of beauty, as in the same place Elgar's genius arrives at its ultimate power of expression.[50]

Squire is quite different here, but less obviously so than in the slow movement. A simple count of the number of portamenti, including the more marginal cases in Harrison and allowing for a margin of error, shows that they use a very similar number (around 38). However, Harrison uses slightly more consecutive portamenti than Squire. She also uses more portamenti overall than Squire in the highly praised *pp* section, especially between rehearsal figures 71–72, although the slides in the final bars of this section are particularly subtle. So in the passage where Elgar finds 'the ultimate power of expression', it is Squire who is the more restrained in his portamento usage. On the other hand, Harrison uses no portamenti in the final *allegro molto*, while Squire uses the two portamenti that have since become almost universal practice (the second bar after 73 and the bar before 74). These two performances therefore resist simple categorization.

Comparison of recordings of Schumann's 'Träumerei' shows an even greater diversity of practice. Cello arrangements of this short piano piece (*Kinderszenen* op. 15 no. 7) were popular from the late nineteenth century onwards. Editions and recordings proliferated.[51] In the period 1904–30 at least ten recordings were made, by seven cellists: Heinrich Grünfeld, Hans Kronold, Rosario Bourdon, Josef Hollman, Victor Sorlin, Boris Hambourg and Pablo Casals (four times).[52] There were at least seven published arrangements in the period 1874–1913,

---

[50] Anon., 'Elgar's Cello Concerto', *British Musician and Musical News*, 5 (1929), p. 37.

[51] Another study of the same piece has compared 28 recordings by 24 pianists, but in the period 1929–90. Bruno Repp, 'Diversity and commonality in music performance: An analysis of timing microstructure in Schumann's "Träumerei"', *Journal of the Acoustical Society of America*, 92 (1992), pp. 2546–68.

[52] Heinrich Grünfeld (vc), un-named pianist (The Gramophone Company Ltd, matrix G.C.-47876x, 1903); Hans Kronold (vc), un-named pianist (Edison, no. 9149, 1905; http://cylinders.library.ucsb.edu [accessed July 2012]); Victor Sorlin (vc), Victor Orchestra (Victor Talking Machine Co. Camden, NJ, matrix 4845, 1906); Rosario Bourdon (vc), un-named orchestra (Victor Talking Machine Co, Camden, NJ, issue no. 4845, matrix B3485, 1906; http://amicus.collectionscanada.ca [accessed July 2012]); Josef Hollman (vc), un-named pianist (Victor talking Machine Co., matrix C-3026-1, 1906); Boris Hambourg (vc), Grace Smith (pf) (Victor Talking Machine Co., Camden NJ, issue no. 60065, 1911; http://amicus.collectionscanada.ca [accessed July 2012]); Pablo Casals (vc), un-named orchestra (Columbia, matrix 37252, issue no. A5679, 1915; The Recorded Cello Vol. 1); Casals, Walter Golde (pf) (reissued Naxos Historical, *Great Cellists – Casals Encores and Transcriptions*, Vol. 4, 8.110986, 2005); Casals, Nicolai Mednikoff (pf) (Victor, matrix no. BE-34075-1, no. 1178, 1926; reissued Naxos Historical, *Great Cellists – Casals Encores and Transcriptions*, Vol. 1, 8.110972, 2003; Casals, Otto Schulhof (pf) (HMV, matrix B♭ 19018-1, no. DA833, 1930; reissued Naxos Historical, *Great Cellists – Casals Encores and Transcriptions*, Vol. 2, 8.110976, 2004).

some by cellists such as Grützmacher, Goltermann and Davidoff, and others by less familiar figures. It is not possible to identify the transcription used in any particular recording, apart from Josef Hollman's. He is the only cellist to use one of Grützmacher's two arrangements, in which the piece is transposed up a fourth to B♭ and five bars are completely recomposed; Hollman also changes one note himself.[53] In any case, the piece is easy to adapt for the cello, and it is quite possible that some of the cellists who recorded it made their own versions. Apart from Hollman's, all these recordings are in the original key. The parallel text (Example 6.8) shows differences of portamento and phrasing, and Table 6.1 summarizes some general statistics. Asterisks mark portamenti unique to one recording.

These performances are all, internally, highly consistent, even regarding phrasing and *rubato*; each cellist nearly always plays the same material in the same way each time it recurs. However, they differ from each other quite considerably.

'Träumerei' – Portamento

Victor Sorlin's portamento is the most extreme of the nine. Even though he omits the first repeat of bars 1–8, he still manages to include 51 portamenti in 24 bars, and therefore it follows that most of the unique portamenti are his. He also combines longer sequences of successive portamenti than any other cellist here. Thus, when he stops using portamento (bar 23) its very absence attracts attention, becoming an expressive device in itself. Sorlin also uses portamento combined with a change of bow much more often than any of the others.

Between them, the earlier recordings cover almost every portamento possibility, which explains why Casals finds only one new one, in one recording – the small 'scoop' to the second a' in bar 22 (1926). Otherwise, Casals uses portamento significantly less than in the earlier recordings, even though it appears very noticeable to modern ears. In this context, it is not only more restrained, but more imaginative. The contrast is especially clear at the end of bar 3, where Hambourg's in particular is very prominent and Casals only adds a small scoop (1915 and 1930). 'Scooping', either to a repeated note, or from below to a lower note, is generally the least used type of portamento here, with only a few examples from Sorlin and Casals. However, Casal's versions explore different possibilities. The two

---

[53]   Grützmacher's other arrangement, in G major, is relatively conservative by his standards: F. Grützmacher (arr.), *Ausgewählte Compositionen von Robert Schumann* (Leipzig: C.F. Peters, [1873]). His version in B♭ was published the following year: F. Grützmacher (arr.), Kinderscenen (Leipzig: Breitkopf & Härtel, [1874]). Other arrangements include those by: G. Goltermann, *Morceaux Célèbres* (Leipzig, London, etc.: Bosworth & Co., n.d.); David Popper (Hamburg: Rahter, [1884]); C.E. Lowe (London: Weekes & Co, [1884]); Carl Yu Davidoff (Offenbach: André, [1887]); Henry Farmer (London, J. Williams, 1892); H. Samuel (London: Augener, [1907]); G.J. Trinkaus (New York: M. Witwark & Sons, 1913).

Table 6.1 'Träumerei', comparisons of tempo, portamento and vibrato (Kronold and Sorlin omit the repeat of bars 1–8)

Year, performer (dates; age)	Total duration	Av. MM (crotchet)	Total portamenti	Average portamenti/bar	Vibrato (general type)
1903 Heinrich Grünfeld (1855–1931; 48)	2'50"	45.5	39	1.2	Only on some longer notes; after portamento
1905 Hans Kronold (1872–1922; 33)	1'56"	50.2	38	1.6	Narrow; often none
1906 Rosario Bourdon (1885–1961; 21)	2'53"	44.4	35	1.1	Narrow; often none; used at highlights
1906 Josef Hollmann (1852–1927; 54)	3'47"	34.1	58	1.8	Continuous
1908 Victor Sorlin (1878–1912; 30)	3'07"	31.1	51	2.1	Nearly continuous; wide; slow
1911 Hambourg (1885–1984; 26)	2'50"	45.5	38	1.2	Often wide; much less on quavers
1915 Pablo Casals (1876–1973; 39)	2'59"	43.2	27	0.8	Sometimes none; narrow; moderate speed
1916 Pablo Casals (40)	3'16"	38.3	32	1	Constant; medium–wide; constant speed
1926 Pablo Casals (50)	3'14"	39.9	30	0.9	Continuous; narrow; moderate speed
1930 Pablo Casals (54)	3'16"	39.9	31	1.0	Continuous; narrow; medium–fast

Example 6.8   Schumann, 'Träumerei', parallel comparison of recordings

expressive highlights of the piece (the dissonant $e\flat'$ in bar 10 and the melodic peak on a'' in bar 22) are treated quite differently. In 1915 he uses a portamento in bar 10, but not in 1926, and in 1930 he reinstates it but in a much more subtle way. He experiments even more at bar 22, with a full portamento and a slur to the first a' (1915 and 1916), separate bows and a scoop to the second a' (1926), and separate bows with no portamento (1930).

Portamento does not in itself lead to slower tempi. Sorlin's extremely slow timing is not primarily due to his portamento, as in general he does not additionally slow down at such places. Rather, it results from his extreme interpretation of the *ritardando* marked in most arrangements in bar 22, and the additional pauses and *molto rit.* that he adds to the final two bars. The more portamento-rich versions by Kronold and Hambourg do not result in slow tempi overall, even when a slow portamento takes time. Kronold prolongs high notes, and adds a heavy *ritardando* in bar 16. He also applies an almost destabilizing *tenuto* to the third note of the theme wherever this phrase occurs, shortens the second note (almost a crotchet in bar 9, which becomes in effect almost a $\frac{3}{4}$ bar), delaying and then speeding up the following two quavers (Example 6.9).

Example 6.9   Kronold, approximate notation of *rubato*

Nonetheless, Kronold is positively brisk overall. Hambourg's *rubato* balances faster phrases with *tenuto*. He accelerates strongly through the rising quaver phrase in bars 1–2, but prolongs the minim every time. But he also uses longer phrases; typically, where Casals plays with two or three quavers per bow, Hambourg plays with four or more, sometimes playing the equivalent of a bar in one bow (bars 3–4).

'Träumerei' – Vibrato

The three earliest recordings are extremely restrained in their use of vibrato, with virtually none in Grünfeld's case. When it is used, it is invariably narrow. Kronold's vibrato is only noticeable at a few places, such as in bars 6 (a'), 7 ($e'\flat$), or 14 ($b'\flat$). Sometimes his vibrato appears randomly applied, such as at the d' in the final bar, but this may be consistent with his tendency to introduce extreme agogic *rubato* combined with vibrato. In the recordings before 1910, two cellists use a continuous vibrato, Hollman and Sorlin. At the age of 54, Hollman is much older than the other pre-war cellists from this period considered here – he was a pupil of Servais, whose vibrato gave such offence to Pavel Makarov. However, Hollman was 14 when Servais died in 1866, so it is hard to say for how long Servais's influence might have persisted, even if he did normally use frequent vibrato. Sorlin's pronounced, continuous vibrato is exceptional in this group of recordings, but it is quite similar to that of the Danish cellist Herman Sandby, probably recorded only a few years later. Hambourg uses a prominent vibrato on longer notes in general, particularly at melodic peaks, but little or none on shorter or less melodically significant longer notes – there is almost no vibrato in the two final bars. The issue of consistency of tone colour when a phrase includes open strings or harmonics arises far less in Kronold's case because he uses little vibrato and no harmonics, and avoids open strings. Hambourg might appear to be using Alexanian's method and minimizing the vibrato on the neighbouring notes.

Casals's vibrato is generally quite narrow, but it becomes a little more prominent at melodic peaks, especially those that are prolonged, such as bars 2, 6, or 14. After a harmonic he generally uses much less vibrato for the next few notes, and the open A string used in the first phrase in his 1915 recording is normally played throughout in a context of less vibrato. At around the same time, Kathleen Parlow's recording of the slow movement of the Mendelssohn Violin Concerto makes no such modification, so that the a″ harmonic and the open A string in the opening bars stand out very clearly as non-vibrated notes.[54] At times in 1915 Casals enhances an expressive note with portamento but not vibrato, unlike Grünfeld, whose few vibrated notes often occur after a portamento. Vibrato in the 1926 and 1930 recordings is more consistent. However, the 1926 version avoids the local expression on prominent notes found in 1915, generally intensifying the vibrato for passages of harmonic interest such as in bars 9–12, but not, for example making a special vibrato effect for the dissonant e′♭ minim in bar 10. Casals in 1930 uses a more intensified vibrato, especially in bars 13–15, where the extra expression even risks distorting the tone on the high b′♭. He also uses more vibrato in the final two bars even though there are several d′ harmonics and here there is no attempt to conceal the change in timbre. In these respects, then, Alexanian's description of vibrato being moderated in the vicinity of an open string to avoid a change in timbre corresponds quite closely with Casals's practice in 1915 (that is, around the time that Alexanian was writing), but less so in 1930.

'Träumerei' – Bowing/Phrasing

Although this chapter is chiefly concerned with vibrato and portamento, the topic of bowing and phrasing is not irrelevant, as these recordings differ noticeably in the use of portamento across changes of bow or phrase-boundaries. Given that this piece is played entirely *legato*, some recordings can present difficulties when trying to determine the bowing used. Apart from some cellists' technical superiority in concealing bow changes, surface noise can also obscure an otherwise audible

---

[54] Mendelssohn, *Violin Concerto* (slow movement), Kathleen Parlow (vn), un-named orchestra (Columbia Graphophone Co., matrix 48665, no. A5843, 1916); http://amicus.collectionscanada.ca [accessed October 2012].

change of bow. The latter is certainly the case in Grünfeld's version, where it is hard to tell whether he is varying the phrasing on the repeat of bars 1–8. The bowing slurs indicated in the parallel text above are based solely on the aural evidence, and no attempt has been made to normalize them in order, for example, to enable down-bows on the most likely notes, or to ensure enough bow space for longer phrases. Nonetheless, some elements are clear. Whereas Schumann's original version and nearly all the published cello arrangements use long phrase-marks or bowing slurs, most of the recordings use quite short bowing slurs. Typically, quavers are grouped in pairs, apart from the three upbeat quavers in bar 1 or bar 6 (*et sim.*). Hambourg sometimes groups in fours, as in the second and third beats of bar 3 and bar 19. Sorlin is the only cellist to use clearly asymmetrical phrasing (bars 3 and 13–14). Grünfeld, Sorlin and Hambourg all use the much longer slur in bars 1/2. However, Sorlin is less consistent here, while Grünfeld and Hambourg generally agree.

From this point of view, Casals's 1926 recording is particularly interesting. His first and last recordings of 'Träumerei' generally agree in phrasing, but in 1926 he experiments with a very clear articulation when playing with separate bows, something none of the other cellists considered here employ – Casals is the only cellist to use separate bows in bar 3. Given the recording quality, it is hard to be certain, but the bow-changes in bars 3 and 10, seem to be combined with what sounds like a more energetic, percussive left-hand action. The combination of the two may constitute what Casals termed 'syllabic diminuendo'. He himself never described this technique in print, but something related to it appears in Alexanian in the context of louder dynamics ('attacks should be reinforced by finger-accents [...] by the withdrawal or striking of the fingers of the left hand').[55]

*   *   *

The range of practices documented in these recordings is striking. While there is an overall change in performing style over this period, it is hard to specify exactly where it occurs. From this point of view it would be fascinating were it possible to compare Grünfeld's 1903 recording with his currently untraceable filmed performance from 1928.[56] Even defining the rough limits of the watershed

---

[55]   Dinan Alexanian, trans. Frederick Fairbanks, *Traité théorique et pratique du violoncelle* (Paris: Mathot, 1922), p. 95. Several of Casals's pupils describe it, principally Christopher Bunting, 'The Syllabic Diminuendo', in *Essay on the Craft of Cello Playing*, 2 vols. (Cambridge: Cambridge University Press, 1982), Vol. 1, pp. 90–95. It is also noted by M. Clynes, 'Expressive microstructure in music, linked to living qualities', in J. Sundberg (ed.), *Studies in Music Performance* (Stockholm: Royal Swedish Academy of Music, 1983), p. 79.

[56]   A three-minute documentary film entitled *Professor Heinrich Grünfeld spielt Träumerei von Schumann*, made by Tobis-Industrie GmbH (Berlin), was passed by the censor in January 1929. See http://www.filmportal.de [accessed July 2012]. No German film archive has a print.

is not easy. In the period under discussion, for example, it is tempting to describe recorded performances in terms of 'old' and 'modern' styles – 'modern' connoting constant wider vibrato and very little portamento, and 'old' connoting occasional narrow vibrato and a considerable amount of portamento. This is very much the approach taken by Mark Katz. In the course of his argument that the 'modern' vibrato was mainly a product of the emerging recording industry, he frequently talks of the old and the new:

> Early twentieth-century recordings of solo violinists corroborate the shift from the old to the new vibrato. [...] After 1920 the new vibrato is apparent in the recordings of most violinists.[57]

While in overall terms it is true that the vibrato of the 1930s is generally a very different thing from that of the 1900s, Katz's claim that the principal force behind this change was the requirements of the recording industry is somewhat one-sided. He cites several examples of continued criticism of the 'new' vibrato as evidence that its adoption was not due to changed aesthetic priorities, but understates the often-criticized prevalence of vibrato among singers in the later nineteenth century, and there is a general lack of a broad historical context for his study. The few later dissenting voices cited by Katz, objecting to 'modern' vibrato, such as Hans Keller, were in fact marginal. Katz also suggests that recordings made players and listeners more aware of imperfect intonation that was then concealed with a heavier vibrato. While this could be ascertained scientifically, vibrato does not in fact work in this way – an out-of-tune note with vibrato is just that.

Recordings that manifest differences in performing styles do not necessarily represent a clash of the 'old' and the 'new'. Timothy Day describes the performance of Bach's concerto for two violins by Arnold Rosé and his daughter Alma in precisely these terms.[58] Rosé *père* uses frequent portamenti and very restrained vibrato, while Alma uses fewer, and lighter, portamenti and more frequent vibrato, so in general terms the 'old'/'modern' distinction appears plausible. However, the clash is as much one of levels of ability as of different performing styles. Alma's intonation is occasionally suspect, and there are rhythm and tempo fluctuations, as distinct from *rubato*, which could explain Arnold Rosé's insistent clarifying accentuation. If Alma's vibrato is rather more apparent that Arnold's, it still could not be called extreme, and there are many cases, especially in the second movement, where the two have clearly agreed to be consistent with portamento. Similarly, the Kreisler-Zimbalist recording of the same work, while clearly performed by two

---

[57]   Mark Katz, *Capturing Sound: How Technology has Changed Music* (Berkeley: University of California Press, 2004), p. 87.

[58]   Timothy Day, *A Century of Recorded Music Listening to Musical History* (New Haven and London: Yale University Press, 2000), p. 144. Bach, *Double Concerto in D Minor*, Arnold and Alma Rosé (vns), (Czech HMV mat. CA 43/47, 1929; reissued *Arnold Rosé and the Rosé String Quartet*, Biddulph Recordings LAB 056-57, 1992).

individual soloists of different generations, does not present problematic stylistic incompatibilities.[59] Indeed, when Kreisler and Ysaÿe played the same work in New York in 1905, the *New York Times* reviewer noted the differences between their playing styles in music that would seem to require complete unanimity of approach, but acknowledged that this did not seriously spoil his enjoyment.

> both Mr. Ysaÿe and Mr. Kreisler have shown sympathy with Bach's music and have interpreted it with authority and amplitude of style, but with a different personal equation. [...] the difference of their artistic individualities was always considerably in evidence. It was nevertheless a performance that gave great pleasure through the many superb qualities it showed.[60]

In the 'Träumerei' recordings, it is the youngest player, Rosario Bourdon, who uses a narrow vibrato at expressive highlights in a way entirely consistent with nineteenth-century practice. Recorded in the same year, Joseph Hollman, at more than twice Bourdon's age, is using a warm continuous vibrato that we might now recognize as 'modern'. Distinct playing styles, with many individual nuances, co-existed for some time in the early recording period, and almost certainly before this. Some cellists used vibrato and portamento in ways that had their roots earlier in the nineteenth century – a light, narrow, fast vibrato applied ornamentally to longer notes, and a range of portamenti as notated in Grützmacher's performing editions from the 1860s onwards. But others did things differently.

This more synchronic, less diachronic, view, could suggest a slightly different conclusion from that reached by David Milsom in his study of early violin recordings:

> The main contrast, then, is between the slight vibrato of the older generation, and the slower and possibly wider vibrato of players such as Hubay. Indeed, Hubay and Drdla seem to represent an important gestational phase in vibrato development, providing a link with the sound-world familiar to modern ears.[61]

For Milsom, there is enough contrast between generations of violinists to justify this diachronic view, and he can speak confidently of the 'clear delineation of players in the 'Franco-Belgian' and the 'German' schools.[62] But the case of the cello suggests that a diachronic analysis in terms of 'schools' of playing, through which influences are transmitted, may have a more limited application. The Russian Wierzbilowicz (aged 54), recorded in 1904 playing Davidoff's *Chanson sans paroles*, was a product of the 'Russian school', and he was strongly associated

---

[59]   Bach, *Concerto in D minor for Two Violins*, Fritz Kreisler and Efrem Zimbalist (vns) (HMV DB 587, matrix 2-07918, 1915; reissued *Great Violinists – Kreisler*, Naxos Historical 8.110922, n.d.). In 1915 Kreisler was 40, Zimbalist 25.

[60]   'Ysaye and Kreisler Play', *New York Times*, 14 March 1905, p. 6.

[61]   Milsom, *Late Nineteenth-Century Violin Performance*, p. 141.

[62]   Ibid., p. 143.

with the violinist Auer both as a pupil and later as a chamber music colleague.[63] Yet Wierzbilowicz's near continuous vibrato and his frequent portamenti clearly conflict with Auer's stern warnings about the over-use of both:

> In any case, remember that only the most sparing use of the *vibrato* is desirable; the too generous employment of the device defeats the purpose for which you use it. The excessive *vibrato* is a habit for which I have no tolerance […] the *portamento* should be employed only when the melody is descending, save for certain very exceptional cases of ascending melody. […] it is the easiest thing in the world to turn this simplest of expressive means into caricature merely by dragging the finger slowly from one tone to the other […].[64]

Another of Davidoff's pupils, Carl Fuchs (who acknowledged his debt to his teacher nearly as often as did Whitehouse vis-à-vis Piatti), uses a rather less obvious vibrato than Wierzbilowicz and considerably less portamento in the movements by Tricklir in Fuchs's only surviving recording.[65] Even allowing for the contrasting character of these pieces, Fuchs has more in common with Whitehouse, and probably Piatti, than with Wierzbilowicz, even though they shared the same Russian teacher. Here, his time in England (he lived there almost continually from 1888) is more significant than his pedagogical descent from Cossmann and Davidoff. In fact, it is hard to generalize about an Auer or indeed a Ševčík 'school', given the wide range of practice evident in their pupils:

> Auer's pupils included not only Zimbalist and Dushkin, who adhered to the traditional, selective use of vibrato as described by Auer, but also players with a more modern view of vibrato, including Elman and, especially, Heifetz […]. Similar inconsistency is found in Ševčík's pupils. These included Jan Kubelík and Marie Hall, who used vibrato sparingly, and Rudolf Kolisch and Wolfgang Schneiderhan, who used continuous vibrato in the modern way. According to Flesch, Hubay's pupils tended to have 'too slow and broad a vibrato'. But Lener's vibrato was much broader and slower than that of Szigeti or d'Aranyi, and they all studied with Hubay. To make matters even more confusing, Hubay had studied under Joachim.[66]

If a synchronic view preserves the diversity of practice at any one time (or relatively narrow time-period) at the expense of a grand narrative, it does at

---

[63]   Carl Davidoff, 'Romance sans paroles', Alexander Wierzbilowicz (vc), un-named pianist (Gramophone & Typewriter Co., matrix 201z, cat. 27886, 1904; reissued *The Recorded Cello*, Vol. 1, CD 2).

[64]   Leopold Auer, *Violin Playing as I Teach It* (New York: Frederick Stokes, [1921]; repr. New York: Dover Publications, 1980), pp. 22–3.

[65]   J.B.Tricklir, Adagio and Rondo, Carl Fuchs (vc), un-named pianist (HMV private recording, matrix 2B4795-1, c.1930; reissued *The Recorded Cello*, Vol. 2, CD 2).

[66]   Robert Philip, *Early Recordings*, p. 104.

least enable simple similarities of style to be seen without the pre-suppositions inherent in terms such as 'the Russian school', the 'German school', 'old', or 'modern'. Exactly how this diversity was replaced by an increasing international standardization in succeeding decades lies beyond the scope of this study, but at least in the first decade of the twentieth century, no style can be clearly privileged above any other. Both Whitehouse's very restrained vibrato and Wierzbilowicz's quite extreme *rubato* were eventually to disappear. What is characteristic of the early recording period as a whole is the diversity of practice, a diversity that, it can reasonably be inferred, was present in earlier decades as well.

The whole discussion of the use and abuse of expressive devices such as portamento and vibrato takes place within what John Potter has called 'the historical ideology of disciplined restraint'.[67] This might be expressed in terms of a 'discourse of expressivity', a 'discourse' that delimits the scope of a topic and controls what is said within these limits, closely allied in this case to the wider discourse of sexuality and the body in the nineteenth century. This may provide a theoretical context for the increasingly *ex cathedra* character of warnings against excess, such as Joachim's:

> This explanation is very important because a clear understanding of the meaning and origin of portamento will be the best means of preventing the pupil from misusing the effect. [...] even when such places are marked glissando or something similar, the use of the portamento must never overstep the limits of the beautiful and degenerate into a whine, as if the intention were to caricature the peculiarities of certain wandering street musicians. [...] The main point is that the pupil should assimilate the counsel given above, and that he should endeavour to train his taste and judgment by frequent comparison of right with wrong, of what is natural with what is affected. [...] the pupil cannot be sufficiently warned against the habitual use of the tremolo, especially in the wrong place. A violinist whose taste is refined and healthy will always recognise the steady tone as the ruling one, and will use the vibrato only where the expression seems to demand it.[68]

Those musicians and critics who so frequently warn about the dangers of excessive expressivity in performance constitute members of a discourse community, entry to which requires the conventional use of certain terms and concepts as well as a basic grasp of appropriate language. Thus, in the case of British music criticism of this period, one finds 'outsiders' – foreigners, or journalists for lower-class newspapers – being roundly mocked for their excessive language, ignorance, or bad taste. There are many cases such as the *Harmonicon*'s disdainful treatment of the *Herald*'s enthusiasm for Max Bohrer (see Chapter 3), but perhaps the most striking

---

[67]   John Potter, 'Beggar at the door: The rise and fall of portamento in singing', *Music & Letters*, 87 (2006), p. 528.

[68]   Joseph Joachim and Andreas Moser, trans. Alfred Moffat, *Violinschule*, 3 vols. (Berlin: Simrock, 1905), Vol. 2, pp. 92–6.

is the *Musical World*'s fit of hysterics at an 1847 American review of Paganini's pupil Camillo Sivori (1815–94), a very long article much abbreviated here:[69]

> As a pendent [sic] to the specimens of American criticism on musical matters which we have already cited [...] we insert the following, *apropos* of our excellent little friend, Camillo Sivori, whose success in the new world appears to be prodigious. It is from the *Daily Picayne* [Picayune] a paper printed at New Orleans, and is signed, 'An Amateur'.
>
> 'To criticise with an unprejudiced mind the sterling worth of an artist [...] *the critic must know something of the art*' – (No! surely?) – 'both as regards its theory and practice [...] The musical world of New Orleans has been recently roused from its comparative state of lethargy by the soul-stirring strains of the LION OF INSTRUMENTS in the hands of the IMMORTAL PAGANINI'S SIVORI [...] When grasped by the Herculean arm of its "Sivori", who by the ARTIST-FINISHED SWEEP (!) of his bow, produces such a SIMULTANEOUS CRASH OF HARMONY (!!!) variegated with a BRILLIANT LIGHTNING DESCENT OF STACCATOED SOUNDS (!!!!) we fairly become bewildered [...] we can almost imagine TEARS OOZE FROM EACH SOFTLY *VIBRATO'D* NOTE (!!!) and our *tender* heart-strings reverberate from their sympathetic effect. [...] when he has played you all his pieces once and recommences THE DYNAMIC, THE RHYTHM OF EVERY NOTE IS INVARIABLY THE SAME, proving that he has depended more upon the contracted rules laid down to him by his masters, than on his genius'.[70]

The *Musical World* highlights in capitals and italics all the most 'excessive' expressions, adding exclamations in parentheses, and concludes:

> What this verbose 'bosh' signifies, we leave it to our American readers to explain. We confess our inability to comprehend a word of it. Nevertheless, it is a good advertisement for our friend Sivori.[71]

In fact, even as quoted, the article appears to make several reasonable points, such as Sivori's lack of innate genius, and the dangers of excessive fame for virtuosi such as Ole Bull. But the *Musical World* prefers to draw attention to the idiosyncratic language of a naïve American amateur who cannot see the absurdity of tears oozing from notes played with vibrato. More surprisingly, however, the article 'quoted' in the *Musical World* appears to have been substantially, if not wholly, invented. In the period January–July 1847 (July being the month of the *Musical World* article) the *Daily Picayune* published programme details for seven concerts by Sivori between 10 February and 12 April, but only one review:

---

[69]   Anon., 'Yankee Criticism Again', *MW*, 22 (1847), pp. 455–6.

[70]   Ibid., p. 456. All emphases – italicization and the use of upper-case – are as the original.

[71]   Ibid.

> We had the pleasure of hearing Sivori for the first time, last evening at the Orleans Theatre, and were delighted with his playing. We are scarcely versed enough in music to pronounce in his favour, with the recollection of other noted artists who have visited this country, and cannot say whether he excels them or not. Certain are we, however, that he is a splendid player [...] there is an inspiration about his manner of playing, combined with the greatest modesty, that enhances the pleasure one experiences in the delicious music he produces. His whole soul seems wrapped in his instrument, and he brings forth from it the softest and most melodious sounds, as if they were indeed the harmonious language of the soul. His bowing is easy and graceful, and there is firmness about it, even in the most delicate touches, that creates a confidence in his ability.[72]

It may be that, not content with mocking an apparently over-written review, the contributor to the *Musical World* actually invented the article for humorous effect. If true, this pastiche could be seen as an attempt to protect a discourse from outside influence, in the context of a post-colonial need to reassert the superiority of the British over the upstart Americans.

But discourse does not simply mean a one-sided exercise of power. A 'discourse of expressivity' need not work solely as a setting of a restriction by critics or teachers of particularly high status. In the case of musical performance, one might argue that performance itself constitutes a competing discourse with different, opposed, boundaries and permissions.[73] Evidence of early cello recordings shows that portamento was used freely until at least the late 1920s, and that vibrato was generally in use from the start – but more importantly, both expressive devices varied considerably in their application. Performers who choose to apply historical findings to their playing will therefore find here, as with the more technical aspects of cello playing in the long nineteenth century, a range of performing practices that, if generalized ('Use some vibrato, some portamento, and some rubato'), become merely superficial, and, if particularized ('Play like Bourdon'), turn the performer into a ventriloquist. A discursive perspective should reassure the historically-aware player that their performance will, whatever their expressive choices, occupy a point on the spectrum between the restraint of Joachim or Auer and the apparent excess of Hans Kronold. Going further, the apparent tension between practice and prescription is a particular case of more fundamental trope of control and resistance that is also manifested in, for example, attitudes towards the relation of music and words in opera, and ultimately in tensions between conflicting gender identities. It is this topic that will be discussed next.

---

[72]   Anon., 'Concert of Sivori', *Daily Picayune*, 11 February 1847, p. 2.

[73]   This approach is explored at greater length in George Kennaway, 'Do as some said, or as most did? – a Foucauldian experiment with nineteenth-century HIP', *Current Musicology*, 92 (2011), pp. 7–29.

Chapter 7
The Manly Cello?

Studies of historical performance practices generally rely on the types of source materials used in previous chapters: instrumental treatises, reviews, pictures, early recordings or printed music. This material is indispensable, but it focuses our attention on, so to speak, means rather than ends, and leaves the study of older performance practices without a cultural context. There are ideas circulating about the cello and its music in the nineteenth century that have wider implications and that require a wider range of sources to substantiate, which can have as direct a connection to concrete performing decisions as scale fingerings, posture, the shape of Romberg's left hand or Grützmacher's portamento markings. Some of these ideas concern the perceived gendered identity of the cello. Although this is interesting for a number of reasons, it will be pursued in this and the following chapter because ultimately it has implications for reception and performance, and it may also suggest ways in which 'historically informed performance' could move in new directions.

There is a very large literature on gender and music (and not only in nineteenth-century musicology), such as studies of music in relation to women and the domestic sphere, or representations of the feminine in music itself. Considerations of space prevent me from rehearsing this now musicologically mainstream material here.[1] Nowadays such topics no longer provoke the heated debate that first greeted the work of McClary, Citron, or Solie. But the historiography of performance practices has remained particularly and peculiarly impervious to discussions of these questions, as it has to the general interaction of critical theory and musicology that has so diversified the academic study of music in modern times. Performance practice research has, indeed, remained predominantly positivist and even pragmatic in its methodology. At a time when so much of this work remains to be done this is entirely understandable. But equally, studies that show how music engages with gender or desire have avoided discussing actual performances in any detail, even though performing choices can crucially obscure, distort or completely redirect the claimed gendered characteristics of the material performed. A few examples will illustrate this point.

---

[1]   See Susan McClary, *Feminine Endings Music, Gender, and Sexuality* (Minneapolis, MN and London: Minnesota University Press, 1992); Marcia Citron, *Gender and the Musical Canon* (Cambridge: Cambridge University Press, 1993); Ruth A. Solie (ed.), *Musicology and Difference: Gender and Sexuality in Music Scholarship* (Berkeley: University of California Press, 1995); Jeffrey Kallberg, 'Gender', *Grove Music Online*.

Andrew Dell'Antonio's intricate and wholly persuasive discussion of the representation of desire in the instrumental sonatas of Dario Castello only briefly cites two recorded performances, finding fault with both as in various ways not conforming to his view of this repertoire.[2] The centrality of the sensual friction of the melodic parts, for which he makes an excellent case, has immediate implications for performance. Sensual friction is central to the very production of sound from bowed string instruments, and there are techniques for intensifying or minimizing its effect, but this practical dimension is not discussed. Marcia Citron's ground-breaking analysis of the implicit critique of gender codes in Chaminade's Piano Sonata op. 21 makes no reference to the effect of performance.[3] When Edward Cone suggested that the 'incorrigibly feminine' dimension of Chopin's A major Polonaise could be concealed by a very specific performance of the cross-rhythms in its concluding bars, Susan McClary's critique was directed towards a conclusion, entirely justified in itself, about masculinizing tendencies in musical analysis. But it did not explore the possibility that the enactment of gender tropes in Western art music might depend to a significant degree on the manner of performance of the works in question.[4] In a similar vein, her account of the floating tonalities of the second movement of Schubert's 'Unfinished' symphony is not offered as a suggested manner of performance; the 'illusion of drifting' she finds is not dependent on, say, the clarity or otherwise of the articulation of the woodwind entries.[5] Suzanne Cusick's exploration of applications of Judith Butler's ideas to music, wondering 'how vocal performance in late twentieth-century North America might be understood to perform sex and gender' with reference to Francesca Caccini's *Primo libro delle musiche* (1618) does not, in fact, consider how this music might be, literally, *performed*.[6]

---

[2]   Andrew Dell'Antonio, 'Construction of desire in early Baroque instrumental music', in Todd M. Borgerding (ed.), *Gender, Sexuality and Early Music* (New York and London: Routledge, 2002), pp. 199–226 (p. 221).

[3]   Citron, *Gender and the Musical Canon*, pp. 145–64. The difficulty of applying a simple gendered approach to sonata-form themes in the nineteenth century has been well demonstrated by James Hepokowski, 'Masculine – Feminine. Are Current Readings of Sonata Form in Terms of a "Masculine" and "Feminine" Dichotomy Exaggerated?', *MT*, 135 (1994), pp. 494–9. In various genres of popular music, gender is discussed in terms of actual performance much more frequently. See, for example, Richard Leppert, 'Gender sonics: the voice of Patsy Cline', in Steven Baur, Raymond Knapp, and Jacqueline Warwick (eds), *Musicological Identities: Essays in Honor of Susan McClary* (Aldershot: Ashgate, 2008), pp. 191–203.

[4]   McClary, *Feminine Endings*, p. 10, referring to Edward T. Cone, *Musical Form and Musical Performance* (New York: W.W. Norton, 1968), p. 45.

[5]   Susan McClary, 'Constructions of subjectivity in Schubert's music', in Philip Brett, Elizabeth Wood, and Gary C. Thomas (eds), *Queering the Pitch: The New Gay and Lesbian Musicology* (New York and London: Routledge, 1994), p. 223.

[6]   Suzanne Cusick, 'On musical performances of gender and sex', in Elaine Barker and Lydia Hamessley (eds), *Audible Traces: gender, identity and music* (Zurich and Los

It is equally true that performers themselves do not, in general, devote rehearsal time to considerations of gender representation, or, indeed, to musical semiotics of any kind; few conductors, if any, try to put into practice McClary's view of Brahms's Third Symphony.[7] Practical considerations such as lack of time are not the only reason for this. Performers in general remain committed to an informal notion of 'the music itself' and look askance at the play of significations that modern musicology reveals (of course, the straightforward mimesis of so-called 'programme music' is unproblematic – conductors vie for the greatest onomatopoeic realism when portraying Don Quixote's sheep). It is not widely appreciated within the academy that full-time classical performers subscribe, consciously or not, to a view of music as autonomous. This view has come under sustained, though not overwhelming, attack outside the concert hall.[8] As Lawrence Kramer memorably put it, 'Persistent sightings notwithstanding, the Autonomous Artwork is dead as Elvis.'[9] This autonomous aesthetic is a manifestation of the modernism that Taruskin perceived as pervading the early music movement of the 1980s, although its roots go much further back.[10] But if music is not autonomous and can have 'cultural meaning', recovered by a musicology that satisfies a demand for 'human interest', then these meanings might help to invigorate and diversify its performance.[11]

During the nineteenth century, where the cello and other instruments such as the violin or the piano are concerned, there were (more or less) explicitly assigned gender identities and roles that were taken for granted. Preconceptions about gender and musical instruments are still current, as many modern studies show.[12] While these gender stereotypes are not now used seriously as tools of

Angeles: Carciofoli Verlagshaus, 1999), pp. 25–49 (pp. 25–6). She refers in this chapter to her earlier paper, 'Feminist theory, music theory, and the mind/body problem', *Perspectives of New Music*, 32 (1994), pp. 8–27.

[7] Susan McClary, 'Narrative agendas in "absolute" music: Identity and difference in Brahms's Third Symphony', in Solie (ed.), *Musicology and Difference*, pp. 326–44.

[8] For a concise summary of the issues, see David Clarke, 'Musical autonomy revisited', in Martin Clayton, Trevor Herbert and Richard Middleton (eds), *The Cultural Study of Music: A Critical Introduction* (New York and London: Routledge, 2003), pp. 159–70.

[9] Lawrence Kramer, *Classical Music and Postmodern Knowledge* (Berkeley, Los Angeles, and London: University of California Press, 1995), p. 227.

[10] Butt suggests a more nuanced perspective in which Taruskin perceives elements of modernism in HIP but uses them in 'a way typical of the postmodernism that [Georgina] Born outlines'. John Butt, *Playing with History* (Cambridge: Cambridge University Press, 2002), p. 129, referring to Georgina Born, *Rationalising Culture – IRCAM, Boulez and the Institutionalisation of the Musical Avant-Garde* (Berkeley and Los Angeles: University of California Press, 1995).

[11] Ibid., p. 1.

[12] See Lucy Green, *Music, Gender, Education* (Cambridge: Cambridge University Press, 1997), and Susan O'Neill, 'Gender and Music', in David Hargreaves and Adrian North (eds), *The Social Psychology of Music* (Oxford: Oxford University Press, 1997),

musical analysis, it is obvious that 'genderedness' cannot be ignored insofar as it is expressed through 'the semiotics of "masculinity" and "femininity"'.[13] So when scholars discuss gender as signified in nineteenth-century music, it is the working of these signifiers at a particular historical period that is being examined, without any additional claim or, worse, an unspoken assumption that they are in any sense 'true'. The cello is no more essentially male than a light-bulb or a desk – if it is perceived as male, that is only because of a social consensus to see things that way, and these things can change. But one can go beyond this conventional disclaimer if one adopts the post-structuralist feminism of Judith Butler: 'There is no gender identity behind the expressions of gender; that identity is performatively constituted by the very "expressions" that are said to be its results.'[14] For Butler, the 'masculine' or 'feminine' is not a submerged entity that breaks through the surface of culture from time to time, like a rarely observed creature from the deep sea. Rather, masculinity and femininity only exist inasmuch as they are 'performed'. Thus, the cello is not masculine or feminine in *any* sense, because these things do not exist as entities 'in themselves'. An assertion of the cello's masculinity is therefore not best seen as a scientifically falsifiable statement, but rather as an assertion of cultural values that determine how the instrument is heard – part of the reception process. The cello only enacts masculinity or femininity (if at all) at the moment when it is being played. Masculinity is also 'performed' when the critic discusses the concert or the composition using those terms that themselves only acquire meaning as the aggregate of innumerable individual performances. The whole of the following discussion should be read in this context.

In the nineteenth century, music itself was seen as both 'masculine' and 'feminine'.[15] According to Lessing (1729–81), poetry was masculine and painting feminine. For Lessing, partly influenced by Burke, the 'masculine' was associated with the sublime, eloquence, an arbitrary sign system that feeds the imagination and a temporal dimension. The 'feminine' connoted silence, beauty, an appeal to the eye and a spatial dimension.[16] While Lessing does not discuss music, it is

---

pp. 46–66. This chapter cites in particular H.F. Abeles and S.Y. Porter, 'The sex-stereotyping of musical instruments', *Journal of Research in Music Education*, 26 (1978) 65–75, R. Bruce and A. Kemp, 'Sex-stereotyping in children's preferences for musical instruments', *British Journal of Music Education*, 10 (1993) 123–34, and J.K. Delzell and D.A. Leppla, 'Gender association of musical instruments and preferences of fourth-grade students for selected instruments', *Journal of Research in Music Education*, 40 (1992), pp. 93–103. A simpler use of gender stereotypes characterizes Atarah Ben-Tovim's *The Right Instrument for Your Child* (London: Weidenfeld & Nicholson, 4th edn 2005).

[13]   Susan McClary, 'Narrative agendas in "absolute music"', p. 332.

[14]   Judith Butler, *Gender Trouble* (New York and London: Routledge, 1990), p. 25.

[15]   See Derek B. Scott, 'The sexual politics of Victorian musical aesthetics', *Journal of the Royal Musical Association*, 119 (1994), pp. 91–114.

[16]   G.E. Lessing, ed. and trans. Edward Bell., 'Laokoön, or on the limits of painting and poetry', in *Selected Prose Works* (London: George Bell and Sons, 1879). See also

clearly masculine within these terms. The unpublished second edition of *Laokoön* suggests that he did indeed see music as similar to poetry.[17] Lessing goes to some lengths to establish a concept of beauty in classical Greek sculpture to which emotion is subjugated and refined:

> all I want to establish is, that among the ancients beauty was the highest law of the plastic arts. And this, once proved, it is a necessary consequence that everything else [...] gave way entirely to it; if incompatible, was at least subordinate. [...] From all such emotions the ancient masters either abstained entirely, or reduced them to that lower degree in which they are capable of a certain measure of beauty.[18]

Hanslick also describes music as more 'masculine' than 'feminine', and is at great pains to assert the irrelevance of music's emotional effect to its aesthetic value. This becomes even more polemical in later editions of *Vom Musikalisch-Schönen*, reacting to the increased prominence of Wagner and Liszt. He concedes that music does have such effects, but they appear to make him uncomfortable:

> I am quite at one with those who hold that the ultimate worth of the beautiful must ever depend upon the immediate verdict of the feelings. But at the same time I firmly adhere to the conviction, that all the customary appeals to our emotional faculty can never show the way to a single musical law.[19]

> Music may, undoubtedly, awaken feelings of great joy or intense sorrow; but might not the same or a still greater effect be produced by the news that we have won first prize in the lottery, or by the dangerous illness of a friend?[20]

Hanslick frequently tells us how emotionally powerful music is, while simultaneously denying the relevance of this effect, and in doing so is enacting a familiar trope. By side-lining the emotionally expressive power of art, both

---

W.J.T. Mitchell, *Iconology Image Text, Ideology* (Chicago: University of Chicago Press, 1986), pp. 109–11. For Burke, see Linda M.G. Zerilli, 'No thrust, no swell, no subject?: A critical response to Stephen K. White', *Political Theory*, 22/2 (1994), pp. 323–8.

[17] Simon Richter, 'Intimate relations: Music in and around Lessing's "Laokoon"', *Poetics Today*, 20 (1999), pp. 155–73. See also Simon Shaw-Miller, *Visible Deeds of Music Art and Music from Wagner to Cage* (New Haven and London: Yale University Press, 2002), p. 8, citing J. Neubauer, *The Emancipation of Music from Language* (New Haven and London: Yale University Press, 1986), p. 136.

[18] Lessing, 'Laokoön', p. 15.

[19] Eduard Hanslick, trans. Gustav Cohen, *On the Beautiful in Music* [Vom Musikalisch-Schönen] (New York: Da Capo Press, 1974; repr. of 7th edn 1885, English version 1891), p. 11.

[20] Ibid., p. 26.

Hanslick and Lessing are exercising a masculine control, a control that has been shown to be exercised in many other musical fields.[21] Giving this essentially abstract art a status above other arts and then subjecting it to male control was tantamount to privileging the masculine.

Music has more often been seen as 'feminine' from Plato onwards, and in our period this was the majority view, subscribed to by Kant, Hegel, Nietzsche and Wagner.[22] For Schopenhauer, music was a way of reconstituting the structure of the world by analogy, recreating emotions by abstracting them so that they could be experienced through a (masculine) aesthetic sensibility. Music was a direct expression of the Will, 'express[ing] the emotions of the will itself', but in an intellectualized form. The emotions caused by music were not, for Schopenhauer, the same things as real sorrow, joy, or fear, and this meant that we could take pleasure from its representation of these emotions without experiencing them directly.[23] Schopenhauer's music appears feminine, but at the same time regulated as being separated from the Will itself. At this relatively simple level, there is a clear connection between Lessing, Hanslick, and Schopenhauer, in the way that they deal with the subjugation of emotion, although the latter's analysis is considerably more complex. These concepts are not only explored by critics and philosophers; they pervaded much writing about music at all levels. Interested amateur musicians would certainly have been aware of them. In 1887, an anonymous female writer in the *Musical Times,* considering who is happiest, 'the worshipped or the worshipper', described music as a willing (female) slave to the dominant (male) composer:

> we may consider it a moot question whether [women], to whom music speaks
> in accents which we have cultivated our ears all our lifetime to understand, and

---

[21]   There are several examples in Susan McClary, *Feminine Endings: Music Gender and Sexuality* (Minneapolis: University of Minnesota Press, 1991), pp. 3–31. Suzanne Cusick has shown how the masculine control of the female eroticism of music extended to the institutional practice of musicology itself, in that while women could pursue music as an art, its scientific study was an activity reserved for men. Suzanne Cusick, 'Gender, musicology, and feminism', in Mark Everist and Nicholas Cook (eds), *Rethinking Music* (Oxford: Oxford University Press, 2001), pp. 471–98.

[22]   See, for example, Herman Parret, 'Kant on music and the hierarchy of the arts', *Journal of Aesthetics and Art Criticism*, 56 (1998), pp. 251–64; Julian Johnson, 'Music in Hegel's aesthetics: A re-evaluation', *British Journal of Aesthetics*, 31 (1991), pp. 152–62; Susan Bernstein, 'Fear of music? Nietzche's double vision of the "musical-feminine"', in Peter J. Burgard (ed.), *Nietzsche and the Feminine* (Charlottesville, VA: University of Virginia Press, 1994), pp. 104–34; Thomas Grey, 'Engendering music drama', in *Wagner's Musical Prose* (Cambridge: Cambridge University Press, 1995), pp. 130–37.

[23]   See Arthur Schopenhauer, trans. R.B. Haldane and J. Kemp, *The World as Will and Idea* (London: Kegan Paul, 1891), Vol. 3, pp. 232 and 235.

which now thrill us to our hearts' core [...] are not equally blest with [men] to whom she shows herself a willing slave, and who bend her to their will.[24]

Music was seen at one and the same time as both as an art dedicated, dangerously, to the representation and recreation of inchoate emotion, and as an abstract, formal discipline of which emotion was an inferior, even embarrassing, by-product.[25] This complex and ambivalent mixture of gender tropes is repeated on a smaller scale with regard to the cello over the course of the nineteenth century. But at the start of this period it was, 'essentially', a manly instrument, and that is where we shall begin.

Whereas the small, curvaceous, high-pitched violin was seen as an inherently female instrument, and the piano acquired a female gender through social practice as an instrument suitable for women to play in the home, the cello was seen as masculine, at least in the eighteenth and earlier nineteenth century. Comparing actors to musical instruments in the late eighteenth century, a certain 'B. Thornton Esq.' observed:

> I shall [...] place [Mr. Mossop] on the Stage nearly in the same Rank that the Violoncello holds in the Orchestra. His elocution to the vulgar part of the Audience may sound harsh and somewhat grating: but there is a noble dignity in it; and like the Instrument just mentioned, at the same time it is Strong, Loud, and Full, is Delectable, Just, and Melodious.[26]

Writing only a year after Mossop (1739–73) had died, 'Thornton' was perhaps being generous. A later theatre historian was less kind about Mossop: 'His syllables fell from him like minute-guns, even in or-din-a-ry con-ver-sa-tion ...'.[27] A 1797 review of T.A. Dahmen's *Three Duetts* criticized the pieces for using the cello's high register too much, saying that 'the rich, manly and generous tones of which it is capable, are resigned for a bad imitation of powers foreign to its own'.[28] A review of Nikolaus Kraft's playing described his tone as 'powerful, manly, full'.[29] In 1823 a reviewer for the *Harmonicon* called the cello 'a rich, manly instrument',

---

[24]   Anon., 'Women as Composers', *MT*, 28 (1887), pp. 80–82 (p. 82).

[25]   For a lengthier discussion of this topic, see Scott, 'The sexual politics of Victorian musical aesthetics'.

[26]   Anon. ['B. Thornton, Esq.' ?], 'An Inspector', in *Miscellaneous and Fugitive Pieces*, 3 vols. (London: T. Davies, 1774), Vol. 3, p. 79.

[27]   Dr John Doran, *Their Majesties' Servants or Annals of the English Stage from Thomas Betterton to Edmund Kean; Actors, Authors, Audiences* (London: Wm. H. Allen, 1865), p. 274.

[28]   Anon., *Monthly Magazine, or, British Register* (1797), p. 149.

[29]   Anon. review, *AmZ*, 28 April 1802, pp. 498–9, quoted in Raymond Monelle, 'The criticism of musical performance', in John Rink (ed.), *Musical Performance a Guide to Understanding* (Cambridge: Cambridge University Press, 2002), p. 215.

an adjective repeated in the same journal the following year: 'We are glad to observe how much progress this manly instrument, the violoncello, is making.'[30]

The Paris Conservatoire's cello method describes this serious, expressive, manly instrument at some length:

> The Violoncello possesses by the nature of its tone, the length of its strings, and the extent of its sounds, a grave, earnest and expressive character. In the execution of melody it loses nothing of its majesty, and when it serves as a regulator in accompaniment we perceive, in the midst of that commanding influence by which it keeps the whole in order, that it will finally yield to expression by taking part in the dialogue. [...] When the Violoncello performs a solo, its tone becomes touching and sublime, not such as points and excites the passions, but moderates them, by raising the mind to a higher region. [...] But there are limits which must not be exceeded: the grave character of the Violoncello will not allow it to execute the wild and violent movements of the Violin ... .[31]

The cello is not only masculine in the simple analogical or mimetic sense that it is quite large, low-pitched and serious. It also maintains order in the instrumental ensemble, counterbalancing the violin's more unpredictable flights of fancy, and controlling the emotions so that the listener can rise above them. This parallels Lessing's gendered distinction between art forms, in which poetry was superior to painting because it did not require external control to restrain its irrational, unconscious power. The trope of the controlling masculine regulating the emotionally excessive feminine is here reiterated in the cellist who manages the unruly instrumental ensemble or soloist. Just such a cellist, it seems, was Josef Merk (1795–1852):

> Herr M[erk] does not play, like Romberg usually does, without having the notes before him, yet one sees that he does not anxiously follow them, that he keeps the orchestra in view, and now and then reins in its turbulence; in short, that he moves with complete freedom and certainty, like a man of the world, not fearfully observing the tradition, but establishing it.[32]

Orchestral cellists could also help regulate the orchestra (itself a highly regulated group):

---

[30]   *Harmonicon*, 1 (1823), p. 2, and 2 (1824), p. 96.

[31]   Baillot et al., *Méthode de violoncelle* (Paris: Janet et Cotelle, 1805), pp. 2–3; trans. A. Merrick, *Method for the Violoncello* (London: Cocks & Co. [1830]), p. 10.

[32]   'Herr M. spielt war nicht, wie Romberg gewöhnlich thut, ohne Noten vor sich zu haben, allein man sieht, dass er sie nicht ängstlich verfolgt, dass er das Orchester im Auge behält und seinen Ungestüm bisweilen zügelt, kurz, dass er sich mit vollständiger Freiheit und Sicherheit bewegt, wie ein Weltmann die feinere Sitte nicht ängstlich beobachtet, sondern sie von selbst übt'. *BAmZ*, 2 (1825), p. 170.

Aside from a necessary general human development, whereby each artist should distinguish himself, and particularly aside from that oft-neglected humanity – which permits neither unkind nor biased comments about the artistic output of others, where superiors are respected but not fawned to, where colleagues are treated with neither common familiarity nor aloofness – punctuality above all is required of cellists, as with every other orchestra member, whereby each shows respect not only for himself, but also for his colleagues. In the orchestra, where order rules, each member should arrive a quarter of an hour before the appointed time, partly to prepare and tune his own instrument, partly too to familiarize himself with the other parts.[33]

The necessities of having everything in order and of knowing the other parts arose from the deplorable tendencies in solo performance:

In our current time, it is essential to have one's instrument [the cello] under control in such a way that one is in a position to deal with every eventuality without trouble and effort; because we, as is well known, unfortunately live in a time where *ad libitum, a piacere, col canto* etc. so predominate that one can not be sure of any beat. Through this, everything is mutilated. – How shamefully misused become the great masters, who cannot themselves deplore this mischief any more! And – what does art profit thereby?[34]

Later social trends also encouraged men to play the cello. In the home, women were playing the violin so much that the cello was seen as a useful instrument for the husband to play:

---

[33] 'Ausser einer notwendigen allgemein Menschenbildung, wodurch sich jeder Künstler auszeichnen sollte, und namentlich ausser jener oft vernachlässigten Humanität, die sich keine lieblosen und parteiischen Aeusserungen über Kunstleistungen Anderer erlaubt, gegen Vorgesetzte sich nicht kriechend, sondern ergeben, und gegen seine Kollegen weder zu familiär noch zu stolz erweist, ist vom zuvördest Pünktlichkeit in seinem Berufe zu erlangen, wodurch sich Jeder nicht nur selbst ehrt, sondern auch seine Kollegen. Bei dem Orchester, wo Ordnung herrscht, soll eigentlich jedes glied desselben eine viertelstunde vor der anberaumten Zeit da sein, theils um sein Instrument gestimmt und in Ordnung gebracht, theils auch, um sich durch einen Ueberblick mit seinen vorliegenden Stimmen vertraut gemacht zu haben.' Anon. [Dehn?], 'Einiges über die Pflichten des Violoncellisten als Orchesterspielers und Accompgnateurs' [On the duties of cellists as orchestral players and accompanists], *AmZ*, 43 (1841), p. 130.

[34] 'In unserer jetzigen Zeit ist es daher unerlässlich, sein Instrument so in der gewalt zu haben, dass man alles Vorkommende ohne Mühe und Anstrengung auszuführen im Stande ist; denn wir leben bekanntlich leider in einer Zeit wo ad libitum, a piacere, col canto u. d. m. so herrschen dass man auch keinen Takt davor sicher sein kann. Alles wird dadurch verstümmelt. Wie schändlich werden die grossen Meister, die sich nicht mehr über diesen Unfug beklagen können, gemissbraucht! und – was gewinnt die Kunst dabei?' Ibid., pp. 132–3.

The demand for […] popular Instruction-books for stringed instruments has so increased within the last few years that we may confidently predict for this latest addition to 'Novello's Primers' an extensive sale. The violoncello is rapidly becoming a favourite amongst those cultivated amateurs who devote themselves more to the performance of classical chamber music than to that of orchestral works; and the use of this instrument in the domestic circle is likely to be still further increased when the first and second violins in quartets become more entrusted to the ladies of a family.[35]

This development in domestic music-making was partly a consequence of a new attitude to music in the education of young men. The Earl of Chesterfield had dismissed it a century earlier:

There are liberal and illiberal pleasures as well as liberal and illiberal arts […]. As you are now in a musical country, where singing, fiddling, and piping, are […] almost the principal objects of attention, I cannot help cautioning you against giving in to those (I will call them illiberal) pleasures […] If you love music, hear it; go to operas, concerts, and pay fiddlers to play to you; but I insist upon your neither piping nor fiddling yourself. It puts a gentleman in a very frivolous, contemptible light; brings him into a great deal of bad company; and takes up a great deal of time, which might be much better employed. Few things would mortify me more, than to see you bearing a part in a concert, with a fiddle under your chin, or a pipe in your mouth.[36]

But in 1866 the *Athenaeum,* reviewing concerts at Wellington College and Marlborough College, was pleased to note that:

It is a significant proof of the changes which have passed over society since the century began, that Music is beginning to make its way, and to hold its own, in the very places where, thirty years ago, it was tolerated at best – ordinarily mocked as an effeminate waste of time – our resorts of collegiate education.[37]

For the two leading historians of the instrument in the late nineteenth and early twentieth centuries the cello was still definitely male. In the late 1880s Wasielewski eulogized the masculine cello as the counterpart of the female violin in terms very similar to those of the Paris method. While it could not match the violin's 'brilliance and agility', and suffered from muffled tone in the lower registers, it had the advantage:

---

[35]   Anon. review of Jules de Swert's cello method, *MT*, 23 (1882), p. 680.

[36]   Earl of Chesterfield, *Letters written by the late Right Honourable Philip Dormer Stanhope, Earl of Chesterfield, to his son, Philip Stanhope, Esq.*, 4 vols (Edinburgh: C. MacFarquhar, 1775), Letter 68 (19 April 1749).

[37]   *Athenaeum*, 6 January 1866, p. 23.

that it lends itself far less to virtuoso exaggerations and confusions, than does the easily portable violin, so favourably disposed for every variety of unworthy trifling. The masculine character of the Violoncello, better adapted for subjects of a serious nature, precludes this. [...] If the violin, with melting soprano and tenor-like voice, speaks to us now with maidenly tenderness, now in clear jubilant tones, the Violoncello, grandly moving for the most part in the tenor and bass positions, stirs the soul by its fascinating sonority and its imposing power of intonation, not less than by the pathos of its expression, which by virtue of its peculiar quality of tone more especially belongs to it than to the Violin. There is no rivalry between the two instruments, but rather do they mutually enhance each other's power.[38]

It is clear from Wasielewski's pejorative language ('unworthy trifling') that this 'mutual enhancement' is still the male domination of the female through its 'imposing power'. This is a trope familiar from Marx's distinction of masculine and feminine subjects in sonata forms, where the 'masculine' first subject controls and shapes the 'feminine' second subject, beneath the semblance of an equal partnership (a more refined version of this view takes into account varied recapitulations that can represent the transformation of the masculine self by the feminine other).[39] More concisely, but to the same end, Edmund van der Straeten asserted in 1914 that:

in 1800 the violoncello as a solo instrument had passed through the first century of its existence, and arrived at the age of manhood.[40]

However, there were other views. It is clear that some performances, and some cello compositions, did not conform to the male stereotype. In 1848 a review of a performance by Servais, while confirming this gender association, also implied that it was widely contradicted:

The [...] welcome [...] given the artist by Viennese audiences in the winter season of 1847/48 [...] was commented on by a foreign correspondent of a Russian periodical. 'Servais is one of the most notable violoncellists of our time,' he wrote, 'his playing is both graceful and bravura. Whereas other cellists absolutely neglect the virile character of the instrument, Servais keeps himself to the middle way: he sings on the violoncello, approaching the highest notes

---

[38]   Wilhelm Jos. D. Wasielewski, trans. Isobella S.E. Stigand, *The Violoncello and its History* (London: Novello, Ewer & Co., 1894; 1st edn 1888), pp. 212–13.

[39]   See Lawrence Kramer, *Classical Music and Postmodern Knowledge* (Berkeley: University of California Press, 1995), p. 45.

[40]   E. van der Straeten, *History of the Violoncello, the Viol da Gamba, their Precursors and Collateral Instruments* (London: William Reeves, 1914, repr. 1971), p. 383.

of its range, but he also reminds his listeners that – the cello has its strong bass strings as well'.[41]

Similar concerns over a weakening of the cello's manly identity were voiced by the reviewer of Kummer's *Elegie* op. 79 in 1845:

> What we find most appealing is that Herr Kummer, has avoided (with very few exceptions) those whining notes of insipid salon-sentimentality; that, in the *Elegie*, the predominant expression of mourning and pain almost throughout remains [that of] a manly composure, healthy, noble, in complete contrast to certain fashionable compositions of this genre, whose sickly affectation and revolting effeminate coquettishness of feeling often cause positive physical discomfort, leaving [anyone with] a strong, pure temperament the most disagreeable feelings.[42]

A less outspoken, but nonetheless condescending attitude was adopted in relation to Josef Stransky's *Morceaux* op. 18, which were described as being 'accommodated to the taste of the Viennese salons' ('sind der Geschmack der Wiener Salons zu accomodieren'). The fifth piece:

> gives all ladies who gladly hear the cello, a 'Souvenir de Bal', which will delight them; because such a thing is naturally not written for men. However, if out of politeness we lower ourselves to the 'ladylike', then we cannot deny that the Waltz is very pretty.[43]

---

[41]   Lev Ginsburg, *History of the Violoncello* (Neptune City, NJ: Paganiniana Publications, 1983), pp. 34–5, quoting *Literary Supplement to Nuvellist*, March 1848.

[42]   'Was uns besonders darin angesprochen, ist, dass Herr Kummer, mit Ausnahme einiger wenigen Stellen, jenen weinerlichen Ton fader Salonsentimentalität vermieden hat, dass der in der Elegie vorherrschende Ausdruck der Trauer und des Schmerzes fast durchgehends ein männlich gefasster, edler und gesunder bleibt, ganz im Widerspruche mit gewissen dieser Galtung angehörigen Modecomposition, deren krankhafte Affectation und widerlich weibische Gefühlscoquetterie oft förmliches physisches Unwohlsein verinsachen, und wovon eine kräftige, unverdorbene Natur sich nur auf's Unerquicklichtest berührt fühlen kann.' 'Recensionen', *AmZ*, 47 (1845), p. 536. It is possible that this 'weibische Gefühlscoquetterie' is a manifestation of a deeper connection in Germany between sexuality and the civic good. See Jeffrey Kallberg, 'Sex, sexuality and Schubert's piano music', in Steven Crist and Roberta M. Marvin (eds), *Historical Musicology Sources Methods, Interpretations* (Rochester, NY: University of Rochester Press, 2004), pp. 219–33, citing amongst others Isabel V. Hull, *Sexuality, State, and Civil Society in Germany, 1700–1815* (Ithaca, NY, and London: Cornell University Press, 1996), pp. 229–56.

[43]   'Nummer 5 gibt allen Damen, welche das Violoncell gern hören, ein "Souvenir de Bal", das sie entzücken wird; denn für Männer ist so etwas natürlich nicht geschrieben. Stimmen wir uns aber aus Galanterie zum "Dämlichen" herab, so könnten wir nicht leugnen, dass der Walzer recht hübschen ist.' *Niederrheinische Musik-Zeitung, Literaturblatt* no. 6, 14 October 1854, p. 21.

The cellists who neglected the instrument's manly nature could well have included the French musicians so regularly criticized by Henry Chorley in the *Athenaeum* for their affected style:

> M. Lebouc, the principal violoncellist of the Conservatoire orchestra, in Paris, – a sound and excellent solo player; sound, we repeat, because free from that tremulousness of tone and finical falseness of expression, which too largely characterizes the stringed-instrument players of the French school.[44]

> [Servais] has power, tone, execution, every requisite for a first-rate player, but carries them all to an extremity which makes both his expression and his brilliancy *troppo caricato* for our tastes, or, we suspect, for him to be given the name of an artist, in its highest sense. [...] In these days, when there is so much danger of music being corrupted, if not utterly destroyed, by extravagance and whimsicality, it cannot be too decidedly laid down, that no forced effects – no passion pushed to its extreme, or delicacy refined into super-delicacy – deserve to be admired, although they may be excused in consideration of the talent of the performer.[45]

> [Servais's] playing was impaired by a certain violence and eccentricity of manner which disturbed the pleasure of the hearer. The deepest expression, the most vehement passion, are still consistent with grace and composure. It should be added, however, that we heard him at a time when the noxious influences of Paganini's personality had not yet become extinct, and when freaks and gesticulations were in fashion, being thought to attest originality and sincerity; and since years have elapsed since this impression was made, it is possible that with Time these extravagances may have been, in some degree, toned down.[46]

Early in the twentieth century a startlingly different perception of the cello can be observed in *The Twenty-Fourth of June* (1914) by the romantic novelist Grace Richmond (1866–1959). She describes domestic chamber music with a mostly traditional allocation of instruments, where the son plays the violin and one of his sisters the harp. But the other sister, Roberta, plays the cello, and somewhat provocatively:

> As [Richard Kendrick] greeted his hosts, Mr. and Mrs. Robert Gray, Judge Calvin Gray, Mr. and Mrs. Stephen Gray, wondering a little where the rest of the family could be, his eye fell upon the musicians, and the problem was solved. Ruth, the sixteen-year-old, sat before a harp; Louis, the elder son, cherished a violin under his chin; Roberta – ah, there she was! Wearing a dull-blue evening

---

[44]   *Athenaeum*, 11 July 1863, p. 57.

[45]   *Athenaeum*, 30 May 1835, p. 418.

[46]   Obituary for Servais, *Athenaeum*, 8 December 1866, p. 759.

frock above which gleamed her white neck, her half-uncovered arms showing exquisite curves as she handled the bow which was drawing long, rich notes from the violoncello at her knee.[47]

Richmond here avoids explicitly making the easy parallel between Roberta's exquisite curves and those of the cello itself, concentrating instead on her ability to make the instrument sound 'rich' through the 'drawing' of the bow. This manly object responds best to coaxing. Later in the novel, there are more pronounced sexual overtones, when Roberta plays once more:

> She lifted her arms, her head up. 'Mother, let's play the Bach Air,' she said. 'That always takes the fever out of me, and makes me feel calm and rational. Is it very late? – are you too tired? Nobody will be disturbed at this distance.' 'I should love to play it,' said Mrs. Gray, and together the two went down the room to the great piano which stood there in the darkness. Roberta switched on one hooded light, produced the music for her mother, and tuned her cello, sitting at one side away from the light, with no notes before her. Presently the slow, deep, and majestic notes of the 'Air for the G String' were vibrating through the quiet room, the cello player drawing her bow across and across the one string with affection for each rich note in her very touch. The other string tones followed her with exquisite sympathy […].[48]

Not only does her self-absorbed playing, in the dark, from memory, cure her fevered condition through her affectionate repeated bow strokes, which draw out a manly ('deep', 'majestic') sound: as if by sympathetic magic, her performance conjures up a real man who appreciates her slow, comfortable and comforting performance:

> But a few bars had sounded when a tall figure came noiselessly into the room, and Mr. Robert Gray dropped into the seat before the fire […]. With head thrown back he listened, and when silence fell […] his deep voice was the first to break it. 'To me,' he said, 'that is the slow flowing and receding of waves upon a smooth and rocky shore. The sky is gray, but the atmosphere is warm and friendly. It is all very restful, after a day of perturbation.'[49]

It is striking that Roberta uses the cello to help her feel 'rational', and that a man pronounces approval on the performance in terms that are nothing if not restrained – he is, after all, her father. By playing Bach's 'slow, deep and majestic' air, Roberta is re-affirming that type of manly cello melody traditionally held to be

---

[47]   Grace L.S. Richmond, *The Twenty-Fourth of June* (Garden City, NY: Doubleday, Page & Co., 1914), Ch. 4, pp. 46–7. The cello 'at her knee' may imply the side-saddle posture, discussed below.

[48]   Ibid., Ch. 10, pp. 168–9.

[49]   Ibid.

the most characteristic and moving. What is new is that she is playing for her own gratification. This early twentieth-century cello is therefore not quite the manly regulator of the passions described a century earlier. To see how this change came about we must first consider the emergence of women as performers on the public concert platform.

During the earlier nineteenth century, public performances by women (other than singers or pianists in an accompanying role) were rare. The piano was considered a suitable instrument for a woman as it could be played at home, was musically self-sufficient, increasingly inexpensive, could be played at a wide range of levels of ability, and was played with a suitably demure posture. The violin, on the other hand, was a site of more complex gender conflict, at least in England, and in ways that make an interesting comparison with the cello. Wilma Neruda (later Lady Hallé) was surprised to find it thought highly unusual for a woman to play the violin in public in England, having been used to a less restrictive climate on the continent:

> When I first came to London, I was surprised to find that it was thought almost improper, certainly unladylike, for a woman to play on the violin. In Germany the thing was quite common and excited no comment. I could not understand – it seemed so absurd – why people thought so differently here.[50]

Only in 1872 was the first woman violinist enrolled at the Royal Academy of Music[51] – by contrast, Camilla Urso, the first woman violinist to enter the Paris Conservatoire, did so in 1850 at the age of eight.[52] The principal apparent objection to women playing the violin in public was that the woman's posture became in some way inelegant and distorted. However, in practice this was often seen as not merely unattractive or distasteful, but as actually disgusting (except, significantly, in the case of female child virtuosi). By contrast, excessively critical reviews of female violinists in German-speaking countries appear to concentrate on repertoire and performing style, rather than sexual impropriety. Zellner's outraged review of the Ferni sisters in 1859 suggests that what mainly provoked him was the masculinization and repression of emotion in their playing:

> Whatever the so-called French school has collected in the way of affectation, piquancy, over-sharpness, and glimmering dust to throw in people's eyes, and by which it has succeeded in thoroughly banishing all truth and nature from art, is exhibited, with exhausting completeness, in these two young ladies' playing. [...] [They] have been subjected to the most refined system of false education,

---

[50] 'Lady Hallé at Home', *The Woman's World*, 1 (1890), p. 171.

[51] Paula Gillett, *Musical Women in England 1870–1914* (New York: St. Martin's Press, 2000), p. 79.

[52] Susan Kagan, 'Camilla Urso: A nineteenth-century violinist's view', *Signs*, 2/3 (1977), p. 727.

which has [...] robbed them of freedom of individual development, as well as independence of feeling and sentiment [...] their artistic taskmasters have [...] pitilessly nipped off every blossom [...] changing into a smooth-shorn wall of leaves the fresh free forest, with all the variety of its naturally sturdy trees [...] as pupils of Beriot and Alard, they have been educated merely to hawk about the tin-pot concert wares of these gentlemen.[53]

Caroline has been turned into a machine:

[S]he is the prototype of a carefully regulated piece of mechanism [...] which hits the same point a thousand times running.[54]

Female cellists were rarer than violinists, but seem to have provoked mild astonishment rather than disgust:

When the young ladies of Madison Female College gave a concert in 1853, John Dwight of Dwight's Journal of Music was there to document the novel event. He took pianists, guitarists and harpists in stride, but expressed shock at '13 young lady violinists(!), 1 young lady violist(!!), 4 violoncellists(!!!) and 1 young lady contrabassist(!!!!).' (5) As the rising chorus of exclamation marks shows, Dwight's tolerance was in inverse proportion to the size of the instrument.[55]

Dwight's triple exclamation marks had already been used by an astonished writer giving a brief notice of Lisa Christiani's 1844 Paris début:

It is said that a female cellist (!!!) is appearing in a Paris salon, with the name Christiani-Berbier, admittedly to great applause. – These are the fruits of female emancipation![56]

However, her appearance in November that year in the Leipzig Gewandhaus (alongside Ferdinand David's quartet) was reviewed in entirely conventional terms, listing her programme and praising her grace and virtuosity.[57] Reviewing the 1860 graduation competition at the Paris Conservatoire, the *Musical World* expressed its own distaste, but coupled with resignation rather than nausea:

---

[53]   L.A. Zellner, 'The Sisters Ferni', *MT*, 37 (1859), p. 54.

[54]   Ibid.

[55]   Beth Abelson MacLeod, *Women Performing Music: The Emergence of American Women as Instrumentalists and Conductors* (Jefferson, NC: MacFarland and Co., 2001), p. 9.

[56]   '(Eine Violoncellistinn !!!) soll sich in einem Pariser Salon produciren mit Namen Christiani-Barbier und zwar mit grossem Beifall. – Das sind die Früchte der Frauen-Emancipation!' *AwmZ*, 4 (1844), p. 276.

[57]   'Nachrichten', *AmZ*, 47 (1845), pp. 818–19.

among the competitors for the violin and violoncello prizes, figured four young
ladies, three violinists and one violoncellist. Lady-fiddlers we are tolerably well
accustomed to, but the attitude of a lady grasping with all her limbs a violoncello
is one to the grotesqueness of which usage has not yet reconciled us. In time, no
doubt, we shall think nothing of it.[58]

At almost the same time, the romantic novelist Anne Brewster suggested that
playing the cello was actually physically damaging for a woman:

one girl with a violoncello and the other with a violin took their position near
the music stands. They were very young; the eldest, the violoncellist, being
apparently about fourteen, the violinist a year or two younger. [...] The figure of
the eldest showed the effect produced by close practice on her heavy instrument;
already one shoulder was partially elevated and her chin was thrown forward,
giving a pained expression to her countenance.[59]

On the other hand, Charles Dickens was not at all disturbed by Elisa de Try, to
whom he paid one of the highest possible accolades:

M. de Try [...] is a masterly performer on the violoncello himself, and, more
than that, has made a mistressly violoncellist of his daughter, Mademoiselle
Elisa de Try. It is not often that a young lady, scarcely seventeen years of age,
reminds us of the tone and expression of Lindley.[60]

Elisa de Try used a tail-pin, as taught by Servais, so it appears that the newer
posture was indeed less offensive. In 1877, the presence of female cellists in the
Vienna Ladies' Orchestra was noted without any comment at all. The cellist Elise
Weinlich (sister of the orchestra's director Amann Weinlich) was reviewed quite
straightforwardly by the *New York Times* when she gave an 'extremely clever'
performance of a *pot-pourri* by Kummer.[61] No special mention was made of the

---

[58]   Anon., 'Music and Theatres in Paris', *MW*, 35 (1860), p. 487.

[59]   Anne M.H. Brewster, *Compensation, Or, Always a Future* (Philadelphia:
J.B. Lippincott & Co., 1860), p. 94. The idea that playing the cello was physically harmful
was still current at the turn of the century. In 1897 the writer Beatrice Harraden was
described as suffering 'much inconvenience from paralysis of the right forearm brought
on by playing the violoncello', and in 1904 it was reported of an 'untiring student' of the
cello that 'constant pressure of the instrument on his leg led to osteo-sarcoma', which in
turn led to amputation and death 'from shock'. 'Notes about Women', *New York Times*, 28
October 1894, p. 18; 'Gave his Life for Music', *New York Times*, 28 August 1904.

[60]   Charles Dickens (ed.), 'Wood-and-straw music', *All the Year Round*, 20 December
1862, p. 353. Robert Lindley had died in 1855.

[61]   Anon., 'A German Fancy Fair', *Times*, 23 September 1873, p. 10; Anon., 'The
Viennese Ladies Orchestra', *New York Times*, 27 July 1874, p. 6.

four cellists in the Dundee Ladies' Orchestra at their début in 1882.[62] On the other hand, female cellists still posed a problem for the BBC Symphony Orchestra as late as the 1930s according to Ethel Smyth:

> But here's a strange thing; in that orchestra [BBCSO] women 'cellists are banned! Why, I cannot conceive! [...] perhaps the attitude of the 'cello player is considered an unseemly one for women? [...] once men's vicarious sense of modesty gets to work you never know where it will break out next. In my youth they strained at that harmless gnat, a girl on a bicycle; since then they have had to swallow something far worse than camels – horses with girls riding them cross-legged! Today, engulfed by the rising flood of women's independence, perhaps they are clinging to the violoncello as the drowning cling to a spar.[63]

In the period from the second half of the nineteenth century until the early twentieth, over forty female cellists can be identified. It has been suggested that the increase in the number of female cellists in the later nineteenth century was due to the spread of the tail-pin, originating with Servais, which initially enabled women to play the instrument side-saddle, and later to adopt the now conventional posture.[64] The supposed inelegance of a woman playing the cello without a tail-pin had been a problem, which Beth Macleod puts in a wider context:

> The obvious impediment to [the cello's] acceptance for women was physical: anything held between the legs – whether horse, bicycle or cello – engendered discussion as to its suitability for women.[65]

The review of the female cellists at the Paris Conservatoire in 1860 has already been cited – it clearly implies that the instrument was held without a tail-pin.[66]

However, a century earlier, this posture had not always been considered grotesque. A female cellist is referred to without any surprise in one eighteenth-century account (although she is admittedly playing in an all-female domestic amateur ensemble):

> But at last, from conversation they went to music, and performed two pieces, as a conclusion to the happy evening. Mrs. *Schemberg* and Miss *Chawcer* sing with the greatest judgment, extremely fine. Miss *West* plays well upon the

---

    62   Anon., 'The Dundee Ladies' Orchestra', *MT*, 23 (1882) p. 82.

    63   Ethel Smyth, *Female Pipings in Eden* (London: Peter Davies, 1933), quoted in Carol Neuls-Bates, *Women in Music* (Boston: North East University Press, 1996), p. 285.

    64   Gillett, *Musical Women*, p. 101, and see Tilden Russell, 'The development of the cello end-pin', *Imago Musicae*, 4 (1987), pp. 335–56.

    65   Beth Abelson Macleod, *Women Performing Music*.

    66   Anon., 'Music and Theatres in Paris', *MW*, 35 (1860) , p. 487.

Violoncello, the little bass violin: and the matchless fiddle of Mrs. *Benlow* being added, they formed a harmony the most excellent and perfect.[67]

Casanova was highly impressed by a female cellist whom he met at a concert in Paris in 1749. A young male cellist having performed a concerto by Vandini, Henriette de Schnetzmann (Casanova's great love) complimented him on his instrument:

[she] told him, with modest confidence, as she took the violoncello from him, that she could bring out the beautiful tone of the instrument still better. I was struck with amazement. She took the young man's seat, placed the violoncello between her knees, and begged the leader of the orchestra to begin the concerto again. […] I was beginning to imagine that she had only been indulging in a jest, when she suddenly made the strings resound. My heart was beating with such force that I thought I should drop down dead. […] well-merited applause burst from every part of the room! The rapid change from extreme fear to excessive pleasure brought on an excitement which was like a violent fever. […] My happiness was so immense that I felt myself unworthy of it.
[…] a Spaniard asked Henriette whether she could play any other instrument besides the violoncello. 'No,' she answered, 'I never felt any inclination for any other. I learned the violoncello at the convent to please my mother, who can play it pretty well, and without an order from my father, sanctioned by the bishop, the abbess would never have given me permission to practise it.'
'What objection could the abbess make?'
'That devout spouse of our Lord pretended that I could not play that instrument without assuming an indecent position.'
At this the Spanish guests bit their lips, but the Frenchmen laughed heartily, and did not spare their epigrams against the over-particular abbess. The 'vox humana' of the violoncello, the king of instruments, went to my heart every time that my beloved Henriette performed upon it.[68]

On the other hand, as late as 1919, Alfred Earnshaw assumed that the lack of a tail-pin proved that only men had played the cello in the past:

It is probably only in comparatively recent times that ladies have taken up the 'cello, and the fact that few, if any, 'cellos were fitted with the sliding peg by

---

[67]   Thomas Amory, *Memoirs of Several Ladies of Great Britain* (London: John Noon, 1755), p. 82.
[68]   Jacques Casanova de Seingalt, trans. Arthur Machen, *The Memoirs of Jacques Casanova de Seingalt 1725–1798*, 4 vols (New York: G. Putnam's Books, London: Elek Books, 1894), Vol. 2, Ch. 2, online, URL : http://www.gutenberg.org/files/2956/2956.txt [accessed January 2012].

which the 'cello could be held up, proves that it was considered only possible for a man to play it.[69]

Even though Servais died in 1866 and toured abroad frequently in his later years, he appears to have taught at least four female pupils: Anna Krull, Rosa Szük, Eliza de Try (she also studied with Franchomme, who is occasionally credited with the first use of the tail-pin) and Hélène de Katow. Krull and Szük are not listed as students of the Brussels Conservatoire, but studied with Servais privately.[70]

There are depictions of women cellists using a tail-pin and playing side-saddle, such as Arthur Hughes's *The Home Quartette* (1882–83).[71] According to Anita Mercier:

> A side-saddle position was popular, with both legs turned to the left and the right leg either dropped on a concealed cushion or stool or crossed over the left leg. A frontal position with the right knee bent and behind the cello, rather than gripping its side, was also used. Feminine alternatives like these were still in use well into the twentieth century. […] a photograph exists of Beatrice Harrison playing in the modified frontal position.[72]

However, the great majority of photographs of Harrison from childhood through to her final years show her in the modern posture. The possibility remains that side-saddle posture was adopted for posed photographs but may not necessarily (or only occasionally) have been used in actual performance. Forino mentions Jeanne Fromont-Delune who 'was a supporter of the old posture for ladies (holding the cello to the side with the right knee below the left)'.[73] However, corroboration is hard to find. The *Musical Times* reviewed a Birmingham concert in 1917 and a Paris recital in 1921 favourably, but did not mention her playing position, even though it was clearly out of date at this time:

---

[69]   Alfred Earnshaw, *Elements of Cello Technique* (London: Joseph Williams, 1919), p. 1.

[70]   Information about Platteau supplied by Peter François of the Servais Society. Van der Straeten claimed that Gabrielle Platteau (d. 1875) also studied with Servais, 'unless we are greatly mistaken', but he was indeed mistaken, as her teacher was Servais's successor in Brussels, Gustave Libotton. E. van der Straeten, *History of the Violoncello*, p. 559.

[71]   Current whereabouts unknown; auctioned at Christies in 2010. See Pamela Todd, *The Pre-Raphaelites at Home* (London: Pavilion, 2001).

[72]   Anita Mercier, 'Guilherminia Suggia' (n.d.): http://www.cello.org/Newsletter/Articles/suggia.htm [accessed 15 February 2008].

[73]   'è partigiana della vecchia posizione per le signorine (tenere il violoncello di fianco col ginocchio destro sotto al sinistro)'. Luigi Forino, *Il violoncello il violoncellista ed i violoncellisti* (Milan: Ulrico Hoepli, 2nd edn 1930), p. 399.

the chief attraction was Madame Fromont-Delune's magnificent violoncello playing [...] M. Louis Delune proved himself to be a performer of high rank.[74]

Very welcome was the concert given by Madame Jeanne Fromont-Delune, a violoncellist of unusual attainments, who displayed a remarkably fine technique, breadth of style and beauty of tone.[75]

Indeed, for any repertoire other than the very simplest, the side-saddle posture is quite impractical. Fromont-Delune's edition of Hekking's left-hand finger exercises, many of which require extreme extensions in double-stops, suggests that she herself was an advanced player. In fact, these exercises cannot be executed with the cello turned round to the right as this posture necessitates, and the more extreme pronation of the left wrist makes octave extensions virtually impossible.[76] A rare photograph of Helene de Katow shows one solution to the possibly inelegant male posture (Figure 7.1).

Figure 7.1   Hélene de Katow, c.1864. Photograph, Servais Collection, Halle (Belgium)

74   Anon., 'Music in the Provinces – Birmingham', *MT*, 58 (1917), p. 276.
75   George Cecil, 'Musical Notes from Abroad – Paris', *MT*, 62 (1921), p. 371.
76   André Hekking, rev. Jeanne Fromont-Delune, *Exercices quotidiens pour la force et l'agilité des doigts* (Paris : H. Hérelle & Cie, [1927]).

Her voluminous dress almost totally conceals the disposition of her legs, so that she can rest the cello against her left leg without inelegance. Indeed, in 1875 her appearance, along with that of her female colleagues, was favourably commented on by the *Chronique musicale*:

> In place of the eternal monotonous black suits and white ties, the public was agreeably surprised to see the concert begin with the appearance of three pretty ladies in ravishing costumes. Mme. de Katow, cellist, Mme. Blouet-Bastin, violin *premier prix* [...] and Mme. Tassoni, a young American pianist, executed with remarkable ensemble a trio by M. Lutzen on motifs from *La traviata*. [...] The Salle Philippe Herz is too small for the immense power of the Mme. de Katow's voice, which sang Gounod's Ave Maria.[77]

Depictions of other women cellists such as Rosa Szük, Lisa Christiani, or Elisa de Try suggest that long, full skirts combined with the use of a tail-pin enabled them to play while retaining an elegant posture. Depictions of other women cellists such as Rosa Szük, Lisa Christiani, or Elisa de Try suggest that long, full skirts combined with the use of a tail-pin enabled them to play while retaining an elegant posture.

At around the same time that the cello was becoming much more widely played in public by women in the later nineteenth century, there is also some literary support for the idea that the cello's 'masculine' character was becoming at least diluted if not actually feminized. A century after the cello's 'ascent to manhood', some re-alignment has clearly taken place – the cello sobs, throbs, gasps and groans, in a manner far removed from the deep, manly, restrained and restraining eloquence appreciated by earlier writers.

French sources are particularly interesting, although they are not the only ones. Alfred Guichon begins his 1875 article for the *Chronique musicale* about the cello with a list of instruments and their principal characteristics:

> Man sings. – The clarinet declaims. – The bassoon growls. [...] The violin dreams. – The cello prays. [...] In effect, the cello has a grave and restrained character; it is moving, majestic, it raises the soul towards the celestial regions. Sublime singer, it knows especially how to descend to the role of accompanist; one has even seen it on frequent occasions lose its voice in the middle of the

---

[77] 'Au lieu des éternels et monotones habits noirs et cravates blanches, le public a été agréablement surpris en voyant le concert débuter par l'apparition de trois jolies femmes en toilettes ravissantes. Madame de Katow, violoncelliste, madame Blouet-Bastin, premier prix de violon [...] et madame Tassoni, jeune pianiste americaine, ont executé avec un ensemble remarquable un trio de M. Lutzen sur les motifs de la Traviata. [...] La salle Philippe Herz est trop petite pour l'immense puissance de voix de madame de Katow, qui a chanté l'Ave Maria de Gounod.' 'Concert Mme. Zegowitz de Katow', *Chronique musicale*, 8 (1875), p. 42.

hundred-voiced orchestra, efface its personality, lose itself in the crowd, humble itself, but still remain useful.[78]

Guichon notes how attractive the cello is when played by a woman, 'so noble, so flattering to a white arm, and in the hand of a virgin or a woman'.[79] He also quotes the composer Emil de Bret in a series of remarks, which include these:

> The cello palpitates continually [...] What instrument can sigh like the cello? [...] What instrument is capable of expressing sadness, serenity, despair, hope, blessing? [...] the cello is the only one of the instruments that can sob. [...] The accents of the singing cello seem scarcely born of this world, and float in foreign realms in order to speak directly to God. [...] The cello does not, it never, charms, because it never addresses the senses, as the other instruments do. It raises the soul, enlarges it and puts it under the Creator's gaze.[80]

The rambling sequence of stories that comprises Dumas's *Les mohicans de Paris* (1854–59, but set in the 1820s) includes the story of a cellist. The philosopher Salvator and his poet companion Jean Robert encounter him by chance:

> their astonishment was great: they heard, all at once, at the moment when the door of the pharmacist's kitchen was opened, in the middle of the silence and calm of the serene night, vibrating, as if by magic, the most melodious chords. Whence came these sweet sounds? From what place? From what heavenly instrument? [...] Had St. Cecilia herself descended from the heavens in that pious house to celebrate Ash Wednesday? In fact, the tune which our two young people heard was, for certain, neither an opera aria, not the joyous solo of a musician returning home after a masked ball. It was perhaps a psalm, a canticle,

---

[78] 'L'Homme chante. La Clarinette déclame. Le Basson gronde. [...] Le Violon rêve. Le Violoncelle prie. [...] Le Violoncelle, en effet, a un caractère grave et recueilli; il est émouvant, il est majestueux, il élève l'âme vers les régions célestes. Chanteur sublime, il sait pourtant descendre au rôle plus modeste d'accompagnateur; on l'a vu même, dans les fréquents occasions, perdre sa voix au milieu des cent voix de l'orchestre, effacer sa personnalité, s'égarer dans la foule, se faire humble alors, mais utile encore.' Alfred Guichon, 'Le violoncelle', *Chronique musicale*, 3 (1875), p. 73.

[79] 'si noble, si avantageuse au bras blanc et à la main d'une vièrge ou d'une femme'. Ibid., p. 74.

[80] 'Le violoncelle palpite continuellement [...] Quel est l'instrument qui puisse soupirer comme le violoncelle? [...] Quel instrument est capable comme lui d'exprimer la douleur, la sérénité, le désespoir, l'espérance, la béatitude? La violoncelle seul est celui de tous les instruments qui puisse sangloter. [...] Les accents du violoncelle qui chante semblent n'être point nés sur cette terre, et planer dans les régions étranges pour s'adresser à Dieu directement. [...] Le violoncelle ne charme pas, ne charme jamais, parce qu'il ne s'adresse jamais aux sens, comme le peuvent faire tous les autres instruments. Il élève l'âme, l'agrandit et la place sous le regard du Créateur.' Ibid., pp. 76–7.

a page torn from some old liturgical book. [...] in hearing that melody, one thought one saw go past, like sad shadows, all the sacred hymns of childhood, all the melancholy religiosities of Sebastian Bach and Palestrina. If one had been obliged to give a name to this touching fantasy, one would have called it 'Resignation'. No more expressive name would have been more appropriate.

Then, by the opening of a curtain, they perceived a young man around thirty years old, sitting on a quite high stool, and playing the cello. [...] They read in him the signs of some terrible struggle! Doubtless the conflict of will against sadness; for, from time to time, his face clouded over, and, all the time continuing to draw the saddest sounds from his instrument, he shut his eyes, as if, no longer seeing external things, he had lost with them his deep sadness. Finally, the cello appeared, like a man in agony, to utter a tearing cry, and the bow fell from the musician's hand. Was his soul overcome? The man was weeping! Two large tears flowed silently down his cheeks. The musician took his handkerchief, dried his eyes slowly, put it back in his pocket, bent over, picked up his bow, and began the song again exactly at the point where he had broken off. The soul had won: the soul soared above the sadness with strong wings![81]

---

[81]   'leur étonnement était grand: ils entendaient tout à coup, du moment que la porte de la cuisine du pharmacien s'était ouverte, au milieu du silence et du calme de cette nuit sereine, vibrer, comme par enchantement, les accords les plus mélodieux. D'où venaient ces sons suaves ? de quel endroit ? de quel instrument céleste ? [...] Sainte Cécile elle-même était-elle descendue du ciel dans cette pieuse maison pour célébrer le mercredi des cendres? En effet, l'air que nos deux jeunes gens entendaient n'était, certainement, ni un chant d'opéra, ni le solo joyeux d'un musicien, au retour du bal masqué. C'était peut-être un psaume, un cantique, une page déchirée de quelque vieille musique biblique. [...] C'était cela; car, en écoutant cette mélodie, on croyait voir passer, comme des ombres plaintives, toutes les hymnes sacrées de l'enfance, toutes les mélancolies religieuses de Sébastien Bach et de Palestrina. Si l'on eût été obligé de donner un nom à cette touchante fantaisie, on l'eût appelée: Résignation. Nul nom plus ou moins expressif ne lui eût mieux convenu. [...] Alors, par une ouverture du rideau, ils aperçurent un jeune homme de trente ans environ, assis sur un tabouret assez élevé, et jouant du violoncelle. [...] Il se livrait évidemment en lui quelque combat terrible ! Sans doute la lutte de la volonté contre la douleur; car, de temps en temps, son front se rembrunissait, et, tout en continuant de tirer les plus tristes accords de son instrument, il fermait les yeux, comme si, ne voyant plus les choses extérieures, il eût perdu avec elles le sentiment de sa douleur intime. Enfin, le violoncelle sembla, comme un homme à l'agonie, pousser un cri déchirant, et l'archet tomba des mains du musicien. L'âme était-elle vaincue? L'homme pleurait! Deux grosses larmes silencieuses coulèrent le long de ses joues. Le musicien prit son mouchoir, s'essuya lentement les yeux, remit le mouchoir dans sa poche, se pencha, ramassa l'archet, le ramena sur les cordes du violoncelle, et reprit son chant juste à l'endroit où il l'avait interrompu. Le cœur était vaincu: l'âme planait au-dessus de la douleur avec les ailes de la force!' Alexandre Dumas, *Les Mohicans de Paris*, 2 vols (Montréal: Le joyeux Roger, 2007; 1st edn Paris, 1854–55), Vol. 1, pp. 93–6.

The explanation for this lachrymose scene occupies the following chapters, as Salvator perceives:

> There is the story you would seek, my dear poet; it is there, in this poor house, in this man who suffers, in this cello that weeps.[82]

This episode appears to have remained current for at least a decade, since it was alluded to by a reviewer of the Hungarian cellist Rosa Szük (1844–1921) on the occasion of her Paris début in 1865:

> You remember the person in the *Mohicans de Paris* who finds in his cello a balm for all heartbreaks, a salve for all sadness, a friend who consoles for absence and solitude? What Justin makes of his instrument in M. Dumas' novel, the Hungarian artist Rosa Szuk does with her cello.[83]

Another weeping cellist and cello appear in Octave Feuillet's play *Dalila*, first performed in 1857. The *savant* Sertorius, a composer and cellist, has promised to play his *Calvaire*, or 'song of Calvary', at his daughter's wedding, but in the end he has to play it in the last act as she is dying. The scene is reported:

> ah! Should I live for a thousand years, I would not forget a single detail of that scene! … During this time, the old man's fingers, placed on the strings, producing by jerks sounds, moans which entered my soul … The young woman awoke ….. . My father, she said smiling, I have a favour to ask of you … play me the song of Calvary! … No, no, he said, also trying to smile, it … your wedding day, little one !… The child looked fixedly at him without replying … He lowered his eyes, he gathered up his hair on his forehead paler than marble, and took his bow … (With lively emotion.) Then I heard the song of Calvary … Ah! The song of Calvary, yes! … While he played I saw large tears fall one by one on his poor thin shaking hands … He cried! The wood and the brass wept! … And I !… Only the child did not weep! …[84]

---

[82] 'Voilà le roman que vous cherchiez, mon cher poète ; il est là, dans cette pauvre maison, dans cet homme qui souffre, dans ce violoncelle qui pleure.' Ibid., p. 96.

[83] 'Vous souvenez-vous de ce personnage des *Mohicans de paris*, qui trouve dans son violoncelle un baume à toutes les blessures de son pauvre cœur, un soulagement à toutes les douleurs, un ami enfin qui le console de l'absence et de la solitude ? Ce que Justin fait de son instrument dans le roman de M. Alexandre Dumas, l'artiste hongroise, Rosa Szuk, doit le faire de son violoncelle.' Anon. review, *La Patrie*, evening edition, 20 March 1866, p. 1. My thanks to Agnes Szabó of the Central Ervin Szabó Library, Budapest, for drawing this press cutting to my attention.

[84] 'ah! Je vivrai dix mille ans, je n'oublierai pas un seul détail de cette scène! … pendant ce temps, les doigts du vieillard, posés sur les cordes, en tiraient par saccades des sons, des plaintes qui m'entraient dans l'âme … La jeune fille se réveilla … Mon père, dit-

Sertorius is transformed from a serious, thoughtful musician into a sobbing, broken man. This is far removed from Dickens's Harold Skimpole in *Bleak House*, an amateur cellist and composer (based on Leigh Hunt) who 'had composed half an opera once'.[85] Skimpole has not one but three daughters, each as frivolous as he. He plays the cello at those times when he is also being particularly irresponsible, and eventually he is the cause of the downfall of Richard Carstone. His effeminacy and narcissism are clearly signalled in Dickens's description:

> There was an easy negligence in his manner and even in his dress (his hair
> carelessly disposed, and his neckerchief loose and flowing, as I have seen artists
> paint their own portraits) which I could not separate from the idea of a romantic
> youth [...]. [86]

Skimpole's cello playing becomes a metonymic signifier of moral laxity, a startling reverse of the stereotype. In Thackeray's *Pendennis*, playing the cello is just one of a whole myriad of activities undertaken by a typical modern metropolitan 'woman of world' in the satirical view of the central character Pen. Among all her social events, charitable works, the education of her children and household management, she 'plays in private on the violoncello, – and I say, without exaggeration, many London ladies are doing this'.[87] There is a clear implication that this type of woman is not one to be emulated. Here the cello itself stands for a secret female vice, and colours the reader's perception of all the woman's other activities, each one respectable or at least harmless in itself. Elsewhere in *Pendennis* the cello is used as a more traditional guarantee of probity:

> 'You forget your poor mother, Fanny, [...]' Mrs. Bolton said. '[...] I'm sure
> he'll come to-day. If ever I saw a man in love, that man is him. When Emily
> Budd's young man first came about her, he was sent away by old Budd, a most

---

elle en souriant, j'ai une grâce à vous demander ... jouez-moi le chant du Calvaire! ... Non, non, dit-il en essayant de sourire aussi, lui ... le jour de ton mariage, petite! ... L'enfant le regard fixement sans répondre ... Il baissa les yeux, il secoua ses cheveux blancs sur son front plus pâle que le marbre, et prit son archet ... (Avec une vive émotion.) J'entendis alors le chant du Calvaire ... Ah! le chant du Calvaire, oui! ... Pendant qu'il jouait je voyais de grosses larmes tomber une à une sur ses pauvres mains amaigries et tremblantes ... Il pleurait! Le bois et le cuivre pleuraient! ... Et moi! ... L'enfant seul ne pleurait pas! ...' Octave Feuillet, *Dalila* (Act 3 sc. 5), in *Théatre complet*, 4 vols (Paris: Calmann Lévy, 1893), Vol. 3, pp. 350–51. Original ellipses.

[85]   Charles Dickens, ed. Norman Page, *Bleak House* (Harmondsworth: Penguin Books, 1971; 1st edn 1853), p. 123 (Ch. 6).

[86]   Ibid., pp. 118–19 (Ch. 6).

[87]   William M. Thackeray, *The History of Pendennis* (London: Smith, Elder & Co., 1880; 1st edn 1848–50), p. 435.

respectable man, and violoncello in the orchestra at the Wells; and his own family wouldn't hear of it neither.'[88]

Arsène Houssaye's *Galerie du XVIIIe siècle* (1858) includes a semi-fictionalized account of a real figure, Felice Blangini (1781–1841), a cellist, singer, and composer of *opéras-comiques* and other vocal music.[89] While most of the narrative concerns Blangini's travels, he appears as a cellist twice, framing the story near its beginning and end:

'From that time he was taken with a lively love for the cello, which was until his death his sweetest and most faithful love. "Look, he said to me, grasping the bow with fire, it is in the cello that, little by little, all my hopes and passions are buried; there are souls in the cello which I can bring back to life as if by a miracle; all my life is there, so that my life is no more than a memory. If I wished, at the first bow-stroke I would see once more appear that adored image of Pauline"'.[90]

I met Blangini for the last time a year ago, at a curiosity shop. I had rather lost sight of him. He was still the same man, sad, smiling, anxious, extravagant, his eye full of fire.
'Well! My dear Blangini, where are the canzonettes?
The canzonettes? Alas! I am at my requiem!
– And your dear cello?
– Ah! my cello, I have covered it well with tears since our journey in the forest! I hope that God will give me the strength to break it at the hour of my death; for, he continued with a sweetly saddened smile, shaking my hand, I do not want another to know the secret follies of my youth … Ah! La Grissini! …'
Blangini was less a musician than a poet. He wrote his hymns with his bow on the cello, the cello, eloquent book which contains the full range of the passions and responds to every beat of the heart. Here lies a poet, here lies a soul which sang, here lies the sound of the wind, as Antipater said at the tomb of Orpheus.[91]

---

88 Ibid., p. 495 (Ch. 51).

89 Arsène Houssaye, *Galerie du XVIIIe siècle deuxième série Princesses de comédie et déesses d'opéra* (Paris: Hachette et Cie., 1858), pp. 145–64.

90 'Il s'était pris dès ce temps-là d'un vif amour pour le violoncelle, qui a été jusqu'à sa mort plus doux et fidèle amour. "Voyez, me disait-il en saississant l'archet avec feu, c'est dans ce violoncelle que se sont enfouies peu à peu toutes mes espérances et toutes mes passions; il y a des âmes dans ce violoncelle que je puis ranimer comme par miracle; toute ma vie est là, car ma vie n'est plus qu'un souvenir. Si je voulais, au premier coup d'archet je verrais appraître encore cette image adorée de Pauline".' Houssaye, ibid., p. 147.

91 'J'ai rencontré Blangini pour la dernière fois, il y a un an, chez un marchand de curiosités. Je l'avais un peu perdu de vue. C'était toujours le même homme, triste, souriant, inquiet, extravagant, l'œil plein de feu. "Eh bien! mon cher Blangini, où en sont

Clearly, the cello that contains a man's entire emotional life, and that should even be destroyed in case it repeats its knowledge to another, is a rather different instrument from the cello that elevates and regulates the passions.

Des Esseintes, the central figure of Joris-Karl Huysmans's *A rebours* (1884), creates a musical instrument that dispenses various liqueurs into small glasses, which he calls his 'mouth organ'. Instead of sounds, this organ generates tastes which can be orchestrated at will:.

> Des Esseintes would drink a drop of this or that, playing interior symphonies to himself, and thus providing his gullet with sensations analogous to those which music affords to the ear.[92]

Among these taste/sounds there are the stringed instruments. The violin is 'fine old liqueur brandy', the viola 'rum [...], more sonorous and rumbling', the cello 'vespetro, heart-rendingly long drawn-out, melancholy and caressing', and the double-bass 'an old, pure bitter'; vespetro is a Swiss liqueur made from angelica, coriander, fennel, lemons, cloves and sugar.[93] Admittedly, there is in general no place in Des Esseintes's narcissistic decadence for simple manly eloquence, so the lack of such associations for the cello here is no surprise. Nonetheless, the choice of adjectives is in general more aligned with these later nineteenth-century views of the instrument.

Emile Goudeau's poem 'Le violoncelle' (1896) is ambivalent, with its increasingly exasperated refrain 'Ça n'en finit plus, ce violoncelle'. Its epigraph is remarkable:

> Yes, the cello! All the dreadful moaning music of Parisian struggles seem enclosed in this box in the shape of a coffin, from where the Bow, living, vibrant, biting, fierce as Destiny and sometimes honeyed like a kiss of feminine light, knows how to draw moans, ritornellos, sobs and hymns, at length, at length, until the final hoped-for silence, like a rest from the madnesses of the Parisian

---

les canzonnettes? – Les canzonnettes? hélas! j'en suis à mon requiem! – et votre cher violoncelle? – Ah! mon violoncelle, j'y ai répandu bien des larmes depuis notre voyage dans le forêt! J'espère que Dieu me donnera la force de le briser à l'heure de ma mort; car, poursuivit-il avec un doux sourire attristé et en me serrant la main, je ne veux pas qu'un autre ait le secret des folies de mon cœur. ... Ah! la Grassini! ... Blangini fut moins un musicien qu'un poète. Il écrivait ses hymnes avec son archet sur le violoncelle, le violoncelle, livre éloquent qui renferme les gamme des passions et répond à tous les battements du cœur. Ci-gît un poète, ci-gît une âme qui chantait, ci-gît le bruit du vent, comme disait Antipater sur la tombe d'Orphée.' Ibid., p. 164.

[92]   Joris-Karl Huysmans, trans. Margaret Mauldon, *Against Nature* [À rebours] (Oxford: Oxford University Press, 1998), p. 39.

[93]   Ibid., pp. 39–40. For a recipe, see Archives départmentales de la Savoie, *Boire et manger en Savoie*: http://www.savoie.fr/archives73/expo_boire_et_manger/pages/32.htm [accessed July 2012].

struggle: the silence of Sleep, the peace of the final Retreat … at least until they
do not recover again and do not recommence, awakening, the eternal theme of
life, heroic and mad.[94]

The cello is associated with an endless emotional nagging and physical contortion.
Its voice is sad ('Tristement va la triste voix', stanza 1/1.2); it sobs ('C'est angoissé
comme un sanglot', 3/3); it rattles ('Soudain grince un son de crécelle', 3/1); it will
not stop ('Tais-toi, violoncelle!' 9/8). Its posture is awkward (stanza. 5):

> A swing, going back and forth!
> Stretch your hands, twist your arms!
> Your brains are full, your eyes weary …
> It is not finished yet, the cello.[95]

The final stanza expresses the despair of the poet as listener/victim:

> But the scraping pesters us:
> It torments, it bites, it grasps;
> The final cadence never comes …
> It is not yet finished, the cello.[96]

Interpreting such a poem as evidence of attitudes to the cello is risky; one would
not use Wallace Stevens's *The Blue Guitar* primarily as source material about
guitars. Its association with the constant sound of urban Paris may be deliberately
shocking, casting the cello in an unfamiliar role perhaps to evoke Baudelaire's
'swarming city' ('fourmillante cité') or Verlaine's 'a vague sound / says that the
city is there which sings its song […] which licks its tyrants and bites its victims'
('un vague son / Dit que la ville est là qui chante son chanson […] Qui lèche ses

---

[94]   'Oui, le Violoncelle! Toute la redoutable et geignante musique des parisiennes
luttes semble enclose en cette boite à forme de cercueil, d'où l'Archet, vivant, vibrant,
mordant, farouche comme le Destin, et parfois miel comme un baiser de féminine lumière,
sait tirer des plaintes, des ritournelles, des sanglots et des hymnes, longuement, longuement,
jusqu'au silence terminal, espéré comme un repos par les affolés de la parisienne lutte: le
silence de Sommeil, la paix de la définitive Retraite … a moins qu'ils ne ressaisissent
encore et ne recommencent, en un reveil, l'eternel thème de la vie héroïque et folle.' Emile
Goudeau. 'Le Violoncelle', in *Chansons de Paris et d'ailleurs Violoncelles – Fifres –
Mandolines* (Paris: Bibliothèque-Charpentier, 1896), pp. 3–5.
[95]   'Un va-et-vient de balancelle! / Tendez vos mains, tordez vos bras! / Les cerveaux
sont pleins, les yeux las... / Ça n'en finit plus, ce violoncelle.'
[96]   'Mais le raclement nous harcèle: / Ça lancine, ça mort, ça tient; / Le point d'orgue
jamais ne vient... / Ça n'en finit plus, ce violoncelle.'

tyrans et qui mord ses victimes').[97] Nonetheless, this sobbing, painful instrument is at least closer to the cello of Dumas, Feuillet or Houssaye, than the reserved manliness of earlier sources.

Marie Corelli's *A Romance of Two Worlds* (1886) has her character Heliobas criticize English taste in string playing:

> 'Everything that people cannot quite understand is called CLAP-TRAP in England; as for instance the matchless violin-playing of Sarasate; the tempestuous splendour of Rubinstein; the wailing throb of passion in Hollmann's violoncello – this is, according to the London press, CLAP-TRAP; while the coldly correct performances of Joachim and the "icily-null" renderings of Charles Hallé are voted "magnificent" and "full of colour."'[98]

A 'throb of passion' is not something that many critics praised in a cellist, but Marie Corelli clearly admired Hollmann, whom she lavishly eulogized in a short article in 1884:.

> Still when I look at Hollmann and his big friend, and note how they love each other, how eloquently they converse together, how they whisper and laugh and murmur, how they fondle and caress each other, I feel again that grand truth, that in the soul of the artist lives a joy which can never be taken from him, a peace which satisfies, a luxury of delight that the wealth of the world can never compass, and compared with which all other pleasures seem poor and mean. Yet it is well that this great London should learn to know its best friends, and that it should honour Hollmann and do him homage as one of the few among the world's chief artists.[99]

Corelli also described the instrument itself in terms that are very much in tune with the later nineteenth-century view of the cello as a sexually charged emotional vehicle:

> the warmth, light and happiness of a sunny summer's day, as well as the melancholy and love-languor of a moonlight night, can be summoned forth from the strings of the heavy, cumbrous thing, which, in the hands of a master, becomes a living, talking being – a being that laughs and weeps, and is capable of quick pulsations of joy and strong shudders of passion near akin to pain.[100]

---

[97]   Charles Baudelaire, 'Les sept vieillards', *Fleurs du mal* (Paris: Poulet-Malassis et de Broise, 2nd ed. 1861); Paul Verlaine, 'Nocturne parisien', *Poèmes saturniens* (Paris: Lemerre, 1866).

[98]   Marie Corelli, *A Romance of Two Worlds* (London: Richard Bentley & Son, new edn. 1890; 1st edn 1886), p. 114 (Ch. 6).

[99]   Marie Corelli, 'His Big Friend', *The Theatre*, 1 August 1884, p. 69.

[100]   Ibid., p. 64.

But the feminized cello was not necessarily the product of over-heated urban *fin-de-siècle* sensuality. Mona Douglas describes Tom Taggart, a cellist from the Isle of Man, known as a 'wise man and a musician'. He played:

> a rather large 'cello, which he always referred to as The Fiddle, or Herself; and it was, to him, quite definitely a personality. Where it came from I could never find out; a question would only elicit from Tom a vague: 'Aw, she's been in the Island a long time – brought by one of them Spaniards, it's like, and she's been here all my time.'

Taggart played hymn tunes for services in Grenaby Church in which he led the singing, and also played folk music:.

> But as a good old-fashioned Methodist, Tom felt rather guilty about these lapses of The Fiddle from 'sacred' music; and I remember him once stroking the brown wood and saying apologetically: 'Herself here has never what you could really call sinned to – but I'm admitting she likes a lively tune!'[101]

If the cello has become during this period 'feminized', or at least less 'masculine', these gender tropes are still being assigned by men, and can be seen as an exploration of otherness, rather than as a complete change of gender. Alastair Mitchell suggests such a possibility when considering Jeffrey Kallberg's view of Chopin nocturnes as a genre that 'embodies a male construction of femininity':

> Can we not find another voice in this socialisation of genre? Is it not possible that men experiencing the nocturne were not just constructing an idealised, patriarchal femininity, but also exploring another subject position, a feminine voice outside the normative codes of masculinity?[102]

These 'feminizing' traits were not sufficiently well established to cause problems of autoeroticism for female cellists like those encountered by female violinists. One possible reason for this is that, unlike the violinist, the cellist faces the audience directly and therefore is less likely to turn away from the listener in an attitude of eroticized self-absorption. Conversely, in the first part of the nineteenth century the 'manliness' of the cello does not appear to have been a significant

---

[101]   Mona Douglas, *This is Ellan Vannin Again: Folklore* (Douglas, Isle of Man: Times Longbooks, 1966), pp. 61–3. The vicar and churchwardens of Grenaby Church donated Tom Taggart's cello to the Manx Museum in 1934. It is now in the collections of Manx National Heritage, Douglas.

[102]   Alastair Williams, *Constructing Musicology* (Aldershot: Ashgate, 2001), p. 54.

cause of the relative lack of women cellists, and neither is there ever a suggestion of problematic auto-eroticism when played by a man in public.[103]

The female cellist with the most striking visual representation, Guilherminia Suggia, stimulated an extraordinary response from *Country Life*, cited below, which brings together many of the different gendered aspects of the cello discussed here. Suggia's photographs were considerably more demure than the famous portrait by Augustus John, and they have something in common with depictions of Christiani and de Try. However, there is a degree of self-absorption which is less evident in earlier pictures of female cellists, and a striking physical intimacy in the photograph of her putting her Stradivarius cello in its case.[104] While reviews of Suggia's concerts generally followed predictable lines, remarking on her technical skill and musicality while occasionally criticizing her small tone, some took a rather wider view. In 1924 the *Musical Times* described her as teasingly flirtatious in Brahms sonatas, written originally for 'big, bushy old Haussmann':

> Madame Suggia is a flashing sylphide. It was a great treat to hear her coaxing and drawing out Brahms, with all a woman's wiles. Now she would languish, and again she would give him a taste of her temper. As for Brahms, sometimes he responded all smiles (the Minuet of Op. 38), but sometimes he couldn't or wouldn't be nice (the fugal Finale of the same) but would insist on being cross as a bear, Andalusian witchery or no.[105]

However, stereotyped gender roles were presented very differently in an extraordinary article about her in 1928:

> It was as if I watched a dance [...] the very imperfections of the visible rhythm kept me aware that the real dance was invisible; that rigid partner of hers forced her to almost ungainly motions, like those of strong rowers with stiff oars in a surge.
>
> In the visible impression, strength dominated always: the tense vibrant body, the powerful shoulders, had nothing of what is called graceful; as for prettiness, it never came within a league of that lady. Beauty, the obvious plain indisputable compulsion of beauty, flashed at you in moments now of motion, now of poise, in the long sweep of the bow, or the half instant of arrest when movement completed itself, and all lines fell together in a harmony. But beauty in the larger

---

[103]   Not even when played by a Scotsman in a kilt, as in David Allan's *Highland Wedding* (1780), which depicts the cellist Donald Gow and his brother, the fiddler Neil.

[104]   These photographs can be seen in Anita Mercier, *Guilherminia Suggia* (Aldershot: Ashgate, 2008), plates following p. 75.

[105]   'C.', *MT*, 65 (1924), p. 1124. The Portuguese Suggia was frequently thought to be Spanish. On at least one occasion, on the other hand, Casals was described as Portuguese (Richard von Perger, 'Music in Vienna', *MT*, 51 (1910), p. 109).

sense […] was always there: the beauty that has roughness and force in it, like some of the hoarse disturbing notes she sent clamouring.

It was a delight to see her, before each bout began, sit up alert, balance and adjust her bow as a fencer balances his foil, then settle herself with that huge tortoise between her knees, like a jockey sitting down to the ride: erect at first and watchful, till gradually, caught by the stream she created she swung with it, gently, sleepily, languidly, until the mood shifted, the stream grew a torrent and the group rocked and swayed almost to wreckage. Or again, she would be sitting forward, taking her mount by the head, curbing it, fretting it, with imperious staccato movements, mastering it completely – letting it free to caracol easily, or once more break into full course, gathering itself in, extending itself, in a wild gallop. She was creating sound till you could see it: the music seemed to flow like running water, up her arms, over her neck; one felt that seated behind her one could see it coursing down her shoulders and her spine, with the whirls and eddies of a mountain river.

Only the face remained apart: in it was something different: the face with its closed eyes belonged to us who were played upon rather than to who played: it was the artist in the artist's other role, her own audience, listening to herself, experiencing first and more than all others the motion which her art evoked. That rapt and passive countenance, that swift ordered disciplined activity of every fibre of her body – disciplined till all was instinctive as the motions of a flying bird – showed once for all the double nature, speaker and listener at once, actor and spectator, which must be the artist's.

And then at the end, with some long-drawn singing fall, or with one abrupt vehement clang of sound, she would finish, would raise her bow high, in a gesture of dismissal, break the magic – and come to the top like a diver, a little breathless and smiling.[106]

The reviewer, Stephen Gwynn, writes as a self-proclaimed non-musician, and he responds to Suggia's performance primarily as a visual experience. The 'masculine' trope of control is present – but here it is exercised by a woman. She is herself disciplined, and is also fully in control of the cello, her 'rigid partner', here presented as an awkward or impetuous animal (tortoise, racehorse). She is transformed into a force of nature, 'a mountain river', and finally emerges from what is surely a self-absorbed sexual experience, 'a little breathless and smiling'. Beneath the exuberant language, this is a description of a self-contained, controlling and sexually dominant woman. The cello is the object of a woman's control, and a means to her own private fulfilment. Gwynn looks on.

---

[106]   Stephen Gwynn, 'When Suggia was Playing', *Country Life*, 26 November 1927, pp. 767–78. Anita Mercier cites a shortened version of this passage, but mainly to demonstrate the importance to Suggia of listening intently to herself, and making a link between the physical energy of the performance described here with the Augustus John portrait. Mercier, *Suggia*, p. 61.

He was not the only person to describe Suggia's intense physical relationship with the instrument. The adult beginner cellist Doris Stevens (1892–1963) quoted Havelock Ellis to similar effect:

> At times […] she [Suggia] seems crucified to the instrument; with arched eyebrows raised there is almost an expression of torture on her face, one seems to detect a writhing movement that only the self-mastery of art controls, and one scarcely knows whether it is across the belly of the instrument between her thighs or across her own entrails that the bow is drawn to evoke the slow deep music of these singing tones.[107]

Ellis saw the cello as ideally suited to a female performer, to the extent that he found it:

> hard to experience complete satisfaction at the spectacle of a woman with a violin […] and conversely […] the spectacle of a man with a violoncello causes a corresponding dissatisfaction.[108]

Stevens herself finds fault with Ellis for 'turn[ing] into the female body everything he likes', and she herself recounts several very conflicting accounts of the cello's gender, given to her by various friends. To the writer Floyd Dell, it was male; Konrad Bercovici, a writer and musician, confidently asserted it to be female; and the poet William Rose Benét 'said with equal finality, "It is clear that the cello is an hermaphroditic instrument"'. The lawyer Clarence Darrow, another friend, simply said '"I know it's a stringed instrument", and shrugged his famous shoulders'.[109]

With Doris Stevens and her prominent friends, the conflicting significations of the cello lead us first into an aporic confusion that is simply sidestepped by Clarence Darrow's shoulder-shrugging. The traditional characteristics of the cello are still present in Ellis's 'slow deep music', something that Doris Stevens is also drawn to. However, within the terms used in this period, the cello has undergone a significant transformation. In her final paragraph, Doris Stevens describes a cello full of memories like Felice Blangini's, an eloquent instrument like the Paris Conservatoire's, one that provides 'wide hearty joy', but a cello whose personal value transcends all this:

---

[107]   Doris Stevens, 'On Learning to Play the Cello', *American Mercury*, 8 (1926), p. 7, citing Havelock Ellis, *Impressions and Comments (2nd Series)* (London: Constable and Company Ltd., 1921), p. 169, describing a concert given by Suggia in May 1919. Stevens was a prominent American suffragist. She amusingly describes how shop assistants assumed that she was buying the instrument for a child or a young man. Hers is probably the earliest account of the experience of being an adult beginner (of either sex) on the cello.

[108]   Havelock Ellis, *Impressions and Comments, Third series* (London: Constable and Company Ltd., 1924), p. 13.

[109]   Ibid., p. 8.

The cello is mine now. It is a storehouse of beauty. It seems to me to have the power of a whole orchestra. Perhaps I endow it with memories. Anyway I no longer feel the pricks of the foolish. The instrument's deep beauty is eloquent and enduring and shrivels the easy prattle of the dead.[110]

The reception of the cello through a gendered filter shows certain significant changes over time. They have been explored here in order to establish a context for the potential application of these ideas to the perception of specific works and to aspects of their construction, and ultimately to issues of historical performance, which are explored in the next chapter.

---

[110] Ibid.

Chapter 8
Gender in Action – Performing the Cello

When a cello composition is played, what is being performed is not only the sonata or other piece; the instrument itself is also being performed. With that act of performance come certain cultural associations (which change or disappear over time), some of which have been outlined in the previous chapter in the context of gender. These associated ideas bear directly on the reception of the performance. Indeed, the audience re-creates the work in the light of these ideas. When certain instrumental forms are themselves seen in terms of gender tropes, the interaction of performer, instrument and musical form can raise issues for performance practice and reception study. This chapter will explore some of the possible consequences of this interaction by looking at compositions by the Bohrer brothers, Romberg and Lalo. The works by Bohrer and Romberg, written earlier in the nineteenth century at a time of relative consensus about the 'character' of the cello, are studied with a view to showing how their differences led to strikingly contrasting reception. The Lalo Cello Concerto, from the late nineteenth century, is examined as an example of how gender issues can become more complex, and can have suggestive implications for performance.

The cello began the nineteenth century as a manly instrument played by men, and entered the twentieth century as a less strongly gendered instrument played by men and women. But the actual music written for it took a rather different path. While tropes of the masculine virtues of restraint, slow eloquence and sublime emotion predominate, cellists rarely followed this rhetorical path in practice when they wrote music intended to demonstrate the cello's (or possibly their own) 'character'. For every slow, deep, dignified melody (such as the initial themes of Beethoven's A major sonata or Brahms's in E minor, or the second theme of Saint-Saëns's A minor concerto), there are scores, if not hundreds of compositions that exemplify precisely the opposite qualities. A cello canon develops very late in the nineteenth century. The 'classical' cello compositions deemed most important in the 1889 edition of *Grove* are the sonatas by Beethoven, Hummel, Mendelssohn (the most highly recommended), Sterndale Bennett and Brahms, the concertos by Schumann and Molique, the Brahms double concerto, Schumann's *Stücke im Volkston* and Mendelssohn's *Variations Concertantes*. Few surprises so far – but the same writer also recommends the duos for violin and cello by the Bohrers, the Rombergs, and Léonard and Servais, and Popper's *Requiem*.[1] The first unambiguous statement of the centrality to the repertoire of any cello sonata

---

[1]   Edward John Payne, 'Violoncello-playing', in Sir George Grove (ed.), *A Dictionary of Music and Musicians*, 4 vols (London: Macmillan and Co., 1889), Vol. 4, p. 301.

only occurs at the very end of the nineteenth century, in Josef Werner's comments on Beethoven's sonata in A op. 69 (which also repeat the 'manly' trope found at about the same time in Wasielewski):

> This sonata by Beethoven, with the motto: 'Inter Lacrimas et Luctum' ('Twixt tears and pain) is the best and most beautiful that the literature of the violoncello can boast of. It is so thoroughly suited to the character of the instrument that [...] the performer can display his artistic capabilities in every direction. The genuine manly character which speaks in the principal theme shows the nobility which distinguished Beethoven from all other composers. Whoever can play this sonata properly deserves the reputation of being a good violoncellist.[2]

Werner, in stressing the manliness of this sonata, could be seen as reasserting the traditional gender trope at a time when it may have begun to have had less force. On this basis, the musical 'character' of the instrument is not clearly established, even assuming that such a concept is valid.

Much of the solo repertoire even in the later eighteenth century clearly sought to imitate violinistic virtuosity, avoiding the lower strings and preferring high passage-work often using the thumb, such as the sonatas by Janson (1765), Lepin (1772) or Bréval (1783).[3] Raoul's *Méthode* (c.1797) also explores high passage-work and particularly complex bowing, often involving intricate combinations of short slurred groups and détaché notes very much in the style of violin virtuosi such as Viotti or Kreutzer, and culminates in a cello transcription of Tartini's virtuosic violin exercises *L'arte dell' arco*.[4]

If we examine some of the numerous cello compositions that do not endorse the traditional manly view of the instrument, some interesting aspects of construction and reception emerge, which can be seen in the light of the gender preoccupations outlined in the previous chapter. Here we will look at works by the Bohrer brothers and Romberg.

A height of violinistic virtuosity is reached in the duets for cello and violin by Anton Bohrer (1783–1852) and his cellist brother Max (1785–1867), composed by the brothers as vehicles for their skills. Anton Bohrer led a quartet in Paris which

---

[2]   Josef Werner, *Die Kunst der Bogenführung The Art of Bowing. op. 43. Supplement No. VII to the Author's Violoncello-Method* (Heilbronn: C.F. Schmidt, 4th edn, 1894), p. 47. The story of the 'Latin motto', supposedly found in a lost autograph MS, originates in Thayer's biography of Beethoven, and is based on Thayer's misreading of an earlier source. See Jonathan del Mar (ed.), *Beethoven Sonaten für Violoncello und Klavier* (Kassel: Bärenreiter, 2004), Critical Commentary, pp. 35–6.

[3]   Jean Baptiste Janson, *Six sonates à violoncelle et basse* op. 1 (Paris: Moria, [1765]); Henri-Noël Lepin, *Six sonates pour le violoncelle* op. 2 (Paris: the author, [1772]); Jean-Baptiste Bréval, *Six sonates à violoncelle et basse* op. 12 (Paris: the author, [1783]).

[4]   Jean Marie Raoul, *Méthode de violoncelle* (Paris: Pleyel, [c.1797]), p. 74, and ibid., 'Airs variés pour Violoncelle et Basse. L'Art de l'Archet de Tartini', pp. 84–93.

in 1830–31 gave some of the earliest performances of Beethoven's late quartets. He was a close friend of Berlioz, who noted his particular affinity with 'des œuvres de Beethoven réputées excentriques et inintelligibles'.[5] Berlioz also esteemed Max Bohrer, 'le célèbre violoncelliste', who, in 1847, offered 'cordialement' to play in Berlioz's Moscow orchestra to bolster a weak cello section.[6] Earlier critics were divided about the merits of Max Bohrer's cello playing. William Ayrton's *Harmonicon* scorned the *Herald*'s enthusiasm:

> And the Herald says, speaking of M. Bohrer's performance on the violoncello, that he 'drew the most charming, tremulous, and harmonic-like tones from that, in few other hands pleasing, instrument.' Tremulous and charming! – and the violoncello only pleasing in few hands! The fact is, I believe, that the simple tones of no instrument are more delicious than those produced from this. When bungling players attempt to execute on it, it is then, I grant, anything but pleasing. In this case, however, the player, and not the instrument, is at fault. But such trash is hardly worth a comment.[7]

This critique can be read in terms of the conflicted gender of the cello: the *Herald* praises the 'charming, tremulous harmonic-like tones' and the implied insubstantial and ethereal sound, while the *Harmonicon*'s prefers 'simple tones' and direct unadorned address to the ear. The *Harmonicon* rarely missed an opportunity to disparage the Bohrers or their unstructured compositions. When an unnamed French critic suggested that they might have more success in England, where 'a taste for futile music is so predominant', the *Harmonicon* disagreed, by siding with the Parisian when he observed of the Bohrers' works that:

> [a]n eternal wandering from subject to subject, adopted without design, and abandoned without motive, can have no other effect than to excite weariness and disgust […].[8]

Indeed, when the Bohrers eventually came to London, the *Harmonicon*'s reviewer used some of the French critic's language himself:

> Eternal motives, resumed and laid aside at pleasure, can have no other effect than to weary and disgust.[9]

---

[5] Hector Berlioz, 'Dixième lettre', *Mémoires de Hector Berlioz*, 2 vols (Paris: Calmann Lévy, 1897), Vol. 2, p. 141.

[6] Ibid., Vol. 2, p. 287.

[7] Anon., 'Diary of a Dilletante', *Harmonicon*, 7 (1829), p. 193.

[8] *Harmonicon*, 6 (1828), p. 110.

[9] Ibid., p. 119.

The English critic even affected French word-order when reviewing the Bohrers at the *Concert Spirituel*: 'Modulations incomprehensible, airs and passages old and feeble'.[10]

However, the *Harmonicon* also suggested an alternative repertoire for the cellist:

> His brother, M. Max Bohrer, has not lost any of his talent, but he would have been better appreciated had he displayed it in a concerto of Romberg.[11]

The *Harmonicon* clearly thought Romberg a better example than Bohrer, judging from a review of the former in Riga:

> the most remarkable [concert] was that given by the celebrated Bernhard Romberg, on his return from [...] a very successful tour in Russia. On this occasion he performed with that effect which an author only can impart to his own works, his grand concerto in B minor [no. 9, op. 56]. This noble picture of tones contains every thing that is consonant with the dignity of the art, and stands as a model of pure excellence in these days of caprice and extravagance.[12]

This contrasting of Bohrer and Romberg is also referred to by van der Straeten:

> He [Romberg] said on one occasion when he heard Bohrer play: 'If I stand at the end of the hall and close my eyes, I imagine myself sitting on the platform, and it sounds to me as if I were playing myself.' A contemporary writing about the two artists says: 'Romberg's playing is that of the purest German school, and as such unparalleled. Max Bohrer as a virtuoso stands outside of any school. His tone is fantasy itself, the earthly echo of the innermost vibrations of his very soul. This gives his style and manner of playing the stamp of originality, and it is so interwoven with his psychical being, so characteristic, light and skilful, that it must be regarded as absolutely individual, unlike everything else, and excluding all comparison. Technically he stands on the same level as Romberg, with whose compositions he usually appears before the public, the two artists being as yet unequalled by any other player'.[13]

Max Bohrer's *L'Amabilité*, and the brothers' jointly composed 16th *Grand Duo Concertant* for violin and cello, give an indication of what it was that so exercised the *Harmonicon*, charmed the *Herald,* and perhaps prompted the un-named writer

---

10   Ibid., p. 141. This is all the more significant given the *Harmonicon*'s frequent antipathy towards French music and criticism.

11   Ibid.

12   *Harmonicon*, 4 (1826), p. 61.

13   Edmund van der Straeten, *A History of the Violoncello, the Viol da Gamba, their Precursors and Collateral Instruments* (London: William Reeves, 1914), p. 244.

quoted by van der Straeten. The following discussion will set out some of the characteristic features of these works.[14]

L'Amabilité is in that popular earlier nineteenth-century form, a set of variations. It begins with a short slow *pp* introduction, featuring double-stopped harmonics on the cello over a simple dotted-rhythm *arpeggio* figure in the piano part that prefigures the opening notes of the principal *allegro* theme. Though lacking melodic or harmonic interest, the piano part creates a particular atmosphere through the generous use of the sustaining pedal, rapid flourishes in the high register and the final *tremolando* in the bass. The banal *tempo di marcia* theme, which slightly resembles that from Rossini's *Mosè in Egitto* used for Paganini's set of variations on one string, concludes with an amusing, *piano subito*, *delicato* sequence of trills. Variation 1 is a virtuosic display, not for the cello, whose part is confined to rudimentary pizzicato, but the piano (Example 8.1). The Bohrer brothers were often accompanied by Anton's wife Fanny (née Lebrun), and it is quite possible that she composed the piano parts, which include detailed fingering. There was a considerable keyboard tradition on the female side of the Bohrer family. Fanny Lebrun (b.1807) was the daughter of the well-known pianist Sophie Lebrun and the piano maker J.L. Dülcken, and her sister Louise married Max Bohrer. Both Sophie Lebrun and her sister Rozine studied the piano with Andreas Streicher,

Example 8.1   Bohrer, *L'amabilité*, variation 1

¹⁴   Max Bohrer, *L'Amabilité, Duo Concertant pour piano et violoncelle* op. 14 (London: Wessel & Co. [1832]); Les Frères Bohrer, *16me. Grand Duo Concertant, pour violon et violoncelle* op. 47 (London: Wessel & Co., [1832]).

the husband of Nanette Streicher, of the famous Viennese piano-manufacturing firm. Max Bohrer's daughter, also named Sophie, was a keyboard virtuoso who made her debut at the age of nine; their son Henry was also a pianist.[15] Variation 2 gives the piano the simple statement of the theme, with the cello adding arpeggio flourishes on one string (Example 8.2). Variation 3 has the cello and upper piano part playing mostly in thirds, in triplet quavers that are slurred, *détaché*, and, in the case of the cello, sometimes played in up-bow staccato groups. However, in the second half of this variation the piano part becomes increasingly virtuosic, culminating in a passage of broken double octaves before fading away into an entirely new *andante* section in F major. But no sooner has this begun than the piano has a cadenza; only after this does the cello play the new theme. For a few bars, the piano takes over, with a florid melody swathed in sustaining pedal over a comically contrasting *buffo* cello accompaniment (Example 8.3). The cello returns to the *andante* theme, but soon this modulates dramatically from F to the dominant of B minor, *con fuoco*. A gradually descending cello trill combines with diminished and dominant sevenths, '*tremulo*', in the piano, dying away on the dominant of the original theme. The main theme is then repeated in full, but the earlier *delicato* trills are interrupted this time by a silent bar. From here, an extensive coda featuring *ponticello* bariolage and broken octave passage-work for the cello leads to a repeat of the opening *adagio* introduction (with its double-stopped harmonics) and a brisk *allegro vivace* conclusion.

This composition contradicts almost all conventional perceptions of the character of the cello at this time. The lower registers are largely avoided, other than for short sections where the cello plays an accompanying bass figure. Dynamics are very restrained, in curious contrast with the piano part, which almost appears designed to be too loud for the cellist (even bearing in mind the less powerful instrument of the period). There is much use of harmonics, both sustained and in passage-work, some *ponticello* and some left-hand pizzicato. A passage of triplet broken octaves is marked a diffident *mezza voce*, surprising from a cellist whose octave playing was often singled out for praise. Other cellists would indicate something more assertive; a very similar passage in Goltermann's Concerto in D minor (1861), is marked *mf* with repeated *crescendi*/*diminuendi* hairpins.[16]

For a composition intended as a virtuoso showpiece for the cello, the piano part is far more than a mere accompaniment (while there may some influence of the 'accompanied sonata' genre here, no review suggests that these pieces were seen primarily as anything other than cello solos). It takes the main role in the first variation (using rapid crossed hands at one point) while the cello provides the simplest possible accompaniment, and its elaborate cadenza is much more impressive than anything the cello is required to do. The piano's upper pitch range is particularly high, often using f′′′′ but going no lower than G♯′ (the upper limit

---

[15] Robert Munster, 'Sophie Lebrun', and Margaret Cranmer, 'Streicher', in *Grove Music Online* [accessed January 2012].

[16] Georg Goltermann, *Concerto no. 2* op. 30 (Offenbach: André, [1861]).

Example 8.2   *L'amabilité*, variation 2, first part (easier alternative cello part omitted)

Example 8.3   *L'amabilité, andante*, piano solo episode

is not by any means unknown at this time, but many pianos were still being made with a top note of only c''''). [17] Not only, then, is the cello part itself rather light-weight, avoiding the more resonant and 'characteristic' registers, but its effect is further weakened by the extremely virtuosic accompaniment – its lack of *gravitas* is only underlined by the frivolous piano part.

Similar tendencies can be observed in the Bohrers' sixteenth *Duo Concertant* for violin and cello. Very high natural harmonics, double-stopped harmonics, combinations of left- and right-hand pizzicato, complex string-crossings, playing in very high positions on lower strings, rapid arpeggios on one string, rapid multiple same-finger shifts, a tendency towards quieter dynamic markings, and the near-total avoidance of anything resembling a straightforward *cantabile* melody, mean that the 'accepted character' of the cello is contradicted if not actually subverted. The cello, in these compositions, becomes an epigone of the violin. Indeed, most of the features of the cello part in the *Duo Concertant* are present in the violin part as well, including the rapid sequences of same-finger shifts (the string and piano parts of both Bohrer works examined here are thoroughly marked with performance instructions such as fingerings, bowings, and pedal marks). This duo maintains an equal balance of interest between the parts to a greater degree than *L'amabilité*. They also generally avoid up- or down-bow staccato and complex combinations of slurred and *détaché* bowing. The equality of the violin and cello parts means that at times both instruments appear to be busy with elaborate accompanying figures, while no melody is present, so that the effect is of a proliferation of subsidiary material in the absence of a principal idea.

Contemporary opinions varied about both the inherent qualities and the aesthetic merits of the Bohrers' compositions. An 1822 concert in Vienna was reviewed at some length, with particular attention paid to the cellist, whose virtuosity was spoken of along with that of the 'unforgettable Romberg', and whose reputation had raised high expectations. [18] Max Bohrer was praised for his 'special certainty and skill, combined with a regulated use of the bow [...], his beautiful trills, precision in the low strings, and the purity of his harmonics'. [19]

---

[17]   Martha Novak Clinkscale, *Makers of the Piano 1700–1820* (Oxford: Oxford University Press, 1993), p. 289. Clinkscale shows that pianos by Streicher after 1810, and most of those by Wachtl, reached f'''', but only some Broadwood grands and uprights did so, and Stodart's mostly did not.

[18]   'Der Ruf, welcher diesen beyden Künsltern vorausging, und besonders jener des Violoncellisten, von dessen Virtuosität selbst noch bey der letzten Anwesenheit des uns unvergesslichen Rombergs viel gesprochen wurde, musste die gespannteste Erwartung des ganzen Publicums rege machen, welches auch die Lösung ihrer Aufgabe nur um so schwieriger machte.' *AmZmbR*, 6 (1822), p. 629.

[19]   'Eine besondere Sicherheit und Fertigkeit, verbunden mit einer geregelten Bogenführung zeichnen ihn besonders aus, so wie auch sein schöner Triller, die Deutlichkeit auch in den tiefen Corden, und die Reinheit seines Flageolets äusserst lobenswerth erscheinen.' Ibid.

However, neither his tone quality nor his *cantabile* production merited such praise; these should have been better, Bohrer being 'in the prime of life' ('in der Blüthe seiner Jahre') as far as strength and feeling were concerned.[20] It is hard to think of a female performer being described in such terms, which suggest that Max Bohrer is really being criticized for a lack of manliness. The concert was 'somewhat old-fashioned, [appearing] to belong to an earlier period' ('etwas veraltet, und scheint der frühern Epoche desselben anzugehören'), but the audience response was much greater than for other musicians:

> The two cadenzas, in which this artist proved to us the whole range of his skill and security in leaps and runs, could not therefore likewise restrain the overflowing applause, because such exercises are more for the assembly of difficulties, as must apply for cadenzas.[21]

The unity of the Bohrers' ensemble was frequently praised, both in parallel passages ('gleichlaufenden Passagen') and in 'insurpassable individual solos' ('unübertrefflich waren die einzelnen Passagen'), particularly the cellist's difficult octave runs ('besonders die so schwierigen Octavengänge des Violoncells'). However, just as with the *Duo concertant* above, so here too the variation technique obscured the principal theme:

> The theme is quite beautiful, and one wants to hear the principal melody more often than the variations allow it to appear.[22]

This review also singles out one surprising aspect of the Bohrers' playing for special praise – their accents:

> The duo's purity in ensemble, often so beautifully produced (which was only more increased through really beautiful and interesting accents [*Drucker*] and *rinsforzandi*), sounded like a complete harmony.[23]

---

[20]   'Wir bedauern nur ihm unsere volle Anerkennung seines Verdienstes nicht in demselben Grade, auch in Hinsicht des Tones, so wie auch in Bezug auf die Führung des Gesanges zu können, da er doch in der Blüthe seiner Jahre, sowohl hinsichtlich der Kraft, als des Gefühls, zu dieser Erwartung berechtiget hätte.' Ibid.

[21]   'Die beyden Fermaten, in welehen uns dieser Künstler die ganze Fülle seiner Fertigkeit und Sicherheit in den Sprüngen und Läufen bewiessen hat, konnten ebenfalls desshalb nicht zum überströmenden Beyfall reitzen, weil derley Excercitien mehr für Agregat von Schwierigkeiten, als für Fermaten gelten müssen.' Ibid., p. 630.

[22]   'Das Thema ist recht anmuthsvoll, und man möchte öfter seinen Haupstgesang hören, als die Variationen ihn zum Vorschein kommen lassen.' Ibid.

[23]   'Die Reinheit ihres im Ensemble oft so schön geführten Duo's, welche durch recht anmuthige und interessante Drucker und Rinsforzando's nur noch mehre erhöht wurde, klang gleich einer vollständigen Harmonie.' Ibid., p. 631.

A concert in Dresden was treated quite favourably, with praise for Max Bohrer's clarity in low registers (even though his compositions do not often exploit this), purity in fast passage-work, confident shifting, and other technical aspects of the performance, but the 'final cadenza clashed horribly with the whole'.[24] The programme consisted of a Mozart overture, a Rossini aria and four items by the Bohrers. The last item, a *Capriccio* on a French song, was seen as a weak conclusion, 'full of difficulties yet with no real effect' ('als Schlussstück zu matt, voll Schwierigkeiten und doch kein wahrer Effect').[25]

On the other hand, the almost literal equality of the violin and cello parts in their duets prompted one reviewer to see them as a particular sub-genre of duet:

> Duets in the strictest sense (i.e. where the composition is purely in two parts, each part is a leading voice and the motives are skilfully developed), are as rare as they are difficult to devise, particularly for instruments of a single type, and are not as highly valued by the multitude as they deserve to be. It may be for this reason that Mozart, the two Rombergs and many others do not exclude polyphonic textures from their Duets, and use it in alternation with two-part counterpoint, though conforming otherwise with all critical demands of this sort of composition. The addiction of virtuosi to writing for their instruments, even without a previous thorough study of composition, has led to the emergence of a third genre of so-called Duos, which could really be called solos for two instruments and are comparable with a poem which two people divide up and recite. […] In [these duos], both instruments are meaningfully used and require good players, especially as concerns execution; in such hands the first two Duos, despite their manifold weaknesses of execution, their motives, modulations etc., will go down well everywhere; the third, however, which aspires to erudition, will not please anyone, under any circumstances.[26]

---

24   'die am Schlusse angebrachte Ferma passte aber zum Ganzen wie eine Faust auss Auge.' *BAmZ*, 6 (1822), p. 679.

25   Ibid., p. 680.

26   'Duetts, im strengsten Sinne des Worts, so dass der Satz rein zweistimmig, jede Stimme Hauptstimme ist, und die Motive kunstgemäss ausgeführt sind, findet man eben so selten, wie sie schwer, besonders für Instrumente einerlei Gattung, zu erfinden sind, und von der Menge nicht so geachtet werden, wie sie es verdienen. Aus diesem Grunde mögen wohl Mozart, die beiden Romberge u. a. m. den mehrstimmigen Satz in ihren Duetten nicht ausgeschlossen haben, und lassen ihn mit dem zweistimmigen Satze, übrigens aber alle Forderung der Kritik an Kompositionen dieser Art erfüllend, abwechseln. Die Sucht der Virtuosen, auch ohne vorhergangenes gründliches Studium der Komposition für ihre Instrument zu schreiben, hat noch eine dritte Gattung sogenannter Duos zu tage gefördert, die eigentlich nur Solos für zwei Instrumente genannt werden können und einem Gedicht vergleichbar sind, in welches sich zwei theilen und so recitiren. Dass auch auf diesem Wege von talentvollen Männern manches unterhaltende Tonstück für kleine Zirkel gewonnen wird, beweisen vorliegende Duos, welche schon durch den herrlichen Vortrag ihrer Autoren dem musikalischen Publikum auf das vortheilhafteste bekannt sind. Beide

Surprisingly, this review of the Bohrers' *Trois duos concertans* op. 3 was supplemented by a much longer discussion of the same music in the same journal, but by a different writer ('v. d. O.'), and with different conclusions.[27] This second reviewer struggles with the concept of two brothers writing one composition. 'V. d. O.' cites the unrelated Reichardt and Naumann who wrote one act each of an opera, and the Stolberg brothers who published poetry jointly, but then goes on to say that for 'two brothers [to] compose one composition, one and the same allegro, is really unprecedented'.[28] In fact it was not quite unprecedented. The Rombergs' *Trois duos concertans* op. 2 had appeared c.1801, although they were admittedly cousins, not brothers, and the brothers Moritz and Leopold Ganz appeared as soloists together often in the 1830s and 1840s performing their own duos.[29] After extolling the Bohrers' presumed upbringing, unanimous taste and feeling, 'v. d. O.' suggests a counter-theory that the duets might have been composed by, say, one of the brothers who only included the other's name out of brotherly affection ('aus brüderlicher Liebe'). This theory is then immediately dismissed because each part is individually treated with great knowledge of the instrument, and therefore 'each [part] owes its origin only to its master and to its virtuoso' ('dass eine jede nur ihrem Meister und ihrem Virtuosen den Ursprung verdankt'). In spite of this eulogy, this reviewer's final assessment is oddly ambiguous:

> Did the two brothers compose this duo together? Probably not. – There blows therein the spirit of a great shared feeling. Nevertheless, it can surely be said: one created it, but both prepared it.[30]

Instrumente sind in denselben bedeutend beschäftigt und verlangen gute Spieler, besonders, was den Vortrag betrifft; in solchen Händen aber werden die zwei ersten Duos, trotz ihrer mannigfaltigen Schwächen rücksichtlich der Ausführung, der Motive, Modulation etc., überall eine recht freundliche Aufnahme finden; das dritte aber, welches Anspruch auf Gelehrsamkeit macht, wird unter keiner Bedingung irgend Jemand aussprechen.' 'Fiaccola', *BAmZ*, 1 (1822), p. 402, reviewing the Bohrers' *Trois duos concertans* op. 3 (Berlin and Paris: Schlesinger, [1822]).

27 'v. d. O.', *BAmZ*, 1 (1822), pp. 403–5.

28 'aber dass zwei Brüder an einem Werke, an ein und demselben Allegro komponirten, ist wol nicht vorgekommen.' Ibid., p. 403. Friedrich Leopold (1750–1819) and Christian Stolberg (1748–1821), joint publications: *Gedichte* (1779); *Schauspiele Wait Choren* (1787), *Vaterlandische Gedichte* (1815). Johann Friedrich Reichardt and Johann Gottlieb Naumann composed Acts 1 and 2 respectively of *Protesilao* (1789, rev. 1793).

29 Andreas and Bernhard Romberg, *Trois duos concertans* op. 2 (Leipzig: Breitkopf & Härtel, [1801]); 'Les frères Ganz', *Duo concertant* op. 11 (Leipzig: Hofmeister, [1832]). Moritz Ganz became principal cellist in the Royal Court Chapel in Berlin in 1826, following Duport, Romberg and Bohrer. Anon., 'Memoirs of the Brothers Moritz & Leopold Ganz', *MW*, 5 (1837), p. 148.

30 'Ob die beiden Herren Brüder auch wol dieses Duo zugleich erfunden haben? Wohl nicht. – Es weht darin nur der geist einer grossen mitgetheilten Empfindung. Man kann wol immerhin behaupten: einer habe es erfunden, aber beide es ausgearbeitet.' Ibid., p. 405.

V.d.O. has mixed feelings about the music itself. On one hand it is almost amusingly predictable:

> The cellist says, 'I will take the theme and play a solo, you accompany the cello.' Said; done. Bravo! The violinist says, 'Now it's my turn, you accompany.' So the first repeat is done just like this, the movement taking off, but tastefully and always interestingly designed, and the whole movement following sonata form. It is certainly not an original duo, in which both parts have melody and the harmony is justified on contrapuntal principles.[31]

But those who like their chamber music with a large solo element will not be disappointed:

> whoever loves the nine quartets of B. Romberg, in which the cello is validated as a concertante soloist, and quartets for the [solo?] violin by Spohr, will, in this sense, not fail to applaud our present duo.[32]

The second duo is 'designed with great virtuosity, efficiently accomplished and in every respect to be called a great duo, but not an original one'.[33] However, the two reviews differ most when discussing the third duo (a prelude and fugue). The first reviewer dismisses it as a work that would not please anyone at all, but for 'v. d. O.' it is the best, especially the prelude:

> However the reviewer gives the absolute preference to the prelude, effectively arranged though the fugue is. It is rich in the noblest song, the clear two-part [writing] always shines out and is only provided with essential long sustained filling notes, nonetheless this only gives more charm to this outstanding duet. The dominant key is C major, however it modulates in the style of the prelude (free fantasia) but nonetheless naturally in various keys (apart from bars 10 and 11).

---

[31] 'Der Cellist sagt: "ich will das Thema nehmen und ein Solo spielen, begleite Du auf dem Cello." Gesagt, gethan. Bravo! Der Violinist sagt: "Nun komm ich, begleite Du." So ist die erste Reprise in etwas zu geraden, absetzenden Sätzen, aber geschmackvoll und immer interessant entworfen und der ganze Satz in Sonatenform gehalten. Ein Original-Duo, in welchem beide Stimmen Melodie haben und nach kontrapunktischen Grundsätzen Harmonie begründen, ist es freilich nicht.' Ibid., p. 404.

[32] 'Wer aber die neun Quartetts des B. Romberg, in welchen das Violoncell allein koncertirend geltend gemacht wird, liebt, und manche Quartette für die Violine von Spohr, der wird in diesem Sinne auch unserm [unsern?] vorliegenden Duo seinen Beifall nicht versagen.' Ibid.

[33] 'Es ist mit hoher Virtuosität entworfen, tüchtig durchgeführt und in jeder Beziehung ein grosses Duo zu nennen, aber nicht Original-Duo'. Ibid.

Through this, it had a high, noble and serious feeling, so that it must produce *a peculiar effect of the evening darkness.*[34]

Although neither the fugal subject nor its passage-work are original, the fugue is competently written and makes an excellent impression. The reviewer singles out the use of inversion, the test of a worthy contrapuntist ('mit vielen Umkehrungen, den wackern Kontrapunktisten bewährt'), and concludes by commending the set of duos as a whole:

The first two likewise cannot be recommended enough for study, and will give to connoisseurs and amateurs, who wish to build up their playing on each instrument, a rich spiritual nourishment.[35]

What is striking in the review by 'v. d. O.' is the combination of conventional musical description with a flash of poetic evocation, and the overall attempt to praise even when pointing out weaknesses or lack of originality. This reviewer is most impressed by the mood of the third duo's prelude, prompting the analogy with twilight, 'etwa des Abends im Dunkeln'. However, this small flight of fancy is easily outdone by the reviewer for the 1822 *AmZmbR*:

These artists are on the path, which they have followed well and rapidly for many years; we mean a correct and sound treatment of the violin and the cello. Bowing, fingering, and presentation, they themselves mark every bow-stroke with the finest security, sweetness and inner feeling [*Innigkeit*]; they are the van der Werfs, the Houwalds among musicians. And it is this combination of the two which arouses new interest in the listener. One can hear no more complete ensemble; it is at the same time a unanimity of feeling [*Zusammenfühlen*] and so must affect the hearer, with sensibility, more strongly. Also in their compositions the brothers' individuality remains the same. Everywhere loveliness and tender colouring, and the same in the *Symphonie militaire concertante* [...], with a rondo on Dutch national themes, which smells of a pot-pourri of violets, mayflowers and primroses, beneath which only a timpani-stroke stands out (like

---

[34] 'Rec. giebt aber dem Präludio unbedingt den Vorzug, so tüchtig auch die Fuge gearbeitet ist. Es ist reich an dem edelsten Gesange, der immer rein zweistimmig erscheint und nur mit langgehaltenen Füllnoten versehen ist, die dem eigentlichen, dennoch hervortretenden Duett nur noch mehr Reiz geben. Die herrschende Tonart ist C-dur, es modulirt aber in der art der Präludien (freien Fantasien) überaus natürlich (ausgenommen den 10. und 11. Takt) in mancherlei Tonarten. Dabei hat es eine hohe, edle und ernste Empfindung, so dass es etwa des Abends im Dunkeln, in einer eigenthümlichen Effekt hervorbringen müsste.' Ibid. Italics added.

[35] 'Die andern beiden ersten sind ebenfalls zum studium nicht genug zu empfehlen und werden Kennern und Liebhabern, die sich für das höher im Spielen der beiden Instrumente ausbilden wollen, eine geistreiche Unterhaltung gewähren.' Ibid., p. 405.

dog-roses). May these true virtuosi remain with us for quite a long time; they will always find grateful listeners.[36]

These reviews from the earlier 1820s suggest that while the identity of the respective instruments remains, with the cello and violin parts each idiomatically conceived, this character is also transcended, so that the correct way of writing for the instrument produces sounds that can only be described by means of floral analogy and literary allusion.

The assertion that the individual character of each instrument is preserved is puzzling in the light of the *Duo Concertant* op. 47, where there seems to be little that distinguishes either part from the other. The simplest explanation would be that some listeners thought that Max Bohrer's style of composition and performance did indeed represent the true character of the cello. Whatever the case, at least one later critic disagreed. In 1830, echoing the *AmZmbR* reviewer of Bohrer's 1822 Vienna concert, *BamZ* praised Max Bohrer's 'praiseworthy skill' ('bewunderungswürdiger Fertigkeit') but with an important reservation:

> One makes a criticism of Herr Bohrer, that he is unable to produce the loveliest characteristic of his instrument, consisting of a singing tone, though the tone of the cello has the greatest affinity with the male voice.[37]

Yet another review even saw Bohrer's apparent contradiction of the character of the cello as a positive virtue:

---

[36] 'Diese Künstler sind auf dem Wege, den sie schon vor mehreren Jahren ganz entschieden betreten, rasch vorgeschritten: wir meinen den, einer correcten und gediegenen Behandlung der Geige und des Cello. Bogenführung, Applicatur, und Vortrag, haben sich bey ihnen zur schönsten Sicherheit, Zartheit und Innigkeit bezeichen jeden Strich; sie sind die van der Werf's, die Houwald's, unter den Musikern. Und diese Vereinigung Beider ist es nun auch wieder, welche ein neues Interesse beim Zuhörer weckt. Man kann kein vollendeteres Zusammenspiel hören; es ist zugleich ein Zusammenfühlen und so muss es auch stärker auf den Zuhörer wirken, der Gefühl hat. Auch in ihren Compositionen bleibt die Individualität der Brüder sich gleich. Überall Lieblichkeit und zartes Colorit, und selbst in der (Sr. Majestät dem König zugeigneten) Symphonie militaire concertante, mit Rondo über holländische National-lieder, duftet ein pot-pourri von Veilchen, Maiblumen und Aurikeln, unter denen nur einige Paukenschlage (als Klatschrosen) hervorstechen. Möchten diese echten Virtuosen recht lange bey uns verweilen; sie werden stets dankbare Zuhörer finden.' Anon., *AmZmbR*, 6 (1822), pp. 25–6. Christoph Ernst von Houwald (1778–1845), German playwright and writer (although his brother Heinrich does not appear to have been a writer); Pieter (1665–1722) and Adriaen (1659–1722) van der Werff, Dutch painters.

[37] 'Man macht Herrn Bohrer zum Vorwurf, dass er die schönste Eigenthümlichkeit seines Instruments, die im Gesangtone bestehe, nicht zu kennen scheine, da der Ton des Violoncello die grösste Verwandtschaft mit der menschlichen Stimme habe.' Anon, *BAmZ*, 7 (1830), p. 40.

Herr Bohrer may be aptly styled the Paganini of the Violoncello, for he conquers a thousand hitherto insurmountable difficulties, and achieves undreamed of things – his tone is mellifluous, his execution brilliant, his fingering rapid and facile, and his bow-hand free and capable of every possible evolution – he makes the instrument more like a violin, or tenor, than a violoncello, and his tone on the two lower strings is almost the reverse of the upper – however, he uses them but rarely [...].[38]

Compared with the next generation of virtuosi, his playing appears to have been found wanting by implication:

Herr Max has a firm tone, and plays *cantabiles* with great neatness and finish. His playing is devoid of the singing-like manner which so highly distinguishes Piatti, Cossmann, and others, but he accomplishes great difficulties; his intonation and phrasing are very correct.[39]

Many reviews, then, suggest that Max Bohrer did not realize the true, masculine, singing character of the cello. Critics agreed that his compositions and performances avoided the conventional cello stereotype, but opinions differed markedly as to why, and to whether or not this was a good thing. Those reviews that resort to particularly *recherché* similes can be read as trying to deal with a repertoire that lies outside conventional discourse. For modern performers trying to recreate the circumstances of early nineteenth-century performance, the asserted masculine qualities of the cello might suggest a certain way of playing, but the works themselves, and some aspects of their reception, might suggest something quite different.

Virtuosic works of this kind, composed by cellists primarily as vehicles for their own technique, can appear broadly similar if viewed from the perspective of the canon. They may look weak when compared with, say, the sonatas of Beethoven or Mendelssohn. However, from a closer viewpoint some interesting distinctions appear, with Romberg's compositions offering the more solid fare. A generation after his death, Romberg was seen as irretrievably *passé*:

Signor Piatti repeated at his concert the *adagio frondo* from Bernard Romberg's 'Swiss Concerto', lately resuscitated by him at one of the meetings of the Philharmonic Society. Music so weakly elegant would not be worth calling from its grave, were it not clothed with fresh beauty by the silvery tones of the Italian violoncellist.[40]

---

[38] Anon., 'Herr Max Bohrer's Concert', *MW*, 17 (1842), p. 309, reviewing a concert at Windsor, 20 September 1830.

[39] Anon., 'Miscellaneous', *MW*, 24 (1849), p. 414.

[40] Anon. [Henry Chorley], *Athenaeum*, 4 July 1868, p. 25.

'Weakly elegant' it may have seemed, but compared to the Bohrers' duos it is relatively substantial. Romberg's musical forms are on a larger scale (he writes far fewer sets of variations), his passage-work and *cantabile* melodies are both more extended, the full range of the instrument is exploited, effects such as harmonics or *sul ponticello* are used much less often (though there are some striking examples of both), and accompaniments remain clearly subordinated to the solo cello. His *Divertimenti* on national themes, at the lighter end of his output, are admittedly uneven. Romberg himself thought highly of the *Nationallieder* genre and discussed its possibilities at some length – note his Herderian distinction between urban and rural folk song:

> If the Composer of such variations has made himself acquainted with the airs upon which they are written, in the country to which they belong, and if he has acquired a knowledge of the musical feeling of the nation, then he may certainly impart a character to the variations which he composes on such airs. The airs with variations of the French, German and Tyrolese, are seldom national […] we must not consider as such, those which have acquired a certain appearance of nationality, by being frequently sung by mechanics and artisans, but only those which take their rise among the peasantry.[41]

The *Divertimento über österreichische Lieder* op. 46 is typical.[42] A short introduction based largely on simple arpeggio figuration (and with no 'national' content) is followed by a succession of triple-time themes: a quaint *ländlerisch* dance, another triple time theme with a contrasting theme from the piano which is taken up later by the cello, a *scherzando* theme with skittish jumps, and a contrastingly broad theme with equal material for both instruments. After a flirtatious linking passage based on the concluding bars of the introduction, the last section of the piece begins with another, more waltz-like, theme. This final section, consisting itself of five new themes, is virtually a pot-pourri of its own. The conclusion consists of simple string-crossing arpeggio figures for the cello under a new theme in the piano part. Although this type of composition is formally loose by nature, it is not quite as arbitrarily constructed as a Bohrer piece. The themes may be fundamentally unconnected, but they share a simple triadic melodic character. Modulation is restrained, and the piece avoids flamboyant instrumental or compositional effects. While reviews of the Bohrer's concerts often mention pizzicato, accents and harmonics, along with a lack of melodic expressiveness, it is clear from works like Romberg's *Nationallieder* that the latter's playing was almost entirely of the opposite kind. Nonetheless, while their playing styles were

---

[41]   Bernhard Romberg, trans. anon. *A Complete Theoretical and Practical School for the Violoncello* (London: T. Boosey & Co., [1840]), pp. 130–31.

[42]   Bernhard Romberg, ed. Friedrich Grützmacher, *Ausgewählte Kompositionen von Bernard Romberg. vol. 1. Drei Divertimenti über Nationallieder* opp. 42. 46 and 65 (Leipzig: C.F. Peters, [1880]).

normally quite clearly distinguished in their day, within a few years they were seen as very similar; in 1849 the *Literary Gazette* described Max Bohrer as 'a cellist of the Romberg school'.[43]

A more substantial composition of Romberg's shows these qualities well. The second cello concerto op. 3 in D, typical of his ten concertos, was particularly widely studied in the nineteenth century. There is a very clear contrast between the first and second subject groups, the latter strikingly restless and contrasting with the first subject's clear orientation around the tonic triad. Both themes are presented along with passage-work of various kinds. The development opens with the first subject in the dominant, slightly modified so that the more decorative passages are not literally repeated, immediately followed by a similarly altered version of the second subject. After more semiquaver passage-work a new theme is introduced in G, which soon modulates towards an extended section of passage-work in B minor, leading to the recapitulation. Romberg omits the first theme and goes straight to a reprise of the passage-work that immediately followed in the exposition, and similarly shortens the second subject group, before finishing with some triplet passage-work. The themes are not particularly individual and rely for their character on the decorative figures which embellish them. The emphasis is clearly on the passage-work material, which uses a small number of ideas sequentially to create larger units. The effect of this method is heightened in the recapitulation by the foreshortening of the principal themes. In general there is a complete avoidance of the tricks used by the Bohrers, and a more integrated structural approach that highlights the soloist's virtuosity while keeping the overall form relatively concise. There are no harmonic surprises – even Romberg's 'dramatic' flattened submediant modulation in the second movement is unconvincing (Example 8.4). The second movement is in a simple ternary form, with an extended middle section. This introduces various short-lived themes which all appear to derive from the initial one, due to the use of short melodic formulae in different combinations (Example 8.5).

Rather like the first movement, the third, a *Rondo tempo di minuetto*, alternates a rather weak theme with successive virtuosic episodes, including an extended Spanish-style fandango utilising the lower strings in high positions (up to a on the C string – see Chapter 3). There are also *ponticello* effects and a few bars in artificial harmonics. Even here, however, the *Passagen* are consistent in character.

Romberg's style of composition strives toward a balance between the basic requirements of musical form and the need for virtuosic display. What should be important thematic material is announced but quite swiftly curtailed, a sensible tactic given Romberg's lack of a real melodic gift. These themes are mostly used as simple structural markers rather than as the source of material for development. Passage-work relies on a few standard figurations derived from scales, arpeggios and sequences of broken octaves, with combinations of short slurred *détaché* groups. High natural harmonics are used in simple arpeggio figures that are

---

[43] Anon., *Literary Gazette*, 33 (1849), p. 468.

Example 8.4   Romberg, Cello Concerto no. 2, slow movement, modulation to C

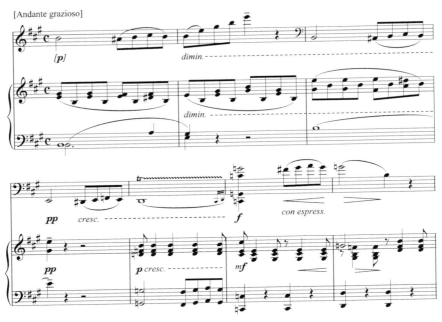

Example 8.5   Romberg, Cello Concerto no. 2, slow movement, themes

extensions of melodic lines rather than sound-effects – once in the high register Romberg does not simply stay there in order to find additional harmonics on other strings as Max Bohrer does. The general impression is therefore of a more integrated style, even if this results from Romberg's limitations.

Critics generally treated Romberg's works quite differently from those of the Bohrers. The *Harmonicon*'s review has already been quoted. Even a more extreme review from *AmZmbR* did not resort to far-fetched poetic similes to describe Romberg's playing. It stressed his effortless technique and the purely musical effect of his performance on his audience, deploying the masculine trope of the controlling cellist:

> Romberg's great freedom in his element shows already in his appearance. Spurning the printed music as an *aide-memoire*, he takes his place, the magic instrument in his hands, and, without hiding himself behind a music stand, presents to the public the whole picture of a free, unrestricted ruler of the kingdom of tones. The left hand flies with a never before seen ease through high and low positions, while the right swings the bow with an unsurpassed calm and security. Not displaying any courageous effort, in spite of the strength of the low strings [when] landing in high positions, the whole bodily strength required by passages of such speed, shows the eye an interesting picture of this artist, such as his marvellously beautiful playing brings to the delighted ear. It sings, to put it in a word, and seizes the listener's soul by the power of its singing. In the *adagio* all hearts admitted themselves overcome by his art, which were already conquered and carried away in the preceding fiery *allegro* by the force of his tones. The applause acknowledged the character of stormy joy, and at the end of the finale hardly seemed to want to end.[44]

Romberg's most 'representational' piece, the so-called 'Swiss' Concerto, no. 7 (performed by Piatti with such a lack of effect in 1868),[45] was received by the *AmZmbR* as a masterpiece of painterly realism with overtones of the sublime:

> His cello concerto, a Swiss picture, showed Romberg's art, which knows how to combine musical painting with high virtuosity. It gives his tone-poem, through

---

[44] 'Romberg's grosse Freyheit in seinem Elemente zeigt sich schon bey seinem Auftritte. Die Noten, als Erinnerungszeichen verschmähend, nimmt er seinen Platz, das zauberische Instrument in Händen, und biethet, ohne sich hinter einem Notenpulte zu verstecken, dem Publikum das ganze Bild eines freyen, unbeschränkten Herrschers in Gebiethe der Töne. Die Höhen und Tiefen der Applicature durchfliegt die Linke Hand mit einer noch nie gesehenen Leichtigkeit, indess die Rechte mit einer unübertroffenen Ruhe und Sicherheit den flüchtigen Bogen schwingt. Keine müthevoll Anstrengung verrathend, da doch die Gewalt der tiefen Saiten sowohl als das Aufsetzen in höheren Tonlagen, bey solcher Schnelligkeit der Passagen die ganze Körperkraft erfordert, biethet dieser Künstler beständig ein interessantes Bild dem Auge, indess sein wunderbar schönes Spiel das Ohr in Entzücken bringt. Er singt, um uns eines Wortes zu bedienen, und ergreift das Gemüth des Zuhörers durch die Macht seines Gesanges. In Adagio bekannten sich alle Herzen für überwunden durch seine Kunst, die schon im vorhergehenden feurigen Allegro von der Gewalt seiner Töne beseigt und mit fortgerissen wurden. Der Beyfall nahm den Charakter der stürmischen Freude an, und schien am Schlusse des Finales kaum enden zu wollen'. Anon., *AmZmbR*, 6 (1822), pp. 25–6.

[45] See n. 41 above.

the tender sounds (not exaggerated in the slightest) which his ear must have overheard carefully in Nature, a decidedly higher poetic worth. One hears in one's breast the sounds, which express gigantic Nature, from the heights of the Jungfrau to the valleys of the Alps, in the most beautiful, but also terrifying, moments, because the music has enough means to give all tender nuances from the whispering wind to the terrifying thunder, representing again and bringing such a beautiful, artistic combination before our fantasy. The alpine song of the beautiful Swiss maiden sounds in the middle of the gale blowing through the rocky ravines, and whispers comfort as it were to the hesitant ear from a distance.[46]

During their lifetimes Bohrer and Romberg were normally seen as different both in their compositional style and in terms of their reception. These differences can be seen partly in terms of differing views of the 'true' character of the cello itself, which in turn reflect its perception as a gendered instrument. When Max Bohrer neglects this masculine character, sympathetic reviewers are driven to use poetic language that is quite at odds with the more measured terms applied to Romberg, while the unsympathetic dismiss Bohrer's music as technically competent but trivial. Romberg's reviews were rarely anything other than eulogistic. However, the Russian critic Odoyevskii observed in 1825 that Romberg's playing had become more powerful, adding that the older generation in the audience disliked this because 'everything strong and virile frightens this lot – they yearn for something delicate, colourless, and senile'.[47] Their compositions themselves can be shown to be different enough in construction to suggest an underlying difference in their approach to their instrument. This difference in approach can also lead to markedly differing reactions from contemporary critics. These reactions become much less differentiated in later periods when this sort of composition is seen as generic virtuosity.

The concept of a performed gender that is achieved, or accumulated through innumerable individual performative acts, rather than simply assigned, is familiar

---

[46]   'Sein violoncell-Concert, ein Schweizer Gemählde, zeigte die Kunst Romberg's, durch welche er die musikalische Mahlerey mit seiner hohen Virtuosität zu vereinigen weiss. Er gibt durch die zarten und nicht im Geringsten übertriebenen Anklänge, welche sein Ohr sorgfältig der Natur abgelauscht haben muss, seiner Tondichtung einen entschiedenen höheren poetischen Werth. Man hört die Laute, welche die gigantischen Natur auf den Höhen des Jungfrauhorns und in den thälern der Alpen in den schönsten, aber furchtbarnsten Momenten aus ihrer Brust hervor drängt, weil die Musik Mittel genug hat, alle zarten Nuançen des säuselnden Windes bis zum furchtbarnsten Donner darstellend wieder zu geben, und in so schöner, kunstvoller Vereinigung vor unsere Phantasie zu führen. Das Alpenlied der schönen Schweizerinn tönt mitten in den die Felsschluchten durchwühlenden Orkan, und flüstert gleichsam dem zagenden Ohre von fern Trost zu'. Ibid., p. 88.

[47]   Vladimir Odoievskii, 'On music in Moscow and on Moscow concerts in 1825', *Moskovskiy Telegraf*, April 1825, p. 132, quoted in Lev Ginsburg, trans. Tanya Tchistyakova, *History of the Violoncello* (Neptune City, NJ: Paganiniana Publications, 1983), p. 353 n. 44.

from Simone de Beauvoir and Judith Butler. In this context, these nineteenth-century gendered views of the cello will appear superficial. No attempt has been made here to examine the wider cultural origins of a gendered view of the violin as feminine or the cello as masculine, or of the refinements and changes to this view evident in the later nineteenth century, or indeed of the eventual disappearance of this view in the twentieth. But from the point of view of cello performance practice, these ideas can still suggest a fresh perspective. The relevance of historical gender studies for performance issues is that an awareness of gender tropes can inform an interpretative approach in a different, but perhaps more thought-provoking, way compared to more conventional studies of performance practice techniques outlined in earlier chapters. Sometimes, women players were criticized for being insensitive to the feminine aspects of their repertoire. Henry Finck approved of the violinist Maud Powell's later performing style, which avoided this trap:

> When Huneker accused Maud Powell of not sufficiently emphasizing the feminine traits of the music she was playing [in *Violin Mastery Talks with Master Violinists and Teachers* by Frederick H. Martens (1919)], she explained that she did this purposely because of the existing prejudice against women violinists. Subsequently she became the very incarnation of femininity in violin playing although she never forgot how to emphasize the masculine side too. Like Chicago's foremost pianist, Fannie Bloomfeld Zeisler, she showed that a woman player can be forceful and impetuous without being mannish.[48]

Some repertoire was itself considered to be more suitable for a woman performer, so much so that on one occasion it was suggested that Haydn's D major concerto was played quite well for a man:

> Haydn's violoncello concerto in D was the other important work, and M. Grigor Piatigorsky [...] brought out its genial charm. He gave to the finale a rather more marked lilt than women violoncellists usually employ, but though female subtlety may be preferred in this particular concerto this masculine reading was all of a piece and bore the stamp of authority.[49]

We can see, then, that in the case of the cello, there are potentially two gendered perspectives at work – the instrument itself as masculine or feminine (or some combination of the two), and the musical material written for it. If we look at a particular work with these ideas in mind, they may lead us to re-assess the nature

---

[48]   Henry T. Finck, *My Adventures in the Golden Age of Music* (New York and London: Funk and Wagnalls Company, 1926), p. 312. Finck may be slightly distorting Maud Powell's explanation here.

[49]   'Weekend Concerts', Times, 20 October 1930, p. 12. This review is also cited in George Kennaway, 'Haydn's (?) Cello Concertos, 1860–1930: Editions, Performances, Reception', *Nineteenth-Century Music Review*, 9 (2012), pp. 177–211.

of historically informed performance: how far could ideas of gender appear in performance? The Lalo Cello Concerto (1877) is an especially suitable work to examine here.

Marcia Citron cites this striking passage from Vincent d'Indy's composition treatise, on the gendered character of themes:

> Insofar as the two ideas exposed and developed in pieces in sonata form perfect themselves, one notices that in effect they truly behave like living beings, subject to the inevitable laws of mankind: sympathy or antipathy, attraction or repulsion, love or hate. And, in this perpetual conflict, reflecting those in life, each of these two ideas show qualities comparable to those which have always been attributed to men and women respectively. Force and energy, concision and clarity: such are almost invariably the essentially masculine characteristics belonging to the *first idea*: they are imposed in the form of vigorous, brusque *rhythms*, nobly affirming its tonal ownership, one and definitive. The *second idea*, on the other hand, all sweetness and *melodic* grace, almost always affects by its verbosity and vague modulation of the eminently alluring *feminine*: supple and elegant, it progressively spreads out the curve of its ornamented melody; more or less clearly circumscribed in a neighbouring key in the course of the exposition, it will always leave it in the recapitulation in order to take up the initial key solely occupied from the outset by the dominant masculine. It is as if, after the active struggle of the development, the entity [*l'être*] of gentleness and weakness has to submit, be it by violence, be it by persuasion, to conquest by the entity of strength and power.[50]

---

[50] 'A mesure que les deux idées exposés et développées dans les pièces de formes sonate se perfectionnent, on constate en effet qu'elles se comportent vraiment comme des êtres vivants, soumis aux lois fatales de l'humanité: sympathie ou antipathie, attirance ou répulsion, amour ou haine. Et, dans ce perpétuel conflit, image de ceux de la vie, chacune des deux idées offre des qualités comparables à celles qui furent de tout temps attribuées respectivement à l'homme et à la femme. Force et énergie, concision et netteté: tels sont à peu près invariablement les caractères d'essence *masculine* appartenant à la *première idée*: elle s'impose en *rythmes* vigoureux et brusques, affirmant bien haut sa propriété tonale, une et définitive. La *seconde idée*, au contraire, toute de douceur et de grâce *mélodique*, affecte presque toujours par sa prolixité et son indétermination modulante des allures éminemment *féminines*: souple et élégante, elle étale progressivement la courbe de sa mélodie ornée; circonscrite plus ou moins nettement dans un ton voisin au cours de l'exposition, elle le quittera toujours dans la réexposition terminale, pour adopter sa tonalité initiale occupée dès le début par l'élément dominateur, masculin, seul. Comme si, après la lutte active du développement, l'être de douceur et de faiblesse devait subir, soit par la violence, soit par la persuasion, la conquête de l'être de force et puissance'. Vincent d'Indy and Auguste Sérieyx, *Cours de composition musicale*, 2 vols (Paris: Durand et Cie., 1909), Vol. 2, Part 1, p. 262, quoted in Marcia Citron, *Gender and the Musical Canon* (Cambridge: Cambridge University Press, 1993), p. 136. Citron's translation modified by the author.

Citron examines this description (which d'Indy offers in the context of a discussion of Beethoven's remarks to Schindler about the contrasting character of the themes in his op. 14 sonatas) in terms of its implication of 'sexual dominance gone awry', and the essentialism that characterized such statements in the nineteenth century.[51] D'Indy's terms do, however, apply strikingly well to the first movement of Lalo's concerto. After an orchestral introduction punctuated by loud staccato chords and a short cello recitative, the first theme appears. This matches d'Indy's description of a masculine theme almost exactly (Example 8.6), although it is interesting to see that each vigorously rising arpeggio figure almost immediately falls back. Only in the approach to the second group do these arpeggios manage to climb through two octaves and remain at this higher *tessitura* for the second group itself. This theme, in a dominant-inflected relative major, wanders without direction, accompanied only by low sustained notes in the orchestral celli, with the flutes playing

Example 8.6 Lalo, Cello Concerto, first movement, first theme

---

[51] Ibid., pp. 135–7.

occasionally in thirds (Example 8.7). The dotted-rhythm ♩♫ figure is common to the introduction and all the thematic groups in the movement, although it only appears at the start of the second group. It does, however, appear prominently at the *ff* culmination of that section, as if the striving masculine material breaks through. When this theme returns in the development section, in A, it has a clearer shape and is more extrovertly expressive, although moving quickly to a more equivocal A minor (Example 8.8). This suggestion of an extended and more clearly structured theme is not fulfilled, as the theme disappears in semiquaver passage-work. In the recapitulation it appears as the first time, here 'correctly' in D. It reappears finally in the coda with a new continuation, heralded by flutes in thirds, which strives after extra emotional effect but which fails after repeating itself and dissolving again into a stream of D major semiquavers. The final peroration firmly reasserts D minor.

Example 8.7   Lalo, Cello Concerto, first movement, second theme

Example 8.8   Lalo, Cello Concerto, first movement, second theme (development)

This 'seconde idée féminine' is never allowed to realize its potential, confirming a dominant masculinity. However, there is also a problem in terms of the cello's own masculine/feminine identity. It has been suggested here that the cello moved from a firmly masculine identity in the earlier nineteenth century to a less clearly defined one – that an instrument that began as a regulator of the passions became a vehicle for almost uncontrolled emotional expression. Here in the Lalo concerto the most apparently 'feminine' material is not in fact the most emotionally free, for all the *appassionato* markings. It has been argued by Citron and others that the 'subjugation' of the feminine is true of sonata-form movements in general, in that the recapitulation will enforce the tonic on the return of the second subject group, and this view has been refined in various ways.[52] However, what is proposed here is more a question of emotional subjugation, in the context of a potential tension between the gendered identity of the instrument and its music.

Lalo's publisher Durand was unimpressed by the concerto. It was eventually published in Berlin (without an opus number), partly thanks to Sarasate's advocacy.[53] The première, given by its dedicatee Adolphe Fischer on 9 December, 1877, was not particularly well received. The *Monthly Musical Record* thought it 'agreeable but somewhat pretentious'.[54] Later performances fared slightly better, but there is persistent suggestion that the work is lightweight: 'diffuse and uninteresting',[55] 'delicate and cleverly written',[56] and played 'with charm' in 1900 by the young Jean Gerardy (1877–1929).[57] 'Delicacy' in particular is not a general characterization that strikes the modern player of this piece, and it might possibly reflect an overall impression made by slower-moving, more lyrical material, which rarely reaches any sustained emotional intensity. This was the basis for the *Gramophone*'s criticism of the work when Suggia's 1946 recording was re-issued in 1950:

> On the whole I find the 'Cello Concerto dull and lacking in sufficient tonal contrast – the solo part being confined largely to the middle register. The serious and rhetorical first movement is too self-consciously maestoso; the lyrical second movement with its sprightly contrasting section has charm and one or two nice harmonic touches; the rhythmical Finale has a tendency to make the 'cello sound uncouthly elephantine.[58]

The first recordings of the concerto (by Suggia, Cassadó, Navarra and Nelsova; see Table 8.1) are strikingly varied in their approaches to the first movement.[59]

---

[52] See Lawrence Kramer, *Classical Music and Postmodern Knowledge* (Berkeley, Los Angeles, and London: University of California Press, 1995), Chapter 7, n. 86.

[53] Edouard Lalo, *Concert pour violoncelle* (Berlin: Bote & Bock, [1878]); Lalo, ed. Joel-Marie Fauquet, *Edouard Lalo: correspondance* (Paris: aux Amateurs de Livres, 1989), p. 121 n. 2.

[54] Anon, 'Music in North Germany', *Monthly Musical Record*, 8 (1878), p. 57.

[55] Anon., *MT*, 31 (1890), p. 28.

[56] Anon., *MT*, 40 (1899), p. 20.

[57] Anon, 'Mr. Robert Newman's Symphony and Wagner Concerts', *MT*, 41 (1900), p. 34.

[58] 'R. H.' review, 'LALO. Concerto in D minor for Violoncello and Orchestra', *Gramophone*, November 1950, p. 23. Cassadó solved the problem of limited register by playing the final scale of the first movement an octave higher than written.

[59] Guilherminia Suggia (vc), Pedro de Freitas Branco (cond), London symphony Orchestra (Decca AX349-52, 1946); Zara Nelsova (vc), Sir Adrian Boult (cond), London Philharmonic Orchestra (Decca, LXT 2906, 1953; reissued *Zara Nelsova Decca Recordings 1950–1956*, Decca 4756327, 2004); André Navarra (vc), Emanuel Young

Table 8.1   Comparison of recordings, Lalo cello concerto

Soloist, age, date of recording	First movement overall timing	First group ♩. MM	Second group ♩. MM	Second subject tempo as % of first subject tempo
Suggia, 61 (1946)	14′ 28″	75.1	60.6	80.7%
Nelsova, 35 (1953)	14′ 01″	75.6	54.9	72.6%
Navarra, 45 (1956)	12′ 25″	86.4	72.9	84.4%
Cassadó, 66 (1963)	13′ 33″	77.8	62.6	80.5%

Of these recordings, Suggia and Cassadó adjust their tempi by almost the same proportion, with Navarra making the least alteration and Nelsova the most extreme. Suggia and Nelsova are clearly slower overall in the first movement. Navarra is almost brisk, although still a little slower than Lalo's metronome marking (♩·88) which means that he can conceal the music's relative lack of direction. He observes none of the printed accents in the second subject (which could mean a degree of articulation, possibly combined with vibrato in the Servais manner), ignores *tenuto* markings, and uses a similar amount of portamento to that used in the first subject. His performance is considerably more sophisticated than Cassadó's, but there is still a tendency to treat the second subject as if it fundamentally requires the same sort of expression as the first. Nelsova uses a fast, intense vibrato and a strong tone throughout, these elements remaining virtually unmodified for the second subject. However, she relaxes the tempo so much here that the aggressive return of the orchestra (exaggerated here by the very dry recorded acoustic) is extremely dramatic. Gaspar Cassadó is particularly consistent in some aspects of his performing style, using a heavily articulated *portato* almost from the outset, frequently ignoring *pp* and *dolce* markings, and breaking many of Lalo's slurs. Of the cellists considered here, it is he who most strongly imposes a 'masculine' expression on the second subject, avoiding portamento entirely here, while using it in the first subject. When the second subject ends, Cassadó remains defiantly *forte*, over-ruling Lalo's *diminuendo* to *pp* and therefore reducing the effect of the orchestral *ff* interruption. By undermining the contrast, he almost denies the very possibility of a feminine subject. In this context his avoidance of portamento is not surprising.

Cassadó's approach may be extreme, but it may also reflect a taste for highly 'masculinized' performances of this work. Even Navarra's brisk recording with Emmanuel Young was held to be inferior to his even more focused and vivid recording with Constantin Silvestri:

(cond), Paris Opera Orchestra (Capitol, P8318, 1956); Gaspar Cassadó (vc), Joel Perlea (cond), Bamberg Symphony Orchestra (Vox, PL10.920, 1963).

Navarra sounds an extraordinarily different artist in the two performances of the Lalo. Under Emanuel Young (a repetiteur and occasional conductor at Covent Garden) he is weakish in attack, and the performance as a whole scarcely begins to grip the attention. Under Constantin Silvestri [...] he gives a far more lively and pungent sort of performance – one listens to the music keenly. [...] the general effect of this version is far more vital.[60]

The same reviewer praised Nelsova's 'strong, warm, singing tone' and her 'great poetry and feeling'.[61] Jacqueline du Pré's solution to the problem of tempi for the first and second groups in this movement was characteristically extreme.[62] The second group takes 92″, exactly the same duration as Cassadó, but her first group is one of the fastest on record (average ♩. = 90.9). Her second group tempo is therefore some 69 per cent- of the first, strikingly more different from the first group than in any other performance considered here.

It would be very difficult to argue that the gender stereotypes attached to sonata-form analysis in the late nineteenth century directly influenced any of these performances, and foolish to suggest that women cellists responded differently from men to the 'feminine' second subject. The recorded evidence simply does not support either view. However, the general character of this cello concerto's thematic material corresponds so closely to D'Indy's account of sonata form that it is legitimate to argue that a performance that takes these ideas into account could be, at least, more 'historically aware' than one that does not. If the Lalo concerto is performed with a uniform intensity and a strong sense of tonal organization, erasing the gender tropes embedded in the themes, it is, in this respect, being played unhistorically (as well as, arguably, insensitively). But if the soloist plays the second theme of the first movement as freely as possible, with a less highly projected tone quality, and no clear sense of direction, they could be said to be playing within the gender tropes of the period, and in that specific respect to be historically aware – and this would be the case even though there is no historical evidence that the work was in fact ever performed in that way. This raises some interesting questions about historically informed performance that will be examined in the final chapter.

---

60   'A. P.', review, *Gramophone*, November 1957, p. 8.

61   'A. P.', review, *Gramophone*, April 1954, p. 33.

62   Jacqueline Du Pré (vc), Daniel Barenboim (cond), Cleveland Orchestra (EMI, 1973, remastered 1995).

Chapter 9
Conclusions and Speculations

This examination of cello performance techniques in the long nineteenth century has attempted to capture the ambiguities inherent in attempts to reconstruct older playing styles, and the interpretation of the research that supports this. Not only by considering aspects of posture, the physicality of bowing and fingering techniques, and changing attitudes to expression, but also by exploring how historical performance might incorporate cultural aspects of music, this study has engaged with the data-driven positivism that has characterized most of these studies in the twentieth century and that still continues. It has tried to suggest that it may be time for this field of musicology to look in a different direction. The closer one looks at the data, the less easy it is to see just what would constitute a fully historically informed performance. Does one play like an amateur, a professional, an old-fashioned player, an up-to-date player, an influential teacher, a commercially successful soloist … ? Even using this small number of categories, the potential combinations are numerous. This multiplicity of performing personae can counter such misleading but increasingly widespread shorthand as 'little vibrato; lots of portamento; keep the bow on the string'. It is entirely possible that such a reductive formula will become as pervasive in nineteenth-century performance as the modernist baroque equivalent.

On the other hand, if separated from the consideration of modern historical performance, much of this data – the emergence of the tail-pin and the debates around its use, changing perceptions of the function of the right wrist – has an intellectual interest simply in terms of demonstrating how different ideas can change at different speeds. It is quite possible that as late as the second decade of the twentieth century a cellist could have been taught to play without a tail-pin, with a consequent posture that would have had much in common with cellists of over a century earlier. Changing perceptions of the right wrist, on the other hand, almost certainly owe more to the increasing interest in the later nineteenth/early twentieth century in anatomy for musicians, part of a more 'scientific' pedagogical approach exemplified by Alexanian, which in turn has links with the modernism of the 1920s.[1]

Nowhere in this study has it been assumed that a historically informed performance is by definition the best. Indeed, it may be read by some as an attempt to undermine the concept. Recent trends in historically informed performance

---

[1]   I suggest a modernist context for Alexanian's edition of the Bach cello suites in 'Bach Solo Cello Suites: an overview of editions': http://chase.leeds.ac.uk/article/bach-solo-cello-suites-an-overview-of-editions-george-kennaway/ [accessed November 2013].

have been to avoid making claims for 'authenticity', in the wake of attacks by Richard Taruskin and others. Although the claims of the 'early music' movement were already under fire (as he himself acknowledged), Taruskin's critique has had the most far-reaching results, so that just over a decade ago, performance practice research was being described as an intellectual *cul-de-sac* with little potential for further development:

> It was originally intended to include a chapter on historically informed performance, but it proved impossible to find an author who could feel that there was something useful that could be said beyond a summary of conclusions of arguments current in the 1980s.[2]

Freed from the stringent requirements of 1980s authenticity, when it stood for the elimination of personal interpretation in performance, and taking advantage of the wider ambiguity of the term (authentic audiences? personal authenticity?), the historical performance of baroque repertoires has generally become more experimental. This is particularly so in the case of baroque opera, as the most cursory examination of recordings of Monteverdi's *Orfeo* will show. If authenticity in performance is in retreat, the research that supports this has likewise aimed at more limited goals, such as historical accuracy (both of instruments and of playing styles), defining the sound-world of the composer, or presenting the performance as simply showing what the composer might reasonably have expected to hear given the prior assumptions that influence the notated form of the work. This research can be used to contest the more carefully circumscribed historical claims (sometimes bordering on the disingenuous) made by performers or their record companies. These twin developments have inevitably increased the distance between performers and researchers. 'Authenticity' may have been an illusion, but at least it offered a common starting-point for both parties. The more that researchers accumulate data, the more do performers, freed from the restrictive pursuit of the authentic, become selective towards the same data. This leads to an impasse where performers appear only half-informed (at best) and researchers appear to lack understanding of the performance process. The consequence of this impasse is the objection expressed by Clive Brown when reviewing recordings of nineteenth-century repertoire: 'Despite the interest and efforts of a few bold spirits in the world of commercial performance we have, as yet, made little progress with evolving a more faithful historically informed approach to performing this music in the spirit of its creators.'[3] Strikingly, those researchers who do have substantial professional performing experience, such as Colin Lawson and Robin Stowell, tend to distance themselves from any rigorous application of research to

---

2   Mark Everist and Nicholas Cook (eds.), *Rethinking Music* (Oxford: OUP, 1999, rev. 2001), p. 12 n. 5.

3   Clive Brown, 'Performing 19th-century chamber music: The yawning chasm between contemporary practice and historical evidence', *Early Music*, 38 (2010), pp. 476–80 (p. 480).

performance, stressing the meeting of 'heart and mind, instinct and knowledge, whilst recognizing that instinct changes with habit, usage and redefinition of interpretative parameters'.[4]

There is a fundamental contradiction at the heart of the historiography of nineteenth-century performance practices. What is generally urged is a sense of a wider range of performing possibilities, a greater flexibility, a less literal reading of the text. Put in those terms, a musician could hardly demur in principle (although the degree of additional freedom involved is often considerably greater than 'mainstream' musicians imagine).[5] But this message is itself delivered as categorically true, in a way that by definition excludes as defective almost any performance. Choices are offered, but the choice to ignore or reject one or other historical finding is denied. The ground-breaking work of Clive Brown – essential reading in this field – demonstrates this well. The fundamental purpose of his major work, frequently cited here, is to show that modern performers can

> experiment with more radically different and audacious performance of familiar repertoire, attempting to recover something of the respectful but not excessively reverential attitudes that typified the finest performers of the Classical and Romantic periods […] .[6]

In particular, his over-arching theme is the considerable distance between the notation and performance of this music, and the rejection of a 'slavishly literal' reading as 'unhistorical'.[7] One might add that such a reading would be universally recognized as, first, unmusical, and, second, impossible. Unmusical, because a performance amounting to a mere recitation of the markings in the score bears as much relation to music as the activity of a 'time-beater' does to real orchestral conducting; impossible, because in practice 'slavishly literal' performances will not be identical, even if starting from the same text, and will always include elements which are not notated at all. Nicholas Cook has summed this up well: 'performance routinely involves not playing what is notated as well as playing what is not notated'.[8] Brown pursues the flexibility of notation through each highly nuanced chapter, exploring additional layers of textual ambiguity and contrasting usages, with the intention of expanding interpretative possibilities. This subtle

---

[4] Colin Lawson and Robin Stowell, *Historical Performance: An Introduction* (Cambridge: Cambridge University Press, 1999), p. 160.

[5] The range of possibilities for nineteenth-century piano performance is a very good example: see Neal Peres da Costa, *Off the Record: Performing Practices in Romantic Piano Playing* (Oxford: Oxford University Press, 2013).

[6] Brown, *CRPP*, p. 632.

[7] Ibid., p. 6.

[8] Nicholas Cook, 'Between process and product: Music and/as performance', *Online Journal of the Society for Music Theory*, 7 (2001): http://www.mtosmt.org/issues/mto.01.7.2/mto.01.7.2.cook.html [accessed July 2012].

exegesis strenuously avoids any suggestion of simple rules. And yet, just over a decade later, Brown observed that:

> Although, during the last two decades, scholarly studies have focused increasingly on the performing practices of the 19th century, only a very limited amount of the information presented in scholarly books and articles has had a direct and significant impact on the world of professional performance. A few period instrument groups are seriously committed to understanding more about the ways in which their current manner of performing differs from that of the past, and some individual professional musicians have shown real intellectual curiosity and a willingness to experiment in private. Very few carry much of this experimentation forward into their public performances and recordings. [...] I know of scarcely any that have come to grips with the question of using piano arpeggiation in the performance of late 18th- and 19th-century music where it is not notated in the score.[9]

His convincingly authoritative review demonstrates conclusively that none of the performers in question has wholly engaged with the available research:

> It is [...] disappointing that the majority of the performers on these discs have shown so little commitment to understanding and bringing to life the aural intentions that lie behind the notation in all these works, which would have been clear to the composers and performers of the time, but have been obscured for us by later developments and changes of taste.[10]

But it is striking that in Brown's long list of possible reasons for the apparently wilful ignorance of these performers (professional caution, the influence of older schools of teaching, and many others), he does not consider a further reason: that these performances include those elements of historical style with which the performers can engage, and exclude those that may have no personal meaning for them, with those elements varying from person to person and group to group. Brown himself concedes that he would be happier with a performer who clearly has no interest in historical questions and simply played as their own intuition suggested.[11] He can afford to make this concession, because it amounts to saying that performers can choose 'nothing', rather than 'all', while not undermining his general approach. Thus, greater flexibility in performance is constantly urged, but the freedom to select from among the available historical options is criticized.

On the other hand, some historical performance research is pointedly offered as a disinterested account of older performance practices without any suggestion that modern performers should adopt them. These scholars are unwilling to dictate

---

9   Brown, 'Performing 19th-century chamber music', p. 476.
10   Ibid., p. 476.
11   Ibid., p. 477.

to performers, possibly for fear of a musical fundamentalism characteristic of the earlier stages of the early music movement, but equally possibly because they simply have no wish to do more than inform those who might be interested. They offer information for performers to use as they please, or not at all. The scholarly work engages with performance chiefly as a means of evaluating historically-informed performance (HIP) advertising claims – John Moran's PhD thesis on Viennese string playing adopts this position explicitly.[12] There are many examples of this approach. For instance, Laurie Ongley produces good evidence about the *basso* group in the eighteenth-century Dresden court orchestra, but simply concludes her article: 'Modern performers who want to follow 18th-century practices can confidently use Dresden's instrumentation as an exemplar'; there is no suggestion here that they ought to do so.[13] Lawson and Stowell amass a great deal of detailed organological information and other data relating to Mozart's Serenade for 13 wind instruments K.361, only to conclude that, while the use of original instruments brings out fascinating sonorities, 'although certain elements of the 1784 performance can be recreated, no rendition more than 200 years later can ever be in any sense authentic'.[14] Stowell's earlier monograph on violin performance practice provides encyclopaedic coverage of earlier violin sources with substantial extracts from the more important ones, offered principally as a resource from which performers can draw – much of this material had not previously been available in English. The information is invaluable, but he offers it simply for its own sake. It is significant that even in 1985 Stowell almost invariably put the word 'authentic' in quotation marks.[15] It is undeniably interesting to know how music was performed in the distant past; such studies are clearly broadly humanist in nature. This may lead to David Milsom's striking conclusion that:

> the value system of the period 1850–1900 was wholly different from our own, and the response of the musical aesthetic to the values of its own time leads to a gulf that is not readily traversed [...] a modern 'period performance' of a late nineteenth-century work is going to be little more than an interesting experiment [...].[16]

---

[12]   John Moran, *Techniques of Expression in Viennese String Music (1780–1830)* (Ph.D. thesis, King's College London, 2002).

[13]   Laurie Ongley, 'The reconstruction of an 18th-century basso group', *Early Music*, 27 (1999), p. 280.

[14]   Lawson and Stowell, *Historical Performance*, p. 124.

[15]   Robin Stowell, *Violin Technique and Performance Practice in the Late Eighteenth and Early Nineteenth Centuries* (Cambridge: Cambridge University Press, 1985).

[16]   David Milsom, *Theory and Practice in Late Nineteenth-Century Violin Performance* (Aldershot: Ashgate, 2003), p. 208.

Elsewhere he refers to 'a void of understanding and a plethora of unanswered questions'.[17] Nonetheless, the relation between older musical aesthetics and contemporary values is a valuable object of study, all the more so given the clear differences between the two. But such studies ultimately remain enclosed within given discursive limits. Milsom's distinctive exploration of the 'philosophical orientations' of later nineteenth-century authorities shows how values such as freedom, diversity, or the combination of historical awareness with the values of the (then) present can be inferred from his sources. But he is not concerned with discursive framework of such statements. This means that the very good question he himself poses – '*Why* the writer of a treatise, for example, should pass judgement on matters of "taste"' – cannot be satisfactorily answered. Some studies of historical modes of performance show what was considered obvious at the time and has now become alien to us. But there are also matters that seem obvious to us and were by no means so in earlier times. Returning to the cello, even such apparently arcane topics as changing approaches to scale fingering patterns can show this. The emergence of the 'obvious' can be slow, and the reasons for the persistence of the older fingering can have implications far beyond the simple mechanics of playing the given notes in the given order in tune. The discovery of physically efficient, rationally based, cello scale fingerings depended on the perception that the musical structure of the scale and its effective fingering were two distinct things. But the baffled reception of John Gunn's cello method where these fingerings were first explained (cited in Chapter 2) is not necessarily an example of ignorant reviewing, and the reason for the relatively slow adoption of these fingerings is not because early nineteenth-century cellists were dull-witted. It is a concrete example of how ideas below the theoretical horizon (whether obsolete or innovative) cannot be properly incorporated into the prevailing discourse. The discursive limits that both constrain and generate such a large quantity of discussion of expressive effects and their abuse, and the forces that shift the theoretical horizon, and with it discourse itself, would make up another entire study.[18]

Such abstract issues are not, in the main, urgently relevant to modern musicians. They do not help the player make much more sense of the music in front of them, which is to be performed tomorrow or next week. Many in the academic community do not fully appreciate the full implications of the fact that performers, generally, learn a new work by first engaging with it as music on the stand. That physical exploration, the first attempt to inscribe the music in the performing body, comes before any conceptual knowledge of the historical performing context of the work. Of course, it is modified in countless ways, not least by the player's previous experience and knowledge. But some historical elements, such as, perhaps, Romberg's total posture, will never be absorbed. Such

---

[17]   Ibid., p. 202.

[18]   See George Kennaway, 'Do as some said, or as most did? – a Foucauldian experiment with nineteenth-century HIP', *Current Musicology*, 92 (2011) pp. 7–29.

a posture goes against every physical proprioception that the player has evolved. There is simply no incentive to unlearn a physically healthy posture in order to recreate Romberg's slanted left hand and extreme supination of the right wrist.

Performers, perversely, tend ultimately to go their own way. In baroque performance, many ensembles are now regularly adopting performance practices for which there is no specific historical evidence. The work of groups such as Red Priest could justifiably be seen as 'post-HIP' if not indeed postmodern in their approach to musical texts:

> 'Most things I feel we could justify historically and the rest we could justify philosophically', [Red Priest's Piers] Adams says. He cites contemporary accounts of Baroque musicians' on-stage antics, such as Corelli's eyeballs turning red. 'There were some pretty wild musicians out there'.[19]

Even where instruments themselves are concerned, Paul Laird has shown that almost every prominent modern baroque cellist has taken a more or less pragmatic approach to historical accuracy. This is prompted in some cases by the acoustic requirements of large concert halls, but at least as often by the player's personal preference.[20] Where Red Priest and similar ensembles are concerned, we have an excellent demonstration of how historically informed performance becomes more experimental when there is less and less information available. There can be no doubt that where very recent performances are concerned, perhaps from the 1980s, fully recorded on film with complete information about the instruments used, the historically-informed recreation of such performances would be straightforward enough, in theory – but redundant (at least in art-music terms). Performances of increasingly older repertoires are by definition less historically informed, and more interestingly diverse.

The evidence offered in the preceding chapters suggests, above all, a range of possibilities for performance. For example, the 'impaired' (in modern terms) tonal projection that would have resulted from the generally accepted nineteenth-century posture (with its emphasis on low elbows, a supinated right wrist when playing at the tip of the bow, and an upright stance that meant that the bow's weight fell less naturally on the string) can be seen not simply as a disadvantage or a limitation, but as an invitation to explore the consequences of this posture to find out how these effects might be used in performance. Based on the writer's experience of recreating Romberg's idiosyncratic posture to perform some of his music, the relative lack of tonal projection is at first perceived as a defect, and in any case this posture is physically difficult to sustain. However, once reconciled to this, the interest of the performance lies in finding out by practical experiment just how adapted the music

---

[19]   Philip Sommerich, 'Viva Vivaldi', *Classical Music*, 14 February 2009, p. 40.

[20]   Paul R. Laird, *The Baroque Cello Revival: An Oral History* (Lanham, MD: Scarecrow Press, 2004).

is to the instrument and to this posture.[21] Later in the period under discussion, the older, '*classique*' posture, recommended as a model even when the tail-pin was almost universally used, could suggest a different approach to works from the late nineteenth century normally now perceived as physically demanding, such as the Dvořák Cello Concerto or parts of Strauss's *Don Quixote*. Indeed, a posture for the latter which showed *aisance* and verticality could visually emphasize the *faux*-rococo character of much of the work. Similarly, while the restrained use of vibrato is a shibboleth of historically informed performance practice, it would appear that in some circumstances there are historical justifications for the use of an intensifying vibrato where accent marks are present. Here, the evidence suggests a possibility that a more naïve reading of the accent marking would not necessarily suggest, and while some modern musicians might instinctively do this in any case, others might not. Further, the use of vibrato to reinforce a small *messa di voce* raises the interesting issue of consistency where parallel passages cannot all be played one way or the other. If consistency for its own sake may not have been so important in the nineteenth century, an 'inconsistent' use of vibrato in such a context could be seen as liberating, rather than, say, mere carelessness. Again, while the possibility that a staccato dot need not mean a particularly short note is universally understood (the distinction between 'separate' and 'short' is one which every student understands), the more interesting option, that it may mean that one plays with a firm *détaché* stroke on the string, is not yet generally known. This type of marking is sufficiently ambiguous to suggest executions that differ not only in degree but in kind. This can create an altogether different effect in passages where the modern player's first instinct is to play with a more or less off-the-string stroke – and yet, a fast tempo and a lot of string-crossing can still result in the bow coming off the string somewhat. In this case, the variety of technical terms used to describe a range of bowing styles, and the inconsistency of their application, could suggest to the player that all options are acceptable. However, an imaginative approach, trying out all reasonable possibilities as well as some that appear initially unpromising (such as Duport's *sauté*) can lead to new performing perspectives. In a more general context, rather than relying primarily on evidence derived from instrumental tutors and other similarly 'authoritative' documents, performers can observe the wide discrepancy between such sources and the evidence of reviews and early recordings, and decide where to position themselves on this spectrum – either inclining more towards *wie es eigentlich gewesen ist*, with liberal portamento and widespread vibrato (of various types), or adopting Potter's 'ideology of disciplined restraint' and obeying the warnings given by Joachim or Becker in the face of a rising tide of cheap coffee-house emotionalism.[22]

---

21   George Kennaway, '"Noble and easy attitudes" or a violent embrace? Towards carnality in 19th-century cello performance', conference lecture-recital, *The Musical Body: Gesture, Representation and Ergonomics in Performance*, Royal College of Music, London, April 2009.

22   John Potter, 'Beggar at the door: The rise and fall of portamento in singing', *Music & Letters*, 87 (2006), p. 528, cited in Chapter 6 of this volume.

Therefore, rather than a set of rules (which the evidence simply does not support, and which no musician would accept), or an enforced package of options to be accepted wholesale, the material presented here can offer a variety of stimuli to performers. This is not, however, quite the same thing as the simple *smorgasbord* approach rejected by Brown and cautiously implied by Lawson and Stowell:

> Performers will almost inevitably have to be the final arbiters [...] and devise tasteful solutions to problems [...] for which there are to be no definitive or widely accepted answers.[23]

The reasons why performers appear to pick and choose from the apparent historical options are not, fundamentally, to do with mere capriciousness or thoughtlessness. Of course their choices can be controversial; Sir Roger Norrington's version of Elgar's First Symphony, with the Stuttgart Symphony Orchestra at the 2008 BBC Promenade Concerts, was notable for lacking vibrato, portamento and (to a degree) *rubato*, in the face of Elgar's recorded evidence to the contrary.[24] In the writer's experience, performers respond to creative stimuli more positively than to simple commands. On the one hand – this is a highly speculative generalization – modern performers are less likely than their predecessors to assert publicly that their own interpretations originate in a profound, unarguable conviction that 'this is how the music goes'. They are more historically *aware* (as opposed to informed) than ever before, and this brings with it an increased sense of the pitfalls of subjectivity. This means that what might have been an unquestioned norm of performance at one time is now recreated with a sense of self-awareness and artifice. Elizabeth le Guin's suggestion that the performer's visible demeanour be calculated for a deliberate rhetorical effect, on the grounds that this was conventional in Boccherini's performances, is perhaps an extreme instance, but it still illustrates a general tendency.[25] But our performances of old music are validated both by appeal to historical data and by reference to our own instincts and convictions. The problem is that the latter do not go away – indeed, in many cases, they cannot be ignored (see Roald Dahl's short story 'The Great Switcheroo' for a vivid demonstration of the primacy of physical instinct over knowledge).[26] Consequently, the performer's self-awareness is combined with a need, not for any specific historical justification, nor for naïve encouragement

---

[23]   Lawson and Stowell, *Historical Performance*, p. 41.

[24]   The ensuing controversy was summarised in Daniel Wakin, 'Elgar without vibrato? Fiddlesticks', *New York Times*, 12 August 2008: http://www.nytimes.com/2008/08/13/arts/music/13vibr.html [accessed December 2011].

[25]   Elisabeth le Guin, *Boccherini's Body: An Essay in Carnal Musicology* (Berkeley: University of California Press, 2006), p. 102.

[26]   Roald Dahl, 'The Great Switcheroo', in *Switch Bitch* (London: Michael Joseph, 1974).

to follow one's own simple instincts, but for an imaginative stimulus. Margaret Campbell cites an amusing but pertinent anecdote:

> After a performance of the Haydn D Major [concerto] in Edinburgh, a small boy came backstage and asked Tortelier what images he used for the Haydn? Tortelier sat down and talked for some time to the child about merry-go-rounds and children falling off and so on. The child went away misty-eyed saying he'd always remember that image every time he heard the concerto in future. As closed the door, Tortelier turned to his student and said, 'How leetle does he know that all I think about in the 'aydn is the dangair of the sheefts!'[27]

The stimulus envisaged in this study is not a simple compromise designed merely to avoid the pitfalls of pedantry or of instinctive self-indulgence (assuming for the moment that this is in fact a pitfall). It should encourage performers to see themselves as part of a continuing process of reception, widely defined. Reception documents such as Marie Corelli's novels, or the reminiscences of amateur musicians, or newspaper articles by non-musicians, or indeed the astonishing popular success of Auguste van Biene, tell us something about audience expectations of performances and performers which could not be determined from other sources. In literary studies, reader-response criticism exploring the way in which the reader 'creates' the literary work dates back to I.A. Richards in the late 1920s, but in musicology the majority of reception studies have taken the form of *Rezeptiongeschichten* – the study of, for example, Wagner's reception in Russia, or of Lithuanian art in England.[28] In histories of performing practices, performance reception in this wider context has not been studied to anything like the extent of literary reception, or of the narrower 'expert' musical reception evidence in the form of reviews or other informed commentary. Emerging notions of what the audience (as opposed to the composer) might have expected from the performance could radically influence our performing choices. An audience familiar with accepted social deportment, for example, would recognize the posture of the cellist whose heels were raised from the floor, and – perhaps – take this as an indication of common ground, raising expectations that the performance itself would not overstep polite convention.

Insofar as academic research into performance practices is central to the modern historically-informed performances of musical works, it has been predicated on a view of the musical work as primarily the composer's creation, shaped by the composer's sound-world and expectations of performance as experienced at the time. Historical performance thus becomes a matter of recovering these expectations and sound-worlds, by studying the available treatises and their contextualization, and using the appropriate instruments and

---

27   Margaret Campbell, *The Great Cellists* (London: Gollancz, 1988), p. 219.

28   George Kennaway, 'Lithuanian art & music abroad: English reception of the work of M.K. Čiurlionis, 1912-39', *Slavonic and East European Review*, 83 (2005) pp. 234-53.

associated technologies. But underlying this is an aesthetic of musical works as ideal entities or types, of which individual performances are tokens. While no-one would argue that a particular performance of a work is totally 'right', in the sense that that no further performance is necessary, the historiography of performance appears nonetheless to have designs in that direction – 'right', that is to say, within the historically ascertained boundaries of expressive resources. To be sure, given that individual judgement in matters such as the application of portamento, *tempo rubato*, vibrato, and other elements, is integral to *all* realizations of the score, there are still potentially many different 'right' performances even within historically informed boundaries. But this remains an historically approved degree of variation, and it rests on an essentialism approved by those who see performance as a fundamentally hermeneutic process directed at uncovering 'the' meaning of the score, not creating 'a' meaning. Here, the slightly different approaches of Brown and Lawson/Stowell converge on an imperative:

> We must always be mindful of the dangers of allowing our attempts at stylish interpretation […] to be governed too much by rules and to be conditioned by the styles and tastes of the intervening years; but in our attempts to express ourselves within a style, we must attune our imaginations as closely as possible to the taste of the period of the music. In the final analysis, although intuition is one of a musician's most valuable attributes, it is no substitute for knowledge; and historical research has an extremely important part to play in the performance process.[29]

This is not the only possible view of performance, or of the nature of the musical work. Perhaps the composer's sound-world (instruments and their manner of performance at the time) shapes expectations of performance, and therefore defines the limits of how the work can best be performed. Perhaps, if the musical work is wholly defined by the circumstances of its production, the recovering of those circumstances should be central to its performance now. But, sidestepping the type/token model of the musical work, if the work exists as a *performative* entity, created anew in each performance, rather than as an entity with essential characteristics, then the circumstances of its first or earliest performances become less relevant as constructing the defining criteria of excellence in modern historical performance. The illocutionary force of the composer's score itself can be diluted:

> I once asked the pianist Jorge Bolet how he could justify changing passages in Chopin and he said that he did it because Chopin was concerned with the piece only for a few months, but he [Bolet] had played it for years and thought he knew more about what worked and what did not.[30]

---

[29]   Lawson and Stowell, *Historical Performance*, p. 41.
[30]   Nicholas Kenyon, *Authenticity and Early Music: A Symposium* (Oxford: Oxford University Press, 1988), p. 14.

A performative, reception-based view of music recovers the freedom of the performer to make their own choices in literally creating the work in partnership with the audience. But beyond this, the very discourse of performance itself offers us a context within which to place ourselves as performers or scholars and which defuses the tensions between the two. The pronouncements of figures such as Joachim or Becker on the evils of excessive vibrato or portamento, in the face of the evident widespread use of these devices by many early twentieth-century players, do not, ultimately, constitute an unresolvable paradox for the modern historically-interested performer. The doctrine acts as a Foucauldian 'incitement'; the pedagogical commands and the dissenting performances are in fact joined together. The same thing can be said nowadays of tensions between scholars, with their plethora of data, and performers, who select from it. The wider perspective suggested here, embracing performers and researchers, retaining indispensable positivist research but interpreting it in a way that takes account of its instability and re-engages it with both a wider sense of historical culture and a performative work-concept, could lead not only to *historically-aware* performance, but to historically-aware *performances*.

Select Bibliography

Principal Internet Sources

Bibliothèque nationale français, Gallica: http://gallica.bnf.fr
British Pathé: http://www.britishpathe.com
CHASE project, University of Leeds: http://chase.leeds.ac.uk
Cylinder Digitization and Preservation Project, University of Santa Barbara: http://cylinders.library.ucsb.edu/index.php
Filmportal.de: http://www.filmportal.de
Grove Music Online. Oxford Music Online: http://0-www.oxfordmusiconline.com
Hofmeister XIX: http://www.hofmeister.rhul.ac.uk
Internet Cello Society: http://www.cello.org
Project Gutenberg: http://www.gutenberg.org
The Virtual Gramophone: http://amicus.collectionscanada.ca

Musical Works

Alard, Jean-Delphin. *Les maîtres classiques du violon* (Paris: E. Gérard, and Mainz: Schott, 1862–83).
Bach, J.S., ed. J.J.F. Dotzauer. *Six Solos ou Études pour le Violoncelle* (Leipzig: Breitkopf & Härtel, [1826]).
—, ed. C. Schroeder. *Classical Violoncello Music Book I. J. S. Bach. Sonate I* (London: Augener Ltd, n.d.).
—, ed. F. Grützmacher. *Six Sonates ou Suites, Edition nouvelle, revue et arrangée pour être exécutée aux concerts* (Leipzig and Berlin: C.F. Peters, [1868].
Beethoven, Ludwig van. *XII Variations [...] sur un thème de Händel* WoO. 45 (Vienna: Artaria, [1797]).
—, ed. F. Grützmacher. *Zwölf Variationen über ein Thema auf "Judas Maccabaeus" von Händel* (Leipzig: C.F. Peters, [1870?]).
—, arr. F. David. *Sonaten und Variationen für Pianoforte und Violoncell* (Leipzig: C.F. Peters. [1874].
Boccherini, Luigi, arr. F. Grützmacher. *Konzert in B* (Leipzig: Breitkopf & Härtel, [1895].
Bohrer, Les Frères. *Trois duos concertans* op. 3 (Berlin and Paris: Schlesinger, [1822]).
—. *16me. Grand Duo Concertant pour violon et violoncelle* op. 47 (London: Wessel & Co, [1832]).

Bohrer, Max. *L'Amabilité. Duo Concertant pour piano et violoncelle* op. 14 (London: Wessel & Co., [1832]).

Bréval, Jean-Baptiste. *Six sonates à violoncelle et basse* op. 12 (Paris: the author, [1783]).

—. *Six Solos for the Violoncello & Bass* (London: Longman & Broderip, [1792–98]; 1st edn Paris 1783). Facsimile, ed. P. Obussier (Exeter: Musisca, 1982).

Chopin, Frédéric, arr. A.F. Servais. *Nocturne de Chopin* (Mainz: B. Schott's Söhne, [1863]).

—, arr. A.F. Servais. *Nocturne de Chopin.* Brussels Royal Conservatoire, MS. 45.106(a).11.

—, arr. C. Yu Davidoff. *Mazurkas von F. Chopin* (Leipzig: Breitkopf & Härtel, [1874]).

—, arr. F. Grützmacher. *Ausgewählte Kompositionen von Fr. Chopin* (Leipzig: C.F. Peters, [1880]).

Dotzauer, J.J.F. *Grand Trio pour Violon. Alto & Violoncelle* op. 52 (Hamburg: Jean Aug. Böe, n.d.)

Fuchs, Carl (ed.). *Violoncello-Werke – Violoncello-Works – Oeuvres pour Violoncelle* (Mainz: B. Schott's Sohne, 1911).

Ganz, Les Frères. *Duo concertant* op. 11 (Leipzig: Hofmeister, [1832]).

Goltermann, Georg. *Concerto no. 2* op. 30 (Offenbach: André, [1861]).

Grazioli, G.B., ed. C. Schroeder. *Classical Violoncello Music Book XII. Sonate von G.B.Grazioli* (London: Augener Ltd, n.d.).

Grützmacher, Friedrich. *Trio* op. 6 (Brunswick: G.M. Meyer, [1853]).

—. *Concerto en la mineur* op. 10 (Leipzig: Hofmeister, [1854]).

—. *Quartett* op. 15 (Leipzig: C.F. Peters, [1855]).

—. (ed.). *Transcriptionen classische Musikstücke* op. 60 no. 2, (Leipzig: Kahnt, 1868).

Hainl, François Georges. *Fantaisie sur des motifs de Guillaume Tell* op. 8 (Mainz: B. Schott fils, [1842]).

Hegyesi, Louis. *Romanze* op. 4 (Mainz: B. Schott fils, [1877]).

Janson, Jean Baptiste. *Six sonates a violoncelle et basse* op. 1 (Paris: Moria, [1765]).

Kummer, Friedrich. *Pièce fantastique* op. 36 (Leipzig: Fr. Hofmeister, [1840?]).

—. *Air et Danse suédois nationaux* (Hanover: Bacann, [1851]).

Lalo, Edouard. *Concert pour violoncelle* (Berlin: Bote & Bock, [1878]).

Lepin, Henri-Noëlle. *Six sonates pour le violoncelle* op. 2 (Paris: the author, [1772]).

Lübeck, Auguste Louis. *Vier Praeludien aus Op. 28 von Fr. Chopin* (Berlin: C.A. Challier & Co., [1885]).

Mendelssohn-Bartholdy, Felix, ed. F. Grützmacher. *Felix Mendelssohn Bartholdys Sämmtliche Werke. Compositionen für Violoncell und Pianoforte* (Leipzig: C.F. Peters, [1878]).

—, ed. D. Popper. *Compositionen für Violoncello und Pianoforte* (Vienna: Universal Edition, [c.1901–04]).

Merk, Joseph. *Variations sur un air tirolien* op. 18 (Brunswick: G.M. Meyer jr, and London: J.J. Ewer & Co., [1836]).

Molique, Bernhard. *Concerto* op. 45 (Leipzig: Kistner, [1854]).

Offenbach, Jaques. *Musette. Air de Ballet du 17e Siècle* op. 24 (Berlin: Schlesinger, [1846]).

Popper, David. *Im Walde* op. 50 (Hamburg: Rahter, [1882]).

—. *Zur Guitarre* op. 54 (Hamburg: Rahter, [1886]).

—. *Requiem. Adagio für 3 Celli* op. 66 (Hamburg: Rahter, [1892]).

—. 'Wie einst in schöner'n Tagen'. *Drei Stücke* op. 64 no. 1 (Leipzig: Breitkopf & Härtel, [1892]).

Reinagle, Joseph. *Three Quartetts* (London: the Author, [c.1805]).

Romberg, Andreas, and Bernhard Romberg. *Trois duos concertans* op. 2 (Leipzig: Breitkopf & Härtel, [1801]).

Romberg, Bernhard. *Divertimento über österreichische Volkslieder* op. 46 (Vienna: Haslinger, [1829]).

—, ed. Carl Schroeder. *Concerto no. 4* op. 7 (Brunswick: Litolff, [1879]).

—. *Concerto no. 6* op. 48 (Brunswick: Litolff, [1879]).

—, ed. F. Grützmacher. *Ausgewählte Kompositionen von Bernard Romberg. vol. 1. Drei Divertimenti über Nationallieder* opp. 42, 46 and 65 (Leipzig: C.F. Peters, [1880]).

—. *Concerto no. 6* op. 48 (Leipzig: C.F. Peters, [1881]).

—. *Concerto no. 9* op. 56 (Leipzig: C.F. Peters, [1883]).

—. *Drei Duos* op. 9 (Leipzig: Breitkopf & Härtel, [1890]).

Schetky, Johann Georg Christoph. *Six Quartettos Op. VI To which are Prefixed some Thoughts on the Performance of Concert-Music* (London: R. Bremner, [1770]).

Schumann, R., arr. F. Grützmacher. *Ausgewählte Compositionen von Robert Schumann für Violonell und Pianoforte* (Leipzig: C.F. Peters, [1873]).

—, ed. F. Grützmacher. *Kinderszenen* op. 15 (Leipzig: Breitkopf & Härtel, [1874]).

—. *Stücke im Volkston* op. 102 (Leipzig: C.F. Peters, [1874]).

—. *Zweite grosse Sonate* op. 121 (Leipzig: Breitkopf & Härtel. [1874]).

—, ed. C.E. Lowe. 'Träumerei' (London: Weekes & Co., [1884]).

—, ed. D. Popper. 'Träumerei' (Hamburg: Rahter, [1884]).

—, arr. Carl Yu. Davidoff. 'Abendlied', op. 85 no. 12 (Leipzig: Rahter, [1887]).

—, ed. Carl Yu. Davidoff. 'Träumerei' (Offenbach: André, [1887]).

—, ed. F. Grützmacher. *Robert Schumann's Samtliche Werke. Konzert op. 129 für Violoncell und Pianoforte herausgegeben von Fr. Grützmacher* (Leipzig: Peters, [1887]).

—, ed. H. Farmer. 'Träumerei' (London: J. Williams, 1892).

—, arr. David Popper. 'Abendlied', op. 85 no. 12 (Offenbach: Johann André, 1896).

—, ed. H. Samuel. 'Träumerei' (London: Augener, [1907]).

—, ed. G.J. Trinkaus. 'Träumerei' (New York: M. Witwark & Sons, 1913).

—, arr. G. Goltermann. 'Träumerei', in *Morceaux Célèbres* (Leipzig and London, etc.: Bosworth & Co., n.d.).

Servais, Adrien-François. *Fantaisie et Variations brillantes sur la Valse de Schubert intitulée: le Désir (Sehnsuchts-Walzer)* (Mainz: B. Schott's Söhne, [1844]).

—. *Souvenir d'Anvers* (Mainz: B. Schott's Söhne, [1844]).

—. *Andante cantabile et Mazurka sur un air de Balfe* op. 7 (Mainz: B. Schott fils, [1849]).

—. *Fantaisie burlesque (ou le Carnaval de Venise)* (Mainz: B. Schotts Söhne, [1852]).

—. *Grande fantaisie sur des motifs de l'opéra Lestocq* (Mainz: B. Schott fils, [1852]).

—. *Fra Diavolo 2me. Grand Duo Brillant* (Mainz: B. Schott fils, [1853].

—. *Concerto militaire* op. 18 (Mainz: B. Schott fils, [1860]).

—, ed. E. de Munck. *Concerto militaire* op. 18 (Mainz: B. Schott's Söhne, n.d.).

—. *Duo sur une mélodie de Dalayrac pour deux violoncelles* op. posth. (Mainz: Schott's Söhne, [1876]).

—, ed. F. Grützmacher. *Concerto in B minor* op. 5 (Leipzig: C.F. Peters, [1896?]).

—. *Concerto no. 2.* Autograph MS. Brussels Royal Conservatoire MS. 45.106.

—. *Fantaisie burlesque sur le carnaval de Venise.* Autograph MS. Brussels Royal Conservatoire MS. 45.106.

—. *Fantaisie la Romantique.* Brussels Royal Conservatoire MS 45.106.

—. *Souvenir d'Anvers.* Autograph MS. Brussels Royal Conservatoire MS. 45.106.

—. *Souvenir de Spa.* Brussels Royal Conservatoire MS 45.119.

Spohr, Louis, arr. F. Grützmacher. *Concerto in modo di scena cantante* (Leipzig: C.F. Peters, [1854]).

—, ed. F. David. *Concertos nos. 2. 7 and 8* (Leipzig: C.F. Peters, [1861]).

—, ed. F. David and F. Hermann. *Concerto no. 11* op. 70 (Leipzig: C.F. Peters, [1878]).

—, ed. F. Hermann. *Salonstücke* op. 135 (Leipzig: C.F. Peters, [1885]).

Squire, W.H. (ed.). *Second Violoncello Album* (London: Joseph Williams Limited, 1902).

—. *Fourth Violoncello Album* (London: Joseph Williams Limited, 1913).

Stiastny, J. *Concert pour Violoncelle* op. 7 (Bonn: N. Simrock, [1817]).

Taubert, Wilhelm. *Concert für das Violoncell* op. 173 (Berlin: Simrock, [1870]).

Transcriptions of Standard Vocal Works, 2nd Series (various eds) (London: Augener. 1906).

Vieuxtemps, Henri. *Concerto pour violoncelle* op. 46 (Mainz : B. Schott's Söhne, [1877]).

Vieuxtemps, Henri and Servais, Adrien-François. *Duo brillant* op. 39 (Mainz: B. Schott's Söhne, [1864]).

Wolff, E. and A. Batta. *Les intimes Deux Duos Concertants. No. 2. Fantaisie dramatique* op. 49 (Mainz. Anvers and Brussels: chez les fils de B. Schott, [1844?]).

Anonymous Articles

Anonymous Articles with Titles

'A German Fancy Fair', *Times*, 23 September 1873. p. 10.
'Ancient Concert', *Harmonicon*, 6 (1828), p. 165.
'Concert Mme. Zegowitz de Katow', *Chronique musicale*, 8 (1875), p. 42.
'Concert of Sivori', *Daily Picayune*, 11 February 1847, p. 2.
'Concerts', *Athenaeum*, 2520, 12 February 1876, p. 24.
'Diary of a Dillettante', *Harmonicon*, 7 (1829), p. 193.
'Einiges über die Pflichten des Violoncellisten als Orchesterspielers und Accompgnateurs' [On the duties of cellists as orchestral players and accompanists], *AmZ*, 43 (1841), p. 130.
'Elgar's Cello Concerto', *British Musician and Musical News*, 5 (1929), p. 37.
'Gave his Life for Music', *New York Times*, 28 August 1904, p. 9.
'Herr Max Bohrer's Concert', *MW*, 17 (1842), p. 309.
'Lady Hallé at Home', *The Woman's World*, 1 (1890), p. 171.
'Lady Violoncellists and One in Particular', *MT*, 48 (1907), p. 307.
'M. Ernest de Munck', *The Lute*, 123 (1893), unpaginated.
'Memoirs of the Brothers Moritz & Leopold Ganz', *MW*, 5 (1837), p. 148.
'Miscellaneous', *MW*, 24 (1849), p. 414.
'Mr. Robert Newman's Symphony and Wagner Concerts', *MT*, 41 (1900), p. 34.
'Music in North Germany', *Monthly Musical Record*, 8 (1878), p. 57.
'Music in the Provinces – Birmingham'. *MT*, 58 (1917), p. 276.
'Music and Theatres in Paris', *MW*, 35 (1860), p. 487.
'Nachrichten', *AmZ*, 47 (1845), pp. 818–19.
'Notes about Women', *New York Times*, 28 October 1894, p. 18.
'On the Records', *Musical Mirror and Fanfare*, 11 (1931), p. 25.
'Recensionen', *AmZ*, 47 (1845), p. 536.
Regency Etiquette: The Mirror of Graces (1811) by a Lady of Distinction (Mendoncino, CA: R.L. Shep Publications, 1997. Facsimile of 1st edn).
'The Dundee Ladies' Orchestra', *MT*, 23 (1882), p. 82.
'The Mara Concert', *Gazeteer and New Daily Advertiser*, 24 February 1787, p. 2.
'The Viennese Ladies Orchestra', *New York Times*, 27 July 1874, p. 6.
'Verses for a Violinist', *Punch*, 11 October 1890, p. 169.
Violisten (M/V). Prenten en foto's vam de muziekabfeling (Den Haag: Haags Gemeentemuseum, 1985).
'Weekend Concerts', *Times*, 20 October 1930, p. 12
'Women as Composers', *MT*, 28 (1887), pp. 80–82.
'Yankee Criticism Again', *MW*, 22 (1847), pp. 455–6.
'Ysaye and Kreisler Play', *New York Times*, 14 March 1905, p. 6.

Anonymous Articles without Titles

AmZ, 43 (1841), p. 130.
AmZ, 47 (1845), p. 536.
AmZmbR, 6 (1822), pp. 25–6.
AmZmbR, 6 (1822), p. 629.
AWMZ, 4 (1844), p. 276.
BamZ, 1 (1822), p. 402.
BamZ, 2 (1825), p. 170.
BamZ, 6 (1822), p. 679.
BamZ, 7 (1830), p. 40.
BamZ, 40 (1825), p. 317.
British Journal of Nursing, 24 July 1915, p. 81.
Harmonicon, 1 (1823), p. 2.
Harmonicon, 2 (1824), p. 96.
Harmonicon, 3 (1825), p. 204.
Harmonicon, 4 (1826), pp. 28–9.
Harmonicon, 4 (1826), p. 61.
Harmonicon, 6 (1828), p. 110.
Harmonicon, 6 (1828), p. 167.
La Patrie, evening edition, 20 March 1866, p. 1.
Literary Gazette, 33 (1849), p. 468.
Monthly Magazine, or, British Register (1797), p. 149.
Monthly Review, 12 (1793), pp. 376–381.
Musica d'oggi, 19 (1937), p. 31.
Musical Herald, 1 May 1896, p. 140.
MT, 23 (1882), p. 680.
MT, 31 (1890), p. 28.
MT, 40 (1899), p. 20.
MW, 2 (1837), p. 130.
MW, 4 (1839), p. 29.
MW, 4 (1839), p. 166.
MW, 9 (new ser. 4) (1839), p. 166.
Niederrheinische Musik-Zeitung, Literaturblatt no. 6, 14 October 1854, p. 21.
Punch, 68 (1875), p. 150.
Revue et gazette musicale, 22 (1855), p. 207.
The Monthly Review, or Literary Journal, Enlarged, 12 (1793), p. 326.
The Reader, 7 (1866), p. 452.
Times, 3 February 1928.

Cello Methods, Studies, Exercises and Other Instructional Material

A New and Complete Tutor (London: Preston and Son, [1785?]).

Alexander, Joseph. *Anleitung des Violoncellspiel* (Leipzig: Breitkopf & Härtel, [c.1802]).

Alexanian, Diran, trans. Frederick Fairbanks. *Traité théoretique et pratique du violoncelle* (Paris: A.Z. Mathot, 1922).

Auer, Leopold. *Violin Playing as I Teach It* (New York: Frederick Stokes. [1921]; repr. New York: Dover Publications, 1980).

Azaïs, Pierre-Hyacinthe. *Méthode de basse* (Paris: Bignon, [c.1775]).

Baillot, P., J.H. Levasseur, C.-S. Catel and C.-N. Baudiot. *Méthode de violoncelle* (Paris: Janet et Cotelle, 1805).

—, et al., trans. A. Merrick. *Method for the Violoncello* (London: Cocks & Co. [1830]).

Banger, Georg. *Méthode pratique de violoncelle Praktische Violoncell-schule* (Offenbach am Main: André, [1877]).

Baudiot, Charles. *Méthode pour le violoncelle* (Paris: Pleyel et fils ainé, 1826).

Bazelaire, Paul. *10 Etudes transcendantes d'après des études mélodiques de F. A. Kummer* (Paris: Alphonse Leduc, 1936).

Becker, Hugo and Dago Rynar. *Mechanik und Äesthetik des Violoncellspiels* (Vienna and Leipzig: Universal-Edition, 1929).

Bériot, Charles de. *Méthode de violon* (Mainz: B. Schott fils, 1858).

Bideau, Dominique. *Grande nouvelle méthode raisonnée pour le violoncelle* (Paris: Naderman, [1802]).

Braga, Gaetano (ed.). *Metodo per Violoncello di J. J. F. Dotzauer* (Milan: Regio Stabilimento Ricordi, 1873).

Bréval, J.B. *Traité du violoncelle* op. 42 (Paris: Imbault, [1804]).

—, trans. J. Peile. *Bréval's New Instructions for the Violoncello* (London: C. Wheatstone & Co., [1810]).

Broadley, Arthur. *Chats to Cello Students* (London: 'The Strad' Office. E. Donajowski and D.R. Duncan. 1899).

—. *Adjusting and Repairing Violins, Cellos, &c.* (London: L. Upcott Gill, 1908).

Broderip and Wilkinson's *Complete Treatise for the Violoncello* (London: the Editors, [c.1800]).

Brückner, Oskar. *Scale & Chord Studies for the Violoncello* op. 40 (London: Augener, [1895]).

Bunting, Christopher. *Essay on the Craft of 'Cello Playing*, 2 vols (Cambridge: Cambridge University Press, 1982).

Chevillard, A. *Méthode Complète* (Paris: J. Meissonier, [c.1850]).

Corrette, Michel. *Méthode théorique et pratique* (Paris: Mlle. Castagnery, [1741]).

Crome, Robert. *The Compleat Tutor for the Violoncello* (London: C. & S. Thompson, [1765?]).

Crouch, Frederick. *Compleat Treatise on the Violoncello* (London: Chappell & Co., [1826]).

David, Ferdinand. *Violin-schule* (Leipzig: Breitkopf & Härtel, [1863]).

Davidoff, Carl Yu. *Violoncell-Schule* (Leipzig: C.F. Peters, [1888]).

Dotzauer, J.J.F. *Méthode de Violoncelle. Violonzell-Schule* (Mainz: B. Schott fils, [1825]).

—, trans. G. Minche, *Méthode de violoncelle* (Paris: Richault, [c.1830]).

—. *Twelve Exercises Op. 70. Wessel & Co's Collection of Studies by I.I.F. Dotzauer. Book 4* (London: Ashdown & Parry (Successors to Wessel & Co.), n.d.).

Dressel, Hans. *Moderne Violoncell Schule*, 2 vols (Leipzig, London, Paris and Vienna: Bosworth & Co., 1902).

Duport, Jean Louis. *Essai sur le doigté du violoncelle* (Paris: Imbault, [1806]).

—, trans. August. Lindner. *Anleitung zum Fingersatz auf dem Violoncell und zur Bogenführung. Instruction on the fingering and bowing of the violoncello. Essai sur le doigté de violoncelle et sur la conduite de l'archet* (Offenbach: Jean André. Philadelphia: G. André & Co. Frankfurt: G.A. André. London: Augener & Co, [1864]).

Earnshaw, Alfred H. *The Elements of 'Cello Technique* (London: Joseph Williams Limited, 1919).

Eisenberg, Maurice. *Cello Playing of Today* (London: Novello, 1959).

Eley, Charles F. *Improved Method of Instruction for the Violoncello* (London: Clementi & Co., [1827?]).

Feuillard, Louis R. *Tägliche Übungen. Exercices journaliers. Daily Exercises* (Mainz: B. Schott's Söhne, 1919).

Fuchs, Carl. *Violoncello-Schule Violoncello Method*, 3 vols (London: Schott & Co. Ltd, 2nd edn, 1909)

Grützmacher, Friedrich. *Technologie des Violoncellspiels* op. 38 (Leipzig: C.F. Peters, [1865]).

—. *12 Violoncell-Etuden für den ersten Unterricht* op. 72 (Leipzig: C.F. Peters, [1896]).

—, ed. Willem Welleke. *Daily Exercises* op. 67 (New York: G. Schirmer. 1909).

Gunn, John. *The Art of Playing the German-Flute* (London: the Author, [1793]).

—. *The Theory and Practice of Fingering the Violoncello* (London: the Author, 1st edn [1789]; 2nd edn [1793]).

Hardy, Henry. *The Violoncello Preceptor* (Oxford: the author, [c.1800]).

Hekking, André, rev. Jeanne Fromont-Delune. *Exercices quotidiens pour la force et l'agilité des doigts* (Paris: H. Hérelle & Cie., [1927]).

Hus-deforges, Pierre Louis. *Méthode* (Paris: the author, [1829]).

—, Pierre Louis, trans. anon. *Method for the Violoncello* (London: R. Cocks & Co., [1840]).

Joachim, J. and A. Moser, trans. Alfred Moffat. *Violinschule* (Berlin: N. Simrock, 1905).

Junod, Laurent, trans. F. Clayton. *New and Concise Method for the Violoncello* op. 20 (London: Lafleur, 1878).

Kastner, Georges. *Méthode Élémentaire pour le Violoncelle* (Paris: E. Froupenas & Cie., 1835).

Krall, Emil. *The Art of Tone-Production on the Violoncello* (London: 'The Strad' Office. John Leng & Co., 1913).

Kreutzer, Rudolphe. *40 Etudes ou Caprices* (Paris: Conservatoire de Musique, [1796]).

Kummer, F.A. *8 Grandes Etudes* op. 44 (Dresden: Meser, [1838]).

—. *Violoncelloschule* op. 60 (Leipzig: Hofmeister, [1839]).

—, trans. anon. *Violoncello School* op. 60 (London: Ewer and Co., [1850]).

—. rev. A. Piatti. *Violoncello School for Preliminary Instruction* (Leipzig: Friedrich Hofmeister, 1877).

—, rev. Hugo Becker. *Violoncelloschule* op. 60 (Leipzig: C.F. Peters, 1909).

Laborde, Jean Benjamin. *Essai sur la musique* (Paris: Enfroy, 1780).

Langey, Otto. *Practical Tutor for the Violoncello. New Edition. Revised & Enlarged* (London: Hawkes & Son, 1909).

Lee, Sebastian. *Méthode pratique pour le Violoncelle (Praktische Violoncell-Schule.)* op. 30 (Mainz: B. Schott et fils, [1846]).

—. *40 Etudes mélodiques et progressives* op. 31 (Mainz: B. Schott's Söhne, [1853])

—, rev. H. Becker. *Violoncello Technics* op. 30 (Mainz: B Schott's Söhne [1900–03]).

Lindley, Robert. *Hand-book for the Violoncello* (London: Musical Bouquet Office, [1851–55]).

Muntzberger, J. *Nouvelle Méthode* (Paris: Sieber, [c.1820]).

New and Complete Instructions for the Violoncello (London: Goulding, [c.1787]).

New Instructions for the Violoncello (London: Thomas Cahusac & Sons, [c.1795]).

New and Complete Instructions for the Violoncello (London: Clementi, Banger, Hyde, Collard & Davis, [c.1805]).

Nicholson's Flute Preceptor (London: Davidson. [1845]).

Olivier-Aubert, P.F. *Kurze Anweisung zum Violoncellspiel* (Vienna: Artaria und Comp., [1819]).

Peile, John. *A New and Complete Tutor for the Violoncello* (London: Goulding, D'Almaine, Potter and Co., [1819?]).

Piatti, Alfredo, ed. W.E. Whitehouse. *Dodici Capricci* op. 25 (Leipzig: N. Simrock, [1874]).

—, rev. W.E. Whitehouse and R.V. Tabb. *Violoncello Method*, 3 vols (London: Augener, 1911).

Pleeth, William. *Cello* (London: Macdonald & Co., 1982).

Popper, David. *Hohe Schule des Violoncellspiels 40 Études* op. 73 (Leipzig: F. Hofmeister, 1901–05).

Rabaud, Henri. *Méthode Complète de Violoncelle* op. 12 (Paris: Alphonse Leduc, [1878]).

Raoul, Jean Marie. *Méthode de violoncelle* op. 4 (Paris: Pleyel, [c.1797]).

Reinagle, Joseph. *A Concise Introduction to the Art of Playing the Violoncello* (London: Goulding, Phipps and d'Almaine, [1800]).

Romberg, Bernhard, trans. anon. *A Complete Theoretical and Practical School for the Violoncello* (London: T. Boosey & Co., [1840]).

—. trans. anon. *Méthode de violoncelle* (Paris: Henry Lemoine, [1840]).

——. *Violoncellschule* (Berlin: Trautwein, [1840]).

——, ed. and rev. J. de Swert and H. Grünfeld. *Violoncelloschule* (Berlin: E. Bote & G. Bock, [1888]).

Schetky, J.G.C. *Practical and Progressive Lessons for the Violoncello* (London: R. Birchall, 1813).

Schroeder, Carl. *Neue grosse theoretisch praktische Violoncell-Schule* op. 34 (Leipzig: J. Schuberth & Co, [1877]).

——. *Tägliche Studien* (Hamburg: Aug. Kranz, [1877]).

——, trans. J. Matthews. *Catechism of Cello Playing* (London: Augener & Co., 1893); also published as *Handbook of Cello Playing* (London: Augener, 1889, trans. 1893).

Schulz, August. *Elementar-Violoncelloschule* (Hanover: Louis Oertel, [1882]).

Spohr, Louis. *Violinschule* (Vienna: Haslinger, [1833]).

Straeten, Edmund van der. *Technics of Violoncello Playing* (London: 'The Strad' Office, 1898).

——. *Well-Known Violoncello Solos: How to Play Them with Understanding, Expression and Effect* (London: William Reeves, [1922]).

Stutchewsky, Joachim. *Violoncell-Technik*, Vol. 1 (London: Schott, n.d.).

The Gamut for the Violoncello (London: Henry Waylet, [1750?]).

Thompson's New Instructions for the Violoncello (London: Messrs. Thompson, [c.1800]).

Tillière, J.B. *Méthode pour le Violoncelle* (Paris: Bailleux, [c.1775]).

——, trans. anon., *New and Complete Instructions for the Violoncello* (London: Longman & Broderip, [c.1790]).

Vaslin, Olive. *L'art du violoncelle* (Paris: Richault, 1884).

[Waylet, Henry]. *The Gamut for the Violoncello* (London: Henry Waylet, [c.1750?]).

Weber, Carl (ed.). *The Premier Method for Violoncello from the works of [...] Dotzauer, Bach, Laurent, Romberg [...] and others* (Philadelphia. PA: J.W. Pepper. 1895).

Werner Josef. *Zehn Etuden für Violoncell* (Leipzig: Hofmeister, [1876]).

——, trans. anon. *Praktische Violoncell-Schule* op. 12 (Köln: P.J. Tonger, [1882]).

——, trans. anon., *Die Kunst der Bogenführung. The Art of Bowing. op. 43. Supplement No. VII to the Author's Violoncello-Method* (Heilbronn: C.F. Schmidt, 4th edn, 1894).

——. *40 Studies*. Op. 46. Book II (London: Augener, [1897]).

Winram, James. *Violin Playing and Violin Adjustment* (Edinburgh: William Blackwood & Sons, 1908).

All Other Sources

Abeles, H.F. and S.Y. Porter. 'The sex-stereotyping of musical instruments', *Journal of Research in Music Education*, 26 (1978), pp. 65–75.

Alburger, Mary Anne. *Scottish Fiddlers and Their Music* (London: Gollancz. 1983).

Aldrich, Richard. 'The Philharmonic Society', *New York Times*, 10 November 1922.

Amory, Thomas. *Memoirs of Several Ladies of Great Britain* (London: John Noon, 1755).

Anon. *Habits of Good Society* (London: J. Hogg & Sons, [1859]).

'A.P.', review, *Gramophone*, April 1954, p. 33.

——, review, *Gramophone*, November 1957, p. 8.

Appel, Bernhard R. (ed.). *Schumann Forschungen: Robert Schumann, das Violoncello und die Cellisten seiner Zeit* (Mainz: Schott, 2007)

Archives départmentales de la Savoie. *Boire et manger en Savoie*: http://www.savoie.fr/archives73/expo_boire_et_manger/pages/32.htm.

'B. Thornton, Esq.'. 'An inspector', in *Miscellaneous and Fugitive Pieces*, 3 vols (London: T. Davies.1774).

Baldock, Robert. *Pablo Casals* (London: Gollancz, 1992).

Barzanò, Annalisa Lodetti, and Christian Bellisario, trans. Clarice Zdanski. *Signor Piatti – Cellist Komponist Avantgardist* (Kronberg: Kronberg Academy Verlag, 2001).

Baudelaire, Charles. *Fleurs du mal* (Paris: Poulet-Malassis et de Broise, 2nd edn 1861).

Ben-Tovim, Atarah. *The Right Instrument for Your Child* (London: Weidenfeld & Nicholson, 4th edn 2005).

Berlioz, Hector. *Mémoires de Hector Berlioz*, 2 vols (Paris: Calmann Lévy, 1897).

Blum, David. *Casals and the Art of Interpretation* (London: Heinemann Educational, 1977).

Born, Georgina. *Rationalising Culture – IRCAM, Boulez and the Institutionalisation of the Musical Avant-Garde* (Berkeley and Los Angeles: University of California Press, 1995).

Brewster, Anne M.H. *Compensation, Or, Always a Future* (Philadelphia: J.B. Lippincott & Co., 1860).

Brown, Clive. 'Dots and strokes in late 18th- and 19th-century music', *Early Music*, 21 (1993), pp. 593–612.

——. *Classical and Romantic Performance Practice 1750–1900* (Oxford: Oxford University Press, 1999).

——. 'Performing 19th-century chamber music: The yawning chasm between contemporary practice and historical evidence', *Early Music*, 38 (2010), pp. 476–80.

——. 'The physical parameters of 19th and 20th century violin playing' (updated 2013): http://chase.leeds.ac.uk/article/physical-parameters-of-19th-and-early-20th-century-violin-playing-clive-brown/.

Bruce, R. and A. Kemp. 'Sex-stereotyping in children's preferences for musical instruments', *British Journal of Music Education*, 10 (1993), pp. 123–34.

Burgard, Peter J. (ed.). *Nietzsche and the Feminine* (Charlottesville. VA: University of Virginia Press, 1994).

Butler, Judith. *Gender Trouble* (New York and London: Routledge, 1990).

Butt, John. *Playing with History* (Cambridge: Cambridge University Press, 2002).

'C.' *MT*, 65 (1924), p. 1124.

Campbell, Margaret. *The Great Cellists* (London: Gollancz, 1988).

Carrington, Jerome. 'A Tale of Bibliographic Sleuthing', *Juilliard Journal Online*, XIX no. 4 (December 2003).

Casanova de Seingalt, Jacques,. trans. Arthur Machen. *The Memoirs of Jacques Casanova de Seingalt 1725–1798*, 4 vols (New York: G. Putnam's Books, and London: Elek Books, 1894).

Cecil, George. 'Musical Notes from Abroad – Paris', *MT*, 62 (1921), p. 371.

Cheadle, Eliza. *Manners of Modern Society* (London: Cassell Petter & Galpin, [c.1875]).

Chesterfield, Earl of. *Letters written by the late Right Honourable Philip Dormer Stanhope, Earl of Chesterfield, to his son, Philip Stanhope. Esq*, 4 vols (Edinburgh: C. MacFarquhar, 1775).

[Chorley, Henry]. *Athenaeum*, 30 May 1835, p. 418.

—. *Athenaeum*, 23 June 1855, p. 739.

—. *Athenaeum*, 11 January 1863, p. 56.

—. *Athenaeum*, 28 February 1863, p. 302.

—. *Athenaeum*, 11 July 1863, p. 57.

—. *Athenaeum*, 6 January 1866, p. 23.

—. *Athenaeum*, 8 December 1866, p. 759.

—. *Athenaeum*, 4 July 1868, p. 25.

Citron, Marcia. *Gender and the Musical Canon* (Cambridge: Cambridge University Press, 1993).

Clarke, David. 'Musical autonomy revisited', in Martin Clayton, Trevor Herbert and Richard Middleton (eds), *The Cultural Study of Music: A Critical Introduction* (New York and London: Routledge, 2003), pp. 159–70.

Clynes, M . 'Expressive microstructure in music. linked to living qualities', in J. Sundberg (ed.), *Studies in Music Performance* (Stockholm: Royal Swedish Academy of Music, 1983).

Cook, Nicholas. 'Between process and product: Music and/as performance', *Online Journal of the Society for Music Theory*, 7 (2001): http://www.mtosmt.org/issues/mto.01.7.2/mto.01.7.2.cook.html.

Corelli, Marie. 'Joachim and Sarasate', *The Theatre*, 1 May 1883, pp. 283–6.

—. 'His Big Friend', *The Theatre*, 1 August 1884, pp. 64–9.

—. *A Romance of Two Worlds* (London: Richard Bentley & Son. new ed. 1890; 1st edn 1886).

—. *Ardath: the Story of a Dead Self* (London: Richard Bentley & Son, 9th edn, 1895. 1st edn 1889).

Corredor, J. Ma., trans. André Mangeot. *Conversations with Casals* (London: Hutchinson, 1956).

Coudroy-Saghaï, Marie-Hélène (ed.). *Hector Berlioz: Critique musicale 1823–1863*, 2 vols (Paris:Buchet/Chastel, 1998).

Cowling, Elizabeth. *The Cello* (London: Batsford, 1975).

Cranmer, Margaret. 'Streicher', in *Grove Music Online*.

Cusick, Suzanne G. 'Feminist theory, music theory, and the mind/body problem', *Perspectives of New Music*, 32 (1994), pp. 8–27.

—. 'On musical performances of gender and sex', in Elaine Barker and Lydia Hamessley (eds), *Audible Traces: gender, identity and music* (Zurich and Los Angeles: Carciofoli Verlagshaus, 1999), pp. 25–49.

—. 'Gender, musicology, and feminism', in Mark Everist and Nicholas Cook (eds), *Rethinking Music* (Oxford: Oxford University Press, 1999, rev. 2001), pp. 471–98.

Dahl, Roald. *Switch Bitch* (London: Michael Joseph, 1974).

—. *Feminine Endings: Music Gender and Sexuality* (Minneapolis: University of Minnesota Press, 2002).

—. 'Gender, Musicology, and Feminism', in Mark Everist and Nicholas Cook, *Rethinking Music* (Oxford: Oxford University Press, 1999, rev. 2001), pp. 471–98.

Davidson, Jane W. and Hubert Eiholzer (eds). *The String Practitioner* (Aldershot: Ashgate, 2004).

Day, Timothy. *A Century of Recorded Music: Listening to Musical History* (New Haven and London: Yale University Press, 2000).

De'ak, Steven. *David Popper* (Neptune City, NJ: Paganiniana Publications, 1980).

Dell'Antonio, Andrew. 'Construction of desire in early Baroque instrumental music', in Todd M. Borgerding (ed.), *Gender, Sexuality and Early Music* (New York and London: Routledge, 2002), pp. 199–226.

Delzell, J.K. and D.A. Leppla. 'Gender association of musical instruments and preferences of fourth-grade students for selected instruments', *Journal of Research in Music Education*, 40 (1992), pp. 93–103.

Dickens, Charles, ed. Norman Page. *Bleak House* (Harmondsworth: Penguin Books, 1971; 1st edn 1853).

—. 'Wood-and-straw music', *All the Year Round*, 20 December 1862, pp. 351–4.

'Discus'. 'Gramophone Notes'. *MT*, 66 (1925), pp. 135–6.

—. 'Gramophone Notes', *MT*, 69 (1928), p. 813.

Doran, Dr John. *Their Majesties' Servants or Annals of the English Stage from Thomas Betterton to Edmund Kean; Actors, Authors, Audiences* (London: Wm. H. Allen, 1865).

—. *MT*, 66 (1925), p. 135.

Douglas, Mona. *This is Ellan Vannin Again: Folklore* (Douglas, Isle of Man: Times Longbooks, 1966).

Dumas, Alexandre. *Les Mohicans de Paris*, 2 vols (Montréal: Le joyeux Roger, 2007; 1st edn Paris, 1854–55).

Ellis, Havelock. *Impressions and Comments (2nd Series)* (London: Constable and Company Ltd, 1921).

—. *Impressions and Comments. Third Series* (London: Constable and Company Ltd, 1924).

Everist, Mark and Cook, Nicholas (eds) *Rethinking Music* (Oxford: Oxford University Press, 1999, rev. 2001).

Fabian, Dorrotya. *Bach Performance Practice 1945–1975* (Aldershot: Ashgate, 2003).

— and Emery Schubert. 'Is there only one way of being expressive in musical performance? – Lessons from listeners' reactions to performances of J.S. Bach's music', in C. Stevens, D. Burnham, G. McPherson, E. Schubert and J. Renwick (eds), *Proceedings of the 7th International Conference on Music Perception and Cognition, Sydney, 2002* (Adelaide: Causal Productions. 2002), pp. 112–15 [CD-ROM only].

Fellowes, E. H. *Memoirs of an Amateur Musician* (London: Methuen & Co. Ltd, 1946).

Feuillet, Octave. *Théâtre complet*, 4 vols (Paris: Calmann Lévy, 1893).

Finck, Henry T. *My Adventures in the Golden Age of Music* (New York and London: Funk and Wagnalls Company, 1926).

Flesch, Carl,. trans. Frederick Martens. *The Art of Violin Playing*, 2 vols (New York: C. Fischer, 1930).

Forino, Luigi. *Il violoncello il violoncellista ed i violoncellisti* (Milan: Ulrico Hoepli, 2nd edn 1930).

Foster, Myles B. *The History of the Philharmonic Society of London 1813–1912* (London: John Lane, The Bodley Head, 1912).

François, Peter. *'Ah! Le metier de donneur de concerts! Adrien François Servais (1807–1866) als rondreizend cellovirtuos* (Halle, Belgium: vzw Servais, 2007).

—. Exhibition catalogue, Zuidwestbrabants Museum. *Adrien François Servais 1807–2007 Halse cellist met wereldfaam* (Halle, Belgium: vzw Servais, 2007).

Fuchs, Carl. *Musical and Other Recollections of Carl Fuchs Cellist* (Manchester: Sherratt and Hughes, 1937).

Gillespie, Robert. 'Ratings of violin and viola vibrato performance in audio-only and audiovisual presentations', *Journal of Research in Music Education*, 45 (1997), pp. 212–20.

Gillett, Paula. *Musical Women in England 1870–1914* (New York: St. Martin's Press, 2000).

Ginsburg, Lev. *Istoriya violonchel'novo: iskusstva russkaya klassicheskaya violonchel'naya shkola (1860–1917)* (Moscow: Muziyka, 1965).

—. *Istoriya violonchel'novo iskusstva* (Moscow: Muziyka, 1978); trans. Tanya Tchistyakova, *History of the Violoncello* (Neptune City, NJ: Paganiniana Publications, 1983).

Gorst, Harold. 'Masters of the cello', *The Cremona*, 1 (1904), pp. 31–5.

Goudeau, Emile. *Chansons de Paris et d'ailleurs Violoncelles – Fifres – Mandolines* (Paris: Bibliotheque-Charpentier, 1896).

Gramit, David. *Cultivating Music: The Aspirations, Interests and Limits of German Musical Culture 1770–1848* (Berkeley: University of California Press, 2002).

Green, Lucy. *Music, Gender, Education* (Cambridge: Cambridge University Press, 1997).

Grey, Thomas. 'Engendering music drama', in *Wagner's* Musical Prose (Cambridge: Cambridge University Press, 1995), pp. 130–37.

Grove, Sir George (ed.). *A Dictionary of Music and Musicians*, 4 vols (London: Macmillan and Co. 1889).

Guichon, Alfred. 'Le violoncelle', *Chronique musicale*, 3 (1875), pp. 73–7.

Guin, Elisabeth le. *Boccherini's Body: An Essay in Carnal Musicology* (Berkeley: University of California Press, 2006).

Gwynn, Stephen. 'When Suggia was playing', *Country Life*, 26 November 1927, pp. 767–78.

Hanslick, Eduard. *Geschichte des Concertwesens in Wien*, 2 vols (Vienna: Wilhelm Braumüller, 1870).

—. trans. Gustav Cohen. *On the Beautiful in Music* (New York: Da Capo Press, 1974; repr. of 7th edn 1885, English version 1891).

Hargreaves, David and Adrian North. *The Social Psychology of Music* (Oxford: Oxford University Press, 1997).

Hepokowski, James. 'Masculine – Feminine. Are Current Readings of Sonata Form in Terms of a "Masculine" and "Feminine" Dichotomy Exaggerated?', *MT*, 135 (1994), pp. 494–9.

Hofmeister, F., et al. *Musikalisch-literarischer Monatsbericht: über neue Musikalien, musikalische Schriften und Abbildungen* (Leipzig: F. Hofmeister, 1829–1907).

Houssaye, Arsène. *Galerie du XVIIIe siècle deuxième série Princesses de comédie et déesses d'opéra* (Paris: Hachette et Cie., 1858).

Howell, Edward. *Edward Howell's First Book for the Violoncello adapted from Romberg's School* (London: Boosey & Co., [1879]).

Howes, Patricia, Jean Callaghan, Pamela Davis, et al. 'The relationship between measured vibrato characteristics and perception in Western operatic singing', *Journal of Voice*, 18 (2004), pp. 216–30.

Hudson, Richard. *Stolen Time: The History of Tempo Rubato* (Oxford: Clarendon Press, 1994).

Hull, Isabel V. *Sexuality, State, and Civil Society in Germany, 1700–1815* (Ithaca, NY, and London: Cornell University Press, 1996).

Huneker, James. 'Girls at play', *New York Times*, 15 June 1919, pp. 53–4.

Hurwitz, David. 'Orchestral vibrato':http://www.classicstoday.com/features/ClassicsToday-Vibrato-part1.pdf; http://www.classicstoday.com/features/ClassicsToday-Vibrato-part2.pdf (commenced 2007, continually revised).

Huysmans, Joris-Karl, trans. Margaret Mauldon. *Against Nature* [À rebours] (Oxford: Oxford University Press, 1998).

d'Indy,Vincent, and Auguste Sérieyx. *Cours de composition musicale*, 2 vols (Paris: Durand et Cie., 1909).

Johnson, Julian. 'Music in Hegel's aesthetics: A re-evaluation', British Journal of Aesthetics, 31 (1991), pp. 152–62.

Kagan, Susan. 'Camilla Urso: Aa nineteenth-century violinist's view', *Signs*, 2/3 (1977), pp. 731–4.

Kallberg, Jeffrey. 'Gender', *Grove Music Online*.

Kallberg, Jeffrey. 'Sex, sexuality and Schubert's piano music', in Steven Crist and Roberta M. Marvin (eds), *Historical Musicology: Sources Methods Interpretations*. (Rochester, NY: University of Rochester Press, 2004), pp. 219–33.

—. 'Gender', *Grove Music Online*.

Katz, Mark. *Capturing Sound: How Technology has Changed Music* (Berkeley: University of California Press, 2004).

Kennaway, George. 'Lithuanian art & music abroad: English reception of the work of M.K. Čiurlionis, 1912–39', *Slavonic and East European Review*, 83 (2005), pp. 234–53.

—. 'The phenomenon of the cellist Auguste van Biene: From the Charing Cross Road to Brighton via Broadway', in M. Hewitt and R. Cowgill (eds), *Victorian Soundscapes*. Leeds Working Papers in Victorian Studies 9 (Leeds: LCVS and LUCEM, 2007), pp. 67–82.

—. '"Noble and easy attitudes" or a violent embrace? Towards carnality in 19th-century cello performance', conference lecture-recital, *The Musical Body: Gesture, Representation and Ergonomics in Performance*, Royal College of Music, London, April 2009.

—. 'Do as some said, or as most did? – a Foucauldian experiment with nineteenth–century HIP', *Current Musicology*, 92 (2011), pp. 7–29.

—. Review of Kadri Steinbach and Urve Lippus (eds), *Estonian Sound Recordings 1939* (Tallinn: Estonian Academy of Music and Theatre, 2009). *Fontes Artis Musicae*, 58 (2011), pp. 74–6.

—. 'Haydn's(?) Cello Concertos 1860–1930: editions, performance, reception', *Nineteenth-Century Music Review*, 9 (2012), pp. 177–211.

Kenyon, Nicholas. *Authenticity and Early Music: A Symposium* (Oxford: Oxford University Press, 1988).

Kramer, Lawrence. *Classical Music and Postmodern Knowledge* (Berkeley, Los Angeles and London: University of California Press, 1995).

Krehbiel, Henry Edward. *How to Listen to Music* (New York: Charles Scribner's Sons, 7th edn 1897).

Laird, Paul R. *The Baroque Cello Revival: An Oral History* (Lanham. MD: Scarecrow Press, 2004).

Lalo, Edouard, ed. J.-M. Fauquet. *Edouard Lalo: Correspondance* (Paris: aux Amateurs de Livres, 1989).

Lawson, Colin, and Robin Stowell. *The Historical Performance of Music: An Introduction* (Cambridge: Cambridge University Press, 1999).

Leech-Wilkinson, Daniel. 'Portamento and Musical Meaning', *Journal of Musicological Research*, 25 (2006), pp. 233–61.

—. *The Changing Sound of Music: Approaches to Studying Recorded Musical Performances* (London: Royal Holloway University, 2009).

Leppert, Richard. 'Gender sonics: The voice of Patsy Cline', in Steven Baur, Raymond Knapp, and Jacqueline Warwick (eds), *Musicological Identities: Essays in Honor of Susan McClary* (Aldershot: Ashgate, 2008), pp. 191–203.

Lessing, G.E., ed. and trans. E. Bell. 'Laokoön, or on the limits of painting and poetry', in *Selected Prose Works* (London: George Bell and Sons, 1879).

Littlehales, Lillian. *Pablo Casals* (New York: W.W. Norton & Company, 1929).

Lützen, Ludolf. *Die Violoncell-Transkriptionen Friedrich Grützmachers. Untersuchungen zur Transkription in Sicht und Handhabung der 2. Hälfte des 19. Jahrhunderts*, Kölner Beiträge zur Musikforschung, Vol. 79 (Regensburg: G. Bosse, 1974).

McClary, Susan.*Feminine Endings: Music Gender and Sexuality* (Minneapolis, MN: University of Minnesota Press, 1992).

—. 'Narrative agendas in "absolute music": Identity and difference in Brahms's Third Symphony", in Solie, Ruth (ed.), *Musicology and Difference* (Berkeley: University of California Press, 1993), pp. 326–44.

Macleod, Beth Abelson. '"Whence comes the lady tympanist?" Gender and instrumental musicians in America, 1853–1990', *Journal of Social History* (Winter 1993): http://findarticles.com/p/articles/mi_m2005/is_n2_v27/ai_14903043/pg_1.

—. *Women Performing Music: The Emergence of American Women as Classical Instrumentalists and Conductors* (Jefferson, NC: Macfarland & Co., 2001).

Maillot, Sylvette. *Le violoncelle en France au XVIIIième siècle* (Paris: Champion, 1985).

Mar, Jonathan del (ed.). *Beethoven Sonaten für Violoncello und Klavier* (Kassel: Bärenreiter, 2004).

Markevitch, Dmitry,. trans. Florence W. Seder. *Cello Story* (New Jersey: Alfred Publishing Company, 1984).

Martens, Frederick H. *String Mastery Talks with Master Violinists. Viola Players and Violoncellists* (New York: Frederick A. Stokes Company, 2nd edn, 1923).

Matthews, J. *The Violin Music of Beethoven* (London: 'The Strad' Office, 1902).

'M.-D.C.' *MT*, 64 (1923), pp. 325–26.

Mercier Anita. *Guilherminia Suggia* (Aldershot: Ashgate, 2008).

—. 'Guilherminia Suggia' (n.d.): http://www.cello.org/Newsletter/Articles/suggia.htm.

Milsom, David. *Theory and Practice in Late Nineteenth-Century Violin Performance* (Aldershot: Ashgate, 2003).

Mitchell, W.J.T. *Iconology Image Text. Ideology* (Chicago: University of Chicago Press, 1986).

Moran, John. *Techniques of Expression in Viennese String Music (1780–1830)* (PhD thesis, King's College London, 2002).

Mozart, Leopold, trans. Editha Knocker. *Treatise on the Fundamental Principles of Violin Playing* (Oxford: Oxford University Press, 2nd edn 1951).

Munster, Robert. 'Sophie Lebrun', in *Grove Music Online.*

Neubauer, J. *The Emancipation of Music from Language* (New Haven and London: Yale University Press, 1986).

Neuls-Bates, Carol. *Women in Music* (Boston: North East University Press, 1996).

Neumann, Frederick. 'Dots and strokes in Mozart', *Early Music*, 21 (1993), pp. 429–35.

Novak, Martha Clinkscale. *Makers of the Piano 1700–1820* (Oxford: Oxford University Press, 1993).

Ongley, Laurie. 'The reconstruction of an 18th-century basso group', *Early Music*, 27 (1999) p. 280.

Parret, Herman. 'Kant on music and the hierarchy of the arts', *Journal of Aesthetics and Art Criticism*, 56 (1998). pp. 251–64.

Perger, Richard von. 'Music in Vienna', *MT*, 51 (1910), p. 109.

Petrie, Adam. *Rules of Good Deportment. or of Good Breeding. For the Use of Youth* (Edinburgh: [no publisher], 1720).

Philip, Robert. *Early Recordings and Musical Style: Changing Tastes in Instrumental Performance 1900–1950* (Cambridge: Cambridge University Press, 1992).

Potter, John. 'Beggar at the door: The rise and fall of portamento in singing', *Music & Letters*, 87 (2006), pp. 523–50.

'R.H.' 'LALO. Concerto in D minor for Violoncello and Orchestra', *Gramophone*, November 1950, p. 23.

Rau, Fritz. *Das Vibrato auf der Violine* (Leipzig: C.F. Kahnt, 1922).

Repp, Bruno. 'Diversity and commonality in music performance: An analysis of timing microstructure in Schumann's "Träumerei"', *Journal of the Acoustical Society of America*, 92 (1992), pp. 2546–68.

Richmond, Grace L. S . *The Twenty-Fourth of June* (Garden City, NY: Doubleday, Page & Co., 1914).

Richter, Simon. 'Intimate relations: Music in and around Lessing's "Laokoon"', *Poetics Today*, 20 (1999), pp. 155–73.

Rigby, Stanley. 'Memories', *Music & Letters*, 35 (1954), pp. 140–43.

Rink, John (ed.). *Musical Performance: A Guide to Understanding* (Cambridge: Cambridge University Press, 2002).

Røllum-Larsen, Claus. *Impulser i Københavns koncertrepertoire 1900–1935*, 2 vols (Copenhagen: University of Copenhagen, Museum Tusculanum Press, 2002).

Russell, Tilden A. 'The development of the cello end-pin', *Imago Musicae*, 4 (1987), pp. 335–356.

Sabor, Peter (ed.). *Horace Walpole: The Critical Heritage* (New York: Routledge & Kegan Paul, 1987).

Schopenhauer, Arthur, trans. R.B. Haldane and J. Kemp. *The World as Will and Idea* (London: Kegan Paul, 1891).

Scott, Derek B. 'The sexual politics of Victorian musical aesthetics', *Journal of the Royal Musical Association*, 119 (1994), pp. 91–114.

Seashore, Carl. 'Measurements on the expression of emotion in music', *Proceedings of the National Academy of Sciences*, 9 (1923), pp. 323–5.

—. (ed.). *The Vibrato* (Iowa: University of Iowa, 1932).

Shaw-Miller, Simon. *Visible Deeds of Music: Art and Music from Wagner to Cage* (New Haven and London: Yale University Press, 2002).

Smyth, Ethel. *Female Pipings in Eden* (London: Peter Davies, 1933).

Solie, Ruth A. (ed.). *Musicology and Difference: Gender and Sexuality in Music Scholarship* (Berkeley: University of California Press, 1995).

Sommerich, Philip. 'Viva Vivaldi', *Classical Music*, 14 February 2009, p. 40.

Steinhausen, Friedrich Adolf. *Die Physiologie der Bogenführung auf den Streichinstrumenten* (Leipzig: Breitkopf & Härtel, 1903).

Stevens, Doris. 'On Learning to Play the Cello', *American Mercury*, 8 (1926), pp. 1–8.

Stowell, Robin. *Violin Technique and Performance Practice in the Late Eighteenth and Early Nineteenth Centuries* (Cambridge: Cambridge University Press, 1985).

—, (ed.). *Performing Beethoven* (London: Cambridge University Press, 1994).

—, (ed.). *The Cambridge Companion to the Cello* (Cambridge: Cambridge University Press, 1999).

Straeten, Edmund van der. *A History of the Violoncello, the Viol da Gamba, their Precursors and Collateral Instruments* (London: William Reeves, 1914; repr. 1971).

Swert, Jules de. *Le Mécanisme du Violoncelle* (Berlin: N. Rimrock, [1872]).

—. *The Violoncello* (London and New York: Novello. Ewer and Co., [1882]).

Taruskin, Richard. *Text & Act Essays on Musical Performance* (Oxford: Oxford University Press, 1995).

Thackeray, William M. *The History of Pendennis* (London: Smith,. Elder & Co. 1880; 1st edn, 1848–50).

Todd, Pamela. *The Pre-Raphaelites at Home* (London: Pavilion, 2001).

Turner, Edward. *The Young Man's Companion* (Halifax: Milner and Sowerby, 1861).

'v. d. O.' *BamZ*, 1 (1822), pp. 403–5.

Vadding, M. and Max Merseburger. *Das Violoncello und seine Literatur* (Leipzig: Carl Merseburger. 1920).

Verlaine, Paul. *Poèmes saturniens* (Paris: Lemerre, 1866).

Wakin, Daniel. 'Elgar without vibrato? Fiddlesticks', *New York Times*, 12 August 2008: http://www.nytimes.com/2008/08/13/arts/music/13vibr.html.

Walden, Valerie. *One Hundred Years of Violoncello: A History of Technique and Performance Practice. 1740–1840* (Cambridge: Cambridge University Press, 1998).

—. 'Bernhard Heinrich Romberg', *Grove Music Online*.

Wasielewski, Wilhelm. Jos.. D., trans. Isobella S.E. Stigand. *The Violoncello and its History* (London: Novello. Ewer & Co., 1894; 1st edn 1888).

Wiesenfeldt, Christiane. *Zwischen Beethoven Und Bras: Die Violoncello-Sonate im 19. Jahrhundert. Kieler Schriften zur Musikwissenschaft. band 51* (Kassel: Bärenreiter, 2006).

Wildblood, Joan. *The Polite World a Guide to the Deportment of the English in Former Times* (London: David-Poynter, 2nd edn 1973).

Williams, Alastair. *Constructing Musicology* (Aldershot: Ashgate, 2001).

Zellner, L.A. 'The Sisters Ferni', *MT*, 37 (1859), pp. 54–5.

Zerilli, Linda M.G. 'No thrust. No swell. No subject?: A critical response to Stephen K. White', *Political Theory*, 22/2 (1994), pp. 323–8.

Discography

Bach, J.S. *Double Concerto in D Minor*:
    Arnold and Alma Rosé (vns) (Czech HMV, mat. CA 43/47, 1929;
    reissued *Arnold Rosé and the Rosé String Quartet*, Biddulph Recordings
    LAB 056-57, 1992).
    Fritz Kreisler and Efrem Zimbalist (vns)
    (HMV DB 587, matrix 2-07918, 1915; reissued in *Great Violinists – Kreisler*,
    Naxos Historical 8.110922, n.d.).
Bazzini, Antonio. *La ronde des lutins.* Jan Kubelík (vn), un-named pianist
    (Gramophone&TypewriterCo.matrix408c.catalogueno.07901.1903;reissued.
    The Great Violinists Volume 1. EMI: HMV Treasury. EX 7 61062 1, 1988).
Becker, Hugo. *Minuet* op. 3 no. 3. Hugo Becker (vc), un-named pianist (no
    details, 1908; reissued *The Recorded Cello*).
—. *Gavotte.* Hugo Becker (vc), un-named pianist (Gramophone Company cat.
    no. 048013, c.1908; reissued *The Recorded Cello*).
Biene, Auguste van. 'The Broken Melody':
    John Barbirolli (vc), Rose Barbirolli (pf) (Edison Bell, mat. 298k,
        cat. 2148, 1911; reissued *The Recorded Cello*, Vol. 2).
    Auguste van Biene (vc), un-named pianist (Zonophone, mat. Z-047851, cat.
        A60, c.1908).
    Auguste van Biene (vc), un-named pianist (Edison Bell, mat. 3443,
        cat. 3355, 1912; reissued *The Recorded Cello*, Vol. 2).
    Beatrice Harrison (vc), Margaret Harrison (pf) (HMV, matrix Cc14160-2,
        cat. C1626, 1929) (reissued *The Harrison Sisters: An English Music
        Heritage, Harrison Sisters' Trust*, Claremont GSE78/50/47).
    Cedric Sharpe (vc), un-named pianist (HMV, cat. D436, mat. 07884, 1920).
    W.H. Squire (vc), un-named pianist (Columbia, mat. 3353, cat. L2127, 1928).
Biene, Auguste van. *Kol Nidri* [sic]. Van Biene (vc), un-named pianist (Zonophone,
    mat. Z-047851, cat. A60, c.1908).
Boccherini, Luigi. *Minuet.* Heinrich Grünfeld (vc), un-named pianist (Electrola,
    cat. EG 724, c.1927; reissued *The Recorded Cello*).
Brahms, Johannes. *Clarinet Trio in A minor* op. 114, Haydn Draper (cl), Sir
    Hamilton Harty (pf), W. H. Squire (vc) (Columbia, L 1609, 1925).
Chopin, Frédéric, *Nocturne.* Hans Kronold (vc), un-named pianist (Edison Gold
    Moulded Record 9637, [1907]), online at University of California, Santa
    Barbara Cylinder Preservation and Digitization Project, URL: http://cylinders.
    library.ucsb.edu [accessed July 2012].

Davidoff, Carl. 'Romance sans paroles', Alexander Wierzbilowicz (vc), un-named pianist (Gramophone & Typewriter Co., matrix 201z, cat. 27886, 1904; reissued *The Recorded Cello*, Vol. 1, CD 2).

Elgar, Edward. *Cello Concerto in E Minor* op. 85:

    Beatrice Harrison (vc), Edward Elgar (cond), New Symphony Orchestra (His Master's Voice, D1507-1509, 1928; CD transfer, Naxos 8.111260. 2007).

    W.H. Squire (vc), Sir Hamilton Harty (cond), Hallé Orchestra (Columbia DX117-120, 1930; LP transfer. Imprimatur IMP1, 1981).

Fauré, Gabriel. *Après un rêve*. Pablo Casals (vc), Nikolai Mednikoff (pf) (Victor, mat. BE-31972-12. cat. 1083; reissued Naxos Historical, *Casals Encores and Transcriptions*, Vol. 1, 8.110972, 2003).

Godard, Benjamin. 'Berceuse' from *Jocelyn*. Herman Sandby (vc), un-named pianist (Edison Blue Amberol no. 8220, [1915]).

Greene, Edwin. 'Sing me to sleep'. William Whitehouse (vc), un-named pianist (Gramophone Company cat. no. 02090, matrix no. 1861f, 1907; reissued *The Recorded Cello*).

Handel, George Frideric. '*Largo*' (*Serse*):

    Heinrich Grünfeld (vc), un-named pianist (Gramophone Concert Record G.C. matrix no. 19h, catalogue no. 47875x, Berlin, 1905).

    Hans Kronold (vc), un-named pianist (Edison Gold Moulded Record: 9987, 1908).

    ——. *Largo* and Dunkler, *Humoreske (Chanson à boire)*. W.H. Squire (vc), Hamilton Harty (pf) (Columbia matrices 75851 and 75499. cat. no. L1201).

Hillemacher, Paul. *Gavotte tendre*. Pablo Casals (vc) (*Casals Encores and Transcriptions*, Vol. 1, Naxos 8.110972; orig. recorded 1925).

Lalo, Edouard. *Cello Concerto in D Minor*:

    Gaspar Cassadó (vc), Joel Perlea (cond), Bamberg Symphony Orchestra (Vox, PL10.920, 1963).

    André Navarra (vc), Emanuel Young (cond), Paris Opera Orchestra (Capitol, P8318, 1956).

    Zara Nelsova (vc), Sir Adrian Boult (cond), London Philharmonic Orchestra (Decca. LXT 2906. 1953; reissued *Zara Nelsova Decca Recordings 1950-1956*, Decca 4756327, 2004).

    Jacqueline Du Pré (vc), Daniel Barenboim (cond), Cleveland Orchestra (EMI, 1973, remastered 1995).

    Guilherminia Suggia (vc), Pedro de Freitas Branco (cond), London Symphony Orchestra (Decca AX349-52, 1946; reissued *Guilherminia Suggia Plays Haydn Bruch Lalo*, Dutton CDBP 9748).

Mendelssohn, Felix. *Violin Concerto* (slow movement). Kathleen Parlow (vn), un-named orchestra (Columbia Graphophone Co. matrix 48665. no. A5843. 1916).

Misc. composers. *The Recorded Cello – The History of the Cello on Record, from the collection of Keith Harvey*, 2 vols (Pearl Gemm CDS 9981-86, 1992)

Popper, David. *Im Walde* op. 50 no. 1. 'Entrance to the Forest'. W.H. Squire (vc), un-named pianist (Columbia. matrix no. AX 85. cat. no. L1497).

Puccini, Giacomo. *Madama Butterfly* (selections). Victor Sorlin (vc), un-named orchestra (Edison Amberol no. 818 [1911]).

Saint-Saëns, Camille. *Le cygne*:
Hans Kronold (vc), un-named pianist (Edison cat. 9413, 1905).
Joseph Hollmann (vc), un-named pianist (Victor Record, Victor Talking Machine Co. Camden NJ, matrix no. 64046, 1906).

Schumann, Robert. *Cello Concerto* op. 129. Gregor Piatigorsky (vc), John Barbirolli (cond), London Philharmonic Orchestra (His Master's Voice. mat. B 6931-1. 6933-1. 6934-2. 6935-1. 6935-2. cat. DB 2244, 1934; reissued Naxos Historical. 8.111069, 2005).

—. 'Träumerei', *Kinderszenen* op. 15 no.7:
Rosario Bourdon (vc), un-named orchestra (Victor Talking Machine Co. Camden, NJ, issue no. 4845, matrix B3485, 1906).
Pablo Casals (vc), un-named orchestra (Columbia, matrix 37252, issue no. A5679, 1915).
Pablo Casals, Walter Golde (pf) (1925; reissued Naxos Historical, *Great Cellists – Casals Encores and Transcriptions*, Vol. 4. 8.110986. 2005).
Pablo Casals, Nicolai Mednikoff (pf) (Victor. matrix no. BE-34075-1, no. 1178, 1926; reissued Naxos Historical, *Great Cellists – Casals Encores and Transcriptions*, Vol. 1. 8.110972, 2003).
Pablo Casals, Otto Schulhof (pf) (HMV, matrix B@ 19018-1, no. DA833, 1930; reissued in Naxos Historical, *Great Cellists – Casals Encores and Transcriptions*, Vol. 2. 8.110976, 2004).
Heinrich Grünfeld (vc), un-named pianist (The Gramophone Company Ltd. matrix G.C.-47876x, 1903).
Boris Hambourg (vc), Grace Smith (pf) (Victor Talking Machine Co., Camden, NJ, issue no. 60065, 1911).
Josef Hollman (vc), un-named pianist (Victor talking Machine Co., matrix C-3026-1, 1906).
Hans Kronold (vc), un-named pianist (Edison. no. 9149, 1905).
Victor Sorlin (vc), Victor Orchestra (Victor Talking Machine Co. Camden, NJ, matrix 4845, 1906).

Servais, Adrien-François. *Fantasia über Sehnsucht*. Heinrich Kruse (vc), un-named orchestra (orig. details unknown, c.1915; reissued *The Recorded Cello*).

Sibelius, Jan. 'Valse triste' op. 44. Herman Sandby (vc), un-named pianist (Columbia. matrix WC 34. no. J20, n.d.).

Squire, W.H. *Meditation in C*. W.H. Squire (vc), un-named pianist (Columbia, L 1513, c.1928; reissued *Cello 2: The Definitive Collection of the 19th Century's Greatest Virtuosos*, Ongen Music, B0046PO87Q, 2010).

Steinbach, Kadri and Urve Lippus (eds.), *Estonian Sound Recordings 1939* [with 12 CDs] (Tallinn: Estonian Academy of Music and Theatre, 2009).

Tricklir, J.B. *Adagio and Rondo*. Carl Fuchs (vc), un-named pianist (HMV private recording, matrix 2B4795-1, c.1930; reissued *The Recorded Cello*).

Wagner, Richard. 'Evening Star' ['O du mein holder Abendstern'] from *Tannhäuser*. Victor Sorlin (vc), un-named orchestra (Columbia Phonograph Company no. 1049, 1909).

Index